SECOND EDITION

CULTURE
&IDENTITY

Life Stories for Counselors and Therapists

Anita Jones Thomas
Loyola University Chicago

Sara E. Schwarzbaum
Northeastern Illinois University

Los Angeles | London | New Delhi
Singapore | Washington DC

For information:

SAGE Publications, Inc.
2455 Teller Road
Thousand Oaks,
    California 91320
E-mail: order@sagepub.com

SAGE Publications Ltd.
1 Oliver's Yard
55 City Road
London EC1Y 1SP
United Kingdom

SAGE Publications India Pvt. Ltd.
B 1/I 1 Mohan Cooperative
    Industrial Area
Mathura Road, New Delhi 110 044
India

SAGE Publications Asia-Pacific
    Pte. Ltd.
33 Pekin Street #02-01
Far East Square
Singapore 048763

Printed in the United States of America

Library of Congress Cataloging-in-Publication Data

Thomas, Anita Jones.
Culture and identity : life stories for counselors and therapists / Anita Jones Thomas, Sara E. Schwarzbaum.—2nd ed.
    p. cm.
Includes bibliographical references and index.
ISBN 978-1-4129-8668-7 (pbk.)
    1. Cross-cultural counseling. 2. Identity (Psychology) I. Title.

BF637.C6T489 2011
305.092'273—dc22   2010020002

This book is printed on acid-free paper.

14 15 16 10 9 8 7 6 5 4 3

Acquisitions Editor:	Kassie Graves
Associate Editor:	Leah Mori
Production Editor:	Eric Garner
Copy Editor:	Kristin Bergstad
Typesetter:	C&M Digitals, Ltd.
Proofreader:	Sally Jaskold
Indexer:	Naomi Linzer
Cover Designer:	Janet Kiesel
Marketing Manager:	Stephanie Adams
Permissions Editor:	Adele Hutchinson

Contents

Preface

Nothing is more fascinating than looking at old photographs. We love viewing people captured in time by a photograph as much because of what we see as because of what we do not see and do not understand. The same can be said about the stories that people tell about their lives—to themselves, to others, and to therapists. Stories capture only one moment, one perspective, one snapshot of individuals' lives. This includes not only the individuals' recollections of activities, thoughts, and feelings but also their current understanding of their circumstances and their past. Like the elusive nature of memory, truth, and reality, some recollections stay the same, but others change with each telling of the story. As the future alters the past, some details become lost or forgotten, while others become exaggerated and provide more intrigue, eliciting sympathy or enhancing the humor in the story. Our clients afford us the opportunity to look at them in the same way we look at old photographs, both seeing what is there and also wondering what is missing. Working as a clinician provides us with the joy and the privilege of participating in the reconstruction of clients' stories and in the cocreation of a brighter future. This book is about people's life journeys, the stories they tell about themselves, and a few of the possible clinical applications derived from the stories. The stories provide us with a glimpse into the subjects' pasts and an opportunity to imagine their futures.

As a young child, I, Anita, was raised and encouraged by my parents to embrace my cultural heritage. I vividly remember messages that were given both implicitly and explicitly about being an African American female. Because I was raised in a predominantly White environment, my parents were worried about whether I was developing a positive self-concept in the face of often racist and oppressive experiences. Due to their positive encouragement and diligent effort to protect me and to help me process oppressive experiences, I grew to love, appreciate, and embrace my cultural heritage. Most would say that I have a passion or obsession for cultural issues, and I have dedicated my personal and professional life to helping people understand the importance of culture.

When Anita came up with the idea of coauthoring a book based on autobiographical stories to help emerging clinicians, I, Sara, was eager to get started. I was raised in a multilingual and multiethnic household, and long before I became interested in psychology and psychotherapy, I was curious about people's cultural backgrounds, ethnic affiliations, and language abilities. Close friends and relatives tell me that I am insatiably curious about people's lives, but what I am most interested in are people's cultural lives. One of our favorite courses to teach is the multicultural counseling course. Although training professional clinicians and therapists is rewarding because we are helping people to figure out how best to influence and understand the lives of their clients, the multicultural course stands out because it increases the level of self-awareness of students and encourages them to explore the full influence of culture with its multiplicity of meanings and clinical implications.

We have been confronted with four difficulties in the course that we are sure other instructors, students, and clinicians experience, too. First, many multicultural courses and textbooks focus solely on the racial and ethnic aspects of clinical work with minorities and exclude other cultural factors. This approach helps to build understanding of values, beliefs, lifestyle, and perspectives for each group, but it is fairly limited in promoting an understanding of intragroup differences and may promote stereotyping of groups. The second difficulty is helping students understand the full influence of culture on individuals' functioning and identity. Most courses incorporate the use of popular movies and media to help portray many of the concepts covered. Again, this is often limited to exploring racial or ethnic concerns. Third, although such courses promote awareness of the importance of cultural factors, self-awareness of the clinician, and knowledge of cultural factors, the courses often do not promote culturally sensitive skills, which include the ability to assess and understand the interactional effects of the cultural dimensions on the shaping of a person's identity and the interventions that may be necessary at certain moments in time. Fourth, new clinicians are generally exposed to "cookbook" approaches for understanding culture (Speight, Myers, Cox, & Highlen, 1991), in part because it may be difficult for clinicians to consider the multiplicity and complexity that understanding cultural dimensions of identity demands.

This book attempts to fill these gaps in the multicultural training litera-ture by providing cultural autobiographies from individuals who have contributed their life stories. We selected these contributions to highlight the effect of cultural factors on values, beliefs, and the development of identity and self-concept. These stories also present the interaction of multiple cultural factors including intragroup differences and sociohistor-ical developments that affect individual identity. We collected the stories from students in a graduate program, from professionals, and from ordi-nary people who agreed to share their personal histories. To prepare their contributions for this book, the storytellers used a questionnaire (see Appendix A) as a guide, answering some of its questions and ignoring others, creating personal narratives that give the reader an intimate glimpse of each individual storyteller's life. Each is written to give the reader an understanding of the personal significance and meaning that cultural factors play in the authors' lives, as they perceive them. The iden-tifying characteristics of the storytellers and their families—such as names, locations, and certain characteristics—have been changed to pre-serve their anonymity. The language, punctuation, and style of the stories have not been altered much, however, to preserve the authenticity of the story and to honor the storytellers. We offer these selections as a supple-ment to theoretical textbooks on cultural diversity and as a way to develop culturally sensitive skills for clinicians. We were delighted to hear from instructors and clinicians around the country who feel that we fulfilled this aim in the first edition, and we hope that this second edition will be equally informative.

Organization of the Book

This second edition includes expanded cultural factors and new stories to address them. Each chapter presents a story, a cultural autobiography, and can be used independently of the others. Although stories have been grouped together according to the predominant themes of race/ethnicity, immigration, spirituality, social class, sexual orientation, and disability, other themes, including gender, regional concerns, and educational back-ground, are present within the stories. An introductory section provides a brief overview of the predominant cultural factor. Two sections follow each story: "Content Themes" and "Clinical Applications." The content themes are the issues that appear to be most predominant for the individ-ual in the story. They are extracted from the story and describe cultural concepts and cultural variables and how those variables interact in the individual's life. Some of the content themes are applications of known conceptual ideas pulled from the literature of multicultural theoretical frameworks. Others are less well known conceptually, stemming from the authors' experience as teachers, counselors, and consultants. They are intended to help the reader find applications of the multicultural theory concepts in a real-life story and to understand the complexities of identity formation. The content themes described are not the only ones that can be extracted from these stories. Not all themes that are obvious in a story have been described because, in some cases, those themes are explored in a different chapter. Readers might be able to extract additional content themes, and we wholeheartedly encourage that exploration with the help of the Toolbox Activity at the end of each chapter. The "Clinical Applications" section contains assessment questions, clinical interventions, and cross-cultural countertransference issues. The assessment questions are generally related to the content themes and are intended as guidelines, not as an exhaustive list of the possible topics to be assessed in a clinical situation. They are a way to remind clinicians about topics or issues that might be salient or relevant to a certain client at a certain time, and counselors need to be sensitive to the relevance and timing of the questions. The clinical interventions generally flow from the content themes and the assessment questions, but not always. The clinical interventions are intended to be used in all types of therapeutic encounters, including individual, family, couple, and group therapy. We have tried to present culturally sensitive interventions existing in the literature that are related to the individual experiences of each storyteller but can be extrapolated and used in other similar cases. A complete explanation of the intervention is not possible, but the reader is invited to consult with the original sources for the ideas presented in the section.

The final portion of the "Clinical Applications" section includes a discussion of reactions clinicians may experience when working with diverse clients—countertransference reactions. Therapists carry into their interactions with their clients their character, values, and ideals about a good life, a good marriage, and good parenting; their perspectives on "normal" behaviors drive the treatment goals and the therapeutic process. This experience is even more critical to examine when working with culturally diverse clients because clinicians deal with their own cultural socialization, cultural norms, and standards (Comas-Diaz & Jacobsen, 1991), which affect the clinical situation.

As we were seeking feedback from reviewers, student readers, and others, it became clear to us that the readers' reactions to the stories were influenced by the readers' own life stories, their own cultural factors, and their own experiences. These included a variety of emotions: annoyance, rage, sorrow, frustration, sympathy. Readers also reacted strongly to the authors' choice of content themes, choice of placement of the stories, choice of clinical interventions, and descriptions of countertransferential reactions. This indicated to us that the readers were having their own countertransferential reactions to the cultural issues that we decided to cover or not cover in our book, content themes and clinical interventions we decided to include or exclude, and so on. The reactions of our readers reinforced our conviction that each story needed a section on counter-transference because they are proof of the powerful influences strong personal reactions exert on clinical work with individuals, couples, and families. Countertransference reactions can be understood as useful data that can guide clinicians in their quest to provide culturally sensitive clinical services. Clinicians who do not take the time to wrestle with and become aware of personal reactions to issues presented in therapy engage in unethical professional behavior (Gorkin, 1996; Pérez Foster, 1998).

We encourage readers to engage in an exploration of their reactions to the stories and the clinical applications in this book. This book can be used as a supplement to other textbooks in the field of multicultural theory, as a stand-alone textbook for such a course, or as a book for professionals interested in the stories and their clinical applications. We use the words *therapists, clinicians, providers,* and *counselors* interchangeably because the helping professions are populated by individuals of varied theoretical orientations, degrees, and interests. It is clear from the stories that each individual storyteller has embarked on a journey of growth that has included both joy and pain. It is our hope that readers feel enriched by the stories presented and that they gain a better understanding of the importance that comes from exploring the cultural heritage of their clients.

Acknowledgments

We could not have written this book without the contributions from our storytellers. Thank you for being so open with us and sharing your personal tragedies and triumphs! Your stories inspire and move us. Thank you also for not complaining about all the changes in identity that we had to do to fit our needs and protect your privacy. We hope that we have been able nonetheless to honor your voice and spirit.

Thanks to Kassie Graves for wonderful editorial assistance and guidance for this second edition of *Culture and Identity* and for the expanded text of *Dimensions of Multicultural Counseling: A Life Story Approach.* We would like to express gratitude to the reviewers for their comments and feedback: Saundra Tomlinson-Clarke, Rutgers, The State University of New Jersey; Stephanie F. Hall, Monmouth University; Beth A. Durodoye, The University of Texas at San Antonio; and Kimberly J. Desmond, Indiana University of Pennsylvania. What results is a stronger product. Also, thanks to Veronica Novak for your invaluable assistance.

We thank Kia-Rai Pittman and Rabiatu Barrie for assistance in updating references.

—AJT & SS

One

Framework

Personal identity *is* cultural identity. Culture is a powerful organizer of people's lives. How we view ourselves and who we are as individuals cannot be separated from when, where, and how we grew up. How adults behave, love, work, and make decisions is related not only to their individual psychological development but also to how their individual development intersects with the political, geographical, sociological, and historical factors that precede and surround their lives. Culture is one of the most influential determinants of identity (Waldegrave, 1998), and therapists who do not address cultural meanings in their clients may be engaging in oppressive practices rather than therapeutic ones. The stories in this book provide a window into individuals' lives as they reflect on important aspects of their cultural identity. It is important to view the stories as snapshots along a continuum in the storytellers' lives, one possible view of their journey toward identity development. It is also important to view the stories in the authenticity of the moment for the storyteller. How people decide to tell their story at one moment in life may vary according to their self-concept, their developmental stage, and the contextual dimensions of their lives. Our framework includes a description of human developmental models, together with other areas that must be explored to understand self-concept and cultural identity, such as descriptions of life cycle stages and other contextual dimensions of development.

Human Development

The models of human development teach us about human nature and the formation of identity. When working with clients across the life span, it is important to consider developmental tasks and activities, particularly as they relate to behaviors and functioning. Human development is plastic, fluid, and holistic; occurs within multiple contexts; and is often bidirectional because skills gained during one time period may be lost in another (Berger, 2008). For example, cognitive development is important to consider when understanding cultural identity and individuals' perceptions of themselves as cultural beings. In Piaget's model, for example, when school-age children move from concrete to formal operations, they are engaging in a cognitive shift that allows them to understand the world in logical terms and from multiple perspectives (Berger, 2008). In terms of cultural identity development, it is generally at this stage that children begin to move from a conceptual understanding of race and gender from a physical standpoint to a social perspective, with the beginning notions of the sociopolitical context from which culture is derived (Quintana, 1998; Wright, 1999). In Piaget's final formal operations stage, abstract and rhetorical thinking skills are mastered, allowing individuals who reach it to understand multiple perspectives simultaneously. When examining clients' stories, it is important to consider how cognitive development influences their understanding of the events in their lives and their ability to develop effective coping and problem-solving strategies. The stories in this book reflect the storytellers' shift in their cognitive appraisal of their cultural identity as they tell us about their cognitive understanding.

Erickson's stages of psychosocial development help us to understand development and its relationship to culture (Berger, 2008). As children move through their developmental tasks, the role of cultural factors cannot be ignored. As they move through the stages, they begin to understand the social connotations of their identity. For example, preteens begin to base their friendships solely on gender and develop strict rules for behaviors that signify group membership. Children who may not strictly follow the norms for gendered behavior are often teased and ostracized. The same can be true for other cultural factors. As adolescents try to answer the crucial "Who am I?" question, they begin to assess their role within society, including an understanding of stereotypes and the importance of values. For ethnic minority children, issues around career aspiration and expectation, for example, are colored by their perceptions of reactions and acceptance by others, the presence of role models, and financial concerns. In reading the stories in this book, the reader should be able to comprehend complex relationships between personality development and cultural identity.

The final area of development that serves as part of the framework for the stories is moral development. The three major moral development models (Piaget, Kohlberg, and Gilligan) include the significance of social norms and interpersonal relationships in resolving moral dilemmas (Berger, 2008). Piaget postulates that children develop a sense of right and wrong based on cooperative relationships with each other and conforming to what works best for the group. Kohlberg suggests that children move from avoiding punishment to receiving rewards and social praise for their decisions. Individuals move to an understanding of democratic principles and social norms before developing a set of universal moral principles. Gilligan argues that moral development for women differs from that of men because they are socialized to consider connection and intimacy in decision making (Berger, 2008). No matter which model is considered, it is important to remember that the issues of justice and equity need to be taken into account, particularly for people in oppressed groups. The incongruence that individuals often feel between the sense of these principles and their lived experiences needs to be reconciled in the process of cultural identity development.

Development of the Self

These traditional developmental models are not enough to understand cultural identity because they do not address the richness, complexities, and shifting of an individual's identity (Almeida, Woods, Messineo, & Font, 1998). In addition to understanding the role of human development in personality development and behavioral functioning, it is important to understand the development of the self and the intersection of cultural factors with self-concept. There are generally three components that influence the development of the self: the notion of the self, the ideal self, and the self reflected in the perceptions of others. The first layer of the self includes individual components, including unique personality traits, characteristics, and abilities, along with innate dimensions of temperament. The second layer of the self includes the self-ideal, traits and characteristics that are aspired to, along with goals and aspirations. Additionally, identity is not made up of a self that develops in isolation and holds still but is constructed by the social context a person has been in, is in, and will be in. The view of oneself is not constant but is complex, multifaceted, and reflected by others in the person's life (Tomm, 1989). Identities are shaped through social interactions with others (Rockquemore & Laszloffy, 2003). By the time they reach school age and develop the ability to classify on multiple dimensions, children begin to understand that others have perceptions of them (Quintana, Casteneda-English, & Ybarra, 1999; Selman, 1971), and they begin to incorporate others' perceptions into their perception of themselves. They become hypersensitive to others' perceptions and will often elicit feedback from others on their personality traits, abilities, and characteristics. The knowledge that others have perceptions that may differ from one's own underscores the need for acceptance by peers and the desire to fit in, to be "normal," and to feel validated (Rockquemore & Laszloffy, 2003). School-age children begin to have a solid understanding of group membership, and they become aware that group membership includes social status (Kerwin & Ponterotto, 1995). This is carried into the adult years.

Cultural identity models outline development that includes a sense of reference group orientation along with self-group orientation (Atkinson & Hackett, 2003). During preadolescence and the awareness of the sociopolitical connotations of cultural group affiliations, the pressure for conformity and acceptance increases. Preteens develop rigid definitions of criteria for group membership based on behaviors, dress, speech, and relationships. As you read the stories it becomes clear that the storytellers' sense of identity includes not only how they view themselves but also how others view them or have viewed them in the past and their future aspirations for themselves.

Contextual Dimensions of the Self

Cultural identity and self-concept are developed not only within the context of the consciousness of others' perceptions but also within historical images and stereotypes of culture. Dominant cultural patterns are embedded in our cultural discourses and social institutions, perpetuating certain ideas and ignoring others. Cultural identity is constructed historically and socially within groups and is influenced by the contact with differences within those groups or differences between different groups; it also evolves as ideas and historical times change (Falicov, 1998b). Individuals need to integrate their individual traits, their ideal self, and perceptions of others, including current perceptions and historical stereotypical roles, as they form their self-perceptions across the life span.

Therefore, the sense of self is not developed in a vacuum but within multiple contexts. In the field of psychotherapy, explanations for human behavior have traditionally been individual and psychological in nature and have tended to contain the narrow idea that an individual's or a family's behavioral patterns are regulated by personal decision, with an implicit notion of existential freedom devoid from the shaping of contextual dimensions. Although it is true that individual psychological explanations are important and that people do have the freedom to choose their fate to some extent, these individual dimensions are not enough to understand human behavior, motivation, and change. People do not wake up one day and decide to act in a certain way. Historical, sociological, anthropological, political, and geographical explanations are needed to make sense of a person's life choices, life cycle events, and patterns of individual or relational behavior. If therapists lack the curiosity of an anthropologist to seek out information or do not become interested in the statistics that a good sociologist provides, much harm can be done. Counselors, social workers, and psychologists may feel discomfort facing the daunting task of becoming acquainted with so many other disciplines to understand human behavior. But the discomfort of feeling ignorant may be a preferable reaction to indifference and the illusion that only psychological and individual explanations account for human behavior. As Monica McGoldrick (McGoldrick, Giordano, & Pierce, 1996) pointed out in *Ethnicity and Family Therapy*, the typical middle-class White American, often unaware of his or her own ethnic background, believes that ethnicity is something that other groups have, while the Americans are regular, as if the Western, middle-class, individualistic societies were the norm and not just one possible cultural norm. Our storytellers will not let us forget that.

Shifting Selves

Given that personality development, self-concept, and cultural identity are developed with multiple components and within multiple contexts, it is important to remember that the development of cultural identity is not static but dynamic and fluid as individuals continuously relate to institutions, communities, and other individuals. In this "relational reality"

(Gergen, 1991, p. 242) individuals discover new talents or traits, have a better understanding of the perceptions of others, and become aware of historical images and stereotypes while the self continues to evolve. Although we often think of optimal functioning for development, or compare others against norms and standards, what is clear is that self and identity are perpetual processes.

> Psychologists have proposed that a sense of one's own past, present and future life and identity is created through the telling of life narratives. The properties of the narrative form create a sense of temporality and coherence in an uncertain chaotic world, enabling us to learn from our past and predict aspects of the future. (Ellis-Hill & Horn, 2000, p. 280)

As we mature, grow, and add experiences, our view of self shifts and changes, existing in a state of continuous construction and reconstruction (Gergen, 1991). The storytellers in this book demonstrate this idea in their own narratives. Some of them write about how their sense of self changes across developmental age periods, within particular time periods, and across contexts. It is also certain that engaging in a period of self-reflection, in a way that resembles the self-reflection of a person engaged in a therapeutic relationship, also caused them to shift their views. That leads to a unique reflection and representation of the development of their cultural identity. Others do not write about their shifts, but as they go through the stages of their life cycle, predictions of future shifts are possible.

SECTION I

Race/Ethnicity

In America, race has long been a primary distinguishing cultural factor and a basis for oppression. Indeed, racial bias has underpinned many oppressive acts, including slavery, the removal of Native Americans from their lands to reservations, and the internment of Japanese Americans during World War II. Both subtle and institutional forms of oppression occur due to race. Race is associated with many emotionally laden issues, including racism, affirmative action, race-based quotas, acts of personal prejudice, political correctness, and sentiments against ethnic minorities (Sue & Sue, 2007). The experiences of most racial and ethnic minorities are colored by their status as minorities. The significance of race as a term and concept has been debated. Race has been based on phenotypical differences in skin color, facial features, and hair and has been extended to include judgments on intelligence and other psychological characteristics. These physical differences, however, were determined to be inappropriate measures of separateness, so much so that the American Anthropological Association (1998) issued a statement suggesting that race no longer be used as a biological classification but instead be viewed as a product of sociopolitical issues and economics. Skin color, for example, is probably more a historical adaptation to climate and environmental conditions rather than a representation of genetic differences. Contrary to people's beliefs, purity of the races is a myth (American Anthropological Association, 1998). Race has sociopolitical connotations in this country because race is a reason for political oppression (McGoldrick & Giordano,

1996; Sue & Sue, 2007). Race was used for determining citizenship and land ownership and served as a justification for oppressive acts.

Ethnicity is a broader concept in the field of multicultural theory that affords more depth of analysis than race. Focusing on ethnicity allows for inclusion of various groups categorized within racial groups, such as differences between Japanese and Chinese or Mexicans and Puerto Ricans. The emphasis on ethnicity also allows for the exploration of cultural norms for Whites. Although often associated with nationality and national origin, ethnicity influences functioning, the nature of relationships, and life cycle transitions (Breunlin, Schwartz, & Mac Kune-Karrer, 1997). Phinney (1996) defines ethnicity as an aspect of a person's social identity that is a part of an individual's self-concept that derives from his or her knowledge of membership in a social group together with the value and emotional significance attached to that membership. Ethnicity includes three components: cultural values, attitudes, and behaviors; a subjective sense of group membership; and experiences with minority/majority status (Phinney, 1996). Ethnicity directs actions; thoughts; affective experiences, including work/career, interpersonal relationships, rituals, and traditions; and eating habits and patterns (McGoldrick & Giordano, 1996). Members of ethnic groups differ in the nature of their interpersonal relationships, rules, family and personal dilemmas, and strategies for resolving conflict (Hines, Garcia-Preto, McGoldrick, Almeida, & Weltman, 1992). Although understanding an individual's ethnic group membership may be a good framework for understanding behaviors, values, and beliefs, generalizations could also lead to inappropriate stereotypes and misunderstandings of intragroup differences. Individuals differ in terms of ethnic identity, which includes the sense of membership in the ethnic group, and attitudes and feelings about group membership (Phinney, 1996). Racial identity, a similar concept, is derived from socialization experiences and the psychological and sociopolitical attitudes individuals hold toward their racial group and other groups (Helms, 1995). Racial and ethnic identity models postulate that individuals progress through stages of low salience and awareness of race to integration of values and beliefs prescribed by race (Sue & Sue, 2003). It is important to explore racial and ethnic identity because they explain behaviors and attitudes. Ethnic identity varies in family members (Gushue, 1993), and there are often conflicts in families resulting from differences in ethnic identity and values (McGoldrick & Giordano, 1996).

There are a variety of racial and ethnic identity models (Sue & Sue, 2007). Individuals progress from having neutral or negative and deprecating attitudes toward their own racial group and positive attitudes toward the dominant group to immersion in their own culture, sometimes with accompanying anger toward the dominant group. This is followed by a more sophisticated psychological and cognitive exploration of the meaning of their culture and an integration of cultural values and racial and ethnic identity into self-concept. Racial identity is self-determined and is inclusive of values from both cultural groups. It is important for therapists to determine the identity level of their clients. It should be noted that the racial and ethnic identity process is dynamic and recursive and that individuals may move fluidly back and forth through various stages as a result of experiences, personal growth, and self-awareness.

This section includes four chapters with stories on race and ethnicity. The first story chronicles Julie's experiences with racism, internalized oppression, and racial identity development. The second chapter follows the identity development and functioning of Butch, a multiracial individual. The reader will discover the challenges that he faces in integrating each of the cultural groups that comprise his racial heritage. The third chapter focuses on ethnicity and ethnic identity development, as Betsie chronicles the values from her Jewish family traditions. The fourth story, of Maribel, reflects her struggles with being both Puerto Rican and American.

Two

Julie's Story

So What If I'm a Black Woman?

Race remains one of the most contentious issues in our country. When we are at cocktail parties, race, along with politics and sex, is often a forbidden subject. We are often socialized to pretend that race does not exist, encouraged and rewarded to see people as individuals without color. Yet, for many, particularly ethnic minorities, race is a primary identifier. It provides a sense of pride, a sense of connection and belonging; it becomes an all-encompassing source of identity. One's racial affiliation can determine lifestyle choices and values, and it influences relationships and behaviors. But race can also lead to a sense of shame, discomfort, embarrassment, and fear as individuals encounter experiences of oppression and racism. Race can lead individuals to engage in stereotypical behaviors or behaviors that serve as attempts to fight against stereotypes. Although our relationship to race is a lifelong fling, our connection to it changes with new experiences and with changes in development.

Julie's story is one of exploration and the development of her racial identity. Although she has always had an awareness of her status as an African American woman, race had little salience or meaning until she was confronted with racial concerns and episodes of racism in high school and college, which, according to Erikson (1968), is the time when identity development begins. As you read her story, you should think about the influence that racism can have in shaping identity, an individual's sense of self, and self-esteem. Also, begin to think about how Julie's level of social class interacts and intersects with race, along with the role of gender in her life.

Julie's Story

As a 30-year-old African American female, it feels like I have had to deal with my race and its impact on me and how I view the world since the day I was born. I was raised in a single-parent African American household. My maternal grandfather lived with me most of my life and acted as a surrogate father. I saw my father pretty frequently, and he did give me an allowance and took me shopping; however, I always got the feeling he only did it to please my mother. I viewed my father as being very distant and never looked forward to his constant put-downs and negative comments. When I mentioned this behavior to my mother, she usually defended him and made excuses for his behavior: "He just feels if he says that about you, you'll work harder to prove him wrong" or "He's just having some problems right now. Just ignore him." I soon stopped telling her because the excuses were worse than the comments.

As a young girl, I searched for affirmations of my beauty and intellect. On television I did not see many African Americans, and my earliest dreams of being a career woman were colored by how I thought the "White" people did things. You see, my community was poor and Black. Some of the schoolteachers were White, but for the most part, I didn't interact with Whites until I went to the store with my family outside of our community. I often dreamed of traveling and seeing all the places White people came from. It's funny—visiting Africa never entered my mind until high school. During my search for an identity as a young girl, I remember hating to go get my hair done. We would go to a friend of the family who had a beauty shop in her basement. She was an older woman, and my weekly press and comb was done by her. Here my mother talked and got cooking lessons and life lessons. I always felt I was being tortured and talked about. I have very thick, coily hair, and it was the topic of many discussions. My "bad" hair was difficult and hard to manage, and I was often teased about cutting it off. Although I never said anything, this early experience made me feel I should have been born White. I remember getting mad at my mother on a few occasions and asked her why my daddy couldn't have been White so my hair could be "good."

My mother, probably unable to understand the full magnitude of what I meant, would tell me my father was chosen because he was the person she loved.

As I began to develop and get noticed by men in a sexual way, I went through a very uncomfortable and difficult time, which still plagues me to some degree to this day. At home, my father constantly told me I was fat and would have to be pushed through the door by the time I was 18. My grandfather would yell at me to take off the shorts or whatever else I happened to be wearing, and my mother would just say, "Your father used to tell me I was fat when I was your size, and I look back now and see I wasn't." The only people who seemed to think I was beautiful with coily hair and large hips, thighs, and buttocks were the boys who lived in the area. Because I did not have a great relationship with my father, it's safe to say I didn't trust men, so, thankfully, I did not fall prey to any male sexual advances during this time of turmoil. Also, because I was heavily involved in church activities, I believed that sexual activity before marriage was forbidden, and I was determined to not fall prey to it. Lastly, because my father wasn't around much and my mother was raising me alone, I never wanted a child out of wedlock. I had been called a bastard too many times and never wanted my child to endure such a thing, nor did I want to be the subject of the Supremes' song "Love Child."

All of this physical development and turmoil began when I was 12 years old. During this same time, I got the greatest shock of my young world. One day as I sat in the kitchen eating my dinner alone, my father was in the den (located the next room over) watching television. The doorbell rang. Suddenly my mother appeared to tell my father someone wanted him at the door. Well, this was most unusual because my father did not live with us and most definitely did not receive any visitors. As I peeked out of the window, I saw my father's van double parked and a woman standing near it with her hands on her hips and her head moving from side to side. It was apparent she was yelling from the way her hands would occasionally wave in the air. My mother stood in the darkness on our enclosed porch, listening. I ran back to my seat in the kitchen as my father came past me to get his shoes and prepared to leave. I asked who was at the door, and his only response was, "Who do you think?" After I told him who I thought it was, he said, "Yep," and walked out the door. We were never to speak of her again, and, in fact, my mother and I never spoke of her until a few days before my wedding, when I told her I had reservations because I was not confident a man could be faithful. Her only response was, "I knew you would have problems with this eventually. I just didn't know when."

As a Black woman, this early event had dramatic effects on me. Did only White families have faithful husbands who took care of their families and loving and devoted wives? Was it a Black woman's fate to raise her children alone and to bear them outside of marriage (there sure were a lot of single female parents at church)? Why was I not considered beautiful, and because of my appearance, would I ever meet someone who would love me and think I was beautiful? It's funny, but as I continued to struggle with these issues and entered high school, I remember my father telling me he would not walk me down the aisle on my wedding day. Like the glutton for punishment I was, I asked why. He told me that when I got divorced because the man was no good and could not take care of his responsibilities, I couldn't blame my father for giving me away.

In high school, I attended a magnet school with a very mixed ethnic population. I discovered there were intelligent Blacks and Hispanics as well as intelligent people from other ethnic groups. To me, we got along great. I do not recall having any racial discussions or hearing people put down because of their race. You were considered elite because you were able to get into the school, and if you were able to stay, well, you were destined for greatness, regardless of your race. I never really thought about race during this time. Granted, my time at school was very different from my time at home. At home, I was surrounded by African Americans who engaged in the use and distribution of drugs, there were gang fights and shootings, and many of the young girls my age were pregnant or soon to be, but somehow I wanted to believe I was better than they were. I was going to make it, and in my mind I would be a credit to my race. How awful to admit such a thought, but nonetheless it is what I thought. I began to imitate my White classmates. I spoke proper English and worked very hard at sounding White. I even worked on my accents: British, California Valley girl, and so on. I see now that I wanted to be anything but Black. As I left my neighborhood for school each day, I dreamed of being a doctor or anything else that would take me around the world and make me important. In some of my daydreams, my hair was a bouncy, wavy texture, and my skin was much lighter. I was considered beautiful, and all of the men—White and Black and everything else—thought I was the most beautiful woman they had ever met. See, I knew I was Black, but I hated everything about being Black. I hated the way Black people spoke, and I hated the way they laughed and drank and looked. I hated that they all didn't want to do better, wouldn't go to school, didn't find jobs, had unprotected sex, and so on. I didn't realize it, but I hated me. I didn't like my full figure, and I definitely found nothing beautiful about my skin or my hair. I wanted to be White, and I identified with the White culture. I felt that Blacks were in the shape they were in because of the decisions they made. I was unable to see anything differently. My grandfather would also make comments about the neighborhood gang-bangers or other members of the community, which helped to reinforce my beliefs.

In high school, we were all required to take an African American history class, which I thought was an awful requirement. After all, I was Black, so therefore I didn't need the class. Right? Wrong! I remember feeling overwhelmed at the material and somewhat confused. All of my grammar school history books never even mentioned Blacks. We simply were the slaves. Now here was this new information that said we contributed greatly to the world and to the United States. How could this be? The instructor assigned a research paper for us to write, and I still remember part of it and the changes it began to make in me. We were assigned an African country, and we had to write about the land and its people. Additionally, we needed to first start our research at home, in the family encyclopedia. Well, this was great because, for a poor family, we did own a set of encyclopedias, and I thought I would finish this assignment on Egypt in a hurry. Well, I looked up Egypt and found all the pictures of the people to be drawings of White people. I remember feeling hurt and furious. Were Egyptians White or Black? Then I discovered that they never really said Egypt was in Africa (which I found out later during my research). I was floored. How much did I not know about being Black and why were they (I wasn't sure who *they* were) trying to hide this information?

As I entered college, I still had these grand dreams of being accepted into the White world as one of them. I knew I would have to work hard and felt that every word I spoke or wrote was a reflection on how much like them I could become. I did join the African American student union, but this was only because a Black girl I met during orientation introduced me, and I just began hanging out. I also began to discover that making friends with other people (those who were not Black) was much harder than it had been in high school. In fact, most people wouldn't even talk to me let alone be my friend, but I attributed it to my unattractiveness and not my race.

While walking through the community area one day, I noticed many clubs were attempting to bring in new members. I was looking to move on campus and began to talk to a resident of an off-campus dorm. The dorm had a chef and many other benefits, and they seemed very eager to have me apply. Cool, I thought. I can move in here, and this would be great. I didn't realize they wanted me because they didn't have any Blacks living there and thought it would be a good idea to integrate. I also did not know I was in for some trauma that I was not prepared to deal with on an emotional level. I was accepted and moved in right away. It was the beginning of my sophomore year, and I already had a 3.8 average and wanted to keep up the good work. During the first week of classes, I went to the study area in the dorm and prepared to study. Suddenly, these two humongous White males entered the room and began talking to each other. I didn't know them, and they never introduced themselves to me. I continued to try to study, but they just got louder and louder. Eventually, I asked them if they would quiet down so I could continue studying, and this is when I began to understand who I was to the outside world. The two men came over to my table and began to taunt me. One said, "Oh, it looks like we've made the little nigger mad." The other said, "Yes, I wonder what the nigger thinks she can do about it." Well, I was taken off guard, and I definitely didn't know what to say. I had never been called the "N" word, and I had only heard it used from one Black person to another as a word of affection and familiarity. As these two men continued to call me names, something inside of me began to fall into the pit of my stomach. I wanted to fight, to hit, to scream, to kill them for calling me that horrible name. But instead I said nothing. I picked up my books and left the area, telling myself I couldn't take them both; they were too big. I hid. I hid in my room and began to look at each person in my classes. I soon discovered that in all of my classes I was the only Black person. I became paranoid. I was depressed and petrified. My mother was not speaking to me because I had moved into the dorm, and everyone else in my family seemed so busy. I didn't know where to turn. Meanwhile, life at the dorm just got harder.

My roommate was a white Hispanic. This meant she was Hispanic but looked White. She dated a White male and was very confused about who she was. She acted and thought White and began to make racial comments. Her boyfriend was my most incessant source of grief because on some occasions I would wake up with him looking in my face, making a racial comment about me. At a party he told me he asked everyone to turn the lights on so he could find me. The other women on my floor were just as awful. When I woke up in the morning, they made comments about my hair. When I exited the shower after washing my hair, they made comments about that. The time I blow-dried my hair and it stood out in a huge Afro, they all screamed when I entered my room, where they were waiting to see my hairdo. And let's not forget the time they kept harassing me because they wanted to touch Black hair. I won't even mention the times they made comments about how fat I was, although looking back I know I was considered small by all standards; I just had a fuller, rounder figure than they did. I won't even go into detail about my English composition teacher who, during this same time, wrote on my final paper/presentation that I should consider going into a profession where I could do public speaking, like the entertainment field, because I couldn't write, and my people were not known for their writing ability anyway. But with all of this, my breaking point came when an African American male was allowed entry to the dorm, and he proceeded to rob many of the rooms. I was not home at the time, but later that evening the dorm leaders called a family meeting where the robbery was discussed. Many felt I was in on it because I was Black, and others thought he was my friend and wanted me to go get their items back. I sat there in disbelief, fighting back the tears and horror. I found the courage to ask how I could possibly be involved if I was in class at the time. Someone said the man rang the doorbell and was let in. I asked why.

"He wanted to see you."

"Did he ask for me?"

"No, but he was Black, so I just assumed he wanted you, and I let him enter."

"Oh, that makes sense. I know all the Black people in the world."

"Well, why didn't he take any of your stuff?"

"Because I don't have anything to take except my underwear."

It was after these experiences that I began to change my racial identity. I began hanging out with the other Blacks on campus. I joined and attended Black club meetings. I began to take African American studies courses and became friends with some of the instructors. I ran for office in the clubs and soon began running workshops and bringing prominent

Blacks to the campus to speak to the student body. Suddenly, I hated those White people, and I wanted them to know it. I started fighting back at the dorm. When they made comments, I became sarcastic. When it was my turn to cook dinner, I made African dishes and made them eat with their fingers. For dessert, I made a chocolate pudding pie with the words "Black is beautiful" written on top. I even invited some of my Black friends over, and, dressed in black, red, and green, we stood in front of the dinner table with our fists held high while the various artists' versions of "Lift Every Voice and Sing" played in the background. I hated the Whites, and I picked any opportunity to make comments, to scare them, and to do whatever I could to regain my sense of dignity and self-worth. I played on their stereotypes of me, and I loved it. Soon I saw the dorm as a great place because of the benefits of the chef, unlimited kitchen privileges, the guest rooms, and so on and decided I would take it over and make it a Black dorm. I began a huge crusade to get more Blacks into the dorm, and I was successful. The next year six Blacks moved into the dorm, and with them came their friends. It was great, and many of the Whites began to move out.

One day, one of the senator's nephews who lived there had to be hospitalized for a mental breakdown. The rumor was that the Blacks had driven him crazy. The truth? He made all kinds of racial comments and was constantly confronted. This particular day he was caught writing "Millie and Vanilli" on the room door of a Black girl who was dating an Iranian man. She caught him and physically attacked him, knocking him to the ground and pouncing him. I thought it was great. He called his uncle, and some important looking men came to get him and took him away, while he cried and blubbered like a little baby.

Life began to take a turn when one of my instructors pulled me and several other students to the side for a group discussion one day after class. During class time, we had become upset with a White student's presentation. In it, he showed a home movie where all the people in authority were White and all the villains and down-and-outs were Black. We ate him alive, and he was quite insulted. The instructor wanted us to process what happened and told me and the other Black girl in the group that we would have to apologize to him. I laughed and refused. This began the first of many talks with me on racial identity and how to succeed in a multicultural world.

I would like to say that I left college a changed woman. I would even like to say I got through all the stages, and when I entered the work world I was totally open to a multicultural world and confident in who I was as a Black woman. I can't say that. I did not leave totally aware but hurt and angry and determined not to allow Whites to get close. I had been discriminated against by my peers and quite a few instructors, and I was not going to stand for it. If I thought I was being put down because of my race, I was going to scream and shout. I was accepted into the minority internship within the psychology and sociology departments, and I began to assist with research projects on racism and multicultural issues during my last year of school. It was during this time that I began to see the racial tension in the world not just toward Blacks but toward other ethnic groups. I also began to hear positive overcoming stories from Blacks who were able to navigate life despite being discriminated against.

My first job in my field after college was at a women's treatment facility. One of my coworkers was a young White woman, who was a little older than me. She constantly wanted to talk to me and offered me rides home from work, and it became apparent she wanted to be my friend. One day, I sat her down and told her quite bluntly that I did not want her friendship and that I didn't like White people, so she should leave me alone. She replied, "Some White people must have really hurt you bad. I'm going to show you we're not all that way." She and I are still friends today, and that incident occurred over 10 years ago. Her friendship and my work with clients and on myself helped me to continue to grow and develop a positive racial identity. This actually sounds crazy, but my White coworker affirmed my Blackness every day. She loved and kissed the children of our Black clients, she spoke of adopting Black children, she was always braiding her hair and even wearing beads, and she ignored all the comments and stares by other Whites. She thought I was smart and never seemed to mind that I was Black. She came to my home, met my boyfriend, and was just a cool person. I even went to her all-White suburb, met her biased mom, and sat in her outdoor hot tub with my coily hair frizzing into an Afro (by the way, her mother is like an aunt to my kids, today, and our extended families get along great).

Currently, I work in an affluent, predominantly White town where I am now one of only two Black police officers. In this capacity, I have felt a lot of strain and stress from my coworkers, and although they won't say anything to my face, it is apparent that a lot of them operate on some unspoken racial beliefs about my character, and no matter how hard I work it just isn't good enough for them. I became increasingly conscious of my figure and body image, my hair became an issue, and I started to watch every word I spoke. Recently, I cut my hair into a really short style as a sort of liberation. I wanted to swim and engage in other activities in which my hair requires too much effort and time (which I don't have), and I cut it. I have never felt so free. I also began to allow my coworkers to see me in my street clothes, with my stomach or legs showing, as a way of showing I am proud of my figure and who I am.

As I get older and experience life, I am beginning to love myself for who and what I am. I used to cry and wonder why God would make me Black and then make Black the thing people despised and mistreated. Why make me Black and then make my hair so thick and tangly that I can't comb it or so coily that it sticks straight out? Why make my nose so large along with my buttocks, hips, and thighs? Wasn't one of these enough without having all of them? And then why make the other people like me confused and full of self-hatred, self-destruction, and color consciousness? I may not have all the answers, but I am confident that I will find them and am learning to embrace myself more.

Content Themes

Julie's story, though it is unique in many ways, helps us to understand the process and journey that many undergo in the development of a positive racial identity. Her story suggests that the identity development process can be difficult not only because of stereotypes and experiences of oppression from the mainstream or dominant culture but also because of internalized racism and socialization experiences from family and friends. Her story teaches the difficulties individuals face when oppression and racism are internalized, the impact of stereotypes and racism, the effect of socialization experiences with family and peers, and the importance of self-definition.

Race and Stereotypes

The first issue in Julie's story is the influence that perceptions of race and stereotypes have on identity development and psychological functioning. Julie was raised in a poor, predominantly African American neighborhood. She had few role models of positive African Americans and developed a sense of shame about being Black. Negative stereotypes played a role in her self-concept. Julie indicates that she was concerned about the speech and levels of intelligence of African Americans. The negative image of African Americans was reinforced through her education; it was not until high school that she was exposed to African American history and heritage and more positive role models. This is a typical experience for many racial and ethnic minorities, who are more likely to be portrayed in the media as criminals, on drugs, less intelligent than Whites, unemployed or underemployed, and on public welfare. The media also often portray challenges experienced in families of racial minorities, including single-parent families and absent fathers. Asian Americans are often presented differently as the model minority, high achieving and successful, but this portrayal can be limiting as well and can cause many Asian Americans to be ignored if they are underachievers (Sue & Sue, 2007). All of Julie's behaviors, values, and decisions were influenced by her perceptions of race. She imitated Whites in speech to be perceived as more intelligent and to be accepted by Whites. After she experienced racism on campus, she began to associate more with Blacks and to participate in Black activities on campus.

Interpersonal Relationships

Race also influenced Julie's gender role expectations and views on interpersonal relationships. First, her family experiences caused her to question the role of African American women and men in relationships. This, combined with negative stereotypes of African Americans, led Julie to believe that African American men were unfaithful and that African American women were destined to be single or single parents. It is important to note that her gender role expectations were colored not only by her racial identity but also by her family relationships. If both parents had raised Julie, her perceptions might have differed.

Second, Julie's perception of physical attractiveness was influenced by her race. Julie was faced with images of White women as attractive and was self-conscious about her weight, her hair texture and length, and other features. Her level of concern about her appearance was so great that she dreamed of being more White in appearance. Although her self-consciousness might also be exacerbated by her family dynamics, her experience is not unique. Many racial minorities struggle with standards of beauty set by the dominant culture and may internalize a negative self-perception (Greene, White, & Whitten, 2000). Some dye, perm, or relax their hair or use hair extensions to make it straighter, lighter, or longer. At an extreme, some individuals pursue plastic surgery to gain Eurocentric facial features. Julie's concern with her physical attractiveness certainly influenced her interpersonal relationships and may have placed her in a vulnerable position where men may have taken advantage of her.

Third, racial identity influenced the nature of her friendships and social relationships. During her teenage years, Julie was more interested in being accepted by White people and limited her association with other Blacks. She tried to adopt various speech accents to sound White. The mixed ethnic magnet school allowed her to transcend race, or adopt a raceless persona (Fordham, 1988), an option that is often taken by racial minorities. Her efforts to change her speech, however, suggest that the raceless stance was not always a successful strategy to use. After significant experiences of racism, she changed her relationships to associate only with other African Americans. Julie's racial identity influenced her relationships with authority, particularly teachers. She describes an incident in which a professor attempted to lead her to critically examine her behaviors. However, Julie was too hurt and angry at Whites to benefit fully from this experience. Her relationships with coworkers were equally affected because she was initially mistrustful and distant.

Racism

The most striking component of Julie's story is the experiences with racism that she encountered on her college campus. Although college is often a place for intellectual enlightenment, Julie's story reminds us that this is where students often become more aware of their cultural identity and even more aware of the oppressive and prejudicial opinions of others. The pain from the experiences was intense for Julie and led her to change her perceptions of herself. What is striking in the story is the level of threat that she faced, both in terms of concerns for her physical safety and, more important, the threats to her sense of self. Although it is not clear whether Julie ever felt completely accepted by Whites, the sense of security that she did have was completely shaken by her peers' reactions to her in the dorm. Her concerns about physical differences were constantly stirred, even through small experiences such as exiting the shower. Her problem-solving resources were challenged because she had to overcome negative stereotypes of African Americans and reach out to her peers for support and comfort. It was the accumulation of the experiences, or microaggressions (Feagin & Sikes, 1995), that influenced the intensity of Julie's response. Single episodes of racism may not have a devastating influence on individuals, but repeated experiences and assaults of the self can be damaging.

Julie's college experiences caused her to begin the process of racial identity (Cross & Cross, 2008). This process generally occurs with individuals having neutral attitudes about race, low salience to race, or negative internalized attitudes about their own race. Often, this occurs until the individual has racial encounters, which lead to a shift in attitudes and immersion into his or her racial group. Finally, the individual integrates race and racial identity into self-concept. Julia clearly followed this path as she began to develop her sense of positive racial identity. Julie began her racial identity development as a child with negative attitudes about Blacks and being African American. Entering a magnet school allowed Julie to continue to see herself as different from other Blacks and close to equal with Whites. Julie had two periods in which significant encounter experiences occurred, seeming to propel her into further stages. The first period was when she took an African American history class and was exposed for the first time to positive historical images of Blacks. The second encounter period occurred during her study time in the college dorm, when students called her a racial slur. Julie experienced the typical psychological distress that occurs after significant racial encounters, including paranoia, depression, and fear. These experiences shifted Julie into an immersion phase, in which she joined Afrocentric activities and organizations and changed interpersonal relationships. Julie seems to be continuing to develop her identity and completing tasks in the final stage of integrating her racial identity into her self-concept. She admits that her journey was not complete when she left college, but self-acceptance and pride are increasing as she continues in her adult development.

Self-Definition/Authentic Self

The final theme from Julie's story is the importance of self-definition. Julie spent most of her childhood and adolescence reacting to negative experiences and stereotypes of African Americans. She defined herself in opposition to her negative perceptions of African Americans. Julie changed her speech to sound like and be accepted by Whites. She worried about her physical attractiveness and body size. After experiences of racism, she changed her self-definition and immersed herself in African American activities. Although this seems positive in many ways, her behaviors and attitudes were defined to combat others' perceptions. It was not until she was confronted by a professor and a White colleague that Julie began to examine her behaviors more critically. She changed her hair to a style that is more suitable for her lifestyle without being worried about others and is more comfortable with her body image. She has relationships with people from various racial groups and interacts comfortably with them. And she continues to have pride in her race. It is clear that Julie is in the process of defining herself more authentically and that, although she may continue to experience oppression and racism, she is secure in her identity and will continue to thrive.

Clinical Applications

This section explores the clinical implications from Julie's story for counselors, including assessment of race and racial identity, techniques and interventions to use in treatment, and countertransference concerns.

Assessment

Influence of Race

Race influences identity, behaviors, values, and psychological functioning of individuals. It is important to understand how clients conceptualize group membership and their understanding of the stereotypes and others' perceptions of their race. Values from racial groups should be explored. Clients often internalize racial stereotypes and prejudices and engage in self-fulfilling behaviors or attempt to act in opposition to them. Clinicians should assess the level of internalized oppression of their clients and the relationship between a client's presenting problem and his or her experiences with racism. Therapists should also explore how race intersects with other cultural factors. For example, Julie was raised in a poor neighborhood. What would her experiences have been like if she had been raised in a middle- or upper-middle-class neighborhood? Social class intersects with race and influences expectations of education and careers, exposure to role models, and access to resources. Julie's family did not need public aid, but how would her life be different if she had been raised in poverty? Finally, therapists need to examine the level of racial identity of their clients. Treatment with Julie over therapeutic issues would have been different if Julie had been in the immersion stage for longer periods of time or if her immersion experience would have occurred during high school instead of college.

The following questions may be used to assess race and racial identity. Clinicians should feel comfortable directly asking questions on race because clients will generally not initiate these discussions, even if the issues are related to the presenting problems.

> How important is your racial background to you?

> Have you experienced any incidents of racism or oppression?

> What messages about race did you receive from your family? From peers? From your school? From your community?

> Have you felt negatively about your race?

> Has your race served as a source of strength or resource?

> How is your racial background related to your presenting problem?

Techniques and Interventions

Critical Consciousness and the Authentic Self

One technique for clients dealing with racism is to help them to develop critical consciousness, the ability to assess their experiences in light of the context, and to separate their personal response from societal expectations (Watts & Abdul-Adil, 1997). Once individuals have the ability to examine their experiences critically, they can begin to develop their authentic self—self-concept that is self-defined. The development of an authentic sense of self involves the following process: see it, name it, question it, resist it, and transform it (Isom, 2002).

The first step is the development of awareness of the pervasiveness of oppression—seeing racism for what it is. For Julie, this beginning awareness came in high school when she was exposed to African American history. Therapists should help clients to understand the reality of racism, understand the history of stereotypes and sociopolitical context, and recognize individual acts of oppression as well as the institutional structures that support and maintain oppression. For example, in Julie's story one wonders if the residence hall staff were aware of the oppression she experienced and whether any attempts to intervene were made. Julie may not have seen the staff or university administrators as allies in the process, suggesting that the racism she experienced was a part of the institutional climate. The second step in the development of authentic self is to name it, to define the true nature of oppression as it occurs. It is the process of separating societal influences, thereby allowing correct labeling of the experiences. It was important for Julie to recognize the racism for what it was and to not make personal attributes for her experiences. The third step includes questioning one's experiences, to allow for the externalization of the problem to occur. Questions to be asked include the following: Am I responsible for this image? Did I cause the person to respond to me in a particular way? Julie began to question why information on African Americans was excluded from her textbooks in high school and why Egyptians were portrayed as Whites. She also began to question who was responsible for the misinformation. The fourth step is to resist it, which includes being assertive and defending the self. Resistance may also mean confronting oppressors, letting people know that their comments or behaviors are hurtful. Once oppression is resisted, individuals are freed from the restrictive context of oppression and are not ruled by the stereotypes and biases of others. The process of self-definition can begin, and people are free to behave and react in a way that is authentic.

Racial Heritage

The second recommended technique is to encourage clients to explore their racial history and heritage. Another way to overcome negative stereotypes and perceptions is to replace them with more positive information and images. Julie began to build a more positive self-concept when she began to explore her African heritage. Clients can be encouraged to attend cultural events, to read historical pieces or cultural literature, and to join social activities and organizations that promote racial heritage. Clients also can be encouraged to speak to or interview senior citizens in their racial group about their experiences. The interviews and conversations should focus on problem-solving techniques and available resources. Clinicians should be aware of cultural organizations within their communities as well as cultural leaders. Caution must be used in the timing of this intervention, and clinicians may want to consider the client's level of readiness to explore his or her cultural heritage. The more oppressed the client, the more risk of self-hatred. Assessing the client's level of racial identity may be helpful in determining the appropriateness of this intervention (Cross & Cross, 2008). Clients who feel negatively about their own racial group may benefit from exploring racial heritage but may not be psychologically ready to begin such exploration.

Racial Socialization

Racial socialization is the process of helping racial minority children develop positive self-images within an oppressive community. Research shows that parents give messages in a variety of categories, including the presence and reality of racism, preparation for and overcoming of bias and racism, cultural heritage, racial pride, self-pride, racial equality and humanistic values, mainstream Eurocentric values, and spirituality and coping (Hughes, Rodriguez, Smith, Johnson, Stevenson, & Spicer, 2006). It is important for clinicians to assess the racial socialization messages received by their clients. For example, Julie's grandfather often made disparaging comments regarding the poor African Americans in their community. This affected Julie's perspectives on race and gender roles by perpetuating and reinforcing her internalized negative attitudes. Parents should be especially encouraged to discuss racial issues and the possibility of racism with their children (Hopson & Hopson, 1992). Greene (1992) outlines a model for including racial socialization as part of the therapeutic process. The first step includes helping children to correctly label racism and handle accompanying feelings. The second phase includes the parents serving as role models for dealing with racism. The third step is providing emotional support for the emotional reactions to racism, including anger and powerlessness. The final phase includes helping families to adjust by developing coping mechanisms.

Countertransference

Clinicians may experience a variety of reactions to hearing about racial issues in clients. Race is one issue—along with politics and religion—that individuals are often socialized not to discuss, so many therapists may find it awkward to initiate a discussion about racial identity or experiences of oppression. However, because race is so important it is critical for counselors to explore these factors in their clients' lives and functioning. Clinicians may experience feelings of sadness, anger, frustration, anxiety, and guilt (Comas-Diaz & Jacobsen, 1991).

Reactions to Racism

Julie's story reflects the racism and oppression that occurs from membership in a particular racial or ethnic group. Although Julie's experience occurred in the 1990s, it can be easily dismissed as a historical artifact. One reaction that counselors have is to experience sadness over the mistreatment that clients have experienced. Acts of racism and discrimination can have a negative effect on self-esteem, and counselors may become overwhelmed with feelings over these acts. For example, Julie reports mistreatment by other students in her college dormitory. A clinician who feels sadness for her may express sympathy for her pain in an effort to relieve some of the discomfort of the client and the therapist. It is critical to remember, however, the difference between empathy and sympathy. Although comforting comments may be helpful for the client, if the comment is based more on the therapist's sadness, it may come across as patronizing, which may alienate the client. Sympathy from a counselor in this situation may be experienced by the client as the counselor feeling sorry for the client, leading the client to feel disconnected from the therapist or needing to "help" the counselor by minimizing the pain from the incident. Empathy is the ability to place oneself in the experience of another and to understand it from that person's perspective. Although counselors may not have experience with racism, they can empathize with the feelings of anxiety, depression, or discomfort that may arise.

A second common reaction to racism and acts of oppression may be a rationalization of the event, in which the clinician suggests to clients that perpetrators may have other motives for their behavior. Providing a rationale for perpetrators, however valid an alternative explanation may seem, minimizes the issue for the client and may lead the client to feel invalidated. The end result of an explanation is that it often trivializes the problem and may prevent the client from feeling comfortable in disclosing painful experiences. Underlying this response may be some anger at the client for assuming the victim role or for personalizing the experiences of oppression. The therapist may feel that the client is paranoid or too sensitive to issues. This reaction also may hamper the therapeutic relationship.

Therapists may experience a sense of frustration or hopelessness about the likelihood of racism or oppression ending. One common response is a sense of incredulity about the prevalence of oppression in today's society. When racism is brought up, some White people typically respond that racism is a part of history and that ethnic minorities should move on and not be so sensitive to racial issues. Public and violent acts of oppression, such as the James Byrd and Matthew Shepard killings, remind us all of the continued presence of bigotry and prejudice. While ethnic minorities may be reminded of the importance of being prepared for racism, some Whites may perceive the experiences as isolated events that do not represent the majority's feelings. In many instances, the stories presented by clients stir up feelings of frustration that racism will never end. Some clinicians feel some level of powerlessness and helplessness while listening to the clients' experiences. Powerlessness often serves as a parallel process for the clients who may also be experiencing depression, anxiety, and feelings of hopelessness. Clinicians who experience these feelings may help clients in reflecting on their feelings of helplessness, which validates the experience of the clients and possibly opens the door for further dialogue on personal responsibility and the development of coping mechanisms for oppression.

Race of the Therapist

Some reactions may occur based on the racial background of the client–counselor dyad. White counselors may feel some guilt over being a member of an oppressive group. This sense of guilt may lead to feelings of sadness for the client and attempts to overcompensate for the actions of others. The therapists may feel that clients will blame them for oppression and that the clients may harbor feelings of anger and resentment toward them. This may be a reality for nonvoluntary clients who view the therapist as part of the court and social services systems. This may lead therapists to treat clients in a gingerly fashion, and therapists may avoid confronting clients over tough issues that need to be addressed in treatment. At an extreme, clinicians may engage in unethical treatment of clients by allowing problematic behaviors to go unreported to maintain rapport with clients.

Counselors who are the same race but at a different stage of identity development from the client may experience anger over the client's stories and may suggest problem-solving skills that promote assertiveness or sometimes aggression as a reaction to acts of oppression. Although endorsing active problem solving may be helpful to some clients, a client who is experiencing depression may need to resolve those feelings before moving to problem solving. Same-race therapists may also feel powerlessness and helplessness and may be unable to provide solutions as they experience memories of their own experiences of oppression. Same-race clinicians may also experience overidentification with their clients and project their feelings onto the clients' experiences. When therapists begin to overidentify with their clients, they lose the ability to feel and express empathy as they work to attempt to take care of their own emotions. Clinicians at this point often become frustrated when clients deny the emotional reactions that the client is experiencing. Clinicians of the same race or ethnicity may have difficulty distinguishing between behaviors within the cultural norms and those that are pathological. Finally, same-race counselors may ignore pathological behaviors in an attempt to foster solidarity within the race. The example of the reactions to the Anita Hill trials exemplified this notion: Some African Americans were angry that Anita Hill decided to come forward with her accusations against Clarence Thomas, believing that it should have been kept private to protect an African American man. Many counselors, for example, may ignore signs of abuse to prevent another member of their race from entering social service systems.

TOOLBOX ACTIVITY—JULIE		
Discussion Questions	*Activities*	*Resources*
Content themes What other themes do you see emerging in the story that the author did not identify? **Assessment** Are there any questions you would like to ask Julie? **Interventions** What other interventions could you propose with Julie? **Countertransference** What countertransference reactions were emerging in yourself as you read this story? **Other scenarios** What would have occurred if Julie's father had played a more prominent role in her life and lived with the family? What would Julie have been like if she had been raised in a middle- or upper-class family? What role did strengths such as spirituality and extended family play in Julie's life?	Visit a cultural center or museum that focuses on Native American, African American, Asian, or Latino heritage. Write in your journal about the feelings that are elicited as you visit. How will the experience influence your work with clients?	**Suggested readings** Feagin, J. R., & Feagin, C. (2002). *Racial and ethnic relations*. Upper Saddle River, NJ: Prentice Hall. Rodriguez, R. (2002). *Brown: The last discovery of America*. New York: Viking. Tatum, B. (2002). *Why are all the Black kids sitting together in the cafeteria?* New York: Basic Books. **Videos** *Boyz 'N the Hood* *The Joy Luck Club* *Smoke Signals*

Three

Butch's Story

Who Am I?

Developing racial identity can be complicated for individuals because they must balance self-perceptions, stereotypes and biases, and socialization processes. Racial identity development is more difficult for people with multiple or mixed racial backgrounds. Biracial individuals are the offspring of individuals with differing racial heritage. *Interracial* is the term given to describe the marital process, and *multiracial,* a newer term, describes individuals from two or more heritages (Kerwin & Ponterotto, 1995). The idea of the existence of mixed racial heritage has been troublesome. The prevailing notion was—and still is today—that individuals from mixed racial heritages, particularly Whites and Blacks, would have difficulty functioning. It was also believed that mixing the races would "dilute" Whiteness, leading to an inferior race or group of people. In the early 1800s, interracial marriages began to be outlawed, and it was not until 1967 that the U.S. Supreme Court ruled these laws as unconstitutional (Kerwin & Ponterotto, 1995). Complicating the identity process were laws that defined the notion of race, which varied from state to state, including the one-drop rule for individuals with African heritage, which stated that a person with any African ancestry was categorized as African or African American (Rockquemore & Laszloffy, 2003). The consequences of the negative reactions to racial mixing included the development of a social status classification system, leading to intragroup differences and judgmental attitudes. Biracial individuals were often forced to choose a racial group, but some biracial people attempted to "pass" and be accepted as Whites. The tragic mulatto syndrome, personified in the movie *Imitation of Life,* was a by-product of the attitudes toward biracial individuals; it includes the dilemma of having to choose a racial identity, often as a result of denying a part of one's racial heritage (Kerwin & Ponterotto, 1995). It should be noted that this process included not only the denial of part of one's own heritage but also a denial of family members or associates.

The 2000 U.S. Census data show that 6.8 million individuals, or 2.4% of the population, reported a multiracial heritage, the majority of whom reported two races in their background (Grieco & Cassidy, 2001). The majority of individuals indicating more than one race included White as one race (about 80%), followed by "some other race," Black, Native American, or Asian (www.census.gov). (Hispanics are counted as an ethnic group and can have a variety of racial designations, according to the U.S. Census Bureau.) Although historically more attention has been given to White–Black intermarriages, it is clear that the multiracial category is expanding, and clinicians may be confronted with more biracial and multiracial clients. It is more acceptable today to claim multiracial heritage; however, individuals still need to engage in the complex task of identity development. Butch's story describes this complex process that occurs with people of mixed racial heritage. The reader should pay close attention to the negotiation process that must occur with each component of Butch's racial background, including acceptance from various racial groups, pressures to accommodate to particular racial groups, and intragroup oppression from racial groups.

Butch's Story

Who am I? What race am I? What nationality am I? Where do I fit into American society? Where can I find total acceptance? For most of my 47 years, I have struggled to find answers to these questions. I am an American of multiracial descent and culture. In this aspect, I am not very different from many Americans. The difference for me is that I have always felt an urge to feel and live the intermingling of blood that runs through my veins. American society has a way of forcing multiracial and biracial people to choose one race over the other. I personally feel this pressure every time I have to complete an application form with instructions to check just one box for race category. My own racial and cultural background consists of American Indian from two nations, Lahkota and Creek; African American; Italian American; and Puerto Rican. I am Spanish speaking with some knowledge of the Lahkota language. Possessing such a diverse background has often placed me in a position to hear many insensitive and racist remarks from one group to another; obviously, I have often been the target. In the eyes of White Italian people, I am viewed as a Black person. Blacks often view me as a weak and tainted half-breed. Indians have cautiously accepted or rejected me. The Puerto Rican community has offered the most acceptance.

A family tree would be next to impossible in our family, largely due to secrets (skeletons), question marks, and taboo subjects. The matriarch of our family was my maternal grandmother, Anna, who was half Black and half Creek Indian. My paternal grandfather was Ogalla Lahkota from the Pine Ridge Indian reservation. He was called Jimbo, which was short for Jim Bull. I am told that my mother's father was an Italian immigrant who lived in a "little Italy" neighborhood. My father's mother was Black. Her husband, Jimbo, called her Pipe because she always smoked a pipe. So when all of this was finally sorted out, it looked liked this: My mother, Laura, is one fourth Black, one fourth Creek, and half Italian. My father is half Black and half Ogalla Lahkota.

The Italian side of our family was—and to a large extent remains—a mystery seldom discussed in our family. My mother and her siblings were born and raised in a "little Italy" neighborhood. At about the age of 12 or 13 years, I learned of our Italian ancestry. I received this information through one of our family historians, or storytellers, our Aunt June. Aunt June was one of my mother's younger sisters. Aunt June was very fair skinned with dark eyes and hair. She never had children of her own, and she also had a drinking problem, which I realized after I was grown. While I don't believe she told us everything about the family, she did let us in on many family secrets. Probably because she never had children of her own, it seemed like she really enjoyed spending time with my siblings and me. We have fond memories of Aunt June babysitting for us on the weekends. She loved to watch horror flicks with us, which we thought was very cool since no other adult that we knew did. We would all lie down on the floor together, eating popcorn, enjoying all the old original *Frankenstein, Wolfman, Dracula,* and *Mummy* flicks. After the movie, Aunt

June would tell us old family stories of when she and her brothers and sisters were young children. Sometimes after drinking a few beers, Aunt June would cross the forbidden line and tell us things that my mother and her other sisters had secretly kept hidden in the closet. I can remember my mother and her other two sisters pulling Aunt June in the bedroom, closing the door, and scolding her about talking too much. (Of course, as many children do, we eavesdropped.)

Well, one day, Aunt June pulled out this old wallet-size photo of a dark-haired White man with a Hitler-style moustache. She said to me, "This is your grandfather, my father. You can keep this picture, but don't let my sisters know." Aunt June later went on to tell me that my grandfather was an Italian immigrant from Calabria, Italy. Aunt June didn't seem to know much more about him. With a very sad face and with tears welling in her eyes, she told me that she never knew her father. Even though I never asked her, I always wondered why she chose me to keep the picture instead of my brothers and sisters. In some ways, learning about my grandfather helped me to make sense of some things. Between the ages of 5 and 7 years, I began to perceive and question the differences in skin colors, which were quite evident in our family. My mother and Aunt June were very fair skinned, while Candace, my mother's oldest sister, and Lily were brown and olive. Their brother, Tony, had black skin. So after learning about my Italian grandfather, it took me back to a question I asked my mother about the age of 7 years. I was gazing at a picture of my mother's brother, Tony, when I thought to myself, "If Tony is my mother's brother, then why are they virtually opposite colors?" So, as a child, I popped this question to my mother: "If Uncle Tony is your brother, then why is he so dark, and you are so white?" My mother responded with a quick sharp slap to my face and told me, "It's not your business, and Tony is my brother, and that's that." As I was to learn later in life, this was just the beginning of hard questions to come with no easy answers.

When I was about 11 years old, our family moved to an extension of the "little Italy" neighborhood. While the Italian community didn't exactly throw a welcoming party for us when we first moved there, all in all we were not harassed. We had some Italian childhood friends, although I don't remember being invited into many homes. Our family would go on living here for the next 6 years—years that would challenge our multiracial status like never before.

Ironically, the very neighborhood my mother had been raised in, "little Italy," claimed me as a beating victim. One day, possessing an urge to visit my mother's old neighborhood, I was approached by two grown Italian men who had been standing on their front porch stairs. One of the men appeared to be in his 50s, the other in his mid-20s, probably father and son. The younger man had a metal pipe in his hand. They asked me what the hell I was doing around here. At the time, I was 18 years old and had this feeling of invincibility. So, as they approached me, I stood my ground in defiance and proceeded to ultimately receive a beating that cost me 10 stitches on my head, along with numerous bumps and bruises, mostly on my arms, which I had used to ward off some of the blows aimed at my head. I was to learn later from the "Gents," a Puerto Rican street gang, that they had been warring with some of the Italians. This of course answered why they had called me a dirty Puerto Rico Gent as I was being beaten. Somehow, after what seemed like an eternity, I was able to escape, where I later was picked up, bleeding and dazed, by two plainclothes detectives. After showing the detectives the house where my assailants entered after the beating, I was driven to the emergency room. Shortly before leaving the hospital, I was told by the returning detectives that they couldn't locate the perpetrators. It was apparent that I was the wrong person in the wrong place at the wrong time. It was this incident that created a deep hatred on my part toward Italians. In a sense, it was also the beginning of self-hatred for the Italian side of myself. Afterward, whenever anyone asked what my ethnicity was, I would not mention the Italian blood, which ran through my veins.

I also had trouble with my African American heritage. As the neighborhoods in which we lived continued to become more Black, it became increasingly difficult to cope. My oldest brother, Landon, was forever getting beaten up. The Black girls thought he was gorgeous, which didn't help to ease the hatred that the Black males had toward my brother. Landon was a star athlete in track, basketball, and baseball. Since Landon didn't hang out in the neighborhood in which we lived, I was put in the uneasy position of trying to protect my younger brother, Paul. We were always getting socked on because we weren't quite the same as our friends, according to them. I was, quite frankly, afraid to fight Blacks. The blacker they were, the more afraid I was to fight. I remember being told on numerous occasions that my family was physically weak because we were mixed.

There was one kid in our neighborhood that happened to be our friend, sometimes. But whenever he felt like beating up on two little light-skinned curly-haired boys, there my younger brother and I were, ready to be someone's doormat. One day, like so many others, he felt like taking his rage out on us, so he began beating me up. Paul ran home to get our mother. During the beating, I saw my mother coming, so I knew I had to find some courage to fight back, even though at the same time I was glad that my rescue was on the way. When my mother arrived, she shouted out to me, "Don't you stand there and let him beat you up. Fight back!" Well, I suddenly got this renewed energy and courage and began to try to turn the tide. Unfortunately, it was not to be. I was afraid. I was totally lacking in confidence. I was a victim, buying into the belief that, because of my mixed blood, I was not Black enough; I could not and would not overcome my adversary. It would be years before I would grow to understand and confront my fears.

Another incident that occurred when I was about 12 or 13 years old would leave another deep wound in my already shaken and mixed-up mind. My siblings and I had made friends with the new Black kids who had moved into the neighborhood. At first it seemed that they were very eager to make friends with us. We all seemed to get along well, and we hung out and played together often. One day I got into a fight, for reasons I don't recall, with this kid that everyone else called a nerd. Franky, as he was called, certainly wasn't very popular; he wasn't even part of our little group that regularly hung out together. As I was pinning him down to the ground in a straddle position, I couldn't actually believe it, but it appeared I was winning the fight. Franky meanwhile was swearing at me, telling me that as soon as he got up he was going to kill me. Suddenly, my friends (or so I thought), who had been standing in a circle around us watching, began shouting, "Get up, Franky! You can beat this little light-skinned nigger's ass any day!" At that point, the little confidence and courage I had gained was quickly destroyed. As they continued urging Franky on, I began to panic, and Franky started to sense my panic. He began struggling even harder, even though my growing fear was the only thing that gave me strength to keep Franky subdued.

When I looked up at what had turned into a mob, all I could see was hateful faces, salivating for my ridicule and defeat. In desperation, I scanned the crowd for a sympathetic, helping face. And then, bingo! There it was—the face that seemed to say, "Pity you! What can I do?" Speaking low, hoping that the mob wouldn't hear, I asked this person if he could go and bring my mother back. The person nodded slightly indicating that he would. At the same time, some of the other kids had heard my request and began to tease me and laugh at me. Unfortunately, my would-be messenger was physically threatened and ordered to stay put. About that time, my mother stepped out on the terrace and saw the incident. She rushed down to get me. My ordeal was over, though the fear, pain, and humiliation was for me very real. I was in shock—I really thought they were my friends. After the incident, I stayed inside for about 2 weeks. I was very hurt and embarrassed. But eventually I would go back out and try to be part of the group. I knew I needed to try to fit in some way. It would be difficult because I certainly couldn't change my looks. Why did I go back to these kids, who I knew hated me for who I was? Simply put, I had no choice. It was either adapt or stay locked up at home. I wanted and needed to be accepted. It was at this point in my life that I really wondered why I couldn't have been born Black—Black meaning black in skin color, hair texture, facial features, everything.

From this point, it was pretty much open season on my family and me. At times, things seemed to go well with my friends. Friends? We would play basketball, softball, and follow the leader, and sometimes we would just hang out on each other's front porches. But when things got boring or the right situation presented itself, my family would become a target again. I remember one day we were all sitting out on the front porch, and my mother was walking down the street. As she was going up the stairs to our apartment, one of the guys asked, "Hey Butchie! Ain't your mother White?" Knowing that I needed to fit in, I answered back, "No!" They all laughed in response to my answer and said I was lying. Being very sensitive, I lowered my head and went home.

In the fall of 1963, I began my freshman year at a high school that had a Black student population of about 95%. There were 6 or 7 White students, about 5 Asian students, and approximately 15 to 20 Puerto Rican students. Academics aside, the school was primarily known for its top athletics teams. It was also known for its violence. With my shy, sensitive, introverted personality, I felt even less than a number. During my entire 4 years of high school, I was never able to fit in. My freshman year I decided to take Spanish. I was already partly fluent due to our family's early experience with the Puerto Rican culture. I began learning Spanish at the age of 6 from my mother's fiancé, who had moved to the states from Puerto Rico. I did so well the first year that I was immediately placed in honors Spanish for my remaining 3 years of high school. I struck up a friendship with another student in Spanish class, Sue. Sue was racially mixed, part Dominicano, part Santee Sioux, and part Black. We were the most fluent speakers in honors Spanish and often shared our experiences of trying to fit in. Needless to say, our experiences mirrored each other.

By my junior year, I was able to make friends with a Puerto Rican student, Rosa. Rosa in turn introduced me to the Puerto Rican connection or body of students. I was received very graciously, with open arms. Like myself, the other Puerto Ricans had been beaten up and harassed to and from school. They told me to walk with them to school and invited me to sit at the two lunch tables they had assigned themselves to. Sometimes, I would go out for lunch. There was a small family-owned restaurant that served Puerto Rican food, Mexican food, and the traditional student's fare: hotdogs and hamburgers. The owner's stepdaughter, Cristina, a student from my school, also helped out part-time. I began eating there frequently. Cristina and I seemed to be attracted to each other, began dating, and moved in together. We would later become common-law husband and wife, living together for 16 years. By the time I began dating Cristina, I was totally immersed in the Puerto Rican culture but still tried to relate to the African American side of me.

In my second year of living with Cristina, I began looking for something to connect to. This was a time of soul searching for me. Politically there was a lot going on. The late 1960s and early 1970s was an era of civil strife and unrest. There was the Black Power movement, SDS, the Weatherman, the second battle of Wounded Knee in South Dakota, and the assassinations of King and Kennedy. The list goes on and on. The drug culture was also in full bloom. I had started to affiliate myself with the Black Panther Party and the Young Lords, a Puerto Rican revolutionary group. I would sometimes go to their meetings and help pass out revolutionary literature. It was also a time of the Back to Africa movement. Afros and Dashikis were commonplace. We were all sporting huge Afros. In the 1970s, the African movement struck me as very exciting. I actually felt more of a closeness or kinship with Africans than I did with American Blacks. To me, African Americans were a lost and deculturalized people, segregated from everyone else for so long that anyone different was deserving of being set upon. At any rate, the African thing was very exciting to me. Cristina and I began wearing African clothes and sporting big Afros. I went out and bought a bunch of African records. Later on, I purchased two congas and would go out and beat them with a group of drummers that would congregate in the summer at various beaches. I even wound up giving some of my children African names.

Sometimes, we would visit some of my cousin Roy's closest friends to smoke weed and listen to African music. At first, everything would seem fine. But after a while we would get little side cracks thrown our way, things like "You guys aren't Black enough! If you moved to Africa you wouldn't be accepted." One of Roy's friends, Tim, had a girlfriend named Kenya who saw herself as the African spokesperson (whatever that's supposed to mean). Kenya was very black, with a very short natural hairdo, and she actually looked like she was Nigerian. She would always make some negative comments about Cristina. Kenya would ask Cristina why she was wearing an Afro since Cristina was Puerto Rican. Cristina's shyness exceeded my own, so I usually had to talk up for her. I explained that Cristina's father was dark-skinned Puerto Rican. I also told how African slaves had been taken to Puerto Rico and other Caribbean islands. Afterward, Kenya, along with other members of the group, would tell us not to speak Spanish. (Cristina and I would speak Spanish to each other at times.) Eventually, the negative comments escalated. One day, Kenya told Roy to tell me not to bring Cristina to the group since she wasn't Black. When I angrily called Kenya up to question her about the comment, she added, "You and your cousin Roy are lucky we let you half-breeds in." When I told Roy what Kenya said, he passed it off by saying I was too sensitive, saying Kenya was just joking. Well, that was the last time Cristina and I set foot in their house. But apparently I hadn't learned my lesson.

There was a new revolutionary group of Blacks who were conducting educational and revolutionary seminars. My cousin Roy had attended a few of these meetings and was very excited. One day he asked me to go with him. It sounded very appealing, so I brought a friend named Ricardo. Ricardo was from Puerto Rico and had been in the United States about a year. Ricardo spoke very little English, although he understood more than he could speak. As we entered the building and were waiting in line to be searched, I was explaining to Ricardo in Spanish what the meeting was about. Just then, one of the security guys pointed to Ricardo and said to me, "This guy can't come in!" When I asked why, he told me "This is only for Blacks." I then tried to explain that Ricardo was Puerto Rican with some African heritage. The security guard responded by saying, "You have to be all Black to come in here!" I responded by saying that I wasn't all Black, so I wouldn't go in either. Roy and a couple of his friends went inside, while Ricardo and I waited in the front lobby. Since we all had ridden in the same car, we had no choice. Not long after, Roy's older brother, Randy, showed up. Randy was concerned about our interest in these revolutionary groups and had decided to follow us. When we explained why we were sitting outside, Randy immediately went into the meeting, interrupting the speaker by calling them Black racists who were no better than White racists for refusing Ricardo admittance. Roy, of course, disagreed with his older brother and told Randy that he was off base. Randy thought Roy was completely wrong to have entered the place when Ricardo, our friend, was not allowed in. Randy then told his brother that he was a sucker for punishment, that he was nothing but a mixed-breed high-yellow chump who would never be accepted by Blacks. I agreed in heart.

It was about this time that I began to minimize my social contact with Blacks. I was bewildered, rejected, and abused. On top of all of this, I was quite simply tired of the mistreatment. I began to take a close look in the mirror. Here I was telling Blacks that I was the same as they were with no takers. They saw me as different. I thought to myself, "If they see me as different, then maybe I am different." It hit me right in the face. The coffee was there for me to smell. From that point on, I was never to refer to myself as a Black person. If someone were to ask if I was Black, I would answer by saying, "No. I'm brown. I'm a person of color" or "I'm multiracial." I was comfortable with this. I knew at that point I would no longer allow someone else to tell me who I was. As a human being, I felt it was my God-given right to say who I was. Unfortunately, what I knew right then was that I certainly didn't feel Black anymore. The negative experiences I suffered had pushed the Black side of me to the farthest recesses of my mind, body, and soul, and at the time I wasn't sorry for it.

My very first Indian contact began with my maternal grandmother. We always referred to her as simply "Mama." On the other hand, we called our mother, Laura, by her name. Because our grandmother lived with us from a very young age, we more or less copied our mother and her sisters when referring to our grandmother. Grandmother Jenna was half Black and half Musgogee Creek. Mama's physical appearance pretty much typified a Black woman, although her demeanor was very Indian. Mama often talked of her father, who was of the Eastern Band of the Creek Nation. The Creeks were originally from the southeastern portion of the United States, particularly Georgia. Somehow my grandmother's father settled for a time in Kentucky, although he later went to live with his disconnected relatives in Oklahoma. I can vividly remember the various American Indian foods my grandmother would make, food that today is commonly referred to as soul food. Corn pones, hominy soup, succotash, grits, okra, sassafras tea, Indian sumac lemonade, and wild mustard greens are just a few of the dishes my grandmother made that originally came from the southern Indian nations. I am often surprised that many African Americans who to this day still eat many of these foods are unaware that they are gifts borrowed from Indian America.

While my grandmother viewed herself as Indian and Black, neither my mother nor her three sisters did. I think to this very day they have more or less seen themselves as Black, which in my opinion complicated their lives in regard to the racial prejudice and harassment they endured. In contrast, my mother's lone brother, Tony, also viewed himself as Indian and Black. Uncle Tony was the first male figure in my life who inspired me to dance. Because Tony was always traveling across the country we rarely got to see him. But when he visited, he always performed powwow Indian dances for us. There was one dance he would perform called the stomp dance, which, according to him, originated from the intermarriage of Creeks and Black runaway slaves. This was my first inspiration to dance. Uncle Tony was my second inspiration and influence in regard to the Indian side of our family. The other person who was very influential in instilling Indian culture in my life was my paternal grandfather, Jim Bull, otherwise known as Jimbo. Jimbo was a member of the Oglala band of Teton Lahkota, otherwise known as Sioux. Jimbo was born on the Pine Ridge Oglala reservation around the turn of the century. I was told by a cousin that his tribal name was Short Bull, although the name *Short* was taken out somewhere along the way. My grandfather's agency name was Johnson. An agency name for Indians is like a plantation name was for African American slaves. My grandfather actually lived between three homes: Pine Ridge, South Dakota; Wisconsin; and Chicago. Jimbo in stature was a short man, with olive skin and black wavy hair, which, on the few occasions I saw him, he usually wore in a single ponytail. Because of family infighting, I can count my visits with him on two hands. Even still, the impression he left on me was obviously very strong.

Once when my mother was in the hospital, I remember my grandfather taking me up by Oshkosh, Wisconsin. I can remember us going to a lake, where he baited some fishing lines, and after throwing them in, began to walk through the fields gathering plants, which I was to later learn were for medicinal purposes. Before gathering, he always prayed in his language and left some tobacco. Many tribes use tobacco as an offering to God. I didn't know what I was gathering (I was only 8 or 9 years old at the time). I simply gathered the plants he pointed out. What was amazing was what occurred years later as a young adult. I had always enjoyed the outdoors. When I was about 19 years old, I got this incredible interest and urge to gather and use medicinal plants. Once my own children were old enough, whenever we would go to the woods, I would have them help me gather as well. I continued through the years to follow my urge for medicinal knowledge by studying tribal medicinal lore. To this very day, at the age of 47, I continue to forage for wild plants. For each of the four seasons, there are different plants to gather. And just like my grandfather and grandmother, I carry on the tradition of always leaving an offering of tobacco. Foraging for wild plants is cathartic; for me it is equal to worshipping at a church. There is an inner feeling of peace connecting me to a closer understanding of the creator of life. The physical act of gathering brings on a sense of spiritual and physical healing. When I was about 35 years old, it suddenly occurred to me that I was continuing this tradition of gathering left from my grandparents because I had received a calling. Of all my brothers, sisters, and cousins, why me? In fact, neither of my grandfathers told me that I was the one to carry the torch, and yet now when I gather, it's as if I can sense their approving presence. I would soon learn that this was just the beginning of reconnecting with the disconnected Indian side of our family.

Because my cousin Randy was older than me by about 3 years, he got an opportunity to spend more time with our grandfather. In this way Randy was able to pass a lot of the wisdom and knowledge from our grandparents to me. Randy was very aware of his position as an older grandson. Strangely enough, Randy and I, of the grandchildren, were the only ones who tried to stay connected to our Indian family. We saw ourselves as Indian. The rest of our brothers, sisters, and cousins were very aware that we were part Indian, but they simply thought of themselves as Black. Randy in a sense inspired me to stay connected. During our teen years at summer camp in Indiana, Randy and I performed dances for the campers at night around a fire. We put on our homemade dance regalia and even painted our horses, which we rode into camp bareback. After our camp days, I started to drift away from the things Indian; of course there were lots of distractions. I graduated from high school, started working, and was busy raising a family.

I was also experimenting with drugs while at the same time involving myself with the antigovernment, civil unrest scene, which occupied me into the late 1970s. I'll never forget the date: November 1979. That was the year I reconnected with my Indian self.

It was a Friday afternoon. I was at home with my children when my cousin Randy stopped by. My children were 5, 7, and 8 years of age. Randy said, "Come with me and bring the kids. I want to show you something." We got in the car and drove to the National Armory. When we entered the armory, I was completely awestruck. I had never seen so many Indians in one place in my life.

Randy had taken me to the American Indian Center Powwow. My children and I stood for a long time and watched the various dancers dance around the arena. As I watched, it seemed as if I were dreaming. I immediately thought of my grandparents. I suddenly felt their presence. It felt as though I had been lost for many years and had finally found home. I had arrived at the circle. Randy and I looked at each other. He had brought me here because it was his duty to do so. We didn't need to say anything to each other. We knew that our grandparents had entrusted in us the responsibility of not allowing our Indian family to wither away and die. By the enthusiasm I saw in the faces of my children, I sensed that they, too, felt a strong relationship to the dancers, the sacred drummer, and the circle.

When we left the armory that night, I knew right then that the cultural and spiritual aspects of my life would be greatly affected. Through my cousin Randy, I found out about the American Indian Center (AIC). The AIC was created to address the needs of American Indians who were relocating from reservations. At the monthly fundraiser powwows held at the AIC, there was also a potluck dinner where various participants brought dishes from home. For about 2 years, I brought food for the potlucks. The meals were usually eaten before the dancing. Afterward, someone from the powwow committee publicly thanked all the people who brought food or helped to serve. It wasn't long before I noticed my name was never mentioned. At first, I thought maybe I was accidentally overlooked. But after about 6 or 7 months of attending the fundraiser, it became apparent that the snub was intentional. At that point I began to feel a familiar sense of rejection very similar to the rejection Blacks had tossed my way—except there was one difference in the style of the rejection. The Blacks had rejected and harassed me openly and directly. They were vocal in their feelings toward me and right to the point. In contrast, many of the Indian people at AIC rejected me silently. Usually nothing was ever said directly to my children or me. This in itself was not surprising or new to me. It was the type of stony silence and penetrating looks I can remember from my grandparents. They didn't need to physically discipline us when we stepped out of line. We knew what the look and silence symbolized. But I quickly realized how naive I had been to enter into the Indian community as a mixed-blood, thinking that they would be waiting to accept me with open arms. It was indeed another painful eye-opener for me.

As in the past, instead of confronting the resistance, I slowly began to retreat. There were some people who never spoke to us—some of the elders included—although I remember other elders who didn't have too much to say but would occasionally give me an approving nod when my children would dance. One of the AIC employees, Ron, a Vietnam veteran and a member of the Mesqualic (Sac & Fox) tribe of Tama, Iowa, turned out to be one of my biggest supporters.

Ron began telling me more about the tribal conflicts that had been going on for years at the center. The vast majority of the people who frequent the center are from the Midwest—generally Ojibwa, Winnebagos, Menominees, Potawatomies, and Ottawas. At any given time, other tribes come from farther locations, such as Lahkotas, Mesquakie, Choctaw, Iroquois, and Navajos. But according to Ron, it had always been the Ho-Chunks, or Winnebagos, who controlled the center, to the disdain of the other tribes. In fact, he said that the Ho-Chunks, as far as he could remember, always had this aura that they were better than other Indians. According to Ron, the Ho-Chunks way of thinking was "We're more Indian than you, and we have a monopoly on everything that's Indian. Our ways and customs are more sacred than yours." After receiving this information, I began to notice that many of the people from the center who had given my family a cold shoulder indeed were Ho-Chunks. Ron told me as he ended our conversation, "Don't think the Ho-Chunks dislike you and your family because you're of mixed blood. Those people are prejudiced against anyone who isn't Ho-Chunk."

Like Whites who romanticize Indian people, in a sense I too learned that I was also guilty of romanticizing the Indian side of our family, wondering why I couldn't have been born a full-blood, naively thinking maybe Indian people were perfect, without blemish or flavors. My yearning for Indianness was not one of nostalgia but very much like a homeless person searching for a niche in society. It was what I felt the strongest. Likewise, when the door was slammed in my face, the hurt and pain ran deep. Reality, however, boldly revealed that Indians, like all people, are indeed not perfect. Nor were Indian people perfect before the coming of the White man to these shores. That Whites conquered, and Indians became conquered, is proof enough of imperfections on both sides. On the other hand, it would be safe to say that Indian peoples had fewer imperfections before the White man's arrival. The broken treaties (lies), theft of ancestral lands, the rape and plunder of villages, the implementation of the reservation system, genocide, and the deculturalization process of Indian peoples certainly adds up to just one word—colonialism. The results of colonialism produced things that had never before been recorded, seen, or heard: alcoholism, tuberculosis, fetal alcohol syndrome, unemployment, incest, domestic abuse, child abuse, tribal infighting, fatherless children, reservation and street gangs, and the list goes on. So, with all this in mind, the AIC—indeed, the Indian community—is heir to the results of colonialism from its inception. As I began to learn more about the history of my Indian and African American ancestors, I became less bitter but not less hurt.

Content Themes

Butch's journey demonstrates several important components of racial identity development. There are moments that are quite painful in his story, suggesting that identity development is difficult for biracial individuals. The first component is the importance of examining the multiple contexts in which identity development occurs. The second component is the role of the family, particularly the role of socialization and the family role in confronting and dealing with oppression. The most important component of Butch's story is the nature of intra-group differences. This includes the importance of the sense of acceptance from individuals and cultural groups on identity development and psychological functioning.

Contextual Dimensions

Butch's story illustrates the importance of examining the context of development. The ecosystem framework developed by Bronfenbrenner (1977) is a useful model for understanding the multiple influences. The first level, the individual level, represents the intrapsychic component of identity and includes temperament, personality traits and characteristics, and cognitive processes. The second level, the microsystem, includes all of the immediate influences on individual development, including the nuclear family, peers, and the school system or work community. The mesosystem includes the interactions between the individual and the microsystems. The macrosystem includes more distal systemic influences on development, including immediate and extended family relationships, the neighborhood, legal systems, social services, the community, and community organizations. The exosystem, the next level, includes broader societal influences, including cultural and sociopolitical ideology. Finally, individual development needs to be examined within the particular time perspective, or the chronosystem.

Butch's development is reflective of the process outlined in the model. Throughout his childhood and adolescence, experiences with the microsystem were prominent. He and his siblings were consistently teased by neighborhood children and were the victims of physical violence, allegedly due to race. Butch was accused of not being "Black enough" by both neighborhood children as a child and then by members of an organization as a young adult. These experiences contributed to feelings of shame and doubt about his racial identity. His family seemed to have a more tacit influence on his racial identity. Although his mother was aware of the teasing and violence against him, her response seems to have been more related to his self-defense and protection rather than to messages about his race. The family, according to Butch, did not have overt discussions about race and culture. In fact, his Italian heritage was cloaked in secrecy. It is also not clear whether his mother helped to intervene with his sense of isolation in high school. The active components within the microsystem seemed to contribute to Butch's difficulties in identity development.

The school system, particularly the high school, reinforced mainstream values, and Butch continued to struggle with experiences of oppression within the school, along with feelings of isolation and rejection from his peers. Community organizations and AIC had more of an influence on Butch's adult identity though, again, in a negative fashion. It is also important to understand Butch's development in light of the current events of his time and the cultural ideology within society, the exosystem, and the chronosystem. Butch experienced adolescence and young adult development during the era of the civil rights movement. Butch was able to experience the sense of liberation and racial pride and made attempts to take pride in his Black heritage. Ironically, during the time that he was attempting to be empowered, he experienced within-group oppression and was accused of not being truly Black and therefore not worthy of participating in the movement or empowerment. His story reminds us of how important it is to consider the context in identity development and psychological functioning of individuals.

Family Socialization Patterns

The role of the family is an important consideration in examining the role of race in lives and is often critical in understanding identity functioning of biracial individuals. Butch's story provides an example of the complications that can occur when families have not only different racial backgrounds but also differing values. Butch made attempts to be reconciled with and integrate each of the components of his background into his identity. His family did not have overt discussions about racial heritage. Butch learned about his Italian side from an aunt who secretly told him about his grandfather. For Butch, this answered several questions, particularly the variation in skin colors. When he tried to follow up with questions, however, his mother slapped him, ending his questioning. Butch felt that he could not continue to pursue further questions on this topic. It also seems as if the family did not have overt conversations on his Native American heritage. His cousin introduced him to the Native American culture and encouraged him with his dancing. Yet it seems as if he and his cousin were the only ones interested in learning about the heritage and the culture.

What is interesting about Butch's story is that acts of physical violence occurred due to racial differences. Yet although his mother was aware of the fights, there was no indication that overt discussions about racial issues took place. Butch experienced some very real threats and a sense of social isolation. Neither the nuclear nor the extended family engaged in a socialization process that might have served as a buffer to some of the discrimination. One wonders whether Butch would have been so vulnerable if he had been shielded from some of the oppression or given coping mechanisms or resources to deal with them.

Intragroup Differences

Due to historical factors around multiracial heritage, a caste system has developed involving race and racial group membership. Biracial or multiracial individuals often have to choose a racial identity or affiliation, sometimes at the expense of neglecting or denying another. Because outward appearances are often our first connection to racial group membership, this choice is often reinforced in families through favoritism based on skin color; hair color, texture, and length; or facial features. When Butch began to recognize and understand his multiracial heritage as a child, it seemed linked to the physical differences within the family. It is not clear whether siblings were more favored in Butch's family because of physical appearance, but Butch's skin color led to some of the neighborhood fights. Because of the physical differences between Butch and other family members, he became an easy target for intragroup oppression. African

American children teased him because his mother appeared White and because he was not "Black enough."

The caste system and forced racial group affiliation led to intragroup differences. For example, during slavery, the mulatto children, by-products of slave owners and slaves, experienced preferential treatment and did not have to labor as hard in the fields (Rockquemore & Laszloffy, 2003). Issues of superiority were established as people who were closer to White in terms of racial mixing and skin color and features were given more status and clout. The intragroup difference affected identity for people because both physical and psychological characteristics were used to determine group membership. One example of this consequence is the brown paper bag test African American civic organizations used to determine membership. Even today, there are notions of what constitutes membership within certain groups and the concept that people have to meet criteria to belong to a race. Butch was certainly caught up in this phenomenon. When he was a child, his and his mother's skin color became the benchmark for group membership as African Americans. Because his mother appeared to be White, and Butch was biracial, this precluded his true membership. Butch theoretically could have compensated for the skin color issues through his behaviors, but he was also judged as not behaving Black enough. He did not receive socialization and encouragement from his family to learn to connect to his African American heritage and connect with his peers. Butch continued to be judged harshly when joining Black groups as an adult. When Butch joined the AIC and attempted to reconnect with his American Indian heritage, he experienced similar rejection based on his multiracial heritage. Only the Puerto Ricans in his high school accepted him openly, which may have led to his marriage to a Puerto Rican woman.

Self-Image

The development of identity is complex but more so for multiracial individuals. Kerwin and Ponterotto (1995) developed a model of identity development for multiracial individuals based on research. The first stage, preschool, includes low salience to racial heritage as a component of the self. Although Butch was confused about skin color as a child, he did not base his sense of self solely on racial group membership. Children in this stage are aware of physical differences in parents. The second stage, school age, occurs as individuals feel compelled to select a racial group for membership. Children in the school-age stage are often asked to identify their heritage and select a response usually based on parental messages. Butch's journey through identity development reflects this stage as he, one by one, almost in a sequential fashion, attempts to explore his heritage and integrate it into his self-concept. Preadolescence and adolescence, the third stage, is characterized by the growing awareness of the social connotations of race and is usually triggered by specific environmental circumstances. Butch experienced rejection by Italians, African Americans, and American Indians. This rejection led him at some points in his life to deny his Italian and Black heritage and to feel angry with members of these groups. What complicated this process for Butch was his exposure to the negative stereotypes and biases against certain groups. Butch appears to have internalized the stereotypes, sometimes leading him to be more vulnerable to assault. For example, regarding fights with neighborhood children, he reports he did not have the confidence to fight them because he thought Blacks were stronger. This of course denies a part of his own heritage. The internalized oppression may have made it easier to reject parts of himself.

The fourth stage in the model occurs in college and young adulthood, as individuals continue with immersion in one culture due to rejection of another. Butch continued the exploration of his identity after high school and into early adulthood. Adulthood, the final stage, is characterized by the continuing integration of identity and an appreciation of a variety of cultural groups. Butch seems to have moved in this direction as he proudly proclaims his multiracial status and acknowledges all of his parts.

Clinical Applications

This section explores the clinical applications from Butch's story for counselors, including assessment, techniques and interventions to use in treatment, and countertransference concerns.

Assessment

The assessment of racial issues for multiracial individuals is similar to the concerns for individuals with a single racial heritage. Therapists should examine racial identity stages and understand how race intersects with other cultural variables, including social class and gender. More specific information should be assessed to determine how each racial group heritage influences identity development. The following questions are suggested:

What messages did you receive about each of your racial heritages?

Did you experience pressure to accept or deny any of your racial heritages from family members or peers?

Did you feel more accepted by one or more particular groups?

What historical information did you receive about your racial heritage?

What were the societal messages you received about your racial heritage?

Techniques and Interventions

Myths About Multiracial Individuals

There are three myths associated with being multiracial that should inform treatment and therapy (Kerwin & Ponterotto, 1995). The first myth is that of the tragic mulatto, the notion that multiracial individuals live marginalized lives because they are not fully accepted by any cultural or racial group. Butch's story is a good example of this perspective because at each developmental time period in his life he attempts to reconcile his racial identity and is denied by each racial group. He reports feeling isolated and marginalized in his childhood neighborhood, in his high school, and by community organizations. Many biracial and multiracial individuals, however, are able to find acceptance and understanding from family and friends and are able to integrate each dimension of their heritage into their identity. Therapists should facilitate the integration of identities into self-concept as a goal with clients. The goal of clinicians should be to help clients acknowledge and honor each racial heritage (Rockquemore & Laszloffy, 2003). Although therapists may not be able to foster acceptance by others, they can be instrumental in helping clients find appropriate support groups and resources. For example, when Butch felt rejected by members of the AIC, one of the leaders took him aside and explained the reactions of some of the members, thus depersonalizing the issue. Counselors may also be able to help clients find support groups for individuals of multiracial descent. The second myth is that biracial individuals must choose one racial group. Historically, many were forced to choose one racial group by passing and denying their non-White heritage or by choosing a minority race and being rejected by Whites. Dominant society encouraged individuals to associate race in a dichotomous fashion (Rockquemore & Laszloffy, 2003). Until the 2000 U.S. Census count, individuals were asked to check only one race. Today, the option of identifying with and associating with various groups exists. Clinicians can help clients to research and understand the cultural heritage of both groups, working as cultural brokers (McGoldrick & Giordano, 1996). Clients can be encouraged to participate in and share rituals from one heritage with family members of the differing racial groups.

The third myth is the notion that multiracial individuals do not want to discuss their cultural heritage. Butch's story highlights why the opposite view is so important. Many multiracial children have questions about their heritage, particularly because values, beliefs, and lifestyles of each racial group differ. This was not evident in Butch's story, but often child-rearing difficulties arise based on different cultural values. While courting, a couple may agree to certain principles, child-rearing techniques, and values, but the actual birth of the children may change the priorities and focus. Families often experience more pressure from extended family members to maintain traditional cultural and racial activities (McGoldrick & Preto, 1984). Children often find themselves caught between the cultural struggles, which may influence identity development. Many multiracial children look for opportunities to discuss their racial heritage in an attempt to solidify their development. Rockquemore and Laszloffy (2003) recommend a relational-narrative approach to therapy to allow clients to be able to process and tell their stories.

Family and Racial Socialization Processes

Racial socialization is the process of helping racial minority children to develop positive self-images within an oppressive community. The racial socialization process is even more critical for people of multiracial descent. Therapists should be encouraged to discuss and dialogue with their clients about their racial heritage. The process is more complicated with multiple racial backgrounds because individuals need to be socialized to each of the cultural groups to which they belong. Individuals also need to understand the historical influences on and societal messages about interracial marriages. Finally, clients need to be socialized on intragroup oppression.

Countertransference

There are two areas in which countertransference may occur when working with multiracial clients: myths about multiracial persons, and client self-hatred. As with any other area, it is important for clinicians to monitor the personal reactions that arise when working with clients. Therapists should consider their own perspectives on interracial relationships before working with multiracial clients.

Myths and Misperceptions

One area of countertransference for clinicians working with multiracial clients involves becoming caught up by the complexity of identity development. It is important for therapists not to make the assumptions that their clients are experiencing the tragic mulatto syndrome, that clients live marginalized lives, and that they are not accepted by any group. It is true that multiracial clients may face rejection from racial groups. One reaction to Butch's story is to be moved and feel pain from the rejection that he faced and to be anxious about the violence he experienced. One reaction that therapists may have is to alleviate the pain clients experience from the rejection. This can lead to minimizing the rejection or attempting to make excuses for the other behaviors. Therapists may also be concerned that clients are forced to choose one group over another. Therapists may inadvertently encourage clients to choose one racial group to protect clients from the pain of rejection from another racial group. Although it may be a temporary solution to encourage clients to choose a nonrejecting group and to cut themselves off from groups that are rejecting, this has the long-term effect of clients' denying a part of themselves. Clinicians must monitor the sadness they feel for their client so that they engage in empathy and not sympathy.

It is often believed that multiracial individuals do not want to discuss issues. In fact, multiracial individuals often have the experience of strangers asking, "What are you?" and having to explain their background. It is critical for multiracial clients to talk about their background because it influences their identity and functioning. Similar to individuals with single racial backgrounds, multiracial individuals may not discuss racial issues unless this is initiated by therapists. Avoiding racial discussions may be one way that therapists protect themselves from the secondary pain and discomfort of their clients. These conversations are even more important for therapists who are part of a rejecting racial group and for therapists with multiracial or multiethnic backgrounds.

Issues of Self-Hatred

Finally, therapists may be concerned with levels of self-hated that their clients possess. When clients enter with depressive symptoms, including low self-esteem, issues of self-hatred may be easy to introduce as a treatment goal. However, there may be times when the clients are not able to acknowledge their feelings. For example, when Butch is rejected by the African American group, he decides to reject that part of his heritage. If he were to enter treatment at that point, he might not recognize his rejection as being linked to internalized oppression or self-hatred. The therapist would then be caught in the dilemma of identifying a potential treatment goal that the client might not be willing to accept. Clinicians have to reconcile the ethical requirement of not imposing their own values and standards on clients with the need of promoting optimal functioning for their clients.

TOOLBOX ACTIVITY—BUTCH		
Discussion Questions	*Activities*	*Resources*
Content themes What other themes do you see emerging in the story that the author did not identify? **Assessment** Are there any questions you would like to ask? **Interventions** What other interventions could you propose with Butch? **Countertransference** What countertransference reactions were emerging in yourself as you read this story? **Other scenarios** What would have occurred if Butch had been female? What would Butch have been like if he were only biracial instead of multiracial?	Construct a multiracial genogram, using Butch's story or the story of a famous multiracial individual (Joan Baez, Mariah Carey, Barack Obama). Trace the racial heritage and status of each group represented. Write an essay on the influence of heritage and racial history on the person.	**Suggested readings** Kandel, B., & Halebian, C. (1997). *Growing up biracial: Trevor's story.* New York: Lerner. Katz, K. (2002). *The colors of us.* New York: Henry Holt. McBride, J. (1997). *The color of water: A Black man's tribute to his white mother.* New York: Riverhead Books. Nakazawa, D. J. (2004). *Does anybody else look like me? A parent's guide to raising multiracial children.* New York: DaCapo. O'Hearn, C. C. (1998). *Half and half: Writers on growing up biracial and bicultural.* New York: Pantheon. Rockquemore, K. A., & Brunsma, D. L. (2001). *Beyond Black: Biracial identity in America.* Thousand Oaks, CA: Sage.

Four

Betsie's Story

I Am 100% Jewish

Less visible than race, ethnicity affects lifestyle, values, and identity, regardless of the individual's awareness of its influence. People vary greatly in the way they experience their own ethnicity, from ignoring it to feeling pride or ambivalence or expressing rejection. In a clinical situation, ethnicity is often ignored as a variable (McGoldrick & Giordano, 1996) because it may be less visible or because it creates conflicts between family members or between the clinician and the client that may be difficult to address (Hays, 2001). In this chapter, Betsie tells us about her pride in her Jewish ethnic background, the pressures to conform to her ethnicity, and some of her struggles, including her job-related concerns, her experiences with substance abuse, and her romantic relationships. The reader is encouraged to continue reading in spite of the struggles to follow the complex web of Betsie's family tree. It is important to pay attention to her descriptions of the flavors and noises during her childhood years. Following the story, a wide range of issues related to ethnicity are addressed in the content themes, clinical interventions, and countertransference sections, including the perception of ethnicity of oppressed groups, the relationship between ethnicity and religion, and the reaction of clinicians of similar or different ethnicity than that of the client.

Betsie's Story

I am 100% Jewish, having been born to two Jewish parents, both of them born to Jewish parents. I personally remember my two paternal great-grandmothers and have heard stories about their families and those of my two maternal great-grandmothers, whom I am named after, and their families. My family was seldom dull. I have always felt this way about my family history, which includes my life and the stories of my ancestors' lives that have been passed down to me through my parents and grand-parents. First, I only have three sides of family because my mother's parents were uncle and niece. My grandfather, Bert, married his oldest sister's daughter, Fran, my grandmother. This was in 1926, and they had to get married in Illinois because it was illegal in Indiana. One of the many reasons I do not consider myself a truly White person from European decent is because all of my family (the Frieds from Rumania, the Staks from Poland, and the Nobles from Russia) came to the United States because none of their home countries allowed Jews to become citi-zens. All three families came over between 1900 and 1905. They came both out of fear of the pogroms and for the economic opportunities, which were very limited for Jews in the aforementioned countries at that time. My maternal grandfather's (Bert's) mother died on the crossing from Rumania when my grandfather was only 3 months old, so he was raised by his oldest sister, Ellen, and her husband, Yeshiva, a butcher. It is a Jewish custom to name your children after dead relatives whom you were close to, and my middle name is Ethel, after Ellen, whom my mother knew as her grandmother. My maternal grandmother's (Fran's) parents were my grandfather's next oldest sister, Bluma, and her husband, Abraham, who owned a jewelry and watch repair shop. My first name, Betsie, comes from Bluma. My mother considered naming me Bluma but could not see sticking her head out a window and calling "Bluma, come in for dinner!" So she Americanized Bluma to Betsie.

Bert was always in love with Fran (they were 6 years apart in age), and he used to write love letters to her. The mail in Bloomington used to get delivered twice a day, and Bert would write Fran a love letter in the morn-ing on the streetcar on his way to school, where he got his master's degree in education, and mail it from campus, and Fran would have it in the afternoon mail. She used to show my siblings and me the letters. My mother still has them, and I will eventually inherit them. One quote of my grandfather's I will always remember is "I will always be your knight in shining armor, protecting you and our future family forever." They were very much in love with each other, happily married for 63 years until their deaths, and I think it gave my mother a much romanticized notion of love; I know it did for me. They were both in very good physical shape. Fran wore midriff tops until she died at 83—and looked good. Until the end of their lives, when they took their afternoon 3-mile walk, they did it holding hands. They were both teachers. Bert started out as a mechanical drawing teacher at a vocational school, then got his master's degree and doctorate and ended his career as a professor at Indiana Institute of Technology. He was brilliant, and I know that I got my brains from him. Fran was no slouch either. She was also a teacher at two schools, got two master's degrees, one in reading and one in administration, and ended her career as the assistant principal in charge of discipline. It is from this side of my family that I got the most pressure to do well in school.

I was always the smart one of my siblings, and as far back as I can remember my parents always took it for granted that I would get top marks in grammar school and high grades in junior high, high school, and college. Fran began working in 1928, retiring after 40 years in 1968. She always worked under her maiden name, Miss Brooks. If I ever have a daughter, I will name her Brooke (to honor both of my grandmothers, Brooks and Betsie). Bert and Fran lived right behind Bluma and Abraham. Because Fran worked, Bluma cooked dinner for both families. My mother, Millie, remembers that Bluma often cooked three or four different dishes because she loved to cook what each person enjoyed. Millie and her brother Joshua were both very picky eaters. At one time in their lives, Millie would only eat chicken, and Joshua would only eat lamb chops.

Both sides of my family followed many Jewish ideals, but closeness of family is probably the strongest one on both sides. As I mentioned, my grandparents lived right behind their parents; my father's (Jacob's) mother's (Betsie's) family was even closer. Betsie's parents came over from Kiev, Russia, before she was born in 1903. My great-grandmother's (Martha's) sister had died, leaving Isaac and six children, so Martha married him, as was tradition. I have a million stories about this side of my family, the side I have always been closest to. Martha and Isaac lived in Philadelphia and had six children together. After Isaac died, his brother Abe's wife also died, leaving him with four children, so Martha married him. Betsie always said she had 15 brothers and sisters, even though 9 were first cousins. She was the oldest girl of the second set of six. When Isaac was alive, he was a cantor and a Torah scholar, and Martha ran a restaurant to earn enough money for their family. All of the children lived around their parents. The oldest two girls, Carol and Eve, were opera singers who toured throughout Europe with an international opera company, always sending one half of their money home to the family. With 11 children, the money wasn't enough, so during the 1920s Martha added a speakeasy menu to the restaurant. Betsie was forced to quit school after eighth grade to go to work in a department store to earn money. She looked older and was able to get a job as a clerk. She always had a great love of learning and was a voracious reader until she died at 85 years of age. Meeting her, one would never guess her lack of education because she was self-taught. Betsie's older brothers, Sam and Charley, started a clothing business, which became such a success that they sent Martha and the youngest 11 children to Chicago to own an apartment building and restaurant in the late 1920s. So Martha, Abe, and the 11 youngest children, including Betsie, moved to Chicago. Leah and Hyman and their four children—Samuel, my grandfather Jack, Victor, and Silvia—were tenants in the building that Martha and Abe owned. Hyman was a tailor. Sam fell in love with Betsie, who was engaged to a man, named Samson Cowen, who was going to medical school out East. Sam made a deal with Samson. Sam asked Samson to give him 1 year to woo Betsie while he was away at school; if Sam could not convince Betsie to leave Samson in 1 year, Sam would back off forever. Samson stupidly agreed and left for school, cutting off all contact with Betsie, without telling her anything. She thought he had left her, was heartbroken, and started dating Sam on the rebound.

Sam was a good-looking, smooth-talking dreamer. He was a bellboy at a prestigious hotel, with lots of connections for free tickets to concerts and shows and passes to all the fine restaurants, so he wined and dined Betsie and soothed her broken heart. By the time Samson came back from school, Sam had already asked Betsie to marry him. Samson finally told Betsie the truth. She was so angry with Samson for playing games with her emotions that she married Sam out of anger and spite. Although they did remain married for more than 50 years, until Sam's death, they fought often. I got two things from Grandfather Sam. One was his love of partying and having a good time; the other was his quick temper and big mouth. He yelled, and yelled loudly, a great deal of the time. I can get very angry, sometimes very quickly, but like him, after I let it out (I do it in a more appropriate manner than he did) it is over. I rarely hold a grudge.

Although my mother's family was close, Betsie's family took family closeness to a new art form. When Betsie married Sam, her sister, Sarah, married Sam's brother, Jack. All of Betsie's siblings who moved to Chicago lived near each other as adults, and the two brother–sister couples were no exception: They always lived next door to each other until 1948, when they bought a three flat with another of Betsie and Sarah's sisters and her husband. This was known as "the building." Martha lived with Betsie and Sam for the last 15 years of her life. I get my great love of family from the many weekends spent at the building. Betsie was the most loving, caring, giving person you could ever meet. She loved and accepted everyone, just like her mother Martha had done. Martha's youngest son, my Uncle Maurice, fell in love with a Las Vegas showgirl, an Egyptian woman, my Aunt Jessica. Martha welcomed Jessica into the family. After Maurice's death, Jessica and her new husband, Sam, came to all of our family events and continued to do so for almost 20 years. When my Uncle Jack's son, Chuck, married Sandra, an African American woman, we all welcomed her as well.

If I had to pick one person who influenced my life the most, it was my "Nonny" Betsie. I was her oldest granddaughter, and that made me the luckiest person on earth. She was my best friend and my greatest advocate. She died about 5 years ago, and I miss her terribly. I am crying now as I write these words. I consider myself a third-generation party animal because, with such a large, close family, there was always one event or another happening, and everyone was invited. Every other Friday (Shabbat) night we went to "the building" for dinner, and then my siblings and I slept there overnight. My father's sister's family did the same on the other weeks. At 4 p.m. every afternoon, cocktail and snack time was held. Betsie and her sisters met in one of the kitchens for one glass each of vodka, filled to the top. Each floor was filled with cousins; many were my second or third cousins, but that never mattered. Before they bought "the building," my father, Jacob, grew up very poor. Because Sam worked for tips, money was tight and did not come in on a consistent basis, which had a big impact on Jacob—and hence on me. Sam finished high school but did not go on to college. His brothers, Jack and Victor, went to college and became accountants. Jacob became a certified public accountant (CPA). As a class project, he volunteered to be the accountant for the theater department. He took the elevator to the top floor of the school, which housed all the sets and the dressing and rehearsal rooms. As Jacob got off the elevator, he saw a man carrying my mother, Millie, over his shoulder. The man said to Jacob, "Wanna pinch something nice?" Of course Jacob said yes and pinched Millie's behind, and that is how they met (Millie was a theater major). My smooth-talking father romanced my naive mother, and they were married 2 years later, after my father graduated. Their marriage lasted 15 years. When I look back, I see what they had in common at ages 20 and 21: They both were (are) Jewish, they both were (are) close to their families, they both have a great love of literature and the arts, and in the 1950s they both wanted to do what their parents wanted them to do—raise a family of their own to continue the Jewish traditions.

So you have now read much of my family history, and finally I am born. But just like in the movie *Avalon*, I grew up hearing all of the stories I have just shared, and they have been an important influence on my life. These stories grounded me and gave me my great love and appreciation of history in general, especially my family history and traditions. In 1954, when they were 21 and 20 years old, Millie and Jacob got married. Millie quit school and went to work as a secretary, while Jacob sat for the CPA exam and started working with Victor and Jack in their accounting firm. I was born in 1958. Victor died suddenly in 1959, and Jacob became a partner in the firm. At age 26, he was giving advice to men twice his age about how they should run their businesses. My brother was born in 1960, and my sister in 1961. As I mentioned, Jacob grew up poor, which inspired him to do better for himself and his family. For example, in both the apartment we lived in until I was 4 years old and the house we moved to in the suburbs, we always had air conditioning. Jacob would not buy a house unless it had central air. His dream was to have an office on Market Street and to live downtown. He has accomplished both. He worked extremely hard throughout my entire childhood.

Until I was 7 or 8 years old, he worked 6.5 days a week part of the year and 7 days a week from January to April, tax season. To this day I hate math, and I believe it is because I used to fall asleep to the sound of the adding machine. Whereas the Frieds are very conservative, the Staks are very liberal. When my parents looked to buy a house, my father purposely moved us to a mixed suburban community so that we would live in what today you would call a multicultural neighborhood and attend a multicultural school. My four best friends on my block were Dana (Jewish), Laurie (Japanese), Annie (Chinese), and Betty (Polish). I have always been proud to grow up there. Education is another Jewish value I identified greatly with. Because I was the smart one of my parents' children, it was always expected of me that I would do well in school, and I did. Schoolwork always came very easy for me. My brother was the athlete, so it was okay that he did not have top grades, and although my sister did well in school, she had to work very hard to do so. I have to admit that I was actually rather lazy, but because I caught on to things quickly (I have an almost photographic memory and am able to relax when taking a test) it was very easy for me to get high grades. I was also tested for my music and dance abilities and received high marks. When I was 7 years old, my parents bought a piano. The store that we bought it from had music testing. My parents were told that I had the musical ability of a 16 year old. I took ballet classes at the Jewish Community Center (JCC) near my house. My class was taught by a prima ballerina who, after escaping from Russia, was helped by the Chicago Jewish community and was giving back to our community by teaching dance. She told my mother that I should be taking lessons at a higher level. We could not afford better ballet lessons, and I got lazy about practicing piano, so I did not go much further with either one. I am still a frustrated artist. First, I am always drawn to artists. I got involved in theater in high school and was in the National Thespian Society. Most of my friends from college were theater and music majors. I love to take pictures. I am the one on vacations and at parties who brings out the camera; it is my muse.

Another important aspect of my childhood is that I grew up in the 1960s and 1970s. I lived through and was greatly influenced by the civil rights movement, the hippies, the Vietnam War, and the women's movement. I understand that everyone has some prejudice, but I have always felt that because I am Jewish I know that there are plenty of people in this world who hate me because of my ethnicity. I hate this fact. It scares me, makes me very angry, and bothers me, so I feel like that I can't do that to anyone else. This may sound corny, but I truly believe this. My family was always very politically active, and the historic events of my youth made me even more aware of how important it is to be involved in the political process.

The woman's movement really messed things up for me. Even though Fran worked, she still got married at 18 and had two children. Most of the other adult women in my life were homemakers and mothers, some with part-time jobs. Millie did not work until my sister started first grade and was in school all day. Millie got a job as a secretary in the school district's central office so that she would always have the same days off as we did. All of a sudden, everything changed. Now I was expected to find a career and fight for women to have the right to be trained and work in fields dominated by men—and to earn as much as men—and to have the right to a legal abortion. All of a sudden men and women were supposed to be equal. I remember starting junior high school in the fall of 1969. At that time, girls had to wear dresses or skirts, no slacks or shorts. One day in October, the word went around that all the girls were walking out at 10 a.m. to protest the dress code. We wanted the right to wear pants! At the appointed time, virtually every girl walked out of school. We marched around the school chanting for about 2 hours, and then we went home. The rule was changed, and we could wear pants. This felt so powerful, to have a voice and have it heard.

Another aspect of Jewish women is the notion of Jewish women as nurturers (to the point of worriers), always taking care of their families. Being the oldest, and a girl, I took on this role as soon as my siblings were born. One of the first messages I received as a child was "Take care of your brother and your sister!" And I did. Whenever anyone offered me candy, perhaps at a store or at the doctor's office, I would always ask, "Can I have one for my brother and sister?" My mother loved to tell people about this. Somehow I was able to understand when my sister talked baby talk. When I was 11 years old, I began baby-sitting my siblings when my parents went out. They would pay me a quarter per hour. Kids used to pick on my sister because she was so small. I took care of that. Being 3 years older, I was always bigger than her peers, at least through grammar school. Even once we were all in college, my mother would still call me and ask, "Where is your brother?" The funny thing is, often I would know. We were very close growing up and still are to this day. I talk to my sister almost every day, and I talk to my sister-in-law often also. I would talk to my brother more often, but he is a psychologist and is with clients all day.

The most traumatic event of my life was my parents' divorce. They got divorced when I was 11 years old, in 1970. They seem to have started the trend. When it happened, I only knew one other family with divorced parents. I was devastated. Sometimes I think that I still have not completely gotten over it and wonder if I ever will. I know it is part of the reason that I did not get married until I was 44 years old. My siblings were 29 and 34 years old when they got married. We all say that we will never get divorced. It was very ugly. Jacob was cheating on Millie. They told us about it in December of 1969, and the divorce was finalized in March of 1970. Jacob was married again on April 15th of that year. Fran was cruel. She would always badmouth Jacob. The only good thing to come out of it was that we got to spend more quality time with Jacob. Instead of him coming home late every night, tired and crabby, and doing chores around the house on his days off, he was now responsible for us every Sunday and had to spend time with us, and we still went to Betsie and Sam's every other Friday night and slept over.

Jacob's second wife, Avis, was a wonderful person. She had two daughters, Barbara (5 years older than me) and Lynn (2 years older than me). Lynn and I became very close. Jacob and Avis were married for 5 years. Avis and Lynn were major influences in my life. Lynn was thin and beautiful, and Avis was a former model, so she was beautiful, too. My mother is very good looking, but she is short. Avis was tall and glamorous. Avis had helped her daughter Barbara with her weight problem, and she urged me to deal with mine. At age 13 I was 5 foot 3 inches tall and weighed 179 pounds. I looked 8 months pregnant. My weight brings me to another aspect of what I believe is part of the Jewish culture: food. All the Jewish women in my family were avid cooks who loved to feed us and urged us all to eat, eat, eat. And I loved food, so I did. Also, after years of therapy, I have realized that this was the way that I got love from my mother: She fed me. Because Jacob worked so much Millie was left alone to raise three little children. I was always a good girl. My brother was always mischievous: He would get lost in the grocery store or hide our toys. My sister was a big crybaby and demanded my mother's attention, so I did not get enough attention from Millie. I know that she loves me very much, but as a child what I got most from her was her excellent cooking. Avis gently talked to me about how Barbara had lost weight on diet pills (after all, it was 1971, and pills cured everything), took me to my pediatrician, and started me on amphetamines, and I have been conscious of my weight ever since. My metabolism is such that I was on the verge of needing thyroid medication, so the pills just curbed my appetite; I did not get jumpy or lose sleep.

One negative aspect of my family and the era I grew up in was substance use and abuse. As I mentioned, the three sisters always had their cocktail hour. When my father finally did come home from work, he always had a drink almost immediately after walking in the door. Alcohol was never a big deal for us as kids. We always had wine at Passover and could always try our parents' or grandparents' drinks if we asked. Although drinking was no big deal, smoking pot was much more exotic. I tried pot for the first time at age 12 after being influenced by Lynn. I only smoked once or twice a month for the 5 years I knew her, and though

I stopped in high school, I started up again in college. I believe it was the pressure of trying to do my best and be successful at the University of Chicago. I was a lazy student in high school. If I even put my hand over a book, I would get an "A." I was number 98 out of 647 in my class, I got a 29 on the ACT and an 1150 on the SAT, and I had a great interview, so I was accepted to college. Sometimes I think that maybe I was also filling their Jewish quota. Whatever the reason, there I was surrounded by class valedictorians, feeling like I did not belong. My first 2 years were a disaster. I loved going to class and listening to lectures and participating in discussions. I read the books, but it took me 2 years to really learn how to study and write papers. In the meantime, I got "C's" and "D's," something I had never gotten before. In high school, I got a "C" in typing and one in biology and then finished my last 2 years with straight "A's," so my grades at University of Chicago were ego shattering. I hid them from my parents and had many sleepless nights.

Another message I always got from Millie was "Don't worry, don't get upset!" Pot smoking was the perfect solution for my worry and anxiety. I began smoking every night. At least, I never went to class or tried to study while high; I just smoked instead of studying. I finally developed good study habits my junior year after I was put on probation. I am very proud to have a diploma from the University of Chicago and that I did it in 4 years despite my partying, but I am humiliated about my grades. Once I was out of college, I continued to smoke pot virtually every night for 10 more years. I was still using it as a crutch, this time to ease the pressure of not being successful at a career and my lack of an ability to find a husband. These relate to issues in the Jewish culture, the push for success, which for a woman from my generation means success both in a career and in a relationship.

I always loved history (my major), but in 1980, my senior year, schools were closing, and teachers were not paid nearly as well as they are now. I definitely had the desire to be successful, especially monetarily. I worked on the trading floor of the Chicago Mercantile Exchange as a summer job when I was in college. My uncle was the head of the computer department and got me the summer job. I did not have a clue what he was talking about when he offered me the job, only that it paid much more than minimum wage and that the hours were 7:30 a.m. to 2:00 p.m. I loved being out in the sun during the summer, so having a summer job that ended at 2:00 p.m. was heavenly. I carpooled with two girls from school whose fathers were commodity traders. I remember them telling me on my first day, "Forget every rule of life you know. You are about to enter the trading floor!" And they were right. It was a trip: a room full of thousands of people—most men, most young, and most without a college education—all excited and shouting. I thought, "Hey, I'm a University of Chicago student. I am smart, so I should do really well here!" The object of the game is very easy—buy low, sell high—but playing the game is hard: having the guts to know when to stay in as your money is ticking away or when to get out and cut your losses.

I kept moving up the ladder of jobs, and I helped many people make literally millions of dollars. Many promised me a share, but it never materialized. I had eight different jobs in 10 years. For example, my third to last job was as a personal clerk for an options trader. Commodity options were new, and it actually took some brains, not simply luck, to trade them successfully, so I took the job to learn how to trade options. Rick paid me almost no money (I had to work a second job at a video store to pay my bills), but he promised me he would lease me a seat to trade with him in 1 year if I helped him make money and learned enough about options. In 1 year with my help he went from earning $100,000 to earning $300,000. He gave me a $200 Christmas bonus and promptly went into the florist business with his brother and left the trading floor. I could go on, but needless to say, commodities and options was never a career for me: It was just a fun and exciting job. I met a lot of fun, interesting people, and to get through the nights of feeling like a failure I smoked pot. After performing well and still losing three jobs, I decided that God was trying to tell me something. Millie offered to let me live back at home while I got my master's in education to become a teacher. I did not completely stop smoking pot until 4 years later, but from the time I started in my career in education I only smoked occasionally on the weekends, until I finally stopped for good when I got my first teaching job.

I also felt like I was failing in my attempts to form a marriage relationship. I have a large number of friends, a couple since high school and many since college, but I had difficulty in bonding with a man for a lifelong relationship. Part of the problem I alluded to earlier: I think I had romanticized a relationship with a man after seeing the love letters Bert wrote to Fran. Another part was my lack of confidence in my looks. I grew up with the commercials on television touting "blondes have more fun," and I was never going to be a blonde. I was a tomboy growing up before it was popular for girls to play sports. Sometimes I think my parents fought a great deal after my birth because I subconsciously thought a relationship with a man meant fighting, unhappiness, and divorce, and I sent out negative relationship vibes. I did not wear makeup until I was 26 years old. Until that time, I wore blue jeans and T-shirts most of the time when I was not at work. I was always busy with family and friends, so it was not like I sat home doing nothing. I think that the way I dealt with the pressure from my family was to smoke pot and avoid dealing with it. Since I was not getting an "A" in relationships, I was not going to even try to be in one.

Another aspect in my life that kept me away from relationships was my family experiences with my father. He has been married three times and has had two long-term relationships since his last divorce. His third wife, who was 11 years younger than him, was a jerk. After a 10-year relationship, including 2 years of counseling, they finally came to the same conclusion that I realized the moment I met her: that they had nothing in common. His next relationship was with a woman only 3 years older than me. She looked much older because she was a heavy smoker. Betsie made my father promise that he would not get married again because she got attached to his wives, and all of his divorces hurt her a great deal. She died 5 years ago, and I think he has finally realized that she was right. His most recent relationship has lasted 10 years and will probably last the rest of his life because she is only 51 years old and he is 70. All of the women he has had relationships with were skinny and gorgeous. Maybe part of my problem was that I felt I could never live up to my father's image of a woman.

Finally, at 26 years old I met a man, Tim, on the trading floor. He was 4 years younger than me. He seemed nice and very giving, and he really liked me, so we started dating. He was not Jewish, but he said that he would never ask me to convert and that even though he was raised Catholic and went to Catholic school he did not really believe in religion. I was so relieved to finally have a boyfriend that at first I did not realize that he was taking over my life. It was also nice that he came from a very wealthy family. His uncle owned a large company and was a multimillionaire. They were in the vending machine leasing business. We all went to a convention in Atlantic City, and we stayed in a luxurious hotel and were driven around in limousines. His uncle really liked me and asked us to join him in his limo for the weekend. I felt like I had hit the jackpot: a man who loved me and who would be able to take care of me in style. So what if he had cut me off from most of my family and friends? So what if he was telling me what to wear and how to wear my hair? I had been too much of a tomboy anyway, and I was looking much better. My mother was not thrilled, but I think that she liked the physical change in me. She had always tried to get me to dress up more, and I always fought her. I used to hate shopping, which was unusual for a Jewish girl in my new neighborhood.

Maybe part of why I did not mind Tim taking over my life was because I was used to not having important things my way. So many things had already happened to me that I had no control over. We started living together after 1 year and lived together for 4 years. I was so happy that the pressure was off of me to get married. I finally felt like I fit in. Thank God that one of my college friends married a woman, Tina, who is a therapist who works with battered women. She saw what was going on and talked to me about how unhealthy my relationship was. She began to predict how Tim was going to behave. He started breaking my things, and she insisted that it was only a matter of time before he started to hit me. The turning point came when Tim's father won a trip to Cancun and gave it to us. She had warned me that batterers often begin battering in a place outside the United States because the woman is so distant from her family and friends. She warned me that I better have a credit card with me because Tim would start a fight, and if I tried to call the police they would just laugh at me because I was a "rich, White American girl" and do nothing, so I would have to jump on a plane myself. Sure enough, as we were having dinner one night, Tim started up with me. He had asked me to marry him a few weeks before, and I had said that I would think about it. The only thing he could not get me to change my mind about was raising my children as Jews, which I was determined to do. He agreed to this as long as they could celebrate Christmas and Easter, which I had no problem with. So at dinner he said to me, "How can you think I would ever agree to raise my children Jewish after I went to Catholic school all of my life?" I said, "Because you said you would when we first talked about it." He started yelling at me right there in public, and all of a sudden the light-bulb went off in my head. I realized that this was the fight Tina had alluded to, and I knew right there and then that I had to end the relationship. I did not want a scene. Six months before, when I had talked about ending things with him, he broke a glass table of mine. I did not want more violence to happen. I stopped the argument by agreeing to think about it and started planning how I would leave.

The trip had been in late November. I had very early work hours; Tim worked from 10 a.m. to 6 p.m. Just before Christmas, I pretended to go to work, waited at Jacob's apartment until I knew Tim was gone, and then arranged with a few of my friends to pack up all of my things and move out. I went to stay with Tina. I attended her battered women's group and learned a lot about myself. I got into group and then individual therapy as soon as I got back home. I still struggle with my self-image and self-esteem, but through therapy I have gained enough insight to have a healthy career and a healthy marriage.

When I look back at my life so far, I vacillate between two feelings. On the one hand I feel angry because I have wasted so much time being scared to live a full, adult life. I partied away 10 years of my life in commodities and have only had my real career for the past 10 years. So now I am working my behind off catching up. On the other hand, I look back at all the great experiences I have had and know that I would never have been able to have them if I had begun teaching right after college or had gotten married right away. My family's history, experiences, and lessons will continue to help me in my future.

Content Themes

In this story, Betsie tells us about her pride in her ethnic background, the values transmitted through her family to her, her challenges in upholding some of those values, and her struggles with employment, substance use and abuse, and romantic relationships. In looking at the themes of this story, we also learn how the implicit family norms affected and shaped her identity.

Pride About Ethnic Background

As many individuals do, Betsie speaks proudly about her ethnicity: "I am 100% Jewish." She also exhibits pride in her family history and in the fact that she was named after several of her ancestors. She spends a considerable amount of time writing about how her grandparents met and courted, what she considers was passed on to her from them ("he was brilliant, and I know that I got my brains from him"), and who influenced her the most ("it was my 'Nonny' Betsie"). She does not introduce herself until much later in her narrative and spends the first several pages retelling the stories that grounded her and gave her an appreciation of her family history. Ethnicity is a powerful force that influences identity formation, and how an individual feels about his or her ethnicity, whether pride or contempt, has an enormous impact on the individual's views about his or her sense of belonging and sense of inclusion in a community, and that in turn influences a sense of self. Unlike the racial categories, ethnicity can be less visible. Whether people are conscious of their ethnic identity varies greatly within groups and from one ethnic group to another. Not everyone feels like Betsie about his or her ethnic background.

In general, the more pride an individual has in his or her ethnic identity, the easier the acquisition of self-identity becomes. The more people reject their ethnicity, the harder it is for them to negotiate and deal with the rejected or denied parts of themselves. This is particularly true for oppressed ethnic groups (McGoldrick, Giordano, & Pierce, 1996).

Individual awareness of ethnic background differs according to the status of the ethnic group in a given society. The oppressed, marginalized, and less powerful individuals may shift and increase awareness of their ethnic identity as they interact with members of the mainstream, more dominant groups. Often the shifts in awareness depend on whether the minority/majority groups interact within oppressor/oppressed models or within more egalitarian models of interaction. For example, before Hitler's rise to power, the German Jews were assimilated into the German culture and considered themselves more German than Jewish, in part because, in spite of biases against Jews, they tended to be more accepted by the mainstream German society than the Polish or Russian Jews were in theirs (Elon, 2002). Similarly, in the United States, the rate of assimilation of the U.S. Jews appears to be staggering, with intermarriage the highest and rates of synagogue affiliation the lowest in the history of the Jewish people (Ashemberg Straussner, 2001). This is not surprising, considering that Jewish university quotas, employment quotas, and other discriminatory acts have begun to disappear from American mainstream society since the 1960s.

Similar phenomena occurred at certain historical times with other ethnic groups. In general, the easier the group's immersion into the White cultural and ethnic values, the quicker the group seems to lose its ethnic identity in the following generations. The more the group experiences oppression, discrimination, and stereotyping, the more its members cling to and try to retain their ethnic identity (Iglehart & Becerra, 1995).

The Connection Between Ethnicity and Family Values

It is difficult to separate the ethnic identity of the family from the cultural norms the family transmits. The culture of the family is in part the ethnic identity of the family and has deep ties with it (McGoldrick et al., 1996). Implicit family norms tied to the ethnic identity of the family shape an individual's identity. This has an impact on how people live and the values they hold dear, or reject. The typical Jewish family is a good example of the difficulties that arise in trying to tease out the culture of the family from its ethnic background. Because Jews are not only a nationality and not only a religion, some of the general values can be observed regardless of the national origin or the religiously observant or nonobservant status of its members. That is harder to perceive in White Anglo-Saxon Protestants and has traditionally been easier to observe in other ethnic groups (Irish, Italian, Jewish). But that is because the Anglo-Saxon Protestant is the supposedly regular background against which all the other ethnicities are compared, not because the White Anglo-Saxon Protestant does not have a culture (McGoldrick et al., 1996). No Jewish mother would consider herself a competent mother, for example, if she did not worry about her children and share her suffering openly with the rest of the family (Rosen, 1995). Obviously, non-Jewish mothers worry about their children, too, but they might do so differently; they might not share the worrying with the rest of the family, for example, so as to not worry the others. The offspring of these two different mothers encode worrying differently and react accordingly to their own children. Of course, neither one is right or wrong. They just become the ethnic cultural norms for the individual.

In Betsie we see the transmissions of several family values that she interprets as Jewish family values (e.g., the centrality of the family), which includes the expectation that women will marry, have children, and take care of them; the expectation of financial success and intellectual achievement; the love of food; and, of course, the notion that mothers worry and share that worry with other siblings: "Where is your brother?" Whether or not these are really exclusively Jewish family values is not as important as the fact that Betsie thinks they are.

Pressure to Conform to Ethnic Values

We have just seen how Betsie identifies some core Jewish values and traditions that have been passed down from generation to generation. She feels influenced by them and expresses a desire to abide by and continue in the next generation: "he could not get me to change my mind about raising my children as Jews, which I was determined to do." As Betsie continues telling her story, she begins to describe the pressures those values exerted and how unsuccessful she was at keeping up with them. In the age of the feminist movement, the ancestral push for success meant that now she had to succeed in a career as well as in a relationship. This is consistent with the findings in the literature about Jewish families who describe that despite the impact of feminist ideas, the pressure on Jewish women to find the most appropriate mate is still high. At the same time, the expectations of intellectual achievement and professional success once exerted only on sons now seem to pertain to daughters also. Consequently, a Jewish daughter is now expected to be not only a good wife but also a successful professional (Rosen & Weltman, 1996).

Betsie tells us about difficulties that led to years of pot addiction as a way of dealing with the anxiety and worry of not getting the expected good grades, the unfulfilled expectations of marriage, and the unanticipated financial frustrations in the male-dominated world of commodities trading, in which she was not successful. We know little about the pressure her parents actually exerted on Betsie, but we do know from her story that she feels she has not been able to abide by what she considers to be her family expectations. She felt like she failed to uphold the family prescriptions of success. The cost of her perceived pressure and, as she understands it, her failure to conform to her Jewish values was high.

Sometimes the fluidity of identity does necessitate breaking the family ethnic prescriptions of what constitutes a good life to figure out one's self-identity. Many family conflicts are played out in the form of stricter or less strict adherence to family ethnic rules and expectations, most often in the areas of intermarriage, mate selection, parenting, and education. Often, when the offspring do not adhere to strict ethnic family rules, violent cutoffs and hurtful rejections take place. Because this is a country that continues to absorb many immigrants, there are large numbers of second- and third-generation immigrants dealing with the issue of loyalty to, or separation from, the ethnic origin of the family. These immigrants, while struggling with whether to conform or not conform to the ethnic prescriptions of their ancestors, are making the fluidity of the shifting self-identity a hallmark of our immigrant society.

Relationship Between Ethnicity and Religion

Ethnicity has many points of contact with religious observance, but the two are not the same. The Irish Catholics can be different from the Mexican Catholics, and the German Lutherans can be different from the Slovak Lutherans. Their ethnicity may be intersected with their religion, but not totally. The differences in levels of Jewish observance exemplify this. Families can follow secular Jewish traditions that allow for a strong ethnic identification and at the same time be nonobservant. In contrast, there are many Jews who are religiously observant. Betsie thinks of herself as ethnically rather than religiously Jewish. Also, people may have ambivalent reactions to their ethnicity but tend to cling to their reservoir of ethnic traditions in times of crisis, illness, death, marriages, births, and any other markers of the life cycle. Many of these traditions tend to be grounded in religion so that even people who in everyday life do not appear to lead a life where religion plays a role might suddenly resort to religious customs and rituals because of a renewed need to connect with previous generations, heal losses, make a transition to the future, or repeat a familiar family rite (Imber-Black, Roberts, & Whiting, 1988).

Relationship Between Sociohistorical Contexts and Identity

For Betsie, the historical and social contexts in which she grew up included the feminist movement, her parents' divorce, and the societal expectation of women's attractiveness. These historical and social contexts, and the values that can be derived from them, appear to be in contradiction with the values generated by her ethnic heritage (e.g., expectations of togetherness, marriage and children, emphasis on eating and food). She felt that her life was out of her control, and she understands her choices of an abusive mate and her addiction to pot in light of these contradictions. With intense regret she attributes what she considers to be her personal failures to abide by the prescriptions of her ethnic heritage to the new social movement of her time, the civil rights and the feminist movements. She also talks about being negatively influenced by her father, his numerous wives, and other family members. Because of the way she ends the writing of her story, we do not have a clear sense of how she defines herself today, which aspects of her cultural and ethnic background she continues to embrace, and which ones she has decided to discard. Has her self-identity shifted or does it remain the same?

Clinical Applications

This section starts with assessment questions related to the content themes and continues with interventions useful when working with people who present with stereotypes about ethnicity, either their own or someone else's. This section ends with an extensive discussion about possible countertransference reactions when working with people of similar or different ethnic affiliations.

Assessment

Counselors can be instrumental in helping increase their clients' awareness of their ethnic identity, including awareness of the factors that shape their current values, motivations, and actions. Also, it is important to help clients understand that their self-definition and identity may change over time or remain the same. If people receive negative images of their ethnicity, either in the societal or family context in which they develop, or if they begin to have negative views of their ethnicity as they grow and mature, self-hate and rejections of parts of their self may result. Self-hate can be detrimental to their sense of self, their identity, and their relationships. At the other extreme, people may develop distorted, self-aggrandizing, and ethnocentric views of their own ethnicity and feel superior to people they deem inferior because these people do (or do not) possess a certain ethnic identity. Another possibility is that individuals do not recognize that how they think about themselves, their values, their motivations, and their behavior is based on their ethnicity.

It is important to assess the meanings and expectations associated with clients' ethnicity and its relation to other areas of their lives to get a sense of where they are in their identity development and help them move forward, if they so desire. Also, it is important to assess clients' constraints in relation to their own ethnic identity or the way they understand the ethnic identity of others with whom they interact (e.g., spouses, coworkers, neighbors, in-laws, employees). These therapeutic conversations are important because clients' sense of self and their relationships with others are deeply tied to issues about ethnicity.

Pride About Ethnic Background

How important is your ethnicity in your life?

How do you understand your ethnic background?

Has that view changed over the years or remained the same?

Do other people you interact with share your positive/negative view?

Ethnicity, Family Values, and Pressures to Conform

Have any of your decisions been affected by your ethnic background, in terms of choice of spouse, child rearing, home location, your religious affiliation, and so on?

How difficult were those decisions for you? For your family?

Has your ethnicity constrained or made it easier for you to live your life?

If you identify constraints about how you live your life, how have you dealt with those constraints?

Relationship Between Ethnicity, Religion, Sociohistorical Contexts, and Other Variables

Are you aware of any religious, historical, or social class issues that have affected the way you think about your ethnicity?

Are you aware of how your ethnic background has affected the way you think about other peoples' ethnicity (e.g., your spouse, coworkers, in-laws)?

Are there any constraints in your relationship with your spouse, coworkers, subordinates, or in-laws that you attribute to ethnic differences?

Have you changed the way you deal with those constraints or have your methods remained the same over the years?

Techniques and Interventions

Sometimes people attribute their problems in life to the difference between theirs and their parents', spouses', or in-laws' ethnicity: "He drinks like an Irishman," "She worries like a Jewish mother," "He cheats like a Latin lover," "She is uptight like a German." It is not unusual to hear people speak these ready-made stereotypes to justify and explain, to themselves or their significant others, their disputes, family struggles, or profound differences. When people speak this way, they are using what is known as cultural camouflage: the attribution of ethnicity to problems in a relationship (Falicov, 1995). This way of understanding people's characteristics tends to perpetuate struggles, decrease empathy, and polarize family members, coworkers, subordinates, and in-laws because they tend to present people with paralyzing, one-perspective narratives that do not include empathy for themselves or others. Counselors often do not know how to deal with clients who use explanations based on ethnicity to explain their problems with significant others in their lives.

One useful intervention is the internalized-other interviewing technique developed by Epston (1993) and Tomm (1989) to increase empathy, reduce polarizations, and help people see things from multiple perspectives. In internalized-other interviewing, the therapist asks the client to put him- or herself in the shoes of the significant other and allow the client to be interviewed as if he or she were the other person. In internalized-other interviewing, clients answer questions about the subjective experience of other members of the family being interviewed through the client. This brings awareness to the client of the feelings and needs of the other person, and, therefore, increases the client's empathy for the other person (Ziegler & Hiller, 2001). It can be helpful for clients who are struggling with their in-laws, coworkers, superiors, or subordinates, or with the mate selection of their children in terms of their or the other's ethnicity. One of us (Sara) used this technique with Jan, who attributed her difficulties with her mother-in-law, Ellen, to Ellen's ethnic background. According to Jan, Ellen's ethnicity was the reason they did not get along, why she raised her son (Jan's husband) the way she did, and why she was not a good grandmother to Jan's and her husband's baby. Sara asked Jan to answer questions as if she were Ellen and asked, "Speaking as Ellen, what do you attribute your struggles with Jan to? When was the first time you noticed a difference in the way Jan talked to you? What kind of relationship would you like to have with your grandson? What stops you from having this relationship with your grandson? What do you suppose Jan thinks of you? What would be the first thing you would notice in Jan that would give you a clue that the relationship with her will change? What do you think Jan will notice about you, Ellen, that will give Jan the clue that things are going to be different and better?" At the end of the dialogue, Jan was surprised by her increased level of empathy toward Ellen, her mother-in-law.

Similar techniques are circular questions, reflexive questions, relationship questions, outside perspective questions, and role reversal questions (Tomm, 1988; Ziegler & Hiller, 2001), which can help clients become actively reflective about a particular experience, event, or course of action from a variety of perspectives. Because one of the most valuable tools a clinician has is the art of questioning to elicit self-generating solutions, the reader is invited to explore the wide availability of experience-generating questions that can move clients toward other preferred realities and ways of relating to significant people in their lives (Freedman & Combs, 1995).

Countertransference

When clients present with strong ethnic affiliations, countertransference reactions may depend on whether the clinician is of the same or a different ethnicity than that of the client and how much information about or exposure to the ethnicity of the client the clinician has. Therapists must be aware of their own cultural, religious, or ethnic countertransference (Crohn, 1998).

Similar Ethnicity

If the counselor's ethnicity is similar to that of the client, there is a danger that the clinician will overidentify with the client and miss intragroup differences (Comas-Diaz & Jacobsen, 1991). Sara was supervising an intern who completely missed assessing a severe alcohol abuse issue in one of her clients because she and the client were both Jewish. The stereotype of the Jewish female client is that substance abuse may be less of a problem than it would be if the client were of another ethnic group or a man (Ashemberg Straussner, 2001). Because this coincided with the circumstances of the lack of substance abuse in the intern's family, it did not occur to her that this client might be presenting with an alcohol-related problem. The attractiveness of having a client to whom the counselor can attribute similar backgrounds can mask the ability of the clinician to make accurate assessments, seduced by the idea that the clinician and the client have so much in common. The seduction of the apparent knowledge of the ethnic background of the client is no small advantage. Clients, too, feel more attracted to clinicians with whom they think they have more in common. Another possible countertransference reaction of similar background in the counselor–client dyad is annoyance, disappointment, or impatience if the client is not advancing in the way the clinician thinks the client ought to be progressing. This is quite common when the therapist is of the same ethnic background but of a different social class than the client (Comas-Diaz & Jacobsen, 1991). Having become more educated and more assertive, or having been able to overcome poverty, the therapist may have the expectation that the clients can do it too and overlook the clients' differing expectations of themselves, different contexts, or different personalities.

Sara noticed that as a Latina and immigrant therapist, the clients she has the strongest countertransference reactions with are, paradoxically, those who have a very similar background in terms of cultural context but not in terms of class. For several years, as a single mother with three children, teaching four classes a semester at a university and taking two classes a semester in a doctoral program, Sara used to write her own papers at night and grade students' papers during soccer games, at the doctor's and dentist's office, and while her kids were getting haircuts. Several years after that, Sara worked with a very depressed Latina single mother who continuously and bitterly complained about how her (only) child interfered with her ability to study for one English as a second language class she was taking. It was not until Sara was able to become aware of her annoyance, impatience, and arrogant thoughts (e.g., "If I could do it, why can't she?") and overcome them that she was able to be more helpful to her client.

Different Ethnicity

If the client–counselor dyad is culturally very different, there can be ambivalent discomfort on the clinician's part (Comas-Diaz & Jacobsen, 1991). On the one hand, the clinician is eager to help and demonstrate that he or she is not racist or discriminatory and tries hard to show this to the client by being overly friendly or accommodating. On the other hand, the clinician may be puzzled by some characteristic of the client that the clinician attributes to the client's ethnicity and tends to view these attributes negatively. Often the clinician fails to inquire about these characteristics for fear of being labeled insensitive, racist, or both, by a supervisor, the clinician's peers, or the client. This is not uncommon in client–counselor dyads that correspond to traditional polarizing ethnic pairs—for example, Puerto Rican and Mexican, Irish and Polish, Arab and Israeli— but it is worse when the clinician belongs to the dominant group and the client is a member of a traditionally oppressed ethnic minority, such as between a White therapist and a Hawaiian, Native American, Latino, or Asian client (Gorkin, 1996). The ambivalent discomfort of the clinician may be more prevalent currently than it was in years past because the expectation of political correctness may push the ambivalent discomfort underground.

Another reason the discomfort may exist with dominant group counselors is because many feel disassociated from their own ethnicity. The original European immigrant settlers shaped basic political and civic life in such a broad way that the Anglo-Saxon culture became associated with the ideal by which all subsequent ethnic groups were judged (Giordano & McGoldrick, 1996). When ethnic minorities begin to consider issues of race and ethnicity seriously, many of European descent often express surprise. Lack of acknowledgment, rejection, or denial of the ethnic background is more possible for Whites than for other ethnic groups precisely because they are seen by all groups as the norm in the United States. This is due to several historical and sociopolitical reasons. First, White Americans do not generally perceive themselves as anything other than regular Americans, perhaps in part because they fought the English for the right to be Americans and not English (McGill & Pierce, 1996). Second, to be an American has been initially equated to being White, and although the United States was very diverse from its inception, in general, acculturation meant (and often still means) acquiring White Protestant values and personal characteristics (Giordano & McGoldrick, 1996). Third, having been traditionally the ethnic group with the most dominance in the colonized world, ethnic Whites of different backgrounds have considered themselves to be superior to other peoples viewed as less civilized (Hays, 2001).

As the traditional ethnic group with the privilege and luxuries that power and dominance afford, White Americans have, therefore, been able to deny, reject, or not acknowledge their ethnic affiliation. As a concept, ethnicity is often understood by Whites as something that other ethnic minority people have. It is not often a word a White American would apply to describe him- or herself.

This is obviously an illusion shared by minorities and Whites alike. When we teach a multicultural counseling course, the White students tend to be the ones who have the hardest time figuring out how to answer the questions related to their cultural identity. Interestingly, by the end of the course, they may be the ones with the biggest shift. They may realize that the denial of their ethic affiliation is a luxury and a privilege they have been able to afford since the day they were born, a luxury that individuals in other ethnic groups may not share (McIntosh, 1998).

The lack of awareness of ethnicity is more possible for Whites who have had limited exposure to ethnic minorities during their childhood and adolescence. The invisibility of ethnic minorities for Whites is not uncommon. Contact with ethnic minorities may not have been present in the historical past and in the awareness of most Whites. In spite of continued racial hostility and residentially segregated neighborhoods, for example, racial issues are still not present in the awareness of many Whites, who can continue to be complacent about such important issues (Giordano & McGoldrick, 1996). During the multicultural counseling course, it is not unusual for

White students to be the last to acknowledge that racism, bigotry, and discrimination still exist, in part because these are experiences they tend not to have, due to their privileged position in society.

The ethnic identity of Whites might remain weak or not be relevant for most of the person's life. It might take a significant event to change that, such as intermarriage, a move to a less homogeneous part of the country, or exposure to workplace or classroom diversity. These events sometimes force White individuals to examine their identity as they confront the issue of difference, sometimes for the first time in their lives. Confronted with difference, they may begin to understand, for the first time, that the characteristics of their personality are related to their own White cultural socialization. Clinicians need to be aware of their ambivalent discomfort, if or when it surfaces, as they work with their ethnic minority clients and are encouraged to explore the influence of their ethnicity and ethnic socialization on their own identity development and functioning.

TOOLBOX ACTIVITY—BETSIE

Discussion Questions	Activities	Resources
Content themes What other themes do you see emerging in the story that the author did not identify? **Assessment** Are there any questions you would like to ask Betsie? **Interventions** What other interventions could you propose with Betsie? **Countertransference** What countertransference reactions were emerging in yourself as you read this story? **Other scenarios** If Betsie were Irish, Italian, Mexican, or Polish, would your reactions to the story be the same or different? If Betsie were a Jewish man, would your reactions to the story be any different?	Attend a Jewish religious service or a Passover dinner. Visit Latino, Korean, Polish, Vietnamese, Indian, or Mexican neighborhoods. Find out the differences between Orthodox, Reform, Conservative, and nonobservant Jewish individuals. Interview separately individuals from India and Pakistan, Korea and Taiwan, Japan and mainland China, or Poland and Russia and write in your journal about the differences between the two closely related ethnic groups.	**Suggested readings** Ben-Sasson, H. (1985). *History of the Jewish people*. Cambridge, MA: Harvard University Press. Steinberg, S. (2001). *The ethnic myth: Race, ethnicity and class in America* (3rd ed.). Boston: Beacon Press. Thernstrom, S. (1980). *Harvard encyclopedia of American ethnic groups*. Boston: Belknap Press. **Videos** *Bend It Like Beckham* *Monsoon Wedding* *My Big Fat Greek Wedding* *The Way Home*

Five

Maribel's Story

When Are You Going to Have Kids?

Ethnicity is associated with nationality and country of origin. Examining ethnicity provides clues about individuals' values, beliefs, and behaviors and often yields more information than race, particularly on intragroup differences. This is critical in working with clients of Asian or Latino descent. Generic information on racial characteristics provides a helpful starting place for clinicians, but specific information about ethnicity adds to the richness of understanding. In this chapter, Maribel, a Puerto Rican, describes growing up in a poor, Spanish-speaking household; moving around the country; and feeling like a minority everywhere she went. She talks about what she feels was her double life, her pride in her educational accomplishments, and the price she paid for her acculturation and her gender role shifts. As you read, notice how she experienced the frequent moves of her family as she was growing up and how the exposure to racism affected not only her blended identity but also her decision to become better educated to increase her social status options. Also, notice the losses that came with her gains and how she manages her American identity blended with her identity as a Puerto Rican. Following the story, we explore the relationship between ethnicity and racism, language, social class, gender socialization patterns, and gender role shifts that occur as the identity of the individual shifts. The clinical intervention discusses some ideas for working with ethnic minority couples who are in cultural transition from hierarchical gender roles to more egalitarian modes of relating. Finally, the countertransference section includes a discussion about possible reactions clinicians may have when working with couples who exhibit power imbalances.

Maribel's Story

I am a 30-year-old Latina woman. I was born in Puerto Rico and, beginning at the age of 5 years, was raised in Chicago. My parents are both Puerto Rican—born and raised in Puerto Rico. I have one brother, Osvaldo, and three sisters, Daniela, Debora, and Magdalena. Daniela and Debora are half sisters from my father's side. They have lived in Puerto Rico all their life, not once having visited the United States. Osvaldo and Magdalena both live in Chicago, but Osvaldo was born in Puerto Rico, and Magdalena was born in Connecticut.

I was raised in a Spanish-speaking household. When I was in the first grade, I was taught English and was then placed in a bilingual class. I learned English so well, I was transferred to English-only classes and afterward was only in English-only classes. I was still able to retain my knowledge of Spanish because I spoke English only at school and Spanish only at home. To this day, I am very grateful that I was taught to appreciate the Spanish language, despite my need to learn English. I am proud to say I am very fluent in Spanish: I can read it, speak it, and write it well. Not many people who come to the United States are able to do so because they are faced with the challenge of learning English, abandon the Spanish language, and therefore forget it.

My current religion is Roman Catholic. Many Latinos are Catholic. Growing up I was faced with the dilemma of being in two religions, depending on which side of the family I was hanging out with. It was very bizarre. My mother's side of the family was Pentecostal, and my father's side of the family was Catholic. I was only 5 years old when I learned the hard way that when I entered my grandfather's church, which was Pentecostal, I could not do the sign of the crucifix on my forehead. This was very confusing and painful for me to try to understand at such a young age. If I was visiting my father's side of the family, I was Catholic, but if I was visiting my mother's side of the family, I was Pentecostal, even if for that day only. These two religions are complete opposites of one another. As a child, I visited several churches in search of the religion that I felt comfortable with and understood. I visited Baptist, Evangelical, Pentecostal, and various Catholic churches. I even took a course in the sociology of religion at a university to further understand the different types of religions available. I must say, I thought every religion had something to offer that was of interest to me. I enjoyed reading about them and wish there was a way that I could have all of them in one, but it seems impossible. Hence, I have remained Catholic and visit church every once in a while.

My family migrated to the United States when I was 5 years old. We have lived in the United States ever since. We live in Chicago, but after leaving Puerto Rico, we have also lived in several other states. At the age of 6 years, my family and I moved to Hartford, Connecticut. My father was doing auto-body work, and my mother was a housewife at the time. When I was 10 years old, my family and I moved to Winnie, Texas. A friend of my father's lived in Texas and offered my father a job in auto-body work, so we all moved to Texas in search of a better life. I think we only lived there for about 2 years before returning to Chicago. Later, my mother decided to find employment and became a teacher's aide for a school. She has held this job for about 14 years. It was difficult moving every time my father was offered a better job. We had to adjust to a new state, a new environment, new friends, the loss of family left behind, and new beginnings at another school. My father has worked in auto-body work, mechanics, and carpentry almost all of his life. My mother has been a factory worker, a waitress, and a teacher's aide. Growing up, I found that my family and I were different from other families around us. We lived in "barrios" or ghetto neighborhoods. I grew up very poor and a minority. It seemed that, even though we lived in neighborhoods where other minorities lived, we had to go to institutions, such as school, where there weren't too many minorities. I recall living in Texas and attending grammar school where I was the only Puerto Rican girl. People used to stare at me and say things like, "Is that the Puerto Rican girl? I have never seen one before." I was made fun of in school, and riding the school bus to go to my trailer home was a nightmare. I was picked on because of my race, and I felt like a complete outsider—lonely, uncomfortable, and embarrassed—for being so different and not understanding what it meant. Living in Chicago was quite a different story. I grew up mostly in ghetto neighborhoods and still in the lower class. I did not feel as much as an outsider as I did in Texas because there were other Latinos around me, in my neighborhoods and in school. I was not made fun of because of my race or because I spoke Spanish.

As I continued going to school, I saw that there were opportunities available for my personal growth that mostly came about through education. I participated in school events in grammar school, such as the flag squad and band, so I could belong to groups in which there were people like me—Latino and poor—and feel like I belonged. Later in high school, I felt the need to also become a part of different groups. I attended Washington High School my freshman year even though I wanted to attend Smith Tech High School. I was not allowed entrance into Smith because of my entrance exam grades. As a sophomore, I was able to transfer to Smith Tech High School after being ranked second in the entire freshman class at Washington High. At Washington, I was a member of the ROTC and was the top cadet. I was very happy because I felt that I was somehow better than what I was without this rank. All my life I had felt that I wasn't good enough because of my race, my cultural background, my being different. Having rank in ROTC made me feel that it was okay to be different, that I could still be accepted. I also joined the marching band at Washington, where I was a flute player. When I transferred to Smith, I transferred from ROTC to gym class but remained in the marching band. At that time, the Smith Tech Marching Band was quite an important group. This made me feel so good, like I was part of something special. I was very pleased to graduate from such a prestigious high school as a music major. Graduating from Smith Tech High School made me feel that I was not only intelligent but also able to succeed, regardless of my race or cultural background.

In my college years, I attended several schools, colleges, and universities. In each one of these, I found more variety of cultural groups and more people like me, Latinos, attending and making something out of their lives. I realized that there are many minorities, Latinos as well as other minorities, who have struggled throughout their lives with being different from the majority group and with what we call culture shock. We minorities spend so much time trying to acculturate that we miss our culture, and being the way our culture indicates we are when we are in that place of origin. For example, I am Puerto Rican and feel that I am Puerto Rican at all times. However, I cannot dress for work or school the way I would if I were working or going to work or school in Puerto Rico. For one, the climate is different, and, two, I would create too much attention and would hence feel again how different I am from the majority group. Many times, I miss dressing up in "my clothes" and acting the way I would if I were in Puerto Rico. In this way, I feel like I'm living a double life.

When I graduated as a medical assistant from business school in 1993, I was so proud of myself. I remember so many great things about my graduation, but most of all I recall going on stage to give my valedictorian speech and having a crowd of people, whom I did not know, scream, "Yea! It's a Puerto Rican." I was surprised because I did not know the people in the crowd, and they did not know me, but they were proud that I was representing Puerto Ricans everywhere and that I had succeeded in having a 4.0 GPA. Perhaps, the most I was ever involved in a cultural group was when I went back to live in Connecticut. I moved to Storrs, Connecticut, and attended the University of Connecticut for a couple of years. I became a psychology major and learned about the differences in other cultural groups and about the different people who attended the university with me. I was pleased to find that there were other Latinos becoming educated and advancing their careers by obtaining their bachelor's degree. I joined the Puerto Rican and Latina American Cultural Center (PRLACC) and became very involved with university activities, which promoted the advancement of Latinos. As a group, we were very strong in our beliefs, in our desire to continue improving our lives, and in helping others realize that it is possible for us as minorities to have better lives through education and motivation.

In my family, I am a great role model for those who are still going to school. My mother's side of the family is just as different as my father's side of the family regarding educational background—as different as they are in religious background. Almost all the members of my mother's side of the family dropped out of high school, got married, had children, and either lived as housewives or worked in factories or performed other unskilled jobs. My father's side of the family is filled with educated individuals who almost all have careers and have continued their education to the master's and doctorate levels. I say that I have come to be like my father's side of the family. Growing up was difficult for me not only in terms of my cultural background but also in terms of the problems within my household. I grew up in a family where my mother was oppressed as a woman and practically a slave to my father's needs. My father has been an alcoholic most of his life, and this was difficult for me as well. I saw that part of my cultural background consisted of the woman of the house being a slave to her man and the man of the house being the boss. I did not agree with this and saw that it was very common to the other Latino families around me, whether they were just friends of the family or my family members. I did not understand why it had to be this way and why the women put up with all the things their men would do, such as physically and emotionally abuse them and cheat on them and then come home and expect to be treated like kings of the world. I vowed to not let this become my life, and I have kept my promise to myself to become strong and better so that I do not end up like my mother and other Latina women.

I am currently divorced and have been so since January of this year. I believe that part of my divorce came about because of my cultural background and my experiences in my family as I was growing up. I do not see myself as the typical Puerto Rican woman. I am educated and intelligent, and I take advantages of opportunities to become a better person, more educated and experienced. When I was married, my husband tried to treat me the way my father treated my mother, and that was not the life I was going to live. My ex-husband was not educated in the same manner that I am. He is an intelligent young man in different fields, such as in mechanics; he was a real estate agent and is currently a mortgage loan officer at a bank. However, when we were together, my ex-husband thought that he could be my boss and that I would do as he said. He soon found out that this thinking was a mistake. Another issue that came about in my marriage was my education. I decided to continue my studies to obtain my bachelor's degree after I got married.

When I notified my husband of my decision to pursue a degree, his exact words were, "When you married me, you stopped being a student." I was angry when he said this to me and hurt that the man I had chosen to accept as my husband was not supportive of my desire to continue my education. I saw that he was going to be an obstacle in my path. This made me want to continue my education even more, and I did just that. I registered for school and attended classes against his will, which created tension in our marriage for some time. With time, he tried to convince me that he was supportive of my education, but I saw that it was not true. He attended my graduation where I received my bachelor's degree, and he gave me a very hard time when I wanted to stay and take pictures with my friends before leaving campus. He thought I should graduate and leave, and that was the end of that, whether I liked it or not. I was extremely hurt and felt that it had all been an act. I ended up leaving the university without seeing any of my friends or taking any pictures with them. I lost contact with many of them, and I can't forgive him or myself for allowing him to do that to me. I recall one of his friends telling me that my ex-husband thought I was more intelligent than him, and I honestly believe that my education was a threat to him. In my marriage, I had several issues that brought conflict to the marriage, but I would say that family was one of them as well. I am very family oriented, and my ex-husband, even though he is Puerto Rican also, was not family oriented at all. He became very angry and hostile any time I wanted to spend time with my family. I found myself in the middle, as if I had to choose between my family and my husband. This was extremely stressful, and I believe unnecessary, but it was a very big part of my life. It got to the point that my family stopped visiting because my ex-husband became very hostile when they visited me. My entire life had been about family, and there was no way I was going to let a man separate me from my family. I believe that in the Latino culture men believe they are the bosses and that their women and their children are to obey them. I had conflict in my marriage because I did not let my husband be my boss and because of his beliefs in raising children. In my attempt to become a mother, I lost three pregnancies, either to a miscarriage or to an ectopic pregnancy. These experiences were very painful for me and for my husband at that time. Later, I found out that the only way I can achieve a full-term pregnancy is through in vitro fertilization. This was difficult news for me as a woman and also as a Latina because, to me, Latinas are viewed as fertile and ready to have many kids, but I was the contrary of this stereotype. Another thing that made it difficult was my family's expectations that I would have children. I am the only woman in the family who doesn't have children, and they are very persistent that I have some, even now that I am divorced. It is almost as if I am making them look bad. It sounds crazy, but every time they see me they ask me, "When are you going to have kids?"

My ex-husband wanted children, but while married I found out that I did not like the way he treated his little nephews, and this created problems in our decision to go through the in vitro fertilization. My ex-husband thinks that children need to be raised with threats to prevent them from misbehaving, and I do not agree with this. I was raised without ever being spanked, and I think I turned out just fine. One thing I can say: I am glad I divorced my husband because we definitely kept growing apart, and my experiences as a child growing up in the type of family I have made me attentive to people being treated as people and not being oppressed because of their sex, race, or ethnicity. I later found out that he had a girlfriend, which is when I decided I wanted a divorce. Latin men have a bad reputation for being womanizers, and I definitely was not going to accept him after this. Again, my husband came to find out that I was not the typical Puerto Rican woman who was going to let her man oppress her while he hung out at bars with his friends and kept girl-friends on the side. After all has been said and done, I am glad I continued my education because it is just as I said before: A man will come and go, but I will have my education with me forever, and I can do a lot with that, even if I am by myself.

I am now continuing my education to obtain my master's degree. Even though I am still a minority, I see that my education has done so much for me and always will by giving me opportunities to succeed. I may still be a minority and a woman, but I am a better minority and am very proud of my culture, no longer concerned about my differences being criticized or made fun of. I now laugh because I have found happiness within myself, in my culture, in my not being one of the majority group. Growing up poor and allowing my education to give me better opportunities in employment has allowed me to become what I consider middle class. I don't expect to ever become a member of the upper class, but if I were ever to live again in poverty, I know that I would survive just as I did when I was a child. Changing socioeconomic status has showed me that I can survive in the worst environments if I have to become part of them again. I owe my rise to the middle class to my education and the opportunities it gave me. I am thankful to my parents, *mi familia*, for bringing me to the United States as a child and giving me the opportunity to live a better life than they did. If I ever find the perfect man for me, one who will respect me as a woman and an individual and who is not threatened by my education and my ability to think for myself and stand up for myself, then I will take the opportunity to have children, whether it be through in vitro fertilization or adoption, so that I can teach my children that they too can become somebody in a society where we are just another minority. I will teach them to respect others' differences and take advantage of opportunities to be as successful as those of the majority group so that they too can have a better life than the one I have.

Content Themes

The main themes in Maribel's story are how she manages the blending of her Puerto Rican identity with her American identity, her increasing awareness of the gender role shifts, and her pride in her identity as a Puerto Rican woman.

Ethnicity, Immigration, Social Class, and Racism

Maribel's story reflects the relationship between ethnicity, immigration, social class, and racism as she describes the struggles of her family, who came to the United States to escape poverty. Once in the United

States, the family had to move frequently in pursuit of better economic opportunities. According to statistical data, Puerto Ricans still hold the status of being the poorest among the Latino groups (U.S. Census Bureau, 2000). These statistics can be misleading because, although this fact may be true for residents of New York City, where so many Puerto Ricans live and where the concentration of urban poverty may be higher than in other parts of the country, data show that when Puerto Ricans move to other areas of the country, they fare better economically than other Latinos in those areas. In Texas, for example, Puerto Ricans' rates of high school and college graduation and income are higher than that of other Latinos (Garcia-Prieto, 1996). Other cross-national immigration studies show similar results, implying that a minority group's success or lack of success in a new cultural environment is relative to its relationship with the dominant group, rather than to intrinsic characteristics of the minority group (Green, 1998).

Maribel's family moved to Texas where her father found employment as a mechanic. In times of stress, Puerto Rican families may turn to their extended families for help (Garcia-Prieto, 1996), and this is true of many other ethnic groups whose members help each other in times of crisis. Family members who are in more stable positions usually feel obligated to help, often putting allegiance to the distressed extended family members above the needs of their own nuclear families. This may baffle some people in more individualistic or competitive family structures, whose members would never think of asking relatives for help in times of distress. Maribel's father moved to Texas because his brother had a successful business there and invited him to move. But in Texas, Maribel describes being singled out as a Puerto Rican, and she reports being made fun of in school and feeling lonely, uncomfortable, and embarrassed. This is consistent with the experiences of many Latinos in the United States. Dominant group attitudes toward Hispanics may display racist overtones, especially toward those with darker skin and less money or education. Maribel reflects that in her story.

Ethnicity and Language

Immigrants of various ethnic backgrounds often encourage their children to continue speaking the language of origin, in part because there is a newly recognized need to preserve the cultural heritage, particularly the heritage of oppressed minorities. Children of immigrants whose ethnic identity is plagued by issues of discrimination, stereotyping, or other forms of oppression may resist the parental insistence on preservation of cultural and language heritage. Some may, in contrast, express a strong desire to continue their ties with their ethnic identity and their language as a way to express pride, solidarity, and loyalty to the cultural background. Clearly, Maribel not only retained her Spanish language oral proficiency, but also can read and write in Spanish. The extent to which a language is preserved or lost in the second-generation ethnic minority depends on several variables. Maribel speaks with pride about the preservation of her language abilities and is proud of her written and oral proficiency in Spanish.

The racial, ethnic, and socioeconomic heterogeneity of the Latino population in the United States is well documented (Falicov, 1998b; Gonzalez, 1997; Mezzich, Ruiz, & Muñoz, 1999). However, the percentage of Latinos living below or just above the poverty line is significantly higher than the percentage of Whites living below or just above the poverty line (U.S. Census Bureau, 2000). For a large percentage of Latinos in the United States, loss of cultural roots, ethnic discrimination, language barriers, and difficulties with acculturation are common occurrences (Falicov, 1998b). It is not surprising that someone like Maribel, a person exposed to discrimination and poverty while growing up, and who has strived to achieve social mobility and financial independence, shows interest in continuing her ties with her Puerto Rican cultural background through the preservation and betterment of her Spanish language literacy.

The Double Life of a Hybrid Identity

Even though Maribel has preserved her Spanish language, she exhibits hybridization and alternation between two cultures as she negotiates her identity as both an American and a Puerto Rican (Falicov, 1998b). Maribel says she leads a double life because she cannot dress and act in the United States as she would in Puerto Rico. To live in the United States, she feels like she has to act and dress in a certain American way, even though she feels strongly like a Puerto Rican. This can be a confusing and challenging task. As Maribel's story illustrates, her differing identities do not need to be mutually exclusive or progress in a linear or one-dimensional way. As is true with many second-generation immigrants who attempt to reconcile their various allegiances and ethnic identities, changes in Maribel's representation of self can vary over time, across settings, and within relationships. Because she identifies solidly with both the Puerto Rican and the American groups and settings, she appears to be able simultaneously to hold and merge the two worlds at times. At other times, she might experience a shift in identity from foreground to background (Hays, 2001), depending on the context. It would not be surprising if she were to experience herself as primarily American in her occupational or educational settings and primarily Puerto Rican in her family context. She may alternate or combine the uses of her language, for example, Spanish at home and English at work, or Spanish to count and sing and English to discuss schoolwork. She is also choosing what she judges to be the best from the Puerto Rican culture, what she wants to preserve, and choosing what she would like to discard. This hybridization of ethnic identity is not without its challenges (Falicov, 1998b) because, as bicultural individuals navigate life and relationships, they may be accused of being disloyal by other individuals in the same family, they may have trouble convincing others of the benefits of hybridization or biculturality, or they may be confused about the meanings of their own bicultural status. One of the challenges of alternating identities comes from the individual's simultaneous view of him- or herself as an American and a Puerto Rican.

Gender Role Shifts

Another main theme that emerges in this story is the shifting of the gender roles, from traditional or polarized gender roles to more egalitarian or balanced gender role definitions (Breunlin, Schwartz, & Mac Kune-Karrer, 1997). The struggles that result from the shift in the gender roles take place often between the men and women of a family. Usually, the movement toward gender equity comes as a result of discomforts first identified by the women in the family—the wives or the daughters—which may in turn bring discomfort to the men—the fathers or husbands—who may, as a result, resort to increased control and intimidation tactics to keep the status quo. This is clear in Maribel's case. In authoritarian and collectivistic cultures, differing standards for men and women exist, giving men the responsibility for the welfare and honor of the family, with its concomitant privilege, and assigning women spiritual superiority, self-sacrifice, and a more passive and oppressed role (Comas-Diaz, 1987; Falicov, 1998b). Marriages can be more about the preservation of the family than about the relationship among the members of the couple, and divorce is a worse outcome than staying in an unhappy relationship. In some hierarchical societies, the status of the women may change over time, as women become older mothers, grandmothers, and mothers-in-law themselves (Ingoldsby, 1995). In Maribel's case, she does not see herself as a typical Puerto Rican woman who caters to men's needs. She struggles with the role models of other Latina women, women she sees as slaves of the men in their lives. She promised herself that she would not be like that but instead would become independent and educated. She does not describe personal intergenerational struggles with her father, as other second-generation immigrants do, but is critical of her mother's adherence to traditional gender roles. She did not agree with this role for women and vowed not to end up like her mother.

Maribel feels that her view of her gender role and the shifts she elicited for herself precipitated her divorce. She describes a husband who became increasingly polarized as Maribel's gender awareness became strengthened by her exposure to education and the more egalitarian American cultural milieu. These gender role shifts generally come at a considerable cost for the family. The more freedom and equality the female member of the spousal team aspires to, the more the male may cling to his old patterns and may have more difficulty giving them up, solidifying conflicts in the couple. Maribel may shift in gender role expectations in terms of wanting a more egalitarian relationship and separating herself from what she perceives to be her mother's traditional gender roles, while at the same time expressing a wish to fulfill her own family's gender expectations of her as a mother, as she struggles with the loss of her pregnancies and her spousal relationship.

Clinical Applications

This section describes assessment questions that may be relevant for clients like Maribel. The techniques and interventions focus on gender and class differences in help-seeking behavior, couple's therapy for ethnic minority couples, the engagement of the Latino male in therapy, and ideas for avoiding clinical pitfalls.

Assessment

It is important to assess the identity issues of the client whose ethnicity, social class, and educational family background differ from that of the

White ethnic middle-class majority culture. Is the client resorting to rejection, to acceptance, or to a blend of both cultures? It is also important to assess the relationship between ethnicity, immigration, social class, education, and racism in the client's life and the extent of the gender shifts and the gains/losses that come with it.

Ethnicity, Immigration, Social Class, and Racism

Were/are there any experiences with marginalization, oppression, discrimination, or racism related to the client's ethnicity, social class, or immigration status?

Have there been drastic gender or social class shifts between the client and his or her family of origin or members of his or her extended family?

Have there been shifts in educational attainments between the client and the family of origin?

If there were shifts, how have they affected the client's relationship with members of the family of origin or the extended family?

Hybrid Identity

Has the client accepted, rejected, or blended identities?

Can the client identify what she or he has accepted, rejected, or blended?

Does the client alternate behaviors in different contexts?

If the client feels or acts differently in different contexts, how easy or hard is that?

What is the reaction of the significant people in the client's life to the shifts?

Gender Role Shifts

Were there any shifts in gender roles?

How and by whom were the shifts initiated?

What effect did the shift/lack of shift have on the individual/family?

How were the conflicts around gender shifts handled by the client's parents and spouse?

What were the gains/losses associated with the gender role shifts?

Techniques and Interventions

When traditional gender roles begin to shift, as in the case of Maribel with her former husband, conflicts in the couple may increase (Breunlin et al., 1997). With ethnic minority couples, it is not unusual for women to be the ones requesting therapeutic help. Because a Latina woman may see herself in the role of having to be the one to hold the family together, she may think of herself as a failure if she is not successful (Falicov, 1998b). Her willingness to seek therapeutic help may be in sync with her cultural prescriptions. Female cultural prescriptions and therapy share similar characteristics because talking to a stranger about matters of intimate concern is considered to be the cornerstone of therapy. But it can also be seen as a typical female characteristic (McCarthy & Holliday, 2004). Some men, particularly traditional men in patriarchal or hierarchical family structures, might consider talking to a stranger about intimate family matters as signs of weakness, vulnerability, potential incompetence, and lack of control (McCarthy & Holliday, 2004). It is not unusual for men to come to one therapy session and drop out or refuse to accompany the woman to therapy if the therapist reacts negatively to dropping out by mistakenly accusing him, overtly or covertly, of being resistant to change. There are gender-related issues in help-seeking behavior, particularly with respect to individuals who are embedded in traditional, patriarchal, or hierarchical family structures, and applying traditionally female expectations of therapeutic behavior to men may not be conducive to successful therapeutic outcomes. Many men view therapy as something to be avoided rather than a supportive process (McCarthy & Holliday, 2004) when they are faced with a therapist who makes them feel more embarrassed and less competent than they felt before therapy started. It may be more effective to change the way therapy is offered than to criticize men for not wanting to use it as a means of getting help with their couple problems.

This is not a question of matching client–therapist dyads by gender; there are risks involved either way. Both men and women therapists can be guilty of the same therapeutic mistakes. It may help to point out men's strengths rather than deficits and to use a collaborative stance in which men are viewed as having important opinions about the issues facing the couple. The previous comments are not intended to negate or minimize in any way the power imbalances that often exist in couples' relationships or the important role that power imbalances play in those relationships. The ideas that women in traditional marriages need to be empowered (Vazquez-Nuttall, Romero-Garcia, & De Leon, 1987), or that men's position in society has given them privileges not afforded to women (Comas-Diaz, 1987), or that it is important to understand the implications of a patriarchal culture for the mental health of both women and men (Walters, Carter, Papp, & Silverstein, 1988) are not new. But to be able to have a therapeutic conversation about the effect of the distribution of power in a relationship, there needs to be a strong therapeutic alliance first. Often, couples in traditional marriages do not arrive at that point therapeutically and drop out of therapy early because the therapists may be overtly or covertly critical of the men in therapy or may understand the couple as not moving quickly enough in the direction of more equality and, therefore, may pressure their clients to move faster than they may be prepared to move at that time.

Prolonged and regular therapy may not be the staple of couples therapy with couples of ethnic and social class backgrounds other than White middle class (Falicov, 1998b). Couples may seek help as a result of a crisis, and therapists may have a small window of opportunity to prove to both members of the couple that therapy can be helpful for their problem of differing degrees of acculturation. If the couple becomes a customer (De Shazer, 1988) of therapy, it may be possible to move to other issues pertaining to the power imbalances and lack of equality in the relationship. Some couples may never reach the point of working toward gender equality. Therapists can expect ethnic minority couples to come intermittently, perhaps at the time of a crisis, rather than continuously. If the couple views the therapist as helpful for the problems they face as a family, they may be more inclined to return for more sessions when another crisis arises. The effectiveness of the therapeutic encounter is much more related to the strength of the alliance, which includes the match between client and therapist goals, than to the length of the treatment. Couples can make a lot of progress in one or two sessions (Falicov, 1998b), if they are seen by a therapist who does not judge them for not returning for more and whom the couple sees as helpful in solving their problems.

There are several interventions clinicians may implement in the beginning stages of the therapeutic process that have been successful with couples of varying ethnic and social class backgrounds.

Invite Husband to Therapy

Therapists can phone the husband and invite him to come for a session or two, appealing to his sense of duty and dedication to the family. Alternatively, therapists can appeal to a husband's "expert" knowledge about the nature and motivation of his wife's problems with him and the need to get his advice on how to best understand his wife. This is not a trick intervention; it genuinely implies that the husband may know at least as much about the problem as the wife does and may have an idea of how to solve it.

See Members of the Couple Individually

Therapists can offer to see each member of the couple individually and talk to each separately about how to understand the other member. In hierarchical societies, where direct communication among the members of the couple may be less common or not encouraged (Falicov, 1998a), talking indirectly through the therapist may offer the best option in the beginning. Also, couples seen together may be embarrassed or act as if they need to save face in front of the therapist or each other. Individual members of the couple may be more amenable to individual sessions than to couples sessions. As with family therapy, couples therapy is not about how many people are in the room. Clinicians can provide couples therapy even if only one member attends the session (Weiner-Davis, 1993).

Hypothesize Something Different

When clients present their stories and their dilemmas, therapists may have certain ideas in their minds about the meaning of those stories. Those meanings generate a hypothesis, which in turn generates the questions that follow the hypothesis (Tomm, 1989). The questions that therapists ask are more related to their own hypothesis-making process than to the presenting problems of the client. Therapists can force themselves to imagine a different or contrasting hypothesis, rather than the one they hold in the early stages of the therapeutic relationship, thus generating varied questions.

Countertransference

Reactions to Power Imbalances

When faced with a perceived imbalance of power in a couple, therapists may feel pressured to make the relationship more balanced and less unequal. This can include wishing that women were less submissive, more direct, and more assertive or wishing that men exerted less control. A man may contend that his wife is no longer acting in the way that she used to act in terms of her submissiveness and give examples of his wife's unwillingness to comply with socially prescribed expectations for her gender. The therapist's understanding of this complaint, his or her clinical effectiveness with this issue, and the couple's decision to stay or drop out of therapy depend largely on how the therapist views this problem. A number of possible views come to mind. First, the therapist may view the problem as one of differing cultural and gender transitions and shifts. In this case, the therapist might question the husband about when he first became aware that his wife was changing and what needs he has that are not being met because of the wife's change. Second, the therapist may react with curiosity and as a result try to find out how the husband is affected by the wife's change and what changes he foresees himself making in the future as a result of his wife's change. Third, the therapist who views the husband's complaint as an expression of his need for control and continued oppression of the wife may ask a question that implies a criticism of the male client's position with respect to his wife. Fourth, a clinician may be interested in how the wife puts up with such a difficult husband and ask a question that implies a criticism of her. Because questions imply presuppositions and are prescriptive (Tomm, 1988), what the clinician is curious about and ends up asking, based on the countertransference reactions, has profound effects on the outcome of the counseling process.

A therapist may encounter a couple whose problem is presented in the way that Maribel described the difficulties with her former husband: that he did not support her educational goals and felt threatened by them and that he tried to sever her ties with her family. By using the interventions outlined previously, therapists can avoid the countertransference trap of supporting the wife against the husband, of blaming the couple's problems on the *machista* attitudes of the husband, and of prematurely expecting the wife to increase her assertiveness and reclaim her equal rights in the decision-making process. Because the clinician's countertransference reactions drive the questions asked or not asked, this may precipitate separation or divorce, put women at risk of increased violence, and require women to make drastic changes prematurely without the adequate social support needed to implement them (Falicov, 1998b). The issue is not whether clinicians' are right or wrong about what they think clients ought to do or not do but, rather, whether their therapeutic conversations facilitate or block future changes (Breunlin et al., 1997).

TOOLBOX ACTIVITY—MARIBEL		
Discussion Questions	*Activities*	*Resources*
Content themes What other themes do you see emerging in the story that the author did not identify? **Assessment** Are there any questions you would like to ask Maribel? **Interventions** What other interventions could you propose with Maribel? **Countertransference** What countertransference reactions were emerging in yourself as you read this story? **Other scenarios** What if Maribel hadn't divorced her husband? How would Maribel's life be different if she had not gone to graduate school?	Interview a second-generation Mexican, a Puerto Rican, and a Central American Latino and ask them the following question: What is it like to be a Mexican, a Puerto Rican, or a Central American Latino in the United States? In your journal, write how the answers might affect the way you work with Latino clients of different ethnic affiliations. Find the dictionary definitions of *race* and *ethnicity*. Then, ask people of different race and ethnic backgrounds for their definitions. What conclusions can you draw?	**Suggested readings** Alvarez, J. (1992). *How the Garcia girls lost their accent.* New York: Plume Books. Cisneros, S. (1991). *The house on Mango Street.* New York: Vintage Books. Gutierrez, D. (1995). *Walls and mirrors: Mexican Americans, Mexican immigrants, and the politics of ethnicity.* Berkeley: University of California Press. Waters, M. (1990). *Ethnic options: Choosing ethnic identities in America.* Berkeley: University of California Press. **Videos** *Double Happiness* *The Joy Luck Club* *Mi Familia* *Real Women Have Curves*

SECTION II

Immigration/ Acculturation

In earlier generations, the United States was built on the basis of European immigrants. Before the September 11, 2001, attacks, more than one million mostly legal immigrants arrived annually into the United States. Since the 1960s, and due to changes in immigration policies, the majority have come from Asia and Latin America. Many in the United States are the children or grandchildren of immigrants. Immigration can be an issue for an individual long after the first-generation immigrant in that family took the journey. The ability to cope with the migration process in the first and subsequent generations differs according to the level of choice in migrating, gender and age of the immigrant, proximity to the country or region of origin, educational level, social support, and events that occur after migration (Falicov, 2003; McGoldrick, 2003). Regardless of the reasons for migration, immigrants of the first and second generation face a number of challenges and issues of which providers of mental health services should be aware. First, clinicians need to be aware of the reasons for migrating to this country, the method of migration, and the intent of returning to the country of origin (McGoldrick, 2003). Second, most immigrants experience a sense of loss, which may produce grief and feelings of sadness, regardless of the original intent for migration (Falicov,

2003). Third, immigrants face language issues: strains involved in learning and adapting to English, pressure to retain or eliminate the language(s) of origin, and challenges of accented speech. Fourth, life for the immigrants in the host country ranges from the reality of living in the margins of society to the possibility of mainstream acceptance, depending on whether the immigrants have documented or undocumented status, adequate language skills, and educational or work related opportunities (Daniels, 2002) and to what extent they face racism and discrimination.

Immigrants always struggle with the reorganization of themselves in the context of their host society and face pressure to acculturate or not acculturate from a variety of sources. It is important for therapists to understand the level of acculturation or assimilation that individuals experience (Birman, 1994; LaFrombroise, Coleman, & Gerton, 1993). Acculturation can be defined as the process that occurs as members of one cultural group are exposed to, or come into significant contact with, another (usually the dominant) cultural group. Assimilation can be thought of as the adoption or absorption of one culture by individuals of another and can include the pressure to learn and perform new behaviors. Acculturation cannot be viewed as unidirectional because the dominant culture usually absorbs characteristics of all the cultures it comes into contact with.

Regardless of the speed and nature of cultural adaptation, the process of immigration invariably involves a redefinition of cultural identity at the individual and family levels (Beth-Shalom & Horenczyk, 2003). It is impossible to predict the overall outcome and the effect of the immigration experience on the life of the person. At the same time, and paradoxically, certainly the immigrant's identity is always shaped in no small part by the experience of immigration.

Acculturation and assimilation are complex processes, and the theoretical models that describe and explain them have become more refined, less rigid, and more inclusive over time (Berry, Phinney, Sam, & Vedder, 2006; Rahman & Rollock, 2004; Torres & Rollock, 2004). Older models of assimilation describe an almost forced-choice approach between two opposite poles of a continuum (Falicov, 1998b). According to these older models, immigrants could choose to reject the culture of origin and embrace the new culture or not, navigating the either–or possibilities allowed by where they place themselves along the continuum. Theorists tried to figure out which individuals fared better and came to mixed conclusions (Torres & Rollock, 2004). Some concluded that those who assimilate might have more problems than those who remain connected to their culture. These problems might include individual identity problems, problems with peer groups, and conflicts with family members. Other theorists came to the conclusion that to be successful in the new cultural milieu, the immigrant needs to adopt or absorb, at least in part, the values and behavior of the majority culture.

Researchers have acknowledged that the process of cultural adaptation is complex and multidimensional (Hays, 2001), and that the relationship between acculturation and mental distress is a complicated one (Rahman & Rollock, 2004).

Theorists recognize the relationship between social class, ethnicity, racism, and acculturation and have concluded that the extent and the way people acculturate depend on other variables in addition to those related to the individual decision-making process. For example, it seems clear that the oral and written ability with the English language, the age of arrival, the socioeconomic status of the individual, and the exposure to prejudice and discrimination significantly affect the ability to adapt to a new culture.

There are several approaches to thinking about acculturation and assimilation issues, some of which do not force a choice between two necessary and useful perspectives but allow the possibilities of including hybrid, alternation, and bicultural models while at the same time keeping the acculturation and assimilation models as available options (Falicov, 1998b; LaFrombroise et al., 1993). The variability with which people solve their individual and interpersonal dilemmas; the existence of social, cultural, and political forces that influence individual and family decisions; and the intersection of immigration as a fact with other dimensions such as social class, racial, or ethnic discrimination are factors that influence how people live and what options they have. It is not only impossible but also naive to apply one acculturation/assimilation model to all immigrants.

Individuals migrate to this country for a variety of reasons. Scholars of immigration patterns have used special words to describe the major factors involved in immigration: push, pull, and means factors (Daniels, 2002). Push refers to the forces that exist in the place of origin that encourage or force people to emigrate, for example, poverty or the inability to use acquired professional skills. Pull refers to the attraction that draws the immigrants, or the immigrant's goals. For example, some people emigrated from tsarist Russia to the United States or South America to avoid serving 14 years in the military. That the United States or Argentina did not impose such long military service pulled immigrants out of their countries. Means refers to the ability to migrate and the absence of effective barriers at the destination. Most recent immigrants undertake the journey as a result of push rather than pull factors due to economic hardship, which seems to be at the base of the decisions, even when religious or political reasons appear to be at the top. Because of the availability of affordable transportation and other advantages related to globalization and advances in technology, many recent immigrants are not forced to sever ties with the families they leave behind. Unlike the immigrant of the earlier generations, the recent immigrant may have the opportunity to travel back and forth between countries with ease, enjoying continued contact with family and friends and keeping other cultural ties. This in turn makes it harder to acculturate or resolve the ambivalence about the immigration decision (Daniels, 2002). Obviously, not all immigrants can take advantage of the ease of travel and other means of communication, and many, particularly if they are undocumented, feel quite trapped inside the United States.

Even though the United States is one of the largest recipients of immigrants from all over the world, the U.S. population is generally not seen as the most cognizant of other cultures, languages, and international issues. There is also a lack of information in the general public about several important issues regarding immigrants (Mills, 1994): What is the difference between a legal and an undocumented immigrant? Why do immigrants not learn English? Why do some immigrants have so many children? Is it true that they do not care about education? Are immigrants taking jobs away from Americans? Why do immigrants not act more like Americans? Clinicians do not live in cultural isolation and are exposed to these confusing aspects regarding immigrants. These ideas seep into the counseling room and plant themselves in the middle of the relationship, creating countertransference effects.

Policy makers are currently wrestling with difficult immigration issues, and *ambivalence* may be a good word to describe the current attitude toward immigrants in the United States (Daniels, 2002). There has been a 25-year decline in the admission of immigrants and refugees, in particular since September 11, 2001, which is attributed in part to new security measures and other new barriers and to a continued debate among policy makers who seek to find answers to difficult questions:

- How many immigrants should the United States admit?
- Should the United States continue the present policy of one general quota, or should future immigration be restricted to specific nations or races?

- On what criteria should these policy decisions be based?
- How should these policy decisions be enforced?
- Should undocumented immigrants be given a path to citizenship?

Conflicting and paradoxical attitudes from federal, state, and local governments at different historical times have been the common thread in policies that search for answers to these important questions. Although a description of the history of immigration policy in the United States is beyond the scope of this introduction, some examples of recent policies follow, which describe paradoxical, ambivalent, and confusing legislative measures:

- Since September 11, 2001, immigrants, whether documented or undocumented, have not been allowed a state-issued driver's license. The need for a federally issued social security number has not been waived in many states, and many immigrants, regardless of their immigration status, do not have one. As a result, many immigrants either drive without licenses and without insurance, creating risks to public safety, or do not drive, which presents other, no less challenging problems (Kirkpatrick, 2005; Wald, 2004).
- California's Proposition 187 made illegal immigrants ineligible for public social services, public health care, and public education. It was first passed in 1996. In the late 1990s, most of the proposition was deemed unconstitutional (Nieves, 1999).
- Undocumented immigrants are not eligible to receive federal funding for tuition. However, in many communities, they are eligible to receive English lessons at local state public schools and other community agencies that do receive state funding (Mead, 2004).
- Between 1960 and 1962, the U.S. government supported a clandestine program, Operation Pedro Pan, which brought about 14,000 unaccompanied Cuban children to the United States to "save" them from the evils of communist brainwashing. These children were placed in orphanages and homes. About half of the children never saw their parents again (Daniels, 2002). But the post–Cold War political climate was very different in 1999, when a Cuban boy, Elian Gonzalez, the most publicized refugee in the world, who had survived the ill-fated attempt of his family to reach U.S. soil from Cuba by boat, was sent back on the order of Florida Attorney General Janet Reno (Daniels, 2002).
- In the 1990s, the Immigration and Naturalization Service (now part of the Department of Homeland Security) tripled the funding for border patrol programs (Daniels, 2002). Increased border security resulted, paradoxically, not in fewer border crossings but in more death by heat exhaustion or extreme dehydration (McKinley, 2005). At the same time, the funding for the enforcement of existing immigration laws remained the same. Once border crossers are inside the United States, they can find employment easily in the

fields or in the service industries (Thompson & Ochoa, 2004), with very little oversight of the employers who hire them.
• Although official discrimination is no longer permissible, the majority of the refugees admitted into the United States in the late 1990s were from Eastern Europe and not from Africa, where most world refugees are located (Daniels, 2002).

Though officials of some school districts seem to accept the presence of their immigrant student populations and work hard to provide appropriate services for them, others seem to struggle to accept the reality of the changes in their community.

As Nacha explains to Rosa in the 1983 movie *El Norte,* "Trying to figure out the American ideas toward immigrants will give you a headache" (Nava, 1983). Government policy changes regarding immigrants (especially since September 11, 2001), shifts in the economic and budgetary outlooks, and the cultural differences of immigrants who arrive in the United States all affect public opinion about immigrants. These issues permeate the media, which translate them into bite-size chunks of information that viewers consume, often uncritically. Confusion, lack of knowledge, curiosity, criticism, and compassion may be common reactions to issues presented by immigrant clients in therapy and cannot be ignored by the clinician. It is important for counselors to be informed.

This section contains four stories in which the immigration experience represents the cultural factor with the most salience for the storytellers. The stories constitute a sample of the complexity of identities and of the variability and heterogeneity of the immigration experience. Given the chance to interact with them and hear their stories, any counselor would be struck by their struggles with acculturation and assimilation, their resilience, their strengths, and their immense losses. These accounts chronicle how Vu, Esteban, Maria Luz, and Teresa integrate their immigration stories into the fabric of their cultural identity at the present moment. This view permeates their everyday life, generating new stories that filter into their daily routine, furthering their fluid cultural identity, in a never-ending cycle of loss and resilience that constitutes the human experience. Chapters 6 and 7 are told respectively by Vu and Esteban, who came to the United States as forced child refugees, without their parents. Chapter 8 contains the story of Maria Luz, a first-generation adult immigrant with undocumented status. Chapter 9 contains the story of Teresa, a second-generation immigrant who arrived in the United States as a child with her parents.

Six

Vu's Story

I Am an American

In this chapter, we read the story of Vu, a refugee who left Vietnam at the age of 7 years on a boat, without his parents, and arrived in the United States at the age of 9 years, after spending 2 years as a child refugee in the Philippines. Vu was placed with a foster family who later adopted him. In this story, we read about his journey out of Vietnam and onto American soil. As you read, notice how he writes of his forced migration, his refugee status in the Philippines, and his struggles with second language acquisition in school. Even though he became fluent in English quite rapidly, he struggled with his written proficiency in English for a long time. Pay attention to how he describes his process of acculturation, his socialization into his new American family, and his perception of himself as a successful survivor of the tragic journey. Notice also what he thinks would have happened to him had he stayed in Vietnam.

Vu's Story

In 1987 in Vietnam, my world was centered in the small town of Nha Trang. Life was easy, uncomplicated, and pleasant for me. I was a little boy with few worries. I had no awareness of the turmoil my family suffered at the hands of the communists when my father fought with the Americans against the communists during the Vietnam War. With peace also came the communist rule. Daily life, as well as education, was determined by this government, but I knew no different. We were awakened each day by loudspeakers, which were placed strategically throughout the city and were used to broadcast governmental issues and concerns and even state-approved music. I spent my days in school or skipping school to play on the beach with friends. Education in Vietnam was quite different from what I experienced in the United States. For example, although reading was taught, it was in the context of learning communist dogma and recitations. Math was also a rote subject. Reading for pleasure was not something that children were exposed to, nor something that adults demonstrated. This early learning shaped my school and adult preferences for reading.

When I was 7 years old, one of my sisters took me out of elementary school early one day and brought me home. My parents asked me if I wanted to go to America. This was quite a surprise to me. I had heard stories of America, and it was described to me as the land of extraordinary things, such as wealth, an abundance of goods, and, most of all, opportunities. As a child with limited knowledge of the world, I thought it was a fantasyland. I said yes knowing nothing about the situation that I was getting into. This little incident changed my life forever.

That same night, my father put me on the back of his motorcycle, and we rode to meet a bus. My father put me on the bus, saying that he would be back to meet me later. I trusted him and proceeded onto the bus. Hours later, the bus arrived at a beach around midnight. I could hear people telling one another to be quiet and not to make sudden moves. Within minutes, we all started to quickly get out of the bus one by one. As my feet met the sandy beach, I did not know where to go or what to do, and all I could see was people running toward the high waves. At this point, I was wandering aimlessly and frantically up and down the beach, not knowing where to go and searching for my father. Eventually a couple of men grabbed hold of my arms and started to carry me toward the water. As we reached the water, I could see a large boat that was a few hundred yards out. I looked around for my father, but he was nowhere to be found in the darkness of night. The men placed me into a basket because I could not swim and pushed me out toward the awaiting boat. When we reached the boat, people were swarming in and around the boat, trying to get in, and someone pulled me up. After I was safely on the boat, I searched for a place to keep warm and felt fortunate to find the engine room just below the steering deck, where I stayed for the rest of the night. The next morning when I woke up and saw people walking around on the deck, I looked to the horizon, and land was nowhere in sight. This is when I knew I was on my way to an unknown destination. I felt so lonely and scared, wondering what was going to happen. I became more anxious because I did not have my father to comfort me.

I searched everywhere on the boat for my father. From a child's perspective, I believed he must be somewhere on the boat. I tried to find the people who had helped me earlier, but I could not find them either. I looked everywhere on the boat, from the engine room to the steering room to the bow of the ship, but I did not find my father or the people who had helped me. By now, I was hysterical. I did not know anyone, and I had never been alone before. After 2 days, I was exhausted from the endless searching for my father. I could hear people whispering that he had probably been captured by the Communists. He had never lied to me before, but finally it became evident to me that my father did not get on the boat. I kept wandering around the boat taking in what I could. The expressions on most faces began to alleviate my fears. Some people were excited for the opportunity of a lifetime, and some were sad, not knowing what experience awaited them. For 7 days and 7 nights there were continuous problems: We encountered tremendous thunderstorms, hunger, quarrels, and sudden deaths. I can remember one storm that hit us so hard that parts of the ship fell off. The refugees were asked to help repair the ship. During another storm, we were sent down to the hold of the ship, where we had to stay for more than 2 days. Due to the violent shaking and rolling of the ship, people were sick and terrified, crying and praying.

On the third day, I vividly remember an old man opening up the door to the deck and the sun shining. All of us were so happy just to be alive. After climbing out of the hold and walking around the boat, I talked to some people and began to gain a better understanding. I had begun to accept the situation and was not quite so hysterical; everything started to come together for me. People explained what we were doing, where we were going, and when we might get there. Hunger was not on my mind during my expedition across the South China Sea. When it was time to eat, we were rationed steamed rice, fried fish, and one cup of fresh water. Most of the time I could not eat, so I gave my food away to others. To some, the meal portions were not enough, so they fought for what they could get to satisfy their thirst and hunger.

One incident that still haunts me is the death of a little baby. I remember this very clearly because I was standing next to the family when they dropped their dead child into the ocean. The entire family stood in a circle silently crying. I thought to myself, if something would ever happen to me, would I be thrown into the ocean and never heard of again? How would my parents know how I died? Who would tell my parents since no one on this ship knows me? Death was expected on this journey, and it happened daily. However, this was not the way I had experienced death in Vietnam. There were rituals, prayers, and tributes to the deceased. In this instance, death happened, and the person was disposed of.

On the seventh day when land came into sight, we encountered a ship, which turned out to be a pirate ship, and we were told we were going the wrong way. The pirates wanted us to follow them around an island. Our captain started to follow, but, fortunately, a fishing boat came along. The fishing boat captain told us not to follow the pirate ship but to follow his boat. If the fishing boat had not come by, we probably would have been killed by the pirates, as had so many before us, I later learned. The fishing boat led us to land, but we did not know where we were. We later learned we were in the Philippines. Once on land, the native people helped us by giving us food, water, clothes, and a place to stay. We could not understand their native Filipino language, so we could not answer their questions, but eventually we found a bilingual refugee with us who could translate. The next morning there was a U.S. Navy ship next to ours. I had no idea what this all meant, but the adults appeared overjoyed to be greeted by an American ship. We were taken on board the ship and were brought to Manila in the Philippines. We stayed in Manila for 2 nights at a refugee center, and then we were transferred to the primary refugee camp in Palawan, where I remained for 2 years.

Living in a refugee camp was rigid and different from the home that I knew. After arriving at the camp, I was photographed and interviewed. My refugee status had to be validated. Later, I was placed with a couple who claimed to know my father, but I found out later they did not, so I moved out. I knew of my father's status because the night of the escape my father had given me documents to take along with me. I had kept these documents in case I would need to use them. In this instance, the documentation proved my father's service to the United States. As a child with my father's documentation, many were eager to embrace and care for me, hoping to increase their chances of being granted refugee status or being released from the camp more quickly. People without documentation to qualify them as political refugees often spent many years in Palawan only to be returned to Vietnam. Two years in a refugee camp was devastating for me. I missed my parents, my two younger brothers, and my three older sisters. I wondered why I was the chosen one to leave. Was I unloved? Was I bad? I revisited all the naughty things I had done; all the times I was punished; all the times I skipped school to play; all the times I disobeyed my parents, grandparents, or sisters; and all the times my brothers and I fought. I found out later in my adult life that my parents had wanted me to have a better life. In the camp, I did not receive the love and care that I would have received from a normal family, and the majority of the time I was roaming throughout the camp. I was alone, sometimes living in the unaccompanied children's dorm with many other children.

I was 7 years old when I left Vietnam. Being 7 years old without the presence of parents' guidance is disconcerting to a child, but I was fortunate to be placed in the care of a kind family, where I had many friends, until the day I left for America. The new family made sure that I attended school in the camp and brought me to church. School was not my favorite activity; learning English was a goal, but I seemed to learn only to name items, not to speak conversational English. Soon after arriving in America, I found out that the family I lived with in the camp had used me to obtain extra food rations, and they ultimately claimed that they should accompany me to America to care for me, but this ploy ultimately failed them. In 1989, because of my father's military record, I was able to document my status as a political refugee, and I was accepted as an immigrant through the Unaccompanied Minors Program for resettlement to the United States. Everyone at the camp was so happy and excited for me. It felt like I won the lottery! On May 23, 1989, I arrived in the United States to be greeted by my foster family, the Tylers. I have lived with them continuously for 14 years, which is longer than the time I spent with my biological family in Vietnam. Our emotional ties are permanent, and my foster family has become the family I lost.

Throughout my school years, kids asked me if I was adopted, and most of the time I said yes, knowing deep down I wanted the Tylers to be my permanent family. I always used the Tylers' last name, but when I asked my social worker if I could make their name my permanent last name, he told me that I could not be adopted because my family still loved me and wanted to be reunited with me. I did not understand this. I asked my foster family, and they said that social services would not allow adoption because of the Geneva Accord. I did not understand that either. I wanted a family. My foster mother said that if they tried to adopt me, I would be placed in another home. That frightened me. How many families could I lose? How long would I have to wait to be accepted into a family? How many times could I take the chance on loving? I was very happy and secure with my foster family. I had many friends and was doing well in school.

Living in a suburban town provided me with many advantageous educational opportunities and experiences but no contact with other Vietnamese children. My facility with my native language was quickly diminishing. After 6 months in the United States, I was fully conversant in my new language. It was becoming difficult to read the letters from my parents in Vietnam. Eventually, my foster parents had to find someone who could translate the letters for me. For about a year, I had a Vietnamese social worker who visited me monthly. He reminded me of my culture and the need to remain in contact with my family and practice my language. I had been placed in an English-speaking home. How was I to practice speaking Vietnamese?

Often I would end up crying because of what he would tell me—how lucky I was, how my family was suffering. I learned that my father had been caught trying to escape and had been put in prison—his second time in a "reeducation" camp. Letters from my mother would tell of her struggles to support my brothers and sisters. When he was caught, the communists took my family home away from them, and my family had no home. My mother would beg me to send her money. When my foster family learned of this, they wired money to them through Canada, but the requests for money never stopped. At times my parents' advice to me regarding my newly adopted land was contradictory. For example, in one letter I was told to learn English quickly so I could do well, but other letters admonished me to not forget my language, culture, and family. My parents did not speak or write English, so many letters were translated into English prior to being mailed. Many other letters were written in Vietnamese, which I could read only until my second year in the United States. One letter is particularly poignant. It was written, in English, to my foster family from my father in his jail cell where he was held after the escape attempt. He wrote, "My wife has secretly sent your letter into my prison ward, and my roommate help me to translate this letter. . . . We are ineffable in words, please accept all our boundless gratitude. I cease my pen with our best wishes to you." Still other letters state that I am now the Tylers' son, and they are grateful for my new family's love and care.

When I was 10 years old, my mother wrote that I should quit school and get a job, so I could send money home like other "good" Vietnamese sons who live in America. Eventually, my social worker had to write to explain how important education was in the United States, that children my age could not work, and that to be able to help them I needed a good education. I was very worried about my dad in the prison because I remembered stories my family had told about his previous imprisonment, which resulted after he stole food for us.

When I entered third grade, I wanted to become as Americanized as possible. Spending time with all my new American friends facilitated assimilation into my new culture. Adjusting to my new culture was not difficult for me because of my easygoing personality; making friends and being accepted was almost effortless for me. I had already decided to acquire the new culture as quickly as possible. I know I did not identify myself as Vietnamese, although I am sure my classmates and teachers saw me as foreign. Nevertheless, I do not ever remember experiencing any prejudice. I was invited to all my friends' parties and dated American girls in high school. Most of my friends were American-born, but I denied that I avoided friendships with other Asian students. When my foster parents asked me about my choice of friends, I explained that there were no other Asian students who played athletics, and I identified with athletes.

The nature of my Vietnamese education differed from a traditional American education. I attended 3 years of school in Vietnam. School was in session for only half a day, and I frequently skipped school to play with friends, with no consequences. Lessons in Vietnam consisted of memorization and teacher lectures. Students learned by observation, not by experimentation or participation. The Ministry of Education controlled a national curriculum, which was funded by the government. Students in Vietnam were expected to be orderly, attentive, and quiet; everyone worked on memorizing the same thing at the same time, but not in cooperative groups. The students were fearful of not knowing answers and did not like to be singled out. The teacher was the ultimate authority, but there were no conferences or home–school communication. If the teacher called on the parent, it usually meant that the child had done some terrible wrong. Although I was required to attend school in the Philippines, I did so erratically. I remember that the classes consisted of trying to learn names for things in English. School in America was something I enjoyed. It was so different from what I remembered in Vietnam and in Palawan. The teachers were nice, laughing and joking with the students. It was clear to me that they liked me. My day-to-day needs did not include my primary language. I did not feel a need to have a cultural connection to my native language. At the beginning of third grade, I was fluent enough to fit in to the expected routines of the class. My foster mother says I adjusted well and had many friends and I appeared to meet classroom expectations. I could read, via decoding, most of the class texts. This was confusing to some of my teachers, who indicated they equated reading with the ability to pronounce the words—which I could do—rather than construct meaning—which I could not do. My elementary school offered a newspaper club after school, and I became a contributing member. I saw myself as being able to participate in all activities offered. I used literacy in many ways, even writing memos to myself, especially when I had done something wrong. When writing, I made errors of syntax, grammar, capitalization, and punctuation, and I still do today. Although I was a fluent conversationalist fairly soon after arriving in America, my foster mother believed I needed to master the language of the classroom; she raised the issue of programmatic adaptations to accommodate my emerging language. She was met with surprise and was told that I certainly spoke with no accent. There was never any possibility of a language maintenance program in my school district. The only service to second language learners was an English as a second language (ESL) pullout program, which I attended in third, fourth, and fifth grade. After a short time I, uncharacteristically, complained to my foster mother that I was bored. I told her, "I know 'this is a book,' 'this is a pencil,' and 'this is a chair.'" The program consisted, primarily, of learning the name for items (something I did routinely all day) and reciting simple conversational sentences with a goal of oral language proficiency. My foster mother was employed in my school district as an administrator, so she intervened with my ESL tutor, and my program was changed to fit my needs. My foster mother's influence on the nature of the support I was receiving resulted in my ESL teacher's work to address specifically the vocabulary that I was expected to use in class, such as spelling words and words from content areas. Because I was a strong visual learner, I was always able to successfully memorize the correct spelling of weekly words. Thus my teachers were confounded when I could not successfully use the words in fill-in-the-blank worksheets.

As academic demands became greater, I appeared to struggle more. By fifth grade, increased classroom emphasis was placed on worksheets to be completed independently. None of the assignments improved my English or added to my fount of knowledge. Teachers were concerned because I worked so hard and yet did not successfully complete all assignments independently. They suggested testing, which resulted in a CORE evaluation in 1991. I was found to have no special needs; recommendations were to continue with the same support that I had been receiving for 2 years. During middle school, I continued to struggle with multiple meanings of words, idioms, and the nuances of the language. In eighth grade English, almost 2 full months of classroom instruction were spent in preparation for "Word Master," a national competition that tests students' knowledge of words. This preparation involved memorizing lists of words and their definitions. Class time was spent matching words with definitions and figuring out analogies. I could never get more than one or two correct on the weekly test, and my grade was severely affected. What I needed was to be reading good literature, generating ideas and theories, and participating in discussions. In high school, some English courses offered opportunities to read challenging literature and demanded written responses and essays. At home, I frequently spoke enthusiastically of subjects I was studying. The instruction and assessment that occurred in the classes where I had the most success required active participation, daily writing response to readings, performances/interpretations of readings, and work in cooperative groups.

All my grades were "B" and higher. Again, school was another place where I had to unlearn a cultural lesson. American students would enthusiastically call out answers and actively question the teacher. I was expected to know when I needed help and to ask for it. I was conditioned to not do that. I would never want to make myself known as being unable or unprepared. It took me a long time, with my foster parents' and teachers' help, to assert myself. Nevertheless, my foster mother had to first educate my teachers about my learning needs. Most of my high school courses were at the accelerated level. My teachers stated that I participated in class discussions and was well prepared for class. My homework was always completed on time. They said that I was pleasant and polite and did well in class, but often I performed poorly on exams. Many teachers stated that they were sure I knew much more than the exams exhibited. Teacher comments indicated that my test grades were negatively affecting my report card grade. My success on exams depended on the type of exam administered. Tests that were intended to measure vocabulary competence often consisted of matching items, sentence completions, and identification of antonyms and synonyms. The antonym/synonym items caused me great difficulty. Often the use of multiple choice or fill-in-the-blank tests is for ease of scoring. The discrepancy between success on authentic measures and failure on standardized tests reveals that I was able to construct my own meaning with the text and to express it effectively but that I still experienced difficulty when meaning was expected to be boiled down to specific one-word answers. My scores on standardized tests have never been very high and are not reflective of my true achievement or ability.

I believed that to be successful in America I had to acculturate, forget my previous culture and become part of the new. I knew the only way to fit in was to be just like all my friends and thus spend less time thinking and talking about my past. I did not want to be associated with Vietnam or have anything to do with it. I wanted to be Americanized. I wanted to forget my Vietnamese language and culture—everything from Vietnam. I used my foster family's last name on everything I wrote and began calling my foster parents "Mom" and "Dad." My social worker scolded me for doing that and insisted on notifying my school about my real legal name, asking that my records reflect that name. I was required to show the social worker school papers and report cards to prove that I was not using my foster parents' last name.

At this time, I knew I was being rebellious against my culture, but I could not figure out why. Maybe because of what my biological parents had put me through—not being there when I needed them, sending me away because I felt they did not love me. Eventually, I found out that they did it because they wanted me to have a better life in America.

Accepting the new culture quickly and concealing the old did not concern me, but it worried my foster parents. My foster mom sought me out and dragged me to the cultural events offered by the Unaccompanied Minors Program, but I never wanted to be there. I felt as though I did not fit in; I did not think I was like them. I did not want to listen to Vietnamese music or participate in other Vietnamese cultural celebrations in a nearby city. I did not want to be identified as a refugee, a foster child, a ward of the state, or anything other than an American. As years went by, I began to adapt to my new culture and excel in many things, including sports. My foster family exposed me to skiing, soccer, tennis, swimming, and many other sports, in which I experienced much success and awards. In 1989, I had never seen snow when my foster family took me to a ski mountain where they had a winter home to ski. Within a year, I joined the freestyle ski team, to which my foster brother and sister belonged, and I became a competitor in freestyle skiing, loving skiing, the cold, and the snow. Rushing down mountains, jumping and spinning through the air was a new and wonderful feeling.

I qualified for the freestyle series each year from 1990 to 1997, and ultimately I was invited to compete in the junior nationals in Utah, where I was ranked third in the country in aerials. I was asked to participate in nationals that year. Sports provided me with a way to communicate with my peers. I was so successful, so early, that I gained immediate status and acceptance with the skiing community. During the years I competed, I won numerous meets and enjoyed a national ranking. Self-discovery or introspection showed me that I learned visually, and I achieved my goals easily. Playing sports also placed me in a circle of friends that I would not have had if I had not played sports. Being accepted into this group of athletes ultimately allowed me to forget my own cultural learning, which was in conflict with what I was experiencing. In Vietnam, I was taught not to seek the spotlight or to cause attention to focus on myself. Being considered a star athlete, either in high school sports or in skiing, was exciting yet conflicting. Before coming to America, I remember knowing about an athlete, Michael Jordan, thinking how special and lucky he was. Here I was getting awards. This was very difficult for me; I was not shy, but I did not like to be the center of attention. I did not like going to the podium to receive awards. Ultimately, I conformed to the American culture.

My life has changed dramatically since that dark, frightening night in Vietnam. Had I stayed there my world would have been quite different. My education would have stopped when I was 12 years old; I would have had no opportunity for a meaningful future. Because I was the oldest son in the family, I would have had the responsibilities that are traditionally demanded of the eldest son. I would have been expected to support my parents and any remaining single siblings for the rest of my life. I would have remained living in my parents' house. They would have expected me to give them financial help and, in addition, to help distant relatives in emergencies. After the death of my father, I would have taken over the role of head of the family. To my understanding, this is because I was the first-born son, and traditionally I would be the caretaker of the family. I remember that the family unit is the most important entity, to which one's first loyalty is owed. Extended family members are accorded the same respect as immediate family members. Parents and all adults demand obedience. Children begin to learn of their responsibility toward their families at a young age. Many generations live together, and the young care for their elders. This was expected of me and culturally accepted in the Vietnamese tradition. I probably would have quit school by the age of 10 years and would have learned to repair bicycles and motorcycles as my father did. As a little child, I would sit while he worked on repairs and feel that watching him somehow enabled me to be good mechanically. Many times, I have been able to fix something that my foster mother was about to throw away. It is not a skill I learned in America. American parents are different from Vietnamese parents; they love their children differently. In Vietnam, the children are not the center of the family. A traditional Vietnamese family does not engage children in conversation as equals; children are primarily observers and learn by watching, listening, and imitating. Conformity, obedience, respect, patience, and composure are traits that are valued and expected to be developed. In America, family life revolves around children. In Vietnam, it was expected that parents use physical punishments for wrongdoing. I learned quickly that this is not accepted here. In addition, I had to learn to look adults in the eye when speaking to them. This is contrary to my cultural upbringing. Children in Vietnam show respect by keeping eyes downcast when speaking to an adult. I learned that American parents encourage their children to achieve, in school and in sports, and to set long-term educational and financial goals for themselves. This was unknown to me in Vietnam.

Vietnamese parents never ask for children's opinions or desires. In America, there are so many decisions to be made, such as what to eat, what to wear, where to go, what to play. Children are allowed to voice opinions even when not asked. American children are allowed to set their own bedtime, get monetary allowances, and spend their money as they wish. In Vietnam, I was told what to do and when to do it. If I did not agree or want to obey, I did not voice my objections; I simply did what I wanted and suffered the consequences.

When I came to America, I did not know my birthday; birthdays were not celebrated in Vietnam. The year of birth is important. I know I was born in the Year of the Monkey. Not long after I arrived in America, my mother sent me a birth certificate that differed from the one I left Vietnam with. The new birth certificate indicated I was born in 1978 rather than 1980. Yet I know I was born in 1980 because it was the Year of the Monkey. I later learned that my mother wanted me to appear to be 2 years older, so I would be allowed to quit school and work more easily. This caused me years of trouble. I had to get waivers in sports to remain eligible. When I got my license at age 18—really age 16—I had to explain, with embarrassment, to my friends and on job, scholarship, and college applications why I was so old on my license. When I was legally adopted, the attorney corrected my birth certificate; however, I am still having repercussions from that. My passport is being held up because the dates on my citizenship certificate and birth certificate do not match. In America, we celebrate birthdays. My ninth birthday occurred 3 weeks after I arrived in the United States. I was astonished by the gifts and birthday cake. This was something I never expected and could really learn to like! Years later, in a letter from Vietnam, pictures were included of my family celebrating my sister's birthday. Wow, that surprised me. How could they afford to do that? How did they come to do that? It never happened for me in Vietnam, and I wondered why.

Showing emotion was another new experience for me. Although I would cry when I was hurt in Vietnam, I never remembered displaying sadness or anger or being encouraged to do so. My foster mother had to teach me "grouchy" and that it was "OK" to be out of sorts occasionally and to voice my feelings. I remember one instance when I first arrived to the Tylers' and they took me shopping for new clothes. When my foster mother showed me something that I did not like, my response was "I no like." I came with preconceived notions about how I should dress as an American child but was unsure of how to communicate those desires to them.

My foster family encouraged me to be the most I can be. They pushed me and demanded I stretch myself to achieve, but they never made demands similar to those in my Vietnamese culture. With their encouragement, I participated in all that my school had to offer. At times, it seemed almost impossible to learn a new language and customs and do what my American classmates were doing. There were times when I struggled to do schoolwork because of the language barrier and cultural differences. However, I was able to leave the differences behind and accomplish what needed to be done and move on. Nevertheless, academics, sports, clubs, and social activities have enriched my life. In sports, I played on the varsity level in football, soccer, track, and skiing. These opportunities would not typically happen to foster children. Most foster children leave the system at age 18 years, when the foster parents release them; most are never adopted. I was grateful to my foster family for providing me with a roof over my head, a ski home, a summer ski camp, participation in national competitions, and travel across the United States. I was also accepted to a private college with wonderful scholarships. These are things that I will remember and carry with me for the rest of my life. I became a citizen of the United States in 1997. What opportunities I have been given! I became a citizen of the United States, and all things seem possible. I have also tried to begin to give back some of the many kindnesses I have received.

I volunteered in my town's annual cleanup and at a nursing home. I worked throughout high school with a special education class of severely disabled students. By helping these students, I learned how fortunate I truly am. Things I thought were problems for me were simply difficulties I have been able to overcome with help. Those students will never have the same opportunities as I had because of their disabilities.

I am proud to report that I graduated from a prestigious college and received a well-rounded education. Fifteen years ago, I never dreamed going to college was possible. No one in my Vietnamese family is educated. I have an American family—a mother, a father, a sister, and a brother—who love and believe in me.

A significant event took place on April 18, 2003: my adoption into the Tyler family. I was of legal age, and I was able to choose to be adopted by my former foster family. This is what I have been waiting for since I arrived in America. I now have a forever family with a mother, a father, a brother, a sister, an uncle, and a grandmother, and they all care about me. I know I belong. I can honestly say I have closed a chapter of my early life and have started a new chapter. Furthermore, I am also engaged to marry my girlfriend from high school, who also has a wonderful family who embraced me. An evaluation of the significance of my experiences necessitates putting on many lenses. Through my child's eyes, I used to only see what I lost—a family, a home, a limited education, Vietnamese culture, and my native language, a sense of self, government control, and security. In Vietnam, we were always hungry. Rice and fish were our daily foods, just as they were in the refugee camp. At the dinner table in Vietnam, we were expected to eat in silence and to drink water after the meal. In America, mealtime is a time for conversation, relating the day's events, talking or arguing about events in the news, and planning for fun activities via scheduled play dates or sport events. I learned I could eat and drink as much as I wanted, but I did not like milk. If I were hungry between meals, I could eat then too. Often there was more food on my plate than I could eat. In Vietnam, there was never food remaining on a plate. I have never been hungry in America, and there are so many new, delicious foods to eat.

Through a young adult's eyes, I see what I have gained—family, home, security, freedom, education, a culture, and unlimited opportunities. Because I left Vietnam so young, over time my memory has dimmed about many daily experiences and personal interactions with my family. Surely much of which I learned from my culture in my first 7 years of life are part of me, but not on a conscious level. The culture I identify with is American. I am an American. I live as an American does. I celebrate occasions as an American does. On the boat and in the camp, I grieved openly. The picture of me as a new arrival clearly shows a depressed, distraught, young, thin child. Perhaps I rejected my Vietnamese family because anger replaced grief. Perhaps I identified with the family and country that gave me love and security. As I get older, and more mature, I am more comfortable acknowledging my ethnic background. It took me a long time to enjoy going to a Vietnamese restaurant, which I do now, frequently. There is not really a merging of my two worlds. Was I too young to have a strong imprint of my culture? The lessons I learned regarding respect for my elders, authority, and persons of education have served me well, but these are lessons American children are taught also. I do not consider myself a Vietnamese person but an American. I have also gained a new meaning of life, what my priorities are, and how I can achieve them. I believe that I have lost ties to my Vietnamese heritage, my language, my parents, my responsibilities as the eldest son, and my culture. Today, I try to look at what I have gained more so than what I have lost. What I have gained greatly outweighs, in my mind, what I have left behind. This includes obtaining a wonderful education and graduating from college. I feel I am prepared to adapt and fit in to American society.

Content Themes

The major themes of this story are Vu's forced migration and his status as a refugee, the acquisition of English during his school years, and how he views his process of assimilation and Americanization. In addition, he writes about what he considers his gains and losses, how he views his educational and athletic triumphs, and whom he considers his real family.

Forced Migration and Refugee Status

One of the first themes to emerge from Vu's story is that he was forced to leave Vietnam by his family. Vu recalls his traumatic journey at the age of 7 years. He continues to describe his state of mind during the journey to the United States as a Vietnamese boat refugee as traumatic. After Vu makes it, miraculously, to the refugee camp in the Philippines, he writes that the 2 years in the refugee camp were devastating, in part because he wondered if he had been bad or unloved.

Although the distinctions between voluntary and involuntary immigration are important, the case of the child forced to migrate and become a refugee needs to be singled out and differentiated from the status and characteristics of the other types of immigrants. Immigrants can choose not to leave their country of origin and have time to plan their migration. Refugees, on the other hand, often have to leave suddenly, sometimes in fear for their lives (Breunlin, Schwartz, & Mac Kune-Karrer, 1997; Grinberg & Grinberg, 2000) due to extreme political or economic hardships. The voluntary immigrant can often return to his or her land, and many immigrants do, but in general refugees cannot, as is the case with Vu. The forced immigration usually closes off the possibilities of an eventual return, at least for the foreseeable future (Daniels, 2002).

Vu explains that some people in the refugee camp resorted to fraudulent activities to make it into the United States. The decline in the arrival of refugees into the United States can probably be attributed, in part, to new efforts to combat fraud. This has slowed the processing of applications but should not be seen as indication of a drop in need. There are more than 85,000 refugees worldwide who could have been permitted to enter the United States in the last 2 years to escape hardship and danger but have not entered because of processing issues (Migration Policy Institute, 2004).

After the Vietnam War ended, more refugees began to arrive with no significant amount of money, and many of the so-called boat people were often stripped of what little they did have by pirates or officials in the countries of first asylum (Daniels, 2002), as Vu vividly recounts about his days in the Philippines. Refugees continued to come to the United States in much greater numbers than anticipated throughout the 1990s from the former Yugoslavia, the former Soviet Union, and Vietnam. Vietnamese do not have a long history of immigration to the United States and are different from all the other major groups of recent immigrants from Asia in that they tend to be very young, not well educated, and very poor. Many children, such as Vu, were sent alone by their parents in an effort to save at least one child by giving him or her the opportunity to go to the United States. Refugee and asylum policies are very complex and sometimes contradictory because the United States tries to deal with the problem of defining who qualifies as a refugee and who does not, depending on the kind of political regime of the country of origin and whether the refugee is considered an economic or a political one. As Daniels (2002) contends, these complexities seem to be a permanent part of the once simpler matter of emigrating to America.

Children are the ones with the least amount of choice in the decision to emigrate, and Vu's voyage is one of the most dramatic examples of that fact. Refugees crossed the oceans coming from countries devastated by war or political dictatorships. Their parents made a drastic decision that, in their minds, would save their children's lives. In addition, it seems that in Vu's case at least the parents also imagined that if Vu's economic prospects were to improve, his parents' economic hardships would diminish as well because as soon as Vu would be old enough to work, he could start sending money back to Vietnam to support the rest of the family. This belief is consistent with that of other families in the poorest countries of the world who send some of their male offspring to the United States. The forced emigration of children from Vietnam is not an isolated example or a new phenomenon. There are many other countries from which children are forced to emigrate, and, as a practice, it has been going on for centuries (Daniels, 2002).

Second Language Acquisition

The speed and accuracy of the acquisition of a second language varies according to the age, the level of education, and other circumstances of the immigrant. In Vu's case, he was placed with American foster parents who spoke only English, and he did not have any contact with Vietnamese children, which may have accelerated the loss of his native language; he says that after 6 months in the United States he was fully conversant in his new language. Adolescent immigrant students are generally placed in bilingual education classes of differing quality depending on where the school is located, how it is funded, and the philosophy of the school district. Often immigrant students struggle with second language acquisition issues. Bilingual education is often used erroneously in a one-size-fits-all approach that does not serve the heterogeneous needs of children with second language acquisition issues. As Vu's story demonstrates, in spite of an oral English proficiency acquired early on in his American school years, he continued to struggle with grammar, writing, and reading, and only a persistent and knowledgeable foster parent was able to help him overcome his literacy concerns. There is evidence that the socioeconomic status of the parents affects immigrants' acquisition of English proficiency (Kuo & Roysircar, 2004). Immigrant parents' academic and occupational past and present history have been demonstrated to influence the second language acquisition process of the school-age child (Nieto, 1999). School personnel who are not well trained may miss the reasons for the differences between oral written or reading proficiency in English, may arrive at wrong conclusions, and may suggest interventions that are not well targeted to the immigrant child's needs. Also, schools vary in the degree to which they accept or reject the immigrant child's native culture and language ability, depending on whether the native language is viewed as an asset or a liability (Nieto, 1999). This, in turn, affects the second language acquisition process. Vu's foster (and later adoptive) parents were highly educated and employed all the tools, time, and dedication that upper middle-class comfort affords to deal with Vu's second language acquisition concerns. This clearly had effects on his successful high school and college performance in later years. Other immigrant children are not so lucky.

Acculturation and Assimilation Processes

Acculturation and assimilation are complex, nonlinear processes that are further complicated by the different layers, conscious to unconscious; the different levels, from low to high; and the different contexts. How individuals think about themselves may shift depending on where they are— at home or work—or who they are with—their immigrant or their American friends. In terms of his acculturation/assimilation process, Vu clearly wanted to become Americanized, and in his view he succeeded. He remembers that in the third grade he wanted to become as Americanized as possible and that he avoided friendships with other Asian students. As he grew older, he believed he had to forget his previous culture to become part of the new. However, he also states the older he got, the more comfortable he became acknowledging his ethnic background. Another way of looking at Vu's acculturative process is through his depiction of what he had to learn in his new experiences: showing emotions, asserting himself in school, being more talkative during meals, and learning to express which clothes he liked or disliked. Although he acknowledges that his "old self" might be somewhere there unconsciously, he identifies solely with the American culture. This may have been one way for him to cope with his earlier losses when he found himself to be in a strange new world.

Survivor Guilt

Vu's acculturation processes and coping styles can also be understood from the perspective of his traumatic separation and survival. Many immigrants whose experiences are as traumatic as Vu's need to figure out how to deal not only with their separation from their families of origin but also with having survived, psychologically and physically, especially if their parents or siblings did not survive or do as well as the immigrant. Survivor guilt was first identified as affecting survivors of the Holocaust (Vogel, 1999), who were described as exhibiting an intense sense of guilt, which made it difficult for them to be happy knowing that significant members of their immediate families were not. Vu may have "decided" that his biological parents and his siblings are not his "real" family. His stories of forced migration, of his journey from being hungry most of the time during his childhood in Vietnam to having some of the comforts of an upper middle-class family, and of his encounter with the U.S. school system with its more democratic and less hierarchical treatment of children are all factors that may have contributed to his view of his foster/adoptive as his real parents. Had he not become Americanized, and had he continued to feel and act Vietnamese, how would he have coped with the idea that his parents and siblings were still so poor while he was surviving and thriving in America?

It is not unusual for immigrants, particularly those who arrive very young into the United States and who have the opportunity to be exposed to a good educational environment, to do better occupationally, professionally, and financially than the relatives they left behind, which may increase their survivor guilt.

Clinical Applications

It is important for clinicians to assess their client's status as refugees, their struggles not only with their oral proficiency in English but also with their written proficiency, their experiences in bilingual programs at school, and how they tackle their acculturation/assimilation issues. The interventions include learning the history of the immigrant's country of origin and conducting a psycholinguistic history. Several countertransferential reactions are described.

Assessment

Forced Migration and Refugee Status

What are the stories of the journey from the country of origin?

Tell me about the history of your country as it relates to your story of immigration.

How do you think your life has been shaped by your immigration journey?

How did your story affect others who stayed behind?

Who else was affected by/not affected by your immigration journey?

Second Language Acquisition

How easy/difficult was it for you to learn English?

If you were placed in bilingual education programs, what was your experience with second language acquisition? Were you encouraged to speak or discouraged from speaking your language of origin?

How do you experience your language of origin in your life today?

Acculturation Processes and Coping Styles

What have you adopted/not adopted of the American way of life?

What have you preserved/not preserved of your background in terms of personality styles, communication styles, values, worldview, and so on?

If you have children, what values of your culture of origin are you interested in them preserving/rejecting?

How do you think of yourself in terms of your cultural identity?

Has the way you think about your cultural identity changed or remained the same over the years?

Survivor Guilt

How did the rest of your family members do in terms of their occupation, health, and social class status as a result of the immigration experience?

Were there differences among them in those areas?

How have you felt in relation to them in those areas?

If there were marked differences between you and the members of your family in terms of health, occupational successes, and social class status, how have you dealt with it?

What meanings have you attributed to those similarities/differences?

Techniques and Interventions

Acquire Knowledge of History

It is important for the clinician to acquire knowledge about the history of the country of origin, the recent historical factors that may have influenced the cohort of immigrants from that country, and the overall immigration history to the United States from that country.

First, it is important for the clinician to acquire some basic knowledge of the history of the country of origin, which includes a general overview of its racial/ethnic diversity or lack of diversity, history of colonialism, class issues, and general educational issues. The majority of countries in the world were colonized by at least one empire at some point in their history. For example, Argentina and Chile were colonized by Spain; Brazil by Portugal; India, Syria, and Israel by Great Britain; northern Africa by France; Spain by the Arabs; Korea by Japan; and the United States by Great Britain. This is important because the legacy of colonization explains a good deal of the current racial and ethnic characteristics, idiosyncrasies, sensibilities, political problems, and immigration patterns. Second, it is important to acquire basic knowledge of recent history, particularly recent economic or political history and weather- or disaster-related history. Were there recent wars, border conflicts, or economic or political circumstances that may have affected the people and encouraged them to emigrate? Were there recent hurricanes, earthquakes, invasions, or revolutionary movements? This is important because immigrants and refugees generally do not immigrate in isolation; they are part of a cohort that tends to immigrate at about the same time, a time related to recent historical, economic, or weather-related events. Knowing the context of the particular immigration pattern helps to understand the client better.

Finally, a general knowledge of the history of emigration from that country is necessary to understand which wave of migration the client joined. One of the most dramatic examples is the history of the Cuban immigration to the United States, in part because of its contrasting nature and effect. The first wave of migration was composed of the professional and managerial elite, fleeing the instauration of the Castro regime. They were received with open arms by the U.S. government and were given immediate permanent resident status. Their experiences of material success after arriving in the United States are well documented. Twenty years later, in contrast, the Mariel Boat Lift exodus of 1980 was composed mainly of poor Cubans, whose levels of education were much lower than that of the first wave of immigrants from Cuba. Many of these new refugees came from jails and institutions for the mentally ill. Some did not acquire permanent resident status for more than a decade and continue to struggle in the lower echelons of society (Daniels, 2002). Some were sent back. In the case of Vu, he belongs to the cohort of Vietnamese immigrants who came to the United States as a result of the end of the Vietnam War.

It is generally accepted that it is better to acquire this information from books, movies, journals, magazine articles, and other media, not from the clients. Immigrant clients may believe that counselors who do not know enough about the clients' background will not pay attention to the clinical issues because they are too eager and too curious to gather information from the clients. Once the counselors have the general overview of the main historical facts, the main recent facts, and the immigration cohort, they are better equipped to find out the specifics of the client.

Psycholinguistic History

Counselors may want to inquire about the particulars of first- and second language acquisition to understand clients' past and current struggles and their unique relational and contextual experiences (Pérez-Foster, 1996). The age of acquisition of the two languages, the nature of the relationships with people from whom languages were learned, and the environmental context of language acquisition might help a counselor understand the experience of the self of the client when speaking different languages as well as other important issues that may not otherwise emerge in therapy. When children learn English at an early age, the "forgotten" language is often still there. Clients who at some point were bilingual may want to refer to their early memories, which may include early language memories. People who were bilingual at some point in their lives may have two language codes with which they think about themselves (Pérez-Foster, 1996). Some of their earlier interactions with significant people in their lives may linger in affect, modes of expression, and relational characteristics tied in with their early language acquisition. Childhood memories can be uniquely expressed during the therapeutic process because the original language can be seen as a vehicle for reviving the past with a more fully expressed affect (Javier, 1996). This is particularly important for immigrant clients with a traumatic history. Also, the experience with the acquisition of the English language may allow for the emergence of therapeutic themes, such as rejection/acceptance by peers, that may not otherwise emerge. Allowing clients to tell their experiences with the acquisition of each of their languages, and the contextual relationships associated with them, can be helpful in the therapeutic process.

Countertransference

Clients like Vu may elicit in the counselor an excessive curiosity, particularly in the clinician who is not familiar with the culture of the client. Depending on their ideological position, counselors might be tempted to rush clients into a connection with their cultural background they may not be ready to make.

Excessive Curiosity About the Client's Background

An intriguing foreign culture may affect the therapeutic process if the counselor loses sight of the therapeutic task (Gorkin, 1996). In the therapeutic intervention section, the need for the provider to gather the information from outside sources was discussed. If the counselor does not do that, he or she will have to rely too much on the client as a source of information. Comas-Diaz and Jacobsen (1991) aptly termed this phenomenon *anthropologist syndrome,* during which the clinician may be overly curious about the client's background and spend too much time exploring aspects of the client's culture, at the expense of his or her needs.

Wish to Help Clients Go Back to Their Roots

If a clinician subscribed to the nativist position (i.e., assuming an indigenous or ethnic reaffirmation belief; Falicov, 1998b), he or she would be tempted to challenge Vu to adhere to his Vietnamese culture by returning to his cultural roots after hearing him say, "I am an American." Counselors with this position might be distressed at hearing that Vu is practically disconnected from his real parents, his siblings, and his language and cultural values and might try to convince Vu to embrace his original Vietnamese culture. If the counselor has this ideological point of view, it is necessary to share it with the client and articulate this position as one opinion and not the only possible truth (Falicov, 1998b), or else a client like Vu, who is not interested in an examination of his roots at this time, might drop out of counseling, which the client may have requested for different reasons.

TOOLBOX ACTIVITY—VU		
Discussion Questions	*Activities*	*Resources*
Content themes What other themes do you see emerging in the story that the author did not identify? **Assessment** Are there any questions you would like to ask Vu? **Interventions** What other interventions could you propose with Vu? **Countertransference** What countertransference reactions were emerging in yourself as you read this story? **Other scenarios** What would have occurred if Vu had wanted to keep a close relationship with his Vietnamese family? How would Vu's life have been different if he had been raised in several foster homes instead of one? Imagine that Vu is coming to you either several years earlier or several years from now with a presenting problem. Imagine what that presenting problem could be.	Research on the Internet the recent U.S. laws about acceptance/rejection of refugees and the countries where most refugees are coming from. Interview a bilingual individual and ask where he or she speaks the different languages. Ask whether the individual's experience of him- or herself is the same or different according to the language the individual is speaking.	**Suggested readings** Fong, R. (Ed.). (2003). *Culturally competent practice with immigrant and refugee children and families.* New York: Guilford. Pipher, M. (2002). *The middle of everywhere: Helping refugees enter the American community.* Orlando, FL: Harcourt. Rasco, L., & Miller, K. (2003). *The mental health of refugees: Ecological approaches to healing and adaptation.* Mahwah, NJ: Lawrence Erlbaum. Suarez-Orozco, C., & Suarez-Orozco, M. (2002). *Children of immigration: The developing child.* Cambridge, MA: Harvard University Press. **Videos** *Dirty Pretty Things* *Europa! Europa!* *Los Olvidados (The Young and the Damned)*

Seven

Esteban's Story

Still Uprooted

Esteban tells the story of his displacement and exile from Cuba at the age of 14 years and his subsequent struggles in orphanages and foster homes in the United States after being separated from his family of origin. We learn about what he lost, the strengths he has used to make sense of his losses, and how he sees himself in the context of his life in the United States. As you read this story, notice how he describes the loss of his family, his social and economic status, and his contexts and language. Pay particular attention to his sophisticated use of written English, which contrasts with how he feels about his accented spoken English. Also, notice how strongly he holds on to his identity as a Cuban and how he longs for a return to the paradisiacal and beloved country of his youth.

Esteban's Story

I was born into an upper-middle-class family of European (French and Spanish) origin in Cuba in 1947, during the years prior to Castro's communist revolution of 1959. At the time of my birth, and throughout my childhood, my father was an engineer/administrator, who was the director of a large corporation. My mother was an educator/homemaker, who dedicated herself primarily to raising her children and running our household. My sister—who was 3 years my senior—and I lived in an atmosphere of emotional and financial comfort and stability. In addition, we were the recipients of a sense of psychological security, which was conscientiously bestowed on us by our parents and which simultaneously resulted from our organized style of life.

I experienced my family of origin as a loving, peaceful, nurturing, and well structured system. My parents enjoyed a long, happy, and stable marriage. They formed a successful team and equally distributed their parenting responsibilities so that both parents provided quality time to my sister and me. As a result of my parents' socioeconomic position, my earliest identity was formed against the backdrop of Cuba's upper stratum. This was at once a gift and a tragedy, given the devastating, politically imposed, all encompassing losses that followed Castro's communist revolution of 1959.

The gift was receiving a refined and somewhat privileged reception into human life. The tragedy was that such graciousness did not prepare me for the poverty, emotional devastation, and personal and relational losses I would begin to experience in my early adolescence after the initiation of my forced expatriation.

I, along with more than 14,000 other children, experienced forced expatriation from Cuba in 1962, when I was 14 years old—as an unaccompanied child. My parents sent me into political exile in the United States, through the then clandestine Operation Peter Pan, which was organized and funded by the Catholic Welfare Bureau and led by Monsignor Bryan O. Walsh. This operation facilitated the largest recorded political exodus of children in the Western hemisphere. After arriving in the United States, I was sent to a refugee camp for adolescent Cuban boys, which was located south of the Miami area. We lived in Spartan, barracks-type accommodations, which constituted a marked change from the physical comforts and emotional security to which I had been accustomed in Cuba. During the 3 months I spent in camp, I cried every day under the same pine tree for hours at a time, mourning the loss of part of myself—my family, my comfort, and my existential/phenomenological security.

Subsequently, I received an academic merit scholarship to continue my secondary education in a Catholic high school in Delaware. During the next 2 years, I resided in a group home for boys, which was administered by a Catholic priest, who was also on the faculty of the high school I attended. Thereafter, I was, once again, relocated to a third destination—an orphanage in Omaha, Nebraska, where I completed my final year of high school in 1967. I reunited with my parents in Omaha at approximately the time I completed high school. My sister, Anna, was not able to seek political exile because, by the time my parents were able to obtain exit visas in 1967, she had married and had given birth to her first child. Her husband was of military age and would not be allowed to exit Cuba for at least a decade.

The reunion with my parents—after 5 years of separation—was bittersweet. I was angry and disappointed that Castro's government did not allow my sister, with whom I had been quite close, to leave the island. Furthermore, notwithstanding my intense joy at being reunited with my parents in exile, I had to contend with the realization that things would not be the same as they had been in Cuba. For example, my family would never again be complete, and the privileged socioeconomic conditions that my parents had provided for me in Cuba were gone forever. Thus, I found my parents' vulnerability to the harsh conditions of forced expatriation to be quite devastating. It was excruciatingly painful to see that my father—once the powerful and highly respected administrator of a leading international corporation in Cuba—had to accept an insignificant factory position that had nothing to do with his engineering background or administrative expertise to help the family survive financially. My mother, who herself had been a distinguished educator in Cuba, also had no alternative but to accept factory work, which held no relevance to her profession and personal meaning in reference to her life goals. These profound, transcending wounds have left a long-lasting mark on my sense of self and my developing identity.

I perceived my forced expatriation as a highly traumatic phenomenon, which not only represented a series of profound sociopolitical, economic, and cultural losses but also entailed a long separation from my parents at a very sensitive age and a permanent separation from my sister, which culminated in her premature death at the age of 44 years, the result of an "automobile accident" in Cuba in 1988. As such, these critical elements have constituted the loss of my phenomenological framework and original sociocultural context and have come to represent losses of a transcending and irretrievable nature in my life. For example, gone was the psychological security of having an extended family and a support network. Furthermore, our family system was drastically reduced from a comprehensive constellation, which included grandparents and younger generation aunts, uncles, and cousins, to a nuclear family unit, which was comprised solely by my parents and myself.

My current values are a blend of my mother's and my father's beliefs, life philosophies, and manners of being-in-the-world, and they reflect an unresolved polarity between realistic industriousness and the romantic delusion that one is still a member of the upper class while living in the conditions of near poverty, a state which hundreds of thousands of political exiles encountered upon arrival in the United States. My values also constitute the essence of my "received" identity and of the identity I have actively chosen to incorporate into my sense of self, as a conscious, reflective adult. For example, although given my present status as a full-time graduate student, my income is somewhat limited, but my values, aspirations, social training, and philosophy of life have nothing to do with this temporary category and continue to correspond to the upper socioeconomic grooming I received as a child. Furthermore, the humanistic values, which I received from both of my parents, I believe, characterize most accurately my consciously chosen manner of being-in-the world. This is reflected in my chosen profession, as a "wounded healer," in the field of psychology and in my professional dedication—spanning the past 20 years—to providing culturally sensitive services to the most discriminated against minority populations.

I was brought up as a member of the Caucasian race—both biologically and socioculturally. This has been instrumental in maintaining an intact sense of racial identity in my subsequent experiences as a political exile in a country such as the United States where ethnicity is often absurdly confounded with race and where even the most explicit and obvious Caucasian individuals of Latin American extraction (mostly of the younger generation) are effectively brainwashed into thinking that they, indeed, are not Caucasian because they were born in a Spanish-speaking country. Such individuals have had to contend with ethnic discrimination, notwithstanding that they indeed are members of the Caucasian race, given the issue that they are not, per se, "classic" representatives of what has been denominated as "culturally White" by a collective of powerful and influential—but highly ignorant and uncultivated individuals— who have succeeded in establishing the "rules and regulations" for what is, and what is not, "socioculturally White." These individuals have, moreover, established that Whiteness is a "registered trademark" and a monopoly of exclusively one group of Caucasians in the world—namely, the U.S. Anglo Saxons. In view of these anthropologically absurd antics, which, unfortunately, are widespread, I am quite proud of having arrived in this country as an individual with an already well-developed sense of self, including the dimensions of racial and ethnic identity. I am, further-more, proud that, notwithstanding the social and academic ignorance of mainstream society, I have remained impervious to the indoctrination of the latter and have not succumbed to the betrayal of my identity as a member of the Caucasian race—for the sake of the so-called ease of not having to swim against the preposterous and absurd current of "main-stream" society's collective and all-encompassing ignorance.

In terms of ethnic or national identity, along with tens of thousands of youngsters, I was deprived of growing up on my own soil and within the emotional security of my own cultural infrastructure. Instead, my cohorts and I have grown up as foreigners in the United States, and, notwithstanding our legal status as permanent residents or American citizens, we shall remain as ontological foreigners for the rest of our lives—our cultural identities split forever between two irreconcilable nations. Along with more than one million individuals, my family expe-rienced the total confiscation of our businesses, real estate, private prop-erty, bank accounts, and other assets by Castro's government. Shortly after the revolution, we were exposed to diverse forms of political oppression, such as the abolishment of the freedoms of speech and press, the abolition of governmental elections, the Marxist-Leninist indoctrination of children at school, the persecution of the clergy, and the eradication of free enterprise. As political dissidents, we were per-mitted to exit Cuba with only a few personal belongings and very lim-ited funds (i.e., 5 dollars per person).

Experiencing these devastating events during early adolescence, followed by my attempts to consolidate my original national identity with my newly acquired status as a political expatriate living in a foreign country, resulted in profound existential turmoil and a state of cultural uprootedness. Thus, through the phenomenon of forced expatriation, I, along with hundreds of thousands of exiled Cubans, experienced a resulting, all-encompassing feel-ing-state of phenomenological uprootedness—that is, a lack of cultural, his-torical, and national continuity and stability. Many of us who were exiled at an early age may regard ourselves as the lost generation of the late 20th century—a collective of individuals whose lives were developmentally and phe-nomenologically quartered by the devastating socioeconomic, political, and cultural effects of the communist revolution and the ensuing chaos of politi-cal exile. From a metaphorical perspective, many Cuban expatriates of our generation conceive of ourselves as sociocultural-psychological abortions. This is a state of being that emerges as the result of having lost our original framework to exist (i.e., the conditions of our lives in Cuba, before the communist revolution), as a consequence of not fitting in, either into what Cuba has become under communist rule or, ontologically, into the phenomenological sphere of our adopted country of exile, and as a consequence of having had our existential development interrupted.

In my developmental process, this feeling of cultural displacement—of not having roots anywhere—gradually evolved into a perduring, multidimensional sense of existential alienation from postrevolutionary, communist Cuba and, simultaneously, to some degree, from my country-of-exile, the United States. It is this inescapable presence of alienation, per se, that comes to form an inextricable part of many Cuban exiles' national identity and existential framework: the nauseating feeling of not belonging anywhere—a perpetual state of being in existential limbo persists even after four decades of political exile. I do not feel completely North American, and I do not feel Cuban in the manner in which Cuba exists geopolitically today. Along with many of my exiled cohorts, I remain inexorably Cuban in my identification with a unique society, with its own phenomenological configuration, which ceased to exist in 1959, following the communist takeover.

It is important to distinguish here, between the experience of an immigrant and that of an expatriate. Cuban expatriates do not practice the mentality or philosophy of immigration, which lends itself to a more adaptive attitude on the part of the individual who, as an immigrant per se, is voluntarily seeking an alternative—and permanent—life in a new country. The early-wave Cuban expatriate who belonged to the island's considerably large upper and middle classes would not have left Cuba seeking a better life in the United States because prior to the revolution there was no socioeconomic need for such action given the expatriate's level of professional and fiduciary development.

Along with my family and myself, the overwhelming majority of Cuban expatriates believed that our political exile would be short-lived and temporary and that we would return to Cuba after Castro's demise. Forty-four years after our political exile, many Cuban expatriates still consider the possibility of returning to Cuba after the eradication of communism. For example, many of my peers and I consider it an ethical responsibility as well as a human right and privilege to return to Cuba after Castro's demise and to participate in the long and comprehensive reconstruction process, which will be needed to restore Cuba to the functional first world nation it was prior to Castro's invasion.

The relevant point is that the majority of Cuban expatriates presently residing in political exile throughout the world would not have left their nation for socioeconomic, migratory reasons. Thus, as a first-wave Cuban expatriate, I consider myself to be in exile solely from Castro's totalitarian government, from the ensuing abolition of the basic human rights that are upheld in a democratic system, and from the preclusion of free enterprise as it is recognized internationally, within a capitalistic infrastructure. As such, I am not in exile from the fatherland, in itself, and I shall continue to indefinitely await Cuba's eventual recovery and restoration to democracy, a key and highly present issue in the execution of my daily existence.

This may be the reason why my struggles with the English language were so severe. English was not spoken at home during my childhood and early adolescence. I had difficulties once I arrived into the United States. The acquisition of English has been a painful process and an instrumental component of my identity construction. I have an idiosyncratic speech pattern that embodies my struggles with losing my original and desirable psychosociocultural framework, the "temporarility" of my forced expatriation, and my resistance to the acquisition of (or the serious attempts to learn) Standard English phonemes as a strategy for not being assimilated by the dominant culture, to keep my Cuban identity intact. I know that people still struggle to understand my heavy accent.

Notwithstanding the ravaging experiences connected with my loss of country and forced expatriation, and even after assuming the role of a political exile, my identity was constructed within the values, norms, and structure of an affluent, Cuban-European family. However, even upper stratum Cuban society was still considerably influenced by a phallocentric model of psychosocial development and functioned primarily from a patriarchal perspective. Therefore, gender identity formation and sexual orientation issues were clear: heterosexuality was, unquestionably, the only acceptable sexual orientation for both my sister and for me. Gender roles were clearly delineated for men and women, very much in a parallel manner to the upper class, 1950s society of the United States. In Cuba, as in the United States, a critically differentiating experience in female and male development is generated from the transcultural phenomenon that women are, for the most part, responsible for early child care. Therefore, the development of my masculine traits and my defined male personality took place in relation with and in connection to other individuals to a lesser degree than did my sister's identity formation. As a result, my sister was less individuated than me, and I was more autonomous and self-oriented than her. For example, through the process of early identification with our mother, my sister developed a sense of self that was continuous with others as well as connected to the world. As a consequence of the fact that women are mostly mothered by women, as a female child, my sister developed within a self-in-relation context of relational capacities and needs, in which significant importance was placed on the mother–daughter connection as an empathic unit of ongoing mutual support and on the values of nurturing and caring for others, kindness and graciousness in human transactions, and self-development within a framework of respecting and supporting the simultaneous progress of others.

Conversely, my own gender identity formation was more independent and autonomous and more centered on developing myself as an individual entity versus a being-in-relation-to-others. Decades later, it was the referred independent and autonomous attitude that, in part, contributed to my divorce from my second wife. I now remember that she would often make reference—quite accurately and specifically—to the marked contrast between the manner in which she perceived herself in our relationship (i.e., as a being-in-relationship) and the manner in which she perceived that I behaved in our relationship (i.e., with much less reciprocity and mutuality, focusing more on my personal development vs. our development as a team). In retrospect, I realize that this was a valuable lesson to learn.

Furthermore, from a multigenerational perspective, males played a dominant role in both my paternal and maternal ancestors' lives. These phallocentric gender and societal roles were consistently transmitted across the generations to my own family of origin, wherein males enjoyed more personal freedom, individual autonomy, and decision-making power than females and benefited from certain double standards of behavior. For example, at the age of 12 or 13 years, I had more privileges and personal autonomy than my sister, who was then 16 years old. Whereas I received the message that I was *macho, varón, y masculino* and therefore had the upper hand, she received a message of deference to the masculine sex—a message against which she fortunately successfully rebelled.

Again, these previously held values of male dominance ultimately resulted in significant conflicts in my second marriage to a Cuban woman, whose feminist orientation toward gender equality considerably contributed to my progressive rejection of what I now realize is an unfair and quite primitive value system. As a result of many academic discussions with my second former spouse (who presently remains my closest friend and colleague), and of my own consistent reflections on the subject matter, I have adopted a more humanistic and egalitarian worldview and understanding of human relationships, and understand the critical importance of mutuality in all—not just in marital relationships. In addition, my phallocentric family context affected my first attempt at forming a nuclear family. My daughter, Mabel (from my first marriage), at 10 years old nervously asked me if I wanted or planned to have a son, as if I would not be satisfied with merely having a daughter. By the time Mabel confronted me with this issue, I had divorced my first wife and had remarried, and my value system had evolved to the point that I was able to reassure her that I was ecstatic to have her as an only child and that she would always be my treasured and beautiful offspring.

Another pattern is that all first-born or only sons—including myself—have been consistently and invariably named after their fathers on both sides of the family. Having been given my father's name was at once a great honor and a marked challenge. Given that my father was a highly educated, culturally refined, and sophisticated individual who was gifted in many areas of life, and that he was, simultaneously, a truly accomplished professional in the fields of engineering and technical administration, at times I felt awed by his presence and by the expectation to follow in his footsteps. For example, I was expected to become an engineer and completed 1.5 years of engineering courses. In addition, because both my sister and I inherited our gender-consistent parental names (i.e., Anna and Esteban), I was resolute not to name my daughter, Mabel, after her mother or anyone else in the family. I voted to choose a name that had no antecedents on either side of the families-of-origin, thereby presenting Mabel with the opportunity to develop and formulate her own essence as an individual, without preconceived family notions or expectations from prior personas.

Again, although as a Cuban expatriate I am considered to represent an ethnic minority in the United States, I am aware that my simultaneous membership in the Caucasian race has also entitled me to certain privileges that minority groups of color have not been able to receive, including easier upward mobility and the absence of racial discrimination on an almost daily basis, which is part of other minorities' phenomenological experience. I feel that I have also successfully maintained my identity as a Caucasian individual, despite daily exposure to the absurd stereotyping and social ignorance of mainstream Anglo American society, which postulates that Anglo Saxons are the sole ethnicity with rightful claim to authentic membership in the Caucasian race. This latter ability to maintain an intact identity as a member of the Caucasian race despite the endless brainwashing that takes place through all possible mediums of written and verbal communication in the United States at times feels comparable to swimming upstream against a force equitable to that of Niagara Falls and actually surviving; it is, indeed, a significant accomplishment.

I feel that as an individual I have attained a certain degree of integrated biculturalism (i.e., the ability to be involved in both my culture-of-origin and the culture of my host society without having a blended identity), while maintaining an intact sense of identity as a Cuban expatriate. Having had the subjective experience of forced expatriation from my fatherland, Cuba; having had four decades of life in political exile to consciously analyze and reflect on my context as a Cuban national living in the United States, with all the profound levels of loss and reconstruction such a position in life entails; and, finally, having attained an effective level of integration of the two cultures in reference, I feel comfortable with the experience of encountering and understanding the unique processes of cultural transition and acculturation of other individuals in phenomenological transition.

Finally, as a Caucasian, I have developed an effective working knowledge about racial, ethnic, cultural, and religious differences, and, since the time of my residence in Cuba—a time also marked by ethnic and racial diversity—I have actively and consciously worked on developing a nonracist, humanistically oriented, Caucasian identity. As previously stated, I was raised with humanistic, Christian values, which place emphasis on equality and justice for both genders and for individuals of all races, ethnicities, cultures, and socioeconomic backgrounds. Moreover, my parents believed in social justice and equality and ran their household in a democratic and equalitarian manner. Thus, the principles of racial, ethnic, cultural, and gender equality have been of paramount importance in my upbringing and in the development of my sense of identity as a Caucasian of Cuban nationality.

I have successfully become bilingual and bicultural, and I can function quite capably and efficiently in both the mainstream U.S. culture and in my culture-of-origin, which I consider to be at least as efficient and high functioning as U.S. mainstream culture. I have been able to incorporate many aspects of U.S. culture without forsaking my own ethnic identity and value system. In addition, I have emerged as a stronger, more sensitive, more insightful human being as a result of this process. However, at a deeper, existential level, it would be absurd to deny that there are still unresolved personal and identity issues, which are the natural consequences of the loss of my cultural framework; of the fact that Cuba has not, as yet, been liberated from communism; and of the reality that a democratic process has still not been restored to millions of individuals whose human rights continue to be violated by a totalitarian regime.

Content Themes

In this story, Esteban tells us about the profound effect his losses have had in his life. He describes the sorrow at his loss of country, family, upper middle-class comforts, and language, weaving in the themes of acculturation and ethnicity in his relationship with the American cultural milieu.

Tragic Loss

One of the first themes to emerge in the story of Esteban is the issue of loss. Esteban's reaction to his parents' decision to send him to the United States when he was 14 years old still feels raw, and he understands the experience of "psychological uprootedness" as the most traumatic event in his life. He perceives himself as a "sociocultural-psychological abortion." He recalls that during the first 3 months of residence in the United States, he "cried every day under the same pine tree." Throughout the story, Esteban talks about losing his economic security, his immediate and extended family, his cultural infrastructure, and his cultural identity. Esteban describes his losses from the perspective of a child losing the security and comfort of the world that was known to him. The tragedy of the losses is even more evident in him because Esteban came to the United States as an orphan, uprooted from a known and secure world by a decision his own parents made in an effort to offer him a better opportunity in the United States.

Language Loss

The possibility of loss of the language of origin, and the difficulties with the acquisition of the new language, makes it one of the most salient themes for a first-generation immigrant. A second language is best acquired in the first few years of life. Children and early adolescents learn the fastest, and adults the slowest. After age 12 or 14 years, the acquisition of a new language is more difficult (Berger, 2004; Johnson-Powell &

Yamamoto, 1997). Complete native speaking and writing command of two or more languages is difficult and quite rare. Generally, individuals with bilingual capabilities have to use translation processes as part of their encoding in the second language, and they need to invest attention in how they say things as well as in what they say, which may make them look detached, vague, anxious, and less real (Marcos, 1976; Marcos & Urcuyo, 1979).

When children and adolescents learn English, they may end up having various degrees of proficiency in English and their language of origin. Some immigrants keep their maternal language intact, whereas others, for reasons other than the age at migration, do not. Esteban has kept his Spanish alive. There seems to be a clear relationship between acculturation and language. More acculturated individuals have better command of English and greater losses of the language of origin; however, that relationship is not necessarily linear (Kuo & Roysircar, 2004; Torres & Rollock, 2004). As is evident in Esteban's writing, his command of written English is highly sophisticated, while at the same time his oral command is not; we know his "idiosyncratic speech pattern" is still intact because people still "struggle to understand" his "heavy accent." An interesting characteristic of Esteban's writing style is the high level of cognitive and intellectual sophistication that makes it look almost cerebral and unemotional. This style can be understood as a coping mechanism he is exhibiting to deal with the traumatic events in his life. It could also be related to his strong accent in English. It is not unusual for an individual who comes from a highly educated family to have well-developed written English proficiency not matched by the level of oral proficiency (Torres & Rollock, 2004). Many educated immigrants possess a good command of the written English language. The sophistication of written English may also be a way of compensating for concerns about oral proficiency.

An adult immigrant can be affected by the double language loss. Dual encoding in two contexts affects the acquisition and use of both languages. On the one hand, with lack of practice and an inability to encode new material in the native language after migration, the native language gradually becomes obsolete and stale. Immigrants who do not have the opportunity to use words and expressions of their maternal language may end up with holes in the language that comes from lack of practice. On the other hand, the acquisition of the second language by an adult lacks the depth and completeness of the language acquisition that takes place during early schooling. The first-generation immigrant ends up characteristically having a hybrid English, mixed with words in the language of origin, and a hybrid language of origin, mixed with English. For example, one of us, Sara, cannot articulate in English information first learned in Spanish in the first 30 years of her life, and it is common for her not to be able to articulate ideas in Spanish encoded in the last 20 years of living, learning, and teaching in the United States. If she is speaking to her mother in Spanish about something she learned originally in English in the United States, she has to use English words and has difficulty saying it in Spanish, whereas if she is speaking to her American friends in English about something encoded as a young child in Argentina, she sometimes sounds inarticulate or unintelligent. Language can be one of the most profound losses of an immigrant. Because immigrants are so worried about everything that needs to be learned in the process of assimilation into another culture, the loss can be inconspicuous: Immigrants might not be aware of the loss until they suddenly realize that they really miss the language. Someone like Esteban may miss speaking in Spanish, reading fiction in Spanish, listening to music in Spanish, and speaking Spanish with friends. Language loss is the equivalent of losing an important relationship.

Language, Acculturation, and Ethnicity

The relationship between language, acculturation, and ethnicity is complex and multidimensional. The age of migration and the level of education of the immigrant are not the only factors that influence the magnitude of the loss of the native language. There are other factors in play, such as the degree of ambivalence toward the immigration decision, the level of choice in the decision, the experience after entering U.S. cultural contexts, the degree to which the immigrant wishes to acculturate, and many others. This is clear when Esteban talks about his cultural heritage, his accent, and his ethnicity. Esteban talks about his continued struggles with the language, having never lost his accent. As is not uncommon with other Cuban expatriates who had to leave everything behind, he still sees himself as having a Cuban identity that he would have gladly maintained had it not been for tragic political events. There is then a psychological component in Esteban's issues with his second language acquisition that is related to his experience with his involuntary migration and his acculturation process. This has affected both his acquisition of English and how he makes meaning out of his experience of migration. The wife of the professional husband, who reluctantly follows him to the United States from her native country and who would have preferred not to emigrate, might have a harder time learning English and adapting to the new environment than someone in similar circumstances who has her own motivations to emigrate in addition to accompanying her husband in his professional pursuits. This psychological component in language acquisition can be either conscious or unconscious; can affect the immigrant's acquisition of, and relationship with, the second language; and relates to the process of adaptation to a new cultural milieu.

Esteban tackles his issues with acculturation with a mixture of nostalgia, rage, and a sense of continued alienation. Esteban says that while growing up in the United States he felt without roots and still considers himself to be in exile. Later in his story, he explains that he has incorporated many aspects of U.S. culture "without forsaking" his own ethnic identity and value system. In terms of his ethnicity, Esteban considers himself White but explains that he has absurdly been viewed as a minority by the "ignorant" Anglo American society, feeling at times like he is "swimming upstream against a force equitable to that of Niagara Falls and actually surviving." Seemingly contradictory identity allegiances, opposing views within himself, and contrasting positions in terms of where he stands in relation to the host culture are not unusual ways of coping with the dislocation and the traumatic nature of Esteban's immigration experience; they are connected to his loss of his original language and his acquisition of the new one and his identity as a Cuban, a White male, and a bicultural American.

Immigration and Social Class

Every immigrant's story is in part also a story related to issues of social class. Often immigrants change their social class standing, sometimes quite dramatically. It can go either up or down, rarely staying the same (Breunlin, Schwartz, & Mac Kune-Karrer, 1997; Mirkin, 1998). Sometimes the change in social class status is related to a change in educational status, but not always. Esteban's forced migration carried with it traumatic loss of upper-class comfort. What one defines as social class markers also varies according to habits and customs of the country of origin. The rise in social class can be as dramatic and challenging as its decline. For the poorest immigrant, the encounter with the American shopping experience, with its array of choices and the availability of credit that allows the illusion of material ownership, can be an overwhelming occurrence. The overwhelming difference between the austerity of the country of origin and the vastness, richness, abundance, and megasizes of the United States is a universally shocking experience for the immigrant.

Immigrant families who are less financially successful in the United States than in their country of origin clearly experience stressors (Mirkin, 1998). For the immigrant from a middle-class or upper middle-class background in a non-Western society, coming to the United States can mean a dramatic change downward. It is not uncommon for middle-class families in urban areas of Latin America, Africa, or Asia, for example, to have full-time live-in maids who perform all household duties, a chauffeur, a handyman, delivery people to bring goods to the household, and so on. In hierarchical non-Western societies where labor costs are less expensive, families do not have to be wealthy to have access to inexpensive household help. In the United States, with its more democratic and egalitarian traditions and its high cost of labor, this is not possible except for wealthy families. In Esteban's case, his parents had to work in menial jobs in the United States after having lived a life that a successful managerial position afforded in the Cuba of the 1950s. It is not unusual for professionals or former managers to find that in the United States they cannot use their training. Esteban's sister died never having been reunited with her parents and her brother in the United States. His way of living in existential limbo and not quite acculturating, his difficulties with the language, and his perception of himself in constant angst may be at least in part explained by his anguish related to the family's loss of social class standing. How can he be happy if his family is not? How can he be happy if his family lost everything they had? With his sister still in Cuba, poor and without the chances ever to improve her social class standing, how can he forget that he is really a Cuban at heart from before the Castro dictatorship? In his view, were he to stop waiting for Castro to be deposed and for the longed-for old social-class standing to be restored, he would betray his roots and his own identity as a Cuban.

Clinical Applications

This section includes assessment questions related to the content themes of the story that might be useful to ask with first-generation immigrant clients. The interventions address the technique of language switching, and the countertransference section includes sadness, guilt, denial of the client's culture, and a wish to prove that the clinician is above prejudice.

Assessment

With first-generation immigrant clients like Esteban, it is important to assess language losses, changes in social-class standing, and the clients' view of themselves in terms of their ethnicity and their experiences with the American culture.

Language Loss

Is your writing and oral English proficiency the same or different?

If you have an accent, how do you experience it? Do you recall experiences about how your accent affects other people?

If you are bilingual, how do you experience yourself when speaking the two different languages?

In what language do you dream, count, curse, talk to yourself, or fantasize?

Shifts in Social Class

What do you think about your current economic/social-class standing?

Has the social class or economic status of your family of origin changed? Has it improved? Worsened?

What are the challenges/benefits related to the change/lack of change in social class?

Ethnicity and Acculturation Views

What are some of your experiences with the American cultural milieu that have affected how you view yourself today?

Does your view of your ethnicity coincide with the way Americans view your ethnicity?

Techniques and Interventions

Language Switching and Language Mixing

Acculturated individuals with bilingual skills may function effectively in the professional world, for example, but the emotional connections to the early language may appear in surprising contexts. It is not unusual for a bilingual individual to dream, count, curse, or soothe an infant in the language of origin (Pérez-Foster, 1996). Language switching is not uncommon, and the experience of self while speaking each language can shift dramatically depending on the context (Marcos, 1976; Pérez-Foster, 1996). Because language is associated with cultural meanings, individuals may perceive themselves as two different persons according to the language that they speak (Marcos & Urcuyo, 1979).

Sometimes bilingual clients may have the need to use the reservoir of emotional connections for early-encoded memories or to express current or old losses. One technique is to allow the clients to express in their language of origin the memory or the feeling state they are trying to convey, even if the counselor does not speak the language of the client (Fuertes, 2004; Pérez-Foster, 1996). If the feeling state associated with the memories can be elicited in the language of origin, it might be expressed more fully, more genuinely, and more cathartically, even if the counselors cannot access the meaning of what the client is saying. One possibility is to ask the client to speak first in the language of origin and then ask the client to translate the memories into English. The richness of the memories may emerge more clearly when elicited in the originally encoded language (Javier, 1996). This fosters explorations into how the clients experience themselves in each language (Clauss, 1998). Allowing clients to mix in words in their language of origin with their communications in English may make them feel freer to express themselves without having to censor the first word that comes to their minds. If clients can use words in their language of origin without fearing a negative reaction from the therapists, their expressions might appear more genuine, less rigid, and more natural.

Countertransference

Clients like Esteban may elicit in their counselors intense sadness for their history of childhood uprooting. In addition, counselors may be confused and ambivalent about Esteban's cultural factors. In some respects, he is not like a stereotypical Hispanic male, and in other respects he may appear to be. He is highly educated and sophisticated. Most of the time, he does not consider himself an American and longs to return to Cuba. He expresses himself aggressively about the "ignorant" Americans who treat him like a "colored" minority. Counselors may feel defensively attacked and may wonder whether to, or how to, tackle the issues of Esteban's identity. Some may wish impatiently for him to give up his allegiance to Cuba, and others may prefer to avoid dealing with the complicated aspects of his identity.

Sadness or Guilt

For clients with an immigration story such as Esteban, with their stories of early parental loss, refugee status, and struggles at an early age, sadness or guilt about the circumstance of the client's life may not be an unusual reaction (Comas-Diaz & Jacobsen, 1991). If unaware, the counselor could engage in behaviors that may not be helpful. For example, the clinician might feel too much compassion to be helpful, minimizing issues for fear of being labeled ignorant or insensitive. The therapist might be tempted to extend session time, cross boundary lines, encourage dependency, or have an attitude that places responsibility on the clinician and uses an approach of "I am going to be the person who makes all the wrongs go away" (Gorkin, 1996).

Denial of Culture

Because of the complexity of cultural identity issues like the ones Esteban presents in his story, counselors may deny the existence of the cultural factors in the clients and treat them with the attitude that all people are more alike than different (Gorkin, 1996). If the counselor is of the same ethnic background as the client, the denial of the cultural issues in the client may be related to thinking that the similarities are so great that there is tacit understanding of what is going on without having to go into cultural issues. If the counselor is of a different ethnic background than that of the client, the identification may come from the supposed sharing of social class or level of education. It is not always easy to engage in conversations about culture, ethnicity, and the painful, sometimes accusatory experiences clients have with these issues. Because dealing with Esteban's cultural factors may appear to be complicated, the counselor may avoid it, creating distance and possibly a cultural myopia (Comas-Diaz & Jacobsen, 1991) that affect the therapeutic process.

Wish to Prove That the Clinician Is Above Prejudice

This is an interesting and often overlooked countertransference reaction that may seep into the therapeutic dyad and, when not acknowledged, may lead to disastrous outcomes (Gorkin, 1996). Often clients and counselors have differing family, political, religious, or sexual values. If a client evokes dislike or feelings of superiority in the counselor, the counselor may secretly feel discomfort for thinking that prejudices are coming to the surface. The concomitant push to bury those feelings and thoughts may stem from the intense need to prove that the counselor is without prejudice. Unacknowledged thoughts and feelings of this kind may result in pushing clients out of the therapeutic process or engaging in passive-aggressive behaviors or other unethical behaviors. These reactions may occur in counselors of the same or of different cultural backgrounds than the clients'.

TOOLBOX ACTIVITY—ESTEBAN		
Discussion Questions	*Activities*	*Resources*
Content themes What other themes do you see emerging in the story that the author did not identify? **Assessment** Are there any questions you would like to ask Esteban? **Interventions** What other interventions could you propose with Esteban? **Countertransference** What counter-transference reactions were emerging in yourself as you read this story? **Other scenarios** How would Esteban's life be different had he been able to return to Cuba freely? Would Esteban feel differently about his identity as a Cuban had he been very poor before being forced to move to the United States?	Interview recent immigrants and ask them what they like and don't like about living in the United States. Write your reactions in your journal. Write a two-page narrative about the foods, music, and relationships that you are the most nostalgic about or miss the most in your life. Research recent changes in U.S.–Cuba policy and compare it to the United States' previous policy toward Cuba. What is your opinion about the two?	**Suggested readings** Aciman, A. (2000). *Letters of transit: Reflections on exile, identity, language and loss.* New York: New Press. Dorfman, A. (1999). *Heading south, looking north: A bilingual journey.* New York: Penguin Books. Stavans, I. (2002). *On borrowed words: A memoir on language.* New York: Penguin Books. **Videos** *Coming to America* *The Family Perez* *Moscow on the Hudson* *Rabbit Proof Fence*

Eight

Maria Luz's Story

Here We Are Not Free

Maria Luz, a recent immigrant from a small village in Mexico, describes how she arrived in the United States and what she hopes to accomplish. She was interviewed in March 2004, and Sara Schwarzbaum translated the interview from Spanish. When you read her story, notice the ambivalence about her decision to come to the United States, the description of her struggles as an undocumented immigrant who does not speak English, and her longing for her village, where life is different from life in the United States.

Maria Luz's Story

I'm from a small fishing village in Mexico, where I lived with my parents, two brothers, and one sister, until I came to America 2 years ago. My father does the fishing, and my mother sells the seafood. I used to help my mother sell the seafood in a big city 2 hours away from our village. We used to take the bus several times a week with our bags full of shrimp, crab, and calamari. Once in the city, we had to move from corner to corner. We couldn't stay in one place because we did not have a permit; we could not afford a city permit to set up a permanent stand. We were always running. That's how we made a living, my mom and me. We had to support two brothers who went to school, which was in another town, far away from our village, more than an hour away. We had to pay for their transportation, their lunches, their books, their uniforms. I went to primary school. There was no money to send me to secondary school, and, because I was the oldest, I had to start helping my mom. When I started helping my mom sell the seafood, we made some more money, so we were able to send my brothers and sister to high school and a college preparatory school. My sister works in the marina. She went to the preparatory school, so she's doing better already.

We help my mom from here. We send her some money. My parents are still in Mexico. I decided to come here to find out how it was. I had heard a lot about the United States. Back in my village, I used to hear that in the United States, people were free, that life was better, that you could make a lot of money, that jobs paid well. But I didn't know about the obstacles that exist here. First of all, you have to know English; then, you have to have a "good" social security number to work here. When I got here, I didn't know anything; I didn't know how complicated it would be.

When we first decided to come to the United States, we arranged for work visas. There are contractors from Louisiana who go to our province to hire people to work for the pine growers, and that's how we got here. They hired us to work for 3 months in the pine fields. We were supposed to return to our province after the contract expired, but we didn't return to Mexico. We stayed here. If we had returned to Mexico, we would not have been able to come back to the United States. My husband already had a job here in Colorado. After a few months here, I returned to Mexico because I was pregnant with a baby, but I was not well and lost the baby. I stayed in Mexico for about 9 months without my husband, and then I came back here, but this time, my husband had to pay someone to help me cross the border. I walked for 48 hours in the Sonora desert. There were 20 of us with two *coyotes*. I was the only one trying to get to Colorado; all the others wanted to go to California. The "coyotes" were supposed to help me get to Colorado, but they didn't. They charged my husband $2,000 to get me to Colorado, but they didn't honor that agreement. They took the money and left me in California. I didn't have any money to make it to Colorado. So in California, I had to work in a house preparing meals for workers. I was the only woman. I was there for a month and a half. My husband had to pay again $1,000 to a woman who was to bring me to Colorado. I got here OK, and I started working again.

That was 2 years ago. I worked as a busboy. The restaurant owner paid me $5 an hour. He treated me well. But the waitresses did not. I think they were racists; they used to scream and insult us. I left that job after 7 months because I only made $5 an hour, because the waitresses mistreated me, and because I was pregnant. If I hadn't been pregnant, I would have stayed, but it was hard to take all the screaming and the insults. Also, they used to make me clean with harsh cleaning supplies, even though they knew I was pregnant.

The employers pay very little because they know that we don't have papers, that we can't denounce them or accuse them. That's why they pay less than what they are supposed to pay.

I worked without documents. They just gave me the job without asking for any papers. My husband found his job because of his uncle. He does not have any papers either. We bought a social security number only to be used in the contract because it's an illegal paper. The employer wants it. My husband's job is good. They used to pay him $6.75 an hour. He's been there for about 8 years now. So they pay him $8.75 an hour now. He works 40 hours a week. But the money is not sufficient. We have to be very careful with what we spend. For example, we don't have medical insurance. My daughter was born here. She has public aid because she was born here. I imagined that life here would be beautiful and that we would have more money, that I was going to help my family. It's very different from what I dreamed it was going to be. Here we are not free. In my village, I'm free. I can get out of the house and go wherever I want to go. Here I am trapped between the four walls of my apartment. If we need to go out, we need a car. I don't have a car or friends. I thought we would live better. I wanted to build my house in Mexico. That was my dream when we came: that we were going to be able to work here and make enough money to build the house in Mexico, so we could return there. But it's been almost 3 years, and it has not happened. I would like to go back because I want to see my parents. I can't leave the United States because, if I leave, I cannot come back in. I would have to come back in as an illegal again and pay a lot of money to return. I would like to stay in the United States because of my daughter. She could be well prepared and learn English, and here there are better opportunities for her. Mexico is a very poor country. To study and go to school you have to have a lot of money. Whereas here, we can both work, and she can go to school. At the same time, I would like to go back and see my family. The dream was to come here and work for 5 years to be able to go back home and build our house. We could not have built a house had we stayed there. We didn't mean to start a family here. We wanted to wait, but I got pregnant on accident, so now I cannot work. But we don't make enough money here. Rent, phone, gas, and electric bills are very expensive. We pay $1,039 in rent. This apartment has two bedrooms, but six people live here, so we can share the rent. We take one bedroom, two other guys take the second, and two of my husband's cousins sleep in the living room.

If you have a car, the police stop you because we don't have a driver's license. They are always stopping the cars. One of the guys who lives here does not have a license either. He was detained; they towed his car and took him to the police station. He does not have insurance for his car. He has very bad luck; the police are always detaining him, every month, because he does not have a driver's license. You see, you need a social security number to obtain a driver's license, and none of us has a social security number. My daughter gives me strength. We always have problems, with the English, the lack of money, the constant fear of the police, and the troubles at work. She changes our lives. She makes it possible for us to stay here. Now, we prefer to stay here so that we can give our daughter a better education than the one we got. My husband only went to elementary school because he did not want to study; his parents could give him a better education, but he did not want it. The schools in Mexico are public. They don't have high schools in our area. Only big towns have schools. The cost of public education is high because you have to buy the books and the uniforms and pay the admission fees every year. Education is not mandatory in Mexico, so if people don't want to go to school, they don't. Many kids want to go to school, but they can't. The preparatory school does cost a lot of money. Many people have lots of problems when they come alone, especially women. I came alone. I don't want women to come alone. Something bad happened to me, but with the help of my husband I am getting over it. When it happened, I was not going to tell him. But when I got here, I didn't want him to touch me. Thank God and with the help of the social worker who does the home visits I told him, and he helped me to get over it. When I got pregnant, the social worker also sent me to see a psychologist, who helped me a lot.

The one who raped me was the "coyote." The other two ladies who came with me were also raped. They raped us because they knew that we were traveling alone. The other two were traveling alone, too. Nobody else knows about this, not my mother or my brothers and sister; this will stay in my heart forever. These are things that happened to us while traveling. I would have not said this, but I don't want this to happen to other people. It's very difficult. But if you put this in your book, it might be less difficult for other people.

What I like about being here is the city. It's beautiful. I also like the clothes here. Clothes are cheaper here. After one day of work, we can buy clothes. After one day of work, we can buy a week's worth of groceries. The only difference is that here we have to go to a store to buy everything, whereas back in Mexico we grow everything: oranges, plantains, avocados, garlic, potatoes, cabbage, carrots, chiles, onions, and corn. We plant everything, and then we harvest it. Here we have to buy everything.

What I like about the Americans is that they are blond and blue eyed, so good looking! They have a lot of opportunities here because they were born here. They live better. I wish I could live like them. They are not all rich. There are rich Americans and poor Americans.

I have a lot of problems with English. People call on the phone, and I don't understand what they are saying. I go to the store and want to buy something, and I don't know how to say it. Sometimes to go to the social service program I have to take a taxi. I have had two problems already with two different taxi drivers who have screamed at me because I don't speak English. I am going to school to learn English, but it's very hard. The teacher only speaks English, and there are a lot of things I don't understand. I am making progress. I can read some. I feel like I am learning. But it is very slow. I walk to school because it's close by. The teacher is very good. The center also has computer classes. But I can't go because I already pay $4 for 2 hours of baby-sitting when I go to the English class; I cannot afford another hour of baby-sitting to go to the computer class. The center that offers these classes does not have a babysitting service.

I am very proud of myself because the social worker and the nurse told me that I am a good mom, that I take good care of my daughter, and they both told me that they are very proud of me. I always follow their advice. I go to the program classes. Going to those classes distracts me. I only go once a week. No other moms have cars. We have several friends, but I never see them during the week. We cannot visit each other or talk on the phone. I heard of another person who is having a lot of trouble. The *polleros* left him in the middle of the desert. I heard that he had to walk 48 hours and drink his urine because he didn't have anything else to drink, until he found a truck driver who had other immigrants, and they picked him up. He is also having a hard time here. His relatives make him pay double what he is supposed to pay: double the rent, double the utilities. They borrow money from him, and they never return it. My husband hears about this at work. He gives him the money, so he does not fight with them. It's his own family. They never return the money that they borrow. He has his wife and children in Mexico, and his mother-in-law is very sick, so he keeps working here to send money back to Mexico and help them.

Occasionally I send money to my parents, $100 here and there. With that they can buy uniforms and pay the enrollment fee that has to be paid twice a year. They also need money for books. The school my brother goes to is a bit more expensive, but it's a better school.

A lot of the people from my village don't come here to the West. They go to a border town, where there are factories that employ Mexicans on the Mexican side. They don't have to be here illegally, and they make good money. It's unusual for a person from my village to be here. Most of the people who are here are from other provinces, not mine.

Content Themes

Maria Luz is here but longs for a small house in Mexico. At the same time, she wants to stay in the United States to provide her daughter with the education she did not have access to in Mexico. She was raped in the process of getting to the United States yet seems proud to be the best mom to her daughter. She has worked through some of the trauma, with the help of the social worker, the counselor, and her husband, and seems to function well, albeit with enormous difficulties, knowing that what keeps her going is the hope that she'll see her family again one day. In this section, we explore her ambivalent feelings about her immigration decision, how her voluntary decision to emigrate turned into a trap, her lack of skills in English, the differences between life in suburban United States and life in her village, and, finally, the effects of her undocumented status.

Ambivalence

One of the first themes to emerge from reading this and other immigrant stories is the ambivalence about the emigration decision. The desire to leave coexists frequently with the desire to stay (Daniels, 2002; Falicov, 2003; Grinberg & Grinberg, 2000). Maria Luz expresses the temporary nature of her desire to emigrate, so common to a lot of poor immigrants from Mexico and other parts of the world (Johnson-Powell & Yamamoto, 1997). She wants to emigrate only because she thinks she can earn enough money in the United States, but her goal is to return permanently to Mexico, even though she knows that staying in the United States would give her daughter better educational chances. The ambivalent and conflicting decision to emigrate permeates the stories of so many people who want to or need to leave and yet wished that they did not have to do so.

Whether the immigrant is highly educated or painfully unskilled, an ethnocentric attitude is a common human characteristic: People think that their food, their music, and their streets are the best and rarely want to leave the comfort of familiar sights and sounds (Grinberg & Grinberg, 2000). There has to be something in their country of origin that pushes them to leave (Daniels, 2002). Whether the immigrant comes from such an economically depressed area that leaving is a matter of survival or from an area where physical survival is not at stake, ambivalence is always present.

Voluntary Versus Involuntary Migration

Voluntary migration is frequently understood in opposition to involuntary migration, even though they are far from discrete categories. Voluntary immigration implies a deliberate choice to leave a country of origin to change or improve life, either for financial, political, or religious reasons. Maria Luz's decision to migrate at first appears to fit in the voluntary immigration category. Because of the limited economic potential in Mexico and the need to help support younger siblings in school, traveling to the United States seemed to be the most logical of choices.

In every voluntary immigrant there is an involuntary aspect of the decision to emigrate. If it had been possible for Maria Luz to survive in Mexico, she might not have left. Involuntary immigration is typically associated with forced migration, religious or political persecution, and refugee status. When Maria Luz first migrated, her intention had been to work, support her family, and return to Mexico. But she feels trapped now: The lack of opportunities available to her in Mexico and her current inability to return home, which would force her to be separated from her husband and her child because of her undocumented status, make her an involuntary immigrant.

Documented Versus Undocumented Status

The possibilities for employment and inclusion in the mainstream cultural contexts of a society are largely determined by documented or undocumented status. The majority of immigrants to the United States have documented status. They come equipped with student or work visas, or they receive their documented status as part of family reunification programs or their marital status. Documented status can also often be obtained with asylum and refugee status (Daniels, 2002). Other immigrants may be illegal or undocumented. In spite of media depictions and certain public perceptions, the undocumented immigrant constitutes a small percentage of the overall American immigrant population. Although accurate calculations are obviously impossible to make, one estimate puts the proportion of undocumented immigrants at about 3% of the population of the United States, with major increases occurring in times of economic growth. Many hardships stem from immigrants' undocumented status, including low wages, the general inability to go back to the country of origin for family illness or death, and many others, as Maria Luz describes in her story. An immigrant can start out undocumented, as many who cross the borders from Mexico do, or become undocumented after overstaying a tourist visa, a work visa, or a student visa. Once here, the undocumented immigrant typically finds low-wage employment, and the enforcement mechanisms to ensure that employers do not hire them are minimal or isolated. The issue of being undocumented is related to the availability of resources. Without documentation, procurement of a social security number or work visa is prohibited. Without the documents, immigrants are unable to receive public aid, a driver's license, better wages, and subsidized health insurance, among other benefits. This is clearly reflected in Maria Luz's story. Access to medical care and better working conditions might have prevented her miscarriage.

Other consequences of being undocumented are the additional resources needed for daily living and functioning. Maria Luz and her family are exploited constantly. First, her husband had to pay large amounts of money to have her escorted to this country, which led to her vulnerability to sexual assault. Second, employers are able to pay her less than living wages because the employment situation is illegal. Third, landlords and businesses can charge more for goods and services. Maria Luz addresses these issues in her story.

Language Issues of the First-Generation Immigrant

The acquisition of a second language is more difficult for older immigrants of low socioeconomic status. The ability of the first-generation adult immigrant to learn English is more common in people with higher levels of education and more rare in people with less education (Kuo & Roysircar, 2004). For illiterate or quasi-illiterate adult immigrants, the acquisition of a second language is the most difficult (Berger, 2008). Maria Luz came as an adult. Her level of education is low, and, not surprisingly, her command of English is poor. Additionally, learning a language takes time. Many first-generation immigrants have to work double shifts. Sometimes the low wages they earn do not permit them to make ends meet with just one job. If they also are caring for children, the availability of time to learn English is severely limited. In her story, Maria Luz expresses a strong desire coupled with a difficulty to learn English. In general, the desire to learn English in the first-generation immigrant is very strong and rarely is it true that the immigrant refuses to learn or is not interested in learning English, as some wrongly suspect. It is not uncommon for first-generation immigrants with low levels of education to live in the United States for many years and never learn the language, particularly if they do not have time to learn; if they have language brokers, such as spouses, children, or other relatives to help them; if they live in a community where there are a lot of resources in their language of origin, such as Latino barrios, Chinatowns, or Polish villages; or if they come when they are older.

It is clear that Maria Luz is aware that she suffers many barriers due to her lack of English-speaking skills, and she identifies her lack of fluency in English as a great obstacle in her life.

Immigration and Geographic Origin

The geographic origin of the immigrant sometimes is more salient than the other themes (Breunlin, Schwartz, & Mac Kune-Karrer, 1997). Immigrants born and raised in rural areas, in close contact with nature, or in small towns where everybody knows everybody else may end up in large urban or suburban areas. Traditionally, immigrants to the United States came to the large urban areas, but they often came from rural areas (Daniels, 2002). In the last several decades, immigrants are settling in suburban areas in unprecedented numbers. It is unlikely that immigrants will end up in places that are geographically similar to those they came from. Maria Luz expresses this condition when she states, with nostalgia, that in the United States she has to get everything from a store, instead of growing it herself as she did in her village. That shift can have a more dramatic impact on the experience of immigrants and their adaptation than some of the other dimensions.

Clinical Applications

This section discusses clinical applications for working with undocumented and first-generation immigrants. In the assessment sections, it is important to address recent or undocumented immigrants' potential for dropout from services, among other assessment ideas related to the content themes. The interventions section presents the pretherapy orientation technique as a tool to prepare clients for psychotherapy. The countertransference section describes possible clinician reactions, including areas of discomfort.

Assessment

When working with undocumented or first-generation immigrants, there are a number of issues to consider. First, it is important to assess their familiarity and comfort with participating in therapeutic services. Second, it is important to assess their language issues and preferences and whether they are thinking about staying in the United States or returning to their country of origin. Issues of geographic differences and the influence of these differences on daily living routines and patterns need to be assessed. Finally, documentation status needs to be addressed.

Potential for Dropout From Services

When first-generation immigrants become clients of counseling services, it is important to assess their views of mental health and their ideas about the use of these services very early in the process. Not doing so can result in early dropout from services and an overall impression on the part of the clinician that clients are resistant or unmotivated to receive services. First-generation immigrant clients, regardless of their level of education or their socioeconomic status, may come from areas of the world where counseling is not viewed as the way to solve individual or family problems (Sue & Sue, 2003). Others come from areas of the world where mental health services are available only for the rich or the upper middle class. When they need mental health services, many immigrants are referred by others to counseling services. This other-referred (Schwarzbaum, 1995) client is different from the typical middle-class client of therapy services who is self-referred. The self-referred client already has a belief in the helping potential of psychotherapy and knows what to expect from a therapeutic encounter. As a customer (De Shazer, 1988), the client only needs to find a suitable provider to entrust his or her most intimate concerns because he or she has an overall positive view of the process of therapy. In contrast, the typical other-referred client can be a first-generation immigrant, who may have little command of the English language, and who may have been referred by a doctor, a school, or another agency for a situation related to a child, substance abuse, domestic violence, or other reasons (Schwarzbaum, 2002). "Others" may think this prospective client needs therapy, but the client may not know how therapy works, what is expected of him or her as a client, what therapy entails, or how it can help. Talking to a stranger about matters of the most intimate concern is not always a known (or accepted) practice. The other-referred client places a call to a counseling agency of a mental health center, and the intake worker immediately demands personal information, such as a social security number and income information, that the client may not have been ready or willing to share on the first phone encounter with a stranger. The risk of dropout from counseling is higher for first-generation, other-referred immigrant clients than for self-referred, second-generation, or nonimmigrant clients, particularly if they come in contact with agencies that have an ancillary program and not multipurpose service centers that cater to a particular immigrant community (Schwarzbaum, 2004).

High rates of first-session no-show, dropout after intake, and dropout after the first session are common occurrences in mental health centers across the country (Sue & Sue, 2003). These high dropout rates could be prevented, in part, by assessing the potential for dropout very early in the process. Assessing the risk for dropout in the early stages of the therapeutic process is at least as important as the assessment of the presenting issues. Following are questions to assess the beliefs about mental health practices and the risk of dropout of the first-generation immigrant client followed by questions to assess the issues related to the content themes.

Beliefs About Mental Health Practices

In your country/culture of origin, how do people deal with depression, anxiety, and family problems?

Would anybody you know seek help for these kinds of problems?

What kind of help is available in your community of origin for a person with a concern similar to yours?

Do people in your community ever consult a mental health provider for individual or family problems?

Risk of Dropout From Counseling Services

Do you know anyone who has been helped by talking to a therapist or counselor?

Have you ever been helped by a counselor or therapist?

Do you know what is supposed to happen/not happen in a counseling session?

Do you know what you are supposed to do/not do in a first session of counseling?

In addition to assessing potential for dropout from services, counselors can assess issues related to ambivalence about the immigration decision, language issues, documentation status, and the possible importance of the geographic origin.

Ambivalence About the Immigration Decision

Ambivalence may be related to the presenting problem in overt or covert ways and can affect the clients' process of acculturation/assimilation.

How difficult was it to make the decision to emigrate?

Was that difficulty/ease shared with other members of the family? Originally, did you envision emigrating permanently or on a temporary basis?

Currently, do you wish to return or stay here?

Are the members of your family in agreement about whether to stay or to return?

Has your answer to that question changed over the years? To what do you attribute the change/lack of change?

Language Issues

Clinicians need to assess language concerns of clients. Clients with limited English-speaking ability may need to be referred to a therapist who speaks their language. If the clients are not bilingual, the language barriers may make it impossible to provide services beyond an initial assessment to an appropriate form of help. There are ways to find out what constitutes a good translator along with recommendations for training of translators (Bradford & Munoz, 1993). It may also be important to assess literacy levels in both English and the language of origin. Many clients who appear to speak English because they are able to communicate in a rudimentary way may lead the counselor to think that the clients may indeed speak English when in reality they may speak only a few words or do not speak it fluently enough to conduct a therapy session in English.

What language do you speak at home?

What language do you use to watch TV, listen to the radio, and talk to family and friends?

What language do your children use to watch TV, listen to the radio, and talk to family and friends?

If you don't speak English well, how do you manage?

Do you have language brokers (i.e., people who translate for you or help you figure forms out)?

Importance of Geographic Origin

Differences between the geographic regions of origin and the region in the United States where the immigrant settles may need to be assessed. Geographic differences may influence changes in daily living routines and may be contributing factors affecting the degree of ambivalence about the immigration decision and the overall functioning of the client.

Do you come from a place that looks the same or different from the one you are living in today?

How is your current geographic location different from the one you came from?

How is it similar?

How have you and the members of your family experienced the differences/ similarities in geographic location?

Did you live in an urban or rural area? Are you adjusting to being in a rural or urban area?

Has your daily routine been affected by the change in geographic location?

Documentation Status

Therapists need to assess client's documentation status. Many undocumented clients may be reluctant to reveal their status for fear of being refused services. In most instances, social service organizations do not have restrictions on providing services to undocumented clients, but clients may not know that. If clients have changed from undocumented to documented status over the years, knowing about their past status may help counselors understand better the hardship and resilience factors of their clients. Many clinical issues may be a result of the clients' undocumented status, ranging from increased stress to poor physical well-being. Lack of access to medical insurance and care, difficulty obtaining a driver's license and car insurance, housing issues, and lack of employment opportunities may affect the functioning of clients, their spouses, and their children and the client's use of mental health services.

What is the history of your legal status in the United States?

If you started out with undocumented status, how has the documented status changed your life?

If you have undocumented status, how does it affect your life?

Do the members of your family have the same legal status as you or is it different?

Techniques and Interventions

Pretherapy Orientation

Lack of motivation and resistance to receiving services are common explanations given about other-referred clients who drop out after the initial appointment at a counseling agency. But this view fails to acknowledge that dropout is an interactional or relational occurrence (Beyebach & Escudero Carranza, 1997; Phillips, Munt, Drury, Stoklosa, & Spink, 1997; Walitzer, Dermen, & Conners, 1999). Dropout does not need to be viewed as a negative trait the client possesses but rather as a relational phenomenon that says something about the client–counselor relationship or about the relationship between the client and the organization that offers the help (Lewis & Osborn, 2004; Sue & Sue, 2007). What happens during the initial phone call or during the first hour of contact that prevents so many clients from returning? To what extent is there a fit between the person requesting the services and the clinician/organization offering the help?

The view of the client as unmotivated or resistant to therapy also fails to acknowledge that even though healing as a practice has existed for millennia, the 50-minute hour of psychotherapy is a Western middle-class and relatively recent invention (Sue & Sue, 2007). Talking to a stranger about matters of personal or family concern may not be the preferred mode of help-seeking behavior of the immigrant client referred to therapy. Often clients drop out because the organization they come into contact with is not prepared to deal with immigrants and does not make any special adjustments in the way services are delivered (Sue, 1998).

The initial contact (the phone intake, the in-person first interview, and the first session) is what establishes a relationship not only with the counselor but also with the organization where the counselor works and with the idea of therapy as helpful to solve problems. The initial encounter with the organization sets the parameters of what will follow, regardless of the duration of the treatment process. One way to reduce dropout from therapy is the preparation of the client prior to and during the initial encounter with the mental health agency. Pretherapy orientations are tools designed to prepare clients for the process of counseling and can be presented in different formats: as audiotape-recorded scripts or as videotaped orientations available in English and the language of the immigrant (Rosado, 1992; Schwarzbaum, 1995). Written information is also possible, but it has the drawback that it is not helpful for people with limited literacy. The audiotape or the videotape may contain information about what counseling is and is not, how it can help, and the expected behaviors of both clients and therapists. The audiotape or videotape can be supplemented by a conversation during a first appointment to reinforce issues presented in the audiotape or videotape. For example, having this conversation in the first hour may clarify for the client assumptions that he or she may have about the process. It can also help the counselor clarify his or her assumptions about the willingness or the ability of the client to return for more sessions. Making the assumption at the end of the first session that the client will indeed return may be at the heart of many second-session dropouts of the voluntary, other-referred immigrant client. This conversation can also eliminate or minimize other assumptions about what clients know or do not know and about what clients think of the helping process. The importance of this conversation is at least parallel to the need to inquire about the client's presenting problem (Phillips et al., 1997; Schwarzbaum, 2002). A well-designed pretherapy orientation program can help decrease dropout rates of immigrant clients, even in cases of clients mandated for therapy, because it offers a collaborative, rather than a paternalistic, approach to counseling the reluctant, other-referred client (Lewis & Osborn, 2004).

Countertransference

There are two primary reactions that may occur from reading Maria Luz's story or from working with first-generation or undocumented immigrants. The first area of concern is documentation status, and the second is language, habits, and customs.

First, the media have portrayed undocumented immigrants coming to this country as taking jobs from Americans. Clinicians have to assess their own reactions to undocumented immigrants and immigration policies. Reactions may range from anger over loss of opportunities for Americans to sadness over human rights violations suffered by undocumented immigrants. The second issue is confusion over paperwork for undocumented immigrants. Therapists need to consider billing information and procedures. Therapists may be confused about whether they are legally or ethically responsible for reporting undocumented clients. Parents may be reluctant to participate in treatment with children for fear of deportation. Clinicians who wish for clients to become more acculturated may inadvertently use the documentation status as leverage for finding cultural compromise. For example, therapists may threaten to report child abuse of parents who seem overly strict with their children. Finally, some therapists may romanticize or denigrate the cultural background of the client.

Client's Language, Habits, and Customs

Therapists may have a difficult time with clients' accents in English and may become frustrated by not understanding what clients are saying. Therapists' frustration may also appear if clients do not come to therapy with the information they need to fill out paperwork, such as pay stubs or proof of insurance. If clients are seen in organizations and institutions that are not used to dealing with immigrants, clinicians may expect that immigrant clients will behave in ways that middle-class American clients behave within the "culture" of psychotherapy and react with annoyance to clients who do not (Whiston, 1996). Someone like Maria Luz may come to a meeting with a therapist accompanied by one or more members of the family if she does not drive or needs help with the paperwork or with English. She may also be less punctual, less task oriented, and less businesslike. Indirect styles of communication so common in other cultures (Falicov, 1998a) may annoy the clinician, who is an expert at teaching clients how to communicate directly and assertively.

If clinicians are not used to dealing with immigrant clients, they may appear frustrated, annoyed, and impatient. This may in turn elicit mistrust of the client, which could elicit the labeling of clients as resistant or unmotivated to treatment.

Therapist Discomfort and Positive or Negative Stereotypes

Therapists may have a tendency either to romanticize or to denigrate the culture of the client, depending on their knowledge of, and exposure to, the cultural group, their own worldview and values, or their past experiences with that cultural group (Pérez-Foster, 1998). It is important for therapists to examine their own positive or negative stereotypes about the immigrant group because they might be transmitted and projected to the client in direct or indirect ways. When clients come into the therapy room with their marital, parenting, or relationship problems, therapists invariably project into their clients their hypothesis, interpretations, and solutions based on their own worldview and their own cultural, class, and gender characteristics (Pérez-Foster, 1998). Therapists cannot possibly know about the culture of origin of the clients as much as their clients do, and this may make some therapists uncomfortable. The ambiguity of not knowing what to do with the concomitant discomfort may make therapists more prone to either romanticizing or denigrating the culture of the client. Therapists need to challenge themselves constantly and tolerate their own discomfort over not always knowing what to do with their immigrant clients. Clinicians need to train themselves to see and hear the larger context of ethnicity, gender, and class (Mirkin, 1998). At the same time, they need to train themselves to tolerate the ambiguity and discomfort of not always knowing what to do. These are necessary, albeit difficult, skills to master if clinicians are to become culturally competent.

TOOLBOX ACTIVITY—MARIA LUZ		
Discussion Questions	*Activities*	*Resources*
Content themes What other themes do you see emerging in the story that the author did not identify? **Assessment** Are there any questions you would like to ask Maria Luz? **Interventions** What other interventions could you propose with Maria Luz? **Countertransference** What countertransference reactions were emerging in yourself as you read this story? **Other scenarios** How would Maria Luz's life be different if she were married to an American?	Research the website of the Bureau of Citizen and Immigration Services (BCIS) and find the definitions of the following terms: *resident alien, nonresident alien, refugee, asylee, immigrant, naturalized citizen, illegal immigrant,* and *nonimmigrant.* On the same website, find out the alternatives and requirements for immigrants to reside legally in the United States (e.g., work visas, investor's visas, student visas, tourist visas, family sponsorship programs, visa lottery programs). Research the requirements that foreigners have to fulfill to obtain U.S. citizenship.	**Suggested readings** Lewis, L., & Madlansacay, L. (2003). *How to get a green card: Legal ways to stay in the U.S.A.* (5th ed.). Berkeley, CA: Nolo Press. Sicard, C., & Heller, S. (2003). *U.S. citizenship for dummies.* Indianapolis, IN: John Wiley. Weissbrodt, D. (1998). *Immigration law and procedure in a nutshell* (4th ed.). Eagan, MN: West Publishing. **Videos** *East-West* *El Norte* *Lone Star* *Los Refugiados* *Nowhere in Africa*

Nine

Teresa's Story

I Didn't Want to Go to Church on Sunday

Teresa's story reflects the themes of the second-generation immigrant. Although the immigration story of her parents from Lebanon to the United States is still a powerful organizer of her life and identity, Teresa seems clear on which factors of the Lebanese culture she is ready to reject. As you read, notice how much the story of her parents' decision to immigrate to the United States and the hard work her mother engaged in influence the way she thinks about her own life. Also notice the typical second-generation themes of language choice or rejection and how Teresa has dealt with parental authority and other gender issues in her family.

Teresa's Story

Imagine it is November 1980, and you are a 23-year-old Lebanese woman attempting to travel with four small children who are 6, 4, 3 and 1.5 years without the comfort and support of your family or friends. You're trying to travel from Lebanon to Atlanta; however, you have no means of communication with individuals who do not speak Lebanese. You're also still afraid for your children's safety, and you do not even know if you will be able to make it to your destination.

Furthermore, envision that the first flight you are scheduled to take is 16 hours long, and after you land in Los Angeles you have a connecting flight, which is another 4 hours, before you land in Atlanta. To make the situation even more complicated, you are moving your family to a country where you do not understand the language or cultural expectations. While on the plane, as well as at the airport, people attempt to communicate with you. However, the language barriers are too challenging, making it difficult for you to comprehend, so you begin to feel hopeless, questioning if you will ever make it to your destination. Nonetheless, you try to make the best of the situation, and while you are at the airport, you look around for someone who may be of assistance or may have similar ethnic features to translate your travel needs or confusion (if they look Middle Eastern, they may understand something you're trying to say and help you). After several frustrating hours at the airport with four tired and hungry children, you finally observe a couple who may be of assistance to you; you walk up to the couple and ask in Lebanese to be directed to your connecting flight as you wave your tickets at the couple. You realize you are in luck because the couple speaks the same language as you, and to top it all off they are more than willing to help you out with your frustrating experience. The gentleman assists you with your luggage, and the young lady admires the children as they walk you over to your connecting flight. You can finally breathe because you are on the correct plane, and within hours you will ultimately be reunited with your family members who are already in the United States.

Once you reach your destination, you walk out of the plane and are finally greeted by your son and husband, whom you have not seen in a year and a half, as well as your husband's relatives. You are so overwhelmed you start to cry. You have mixed feelings about landing in Atlanta. You are happy to finally be reunited with your family; however, you are sad that you left your entire family behind. You still embrace the moment and focus on the future to come.

This scenario was a reality for my mother, my siblings, and me when we traveled from Lebanon to the United States. I do not remember the transition, but my mother and older brother have vivid memories of the experience. They often share their thoughts and feelings regarding the journey, but they both agree that they would not change a thing about it.

My parents' desire to travel to another country and move away from family, friends, and the comforts of familiar cultural surroundings began in 1977. My parents began the immigration process after I was born. It was not finalized until 3 years later. My parents learned of the American dream from family members who already resided in the United States. My parents dreamed of having a future filled with freedom and independence for the family. So the journey began in 1978 when my father, along with my oldest brother, moved to this country. My mother was pregnant with my younger sister at the time, making travel difficult for her. It was important for my father to immigrate to the United States prior to the rest of the family to establish a home and make some money. The separation was difficult for my mother, but the outcome was eventually worthwhile.

My aunt, who had already lived in the United States for 9 years, assisted my family with the immigration proceedings. My parents admired my aunt for leaving Lebanon and coming to this country to experience independence and freedom. My parents dreamed of the transition for years prior to moving. The war in Lebanon became too unbearable to raise a family, so my parents planned the ultimate sacrifice and began their journey to America. (The ultimate sacrifice was leaving my mother's entire family behind to start over in a new country. My father's entire family emigrated to the United States years prior to our family's plan to defect.)

The reason my father and brother moved to the country prior to the rest of the family was to establish a home, employment, and schooling for my siblings and me. My father did not understand the language when he first came to this country. My father counted on my brother and aunt to translate formalities, so he could get a job and enroll my brother in public school. Our family reunited after a year and a half. Within that time, my father managed to put our living arrangements in order, he enrolled my brother in the neighborhood grammar school, and he managed to find a job in a factory. However, my father still continued to struggle with the American culture and language.

My parents did not have any special skills or education to highlight because they dropped out of school at an early age. Education was not enforced or emphasized in our culture 25 years ago. Once my mother immigrated to the United States, she immediately began looking for a job of her own. In Lebanon, my mother flourished as the master dressmaker in the family business, which helped her obtain a position in the United States. My mother had friends in this country who assisted her in locating the perfect position. She began working as a dressmaker in a busy theater company. My brother, my sisters, and I hardly ever saw her. She worked from 10 a.m. until 10 p.m. for many years. My siblings and I basically raised ourselves because my father did not contribute to the children's upbringing.

When my mother found a job and established herself, my father injured himself at the factory and eventually quit his job. He realized my mother was able to manage the family as well as the finances on her own, so he did not look for another position. My mother was also receiving monthly government checks to make ends meet, so the lack of income was not that detrimental to the family's budget.

Even with the burden of supporting the family, my mother still was able to thrive in this country. She learned the language and taught herself how to read to survive in the American culture. My siblings and I also thrived effortlessly, acculturating to the American worldviews. In Lebanon, English is taught to all students, so both of my older sisters had an advantage over everyone in the family. Nonetheless, my brother and I were raised in American surroundings and culture. Because we were so young when we immigrated, our transition was smooth.

As years passed, my siblings and I became more Americanized. We aspired for the same privileges as American children. Yet my father attempted to retain the family's cultural heritage. My siblings and I were forced to go to Armenian school on the weekends, as well as Lebanese church Sunday mornings, and we were required to speak only Armenian at home. Traditionally, within Lebanese and Armenian cultures, the children are taught the language and are expected to speak the native tongue within the household. During family gatherings, my cousins and I would sneak away from the adults and converse in English. When adults were present, we would not dare respond to the adults in any language other than Armenian. My cousins would always respond to their mother by saying "yes, Mother" in Armenian; if they did not, they would be disciplined with the dreadful shoe! (Once you see an Armenian or Lebanese mother take off her shoe, you know it is headed straight for your head, and if she missed the first time, you can guarantee the next time she will make her target!) My mother was not that strict about responding in Armenian (she's Lebanese and wanted to learn the language). However, my father would not tolerate or accept us talking in English; he deemed that a lack of respect.

My father was also not accepting of individuals of other ethnic backgrounds. We learned early on that we were expected to marry someone with the same ethnic roots and engage socially with Middle Eastern individuals, but only if he approved of them and their family background. So, needless to say, my siblings and I rarely brought our ethnic friends home. Our social lives revolved solely around school time and activities. Traditionally, in Lebanese and Armenian cultures, the head of the household (usually the man) arranges marriages for their daughters. They socialize with local families looking for eligible husbands. I can recall my father talking to my sisters and me about whether we wanted to meet a nice young man who was available to marry. We basically put my father in his place regarding this situation. I certainly laughed in my father's face, stating I would rather die than have him pick my husband. He was surprisingly not defensive but disappointed that we turned down the offer.

Our childhood was obviously trying. My siblings and I spent most of our time defying our father's strict, domineering rules. We disliked attending Armenian school. We played around during classes, and we eventually expressed our loathing. At first, my father was opposed to us dropping out of school, but with the help of my mother we actually won the battle. Our second battle to overcome was attending Lebanese church. Our family was more spiritual than religious anyway, so it did not take a lot of effort to win this battle. My siblings and I did not understand Arabic very well, which led to boredom during the church proceedings and constant struggles within the family before church. Because my mother was so understanding she did not force the issue. She understood that we sought our independence and would choose to go to church on our own if we were not forced to do so, particularly when we understood and observed the spiritual and religious beliefs.

The majority of all Lebanese Christian Orthodox followers commonly celebrate and acknowledge the strong spiritual faith passed down from generation to generation. My mother has always been considered a spiritual healer. It was not mandatory for her to attend church masses for her to be enlightened with her gift; the power of prayer and her strong spiritual roots have always guided her. As children, we watched my mother remove the evil eye from people's spirits. It was a very powerful and moving experience. While lifting the evil eye, my mother's tears would roll down her face as she yawned. The more she cried and yawned, the stronger the eye was on that individual. My mother always advised us to wear symbols, or charms, on our necklaces, which kept the evil spirits and evil thoughts from others away, so we would not get the evil eye. This sounds a little outrageous, but it is widely known in the Lebanese tradition to own and carry an eye with you at all times. I, on the other hand, do not have an eye currently, but I do have a rosary in my car, which is another religious symbol.

Other traditional celebrations followed by individuals of the Christian Orthodox faith are the elaborate celebrations for Easter, which are celebrated one week after the Americans' Easter. We usually begin the celebration days in advance, making Lebanese cookies, dyeing eggs, and planning the meal for brunch after church. Forty days before Easter, Lebanese Orthodox Christians give up something that they love and cannot live without until Easter. Most people give up meat because Jesus did. The fasting is called Lent.

As years passed, these celebrations were not as elaborate as they were when we were children. The entire family became too acculturated to the American culture. In 1986 my mother, siblings, and I became citizens; my father did not pass the test. The family still embraced our heritage; however, we were no longer forced to do things. We willingly spoke either English or Armenian at home and attended church. Our social interactions with others from different cultural backgrounds were also accepted. My father did not have so much control in the family anymore. The more my mother became acclimated to the laws and culture of the American worldviews, the more control and power she gained over my father. My mother's role in the family was significant.

The roles within the family dynamic were defined by rules depicted in our nuclear family. The women in my nuclear family were taught to be hard workers and the family breadwinners. My mother received all the respect in the family, even though she did not demand it. My father was viewed as a worthless man who did not contribute to the family system financially or emotionally. He was physically available; however, we could not count on him for anything. My father became the poster father for all Armenian men. I viewed all men with an Armenian descent to be deadbeat fathers. This negative image was always reinforced, specifically when I observed my father's friends treating their wives and children similarly to the way I had experienced in my upbringing.

My siblings and I definitely learned some nontraditional male and female roles by observing my parents' behaviors. Through observing my father, we were taught that a woman should serve and pick up after her husband. We were also taught that women were the breadwinners as well as the caretakers. As a result of the constant reminder of a woman's responsibilities, we were taught that the women in the family had to be strong, independent women with an abundance of initiative to succeed.

I'm sure my brother was affected differently. For years he expected my mother, my sisters, and me to take care of him. He also struggled with the image my father implanted in our minds as a useless, incompetent, weak man. He wanted others to know that just because he was my father's son did not mean he was my father. He tried so hard not to be him. My mother continuously talked about the traditional cultural expectations of men and women in our culture to ease all of our minds. She expressed that the situations we observed were not due to cultural traditions but due to her own tolerance. My mother reinforced the notion of shared responsibilities between men and women, even though she did not follow her own advice. She also explained that the traditional norms of men being the breadwinner and women being the sole caretakers no longer existed in Lebanon, especially within Christian religions (Muslims in Lebanon defiantly abided by the religious and cultural beliefs that men are the superior sex).

Keeping in mind the false notion of the man as the sole provider and the woman as the caretaker, my siblings and I looked at the gender roles of members in our extended family. We realized that members of both sides of our family are successful in their own way, regardless of gender. Many individuals in my family own their own businesses. Numerous male and female members of my family have established lucrative businesses without the education typically needed to succeed. Their gender never factored into who was going to run the business or who was going to take care of the children. The idea of joint responsibility was passed down from the older generations and practiced (except in the case of my nuclear family).

Typically, Lebanese and Armenian immigrants come to this county with the intent to start a business. Lebanese families frequently own restaurants, auto clinics, and liquor stores, whereas Armenians customarily own jewelry stores. It is amazing to me that every member on my mother's and father's sides of the family is living a comfortable life financially (without an education). On the other hand, my nuclear family has struggled for 23 years in this country to get to the comfort level we are at now. It took our family approximately 18 years to completely get out of the welfare system. My mother explains that some years were easier than others. Getting off of welfare was not a problem; staying off was the difficulty.

It is also noteworthy to mention that I am the only member of my nuclear or extended family to ever attend and graduate from college and attend graduate school. Moreover, many older individuals in my family system have not attained a high school diploma. Even more surprising, a common pattern that emerged on my paternal side of the family is that, even though they did not continue their education, several family members own their own businesses. My paternal grandfather owned a restaurant in Lebanon. My two uncles and my aunt also started their own businesses in the United States and Lebanon. Relatives on my mother's side of the family are blue-collar workers. They work for others. However, they are very wealthy.

Another common theme in my family that I deem significant to mention is that out of 14 marriages across generations, only one has ended in divorce. The marriages on my mother's side appear to be more centered on love, equality, and friendship. However, the marriages on my father's side appear to be centered on deceit, connivance, and financial dependence. My paternal relatives have been through many cycles of closeness and distance but have never ended in divorce, with the exception of my cousin Tessa. These marriages have defiantly embraced the true meaning of "till death do us part," regardless of the hardship encountered in the marriage relationships. Being raised in America, there are some aspects of my identity that I can relate to Americans more than Lebanese/ Armenians. For example, I can guarantee I would have opted for a divorce if I had been married to my father or several of my uncles. Culture depicts a Lebanese/Armenian woman supporting her husband during moments of weakness, whereas American women quickly get a divorce and seek child support. I have a certain tolerance level for conflict in relationships. However, I do not have the tolerance and patience my ancestors possessed. I could not fathom being married to someone for 35 years (like my parents) and being miserable for the majority of our relationship. I cannot identify with that part of my cultural roots.

Content Themes

Teresa presents the typical second-generation themes of immigrant families. She tells the timeless story of her mother, who, through hard work, sacrifice, and dedication, was able to provide a better future for her children. Teresa also describes her resistance to her father's traditional gender role prescriptions, her achievement of being the first one to attend college in a family of small business owners, and her rejection of some of the prescribed expectations regarding language preservation, religious observance, and decisions about mate selection.

First- Versus Second-Generation Immigrants

In earlier generations, the ambivalent immigrant did not have access to inexpensive transportation, e-mail, or frequent telephone contact, as many do now. Leaving was tantamount to severing ties with family and friends because once they made the decision it was usually irreversible. This was (and can still be) particularly true in cases of immigrants from faraway countries. The reason Teresa describes her mother's voyage to the United States as the "ultimate sacrifice" is related to this sense of irreversibility in the immigration decision. Teresa's mother must have known that once she left the Middle East, her four Lebanese-born children were going to be raised in the United States, were going to attend American schools, and would speak English. They would become the immigrants of the second generation.

A traditional demographic definition of a first-generation immigrant is that of a person who was not born in the United States, whereas a second-generation immigrant is defined as a person who was born in the United States. Sometimes a second-generation immigrant is defined by where his or her parents were born. However, these categories are not so clear-cut. Someone may have been born in a foreign country and function as a second-generation immigrant (Grinberg & Grinberg, 2000). An immigrant child who comes to the United States at the age of 3 years might be considered a second-generation immigrant, whereas an individual who comes at the age of 20 years would be considered a first-generation immigrant, even though neither immigrant was born in the United States. What seems to be important is where the person received early schooling, whether English was the primary or the secondary language in the country of origin, and the amount of exposure to American norms, institutions, and peer groups during the formative childhood years, regardless of where the immigrant was born. Teresa would be considered a second-generation immigrant even though she was born in Lebanon because she came to the United States at a very young age and, most important, because she received most of her schooling in English and in the United States.

Language Issues of the Second Generation: Loss or Rejection

Second-generation immigrants vary greatly in the degree to which they preserve their languages of origin. Several psychosocial and acculturation factors exist. The level of conflict within the family, how favorably or unfavorably the language is viewed by the family and the larger community, and the sociocultural pressures to acculturate are among the factors that are influential in determining language preservation. Teresa's mom learned English quickly, did not enforce Arabic to her children, and acted in ways that encouraged assimilation, for herself and her children, the way the old world emigrants did.

Preschool children who are exposed to only their language of origin at home may initially have some difficulty communicating in English to preschool personnel. Some educators still wrongly believe that the reason children may have a delayed literacy in English is that they are exposed to two languages. However, the vast majority of children exposed to two languages during early developmental stages learn both languages equally well (Johnson-Powell & Yamamoto, 1997; Nieto, 1999). Unless the schools offer true bilingual programs, the reality is that immigrant preschool children will most likely use their language of origin at home and use English at school, which often leads to loss of the maternal language because of lack of practice and because children stop the development of literacy skills in their language of origin. When preschool children are placed in English-only settings, they lose not only their first language but also the ability to communicate effectively with their families (Nieto, 1999). Teresa came to the United States when she was very young and quickly learned English. Even though her father forced her to speak Armenian in the house, she speaks neither Armenian nor Arabic, her mother's language. By the third generation, the language of origin will almost always be completely lost.

Family members, like Teresa's mother and father, often differ considerably in their English proficiency and in their positive or negative regard to the acquisition of English or preservation of the language of origin. These differences sometimes get polarized, with language choice symbolizing different sides of the polarized continuum (Falicov, 1998b). The adolescent who refuses to speak the native language can become entangled in loyalty conflicts with parents who do not learn English. Severe generational conflicts may be played out in the family as a result of language issues. In Teresa's recollections, her father forced the children to continue to speak the paternal language, Armenian, which she didn't want to do. It would be difficult to assess whether Teresa fought speaking the native language because her father forced it on her or whether her father attempted to force it because Teresa was fighting it, more interested in becoming "like the others" of her peer group. What seems clear is that Teresa refused to speak Armenian, her father's preferred language, and rejected her father's idea of keeping the traditions of her culture of origin that he wanted her so much to preserve. She seemed to have had a conflicted relationship with him, and it is not surprising, therefore, that she was not making too much of an effort to please her father. Consequently, she does not speak Armenian. Cohort effects may have already been taking place in Teresa's case. In contrast with Spanish-speaking immigrants, for example, who compose such a large percentage of the American population and who, therefore, might be inclined to continue to use their language, Armenian and Arabic are not as well known or accepted in the United States; therefore, Teresa might not have felt guilty about losing her language of origin.

Some children of the second generation need to act as language brokers (Falicov, 1998b) for their first-generation parents, thus becoming parentified in their roles with their families. When immigrant parents are unable to communicate effectively with their children, they lose the ability to socialize and influence the children, losing intimacy and closeness that comes from passing down values and beliefs (Johnson-Powell & Yamamoto, 1997). This may explain part of the generational conflicts that occur between first- and second-generation immigrants. From this point of view, it is not surprising that Teresa's relationship with her mother seems to have been less conflicted than her relationship with her father, whose command of English was poor.

Intergenerational Conflicts and Gender

Acculturation conflicts may develop for immigrants around shifts in gender and intergenerational roles (Hernandez & McGoldrick, 1999). Parent–child relationships often become more strained in immigrant families because the old coping support networks may not be there and because the new country may foster less patriarchal and more egalitarian gender and intergenerational roles. These changes do not come without great emotional and psychological costs. Sometimes there exists an inverse relationship between the new and the old gender roles (i.e., the more egalitarian the second-generation immigrant becomes, the more the older generation seems to need to cling to traditional values and gender roles and the more polarized the generations become). In Teresa's case, the polarization of the gender roles occurred in the context of the intergenerational struggles. Teresa and her father were at opposite ends of the continuum. The more control her father wanted, the more the children rebelled: "My siblings and I spent most of our time defying our father's strict, domineering rules."

Gender role reversals in cultural transitions are not unusual. Because women generally experience more dissatisfaction with narrow gender roles (Bruenlin, Schwartz, & Mac Kune-Karrer, 1997), immigrant mothers sometimes are more inclined than fathers to become more Americanized (Comas-Diaz, 1987; Falicov, 1998b; Hernandez & McGoldrick, 1999). Teresa describes how her mother seems to reflect that tendency, how she shifted in her gender identity more than her father did. In the way Teresa tells the story, there was a change in her mother and not in her father. Teresa's mother was able to find employment, and her father, perhaps due to his disability but most likely because of his gender socialization, continued to expect adherence to the traditional values: "The more my mother became acclimated to the laws and culture of the American worldviews, the more control and power she gained over my father." Even though in the beginning Teresa was taught that "a woman should serve and pick up after her husband," later she learned that "women in the family had to be strong, independent women with an abundance of initiative to succeed."

Not all women in families struggling with cultural transitions make that shift. Cultural transitions to environments that are more egalitarian and less hierarchical may be very difficult for men who come from cultures with patriarchal family traditions in which women do not work for a living and are not eligible to receive an education and in which adolescents, particularly female adolescents, do not question parental male authority (Breunlin, Schwartz, & Mac Kune-Karrer, 1997). Teresa describes a father who, after making the "ultimate sacrifice" and initially finding housing, employment, and the means to reunite with the rest of his family, eventually and for many reasons lost power and control over his children, who rebelled frequently against him and did not want to adhere to his prescription of the traditional gender roles he had been socialized to support. Losing his ability to work may have forced his wife into more than full-time employment to support the family. In immigrating to America, Teresa's father may have sacrificed more than he bargained for.

Clinical Applications

This section includes assessment of issues that can be a concern for families or individuals of the second generation, a clinical intervention most likely to be useful with conflicts related to the choices of the second generation, and some typical countertransference reactions to these cultural transition issues.

Assessment

It is important to assess whether the clients rejected or lost their language of origin and the reasons for the rejection or loss. It is also important to assess whether there were parent–adolescent struggles that may have influenced the second-generation immigrants' decisions about choice of mate, lifestyle, or employment. The rejection of the language may have been a reflection of polarized conflicts within the family context, cohort effects, or other reasons.

Language Issues With the Second Generation

Were there expectations related to language preservation in your family?

Did you and your parents agree about issues related to language?

Did you and your siblings or other extended family members agree about issues related to language?

Were there any gains or losses of language?

Intergenerational Conflicts and Gender Roles

Were there conflicts around preservation of traditional gender roles?

How are/were parent–adolescent conflicts handled?

Who was most/least affected by the gender role shifts?

What were the gains/losses related to gender role shifts?

Techniques and Interventions

Untangling Family Conflicts Based on Second-Generation Choices

Counselors vary in how they view the acculturation/assimilation process in their clients. Second-generation immigrant clients often seek help in the midst of the turmoil elicited by the gender role shifts and the intergenerational conflicts that parents and their adolescent or young adult children exhibit. A clinician might see a family, an individual, or a couple in the midst of these conflicts where there are frequent fights about role definitions and open demands for changes in beliefs and actions (Bruenlin et al., 1997). Counselors might have strong opinions about what they think clients ought to be doing or not doing to solve their problems. For example, had Teresa and her father been in a counseling situation at the time of their cultural transitions, a counselor who thought Teresa should respect her father's hierarchical role in the family would have acted very differently from one who felt the need to encourage Teresa to avoid and discard the traditional, but old-fashioned, gender role expectations her father had for her. Counselors need to be aware of their own ideologies and personal leanings (Falicov, 1998b) and know where they stand in relation to gender and intergenerational conflicts (Bruenlin et al., 1997). Are they advocates for acculturation? Do they regard assimilation or preservation of cultural roots as the ultimate goal for immigrant families? The presenting problems related to gender role shifts or intergenerational conflicts can be linked to dilemmas of cultural transition by helping clients explore what they are interested in preserving and what they are interested in discarding, rather than the clinician imposing his or her own choices. The clinician can then facilitate clients' choices by acting as a cultural intermediary, helping to build bridges between cultural meanings (Falicov, 1998b), and introducing respectful discussions about the gender constraints that fit the goals of the family (Bruenlin et al., 1997). Falicov (1998b) and Breunlin et al. (1997) describe procedures that include drawing attention to differences, contextualizing the differences, reframing problems as dilemmas of coexisting meaning and cultural transitions, and introducing to families the idea that there are many parts to everyone. These interventions help clients highlight the meaning of differences, paying attention to what each member of the family needs from the others. They also help clients understand how those differences in preferences, thoughts, and lifestyle are influenced by socialization and historical and sociocultural patterns. Most important, the interventions help to reduce mutual blaming and polarization by opening the space for personal choice, even if those choices are not correct by the standards of the therapist. Had Teresa and her father been in a therapeutic situation at the time, a therapist might have drawn attention to their differences, might have reframed their struggles as stemming from the cultural transitions, and might have asked them to define what needs each had that were not being addressed. The therapist and the family may have engaged in conversations that might have brought to the forefront each family member's pain, sorrow, losses, and fears. It might also have been useful to explore historical and sociocultural explanations for their generational differences. This in turn might have had the effect of softening their polarized positions.

Each family can discover and develop its own manner of living with two cultures, whether through acculturation, alternation, hybridization, or a combination of all these. But dilemmas can be articulated and creative solutions found if therapists show interest, curiosity, and respect for each family member (Falicov, 1998b) instead of taking sides, which increases polarization. People can be helped to increase their options and lift their constraints (Breunlin et al., 1997), provided that the family is included in a collaborative way.

Countertransference

Taking Sides

Many immigrant clients seek services because of conflicts between the more acculturated children or young adults and their less acculturated parents. In these cases, members of the same family system seem to be pulled in opposite directions. The request for help may come from the parents, the young adults, or a sibling concerned about the level of distress. For a variety of reasons, many immigrants do not seek help until they are in a time of severe turmoil. A therapist may be pulled in and expected to take sides—and do just that. A common countertransference reaction is that the therapist takes sides with the adolescent against the parents or with the parent against the adolescent (Falicov, 1998b). Taking sides with the client against another member of the family makes some clients feel supported and understood and others feel abandoned, misunderstood, or criticized. Dangerous triangulations occur when clinicians take sides either overtly or covertly (Nichols & Schwartz, 2001). Taking sides with some members of the family against others violates one of the basic clinical skills, namely, the ability of the therapist to act in a way that will make every member of the family, whether present in the room or not, feel supported by the therapist.

These countertransference reactions stem from differing positions of the counselor about the acculturation/assimilation dilemmas. At one end of the continuum, there are counselors who hold the position that immigrant clients need to become Americanized because gender equality, individuation, and individualism are desirable cultural values. Counselors may openly or covertly despise women who stay with men who exhibit more traditional gender roles and expectations or be openly or secretly critical of parents who hold on to stricter standards to control their rebellious adolescents (Falicov, 1998b). Clinicians with this orientation who had Teresa as a client might have sided with her against her father.

At the other end of the continuum are counselors who assume a position of preservation of ethnic values and heritage (Falicov, 1998b). They may believe that a connection with traditional cultural values, language, and ethnicity is better for the mental health of the client and openly or covertly encourage clients to find their cultural roots, discourage liberation from oppressing values, and promote ethnic pride and resistance to ethnic blending and Americanization. A therapist with this position may have sided with Teresa's father against her. Either of the two extreme positions may constitute a form of cultural imperialism (Falicov, 1998b). The more covert or secret this agenda is, the more damaging its effect on the clients and on the therapeutic situation. Clinicians may have these reactions regardless of the type of counseling they engage in and regardless of how many people attend a session. Counselors can polarize families or couples even if they are conducting individual counseling and may have important influencing effects on the decision-making process about future actions of individual clients.

TOOLBOX ACTIVITY—TERESA		
Discussion Questions	*Activities*	*Resources*
Content themes What other themes do you see emerging in the story that the author did not identify? **Assessment** Are there any questions you would like to ask Teresa? **Interventions** What other interventions could you propose with Teresa? **Countertransference** What countertransference reactions were emerging in yourself as you read this story? **Other scenarios** How would Teresa's life be different if she had emigrated as an adolescent instead of as an infant? If Teresa's father hadn't been disabled, how would the life of Teresa's family have been different?	Use the Internet to find the percentage of Muslim immigrants in the United States. What are some of the names of the countries they come from and the languages they speak? Find information about lesser known immigrant groups, such as Armenians, Macedonians, and Ethiopians.	**Suggested readings** Portes, A., & Rumbaud, R. (2001). *Legacies: The story of the immigrant second generation*. Berkeley: University of California Press. **Videos** *Avalon* *Coming to America* *Double Happiness*

SECTION III

Religion

According to the Gallup polls, about 6 out of 10 Americans report that religion is a very important part of their lives and believe that religion can answer most of today's problems. Many Americans say they attend religious services at least once a month, and one third of Americans go to services every week. Of those in the surveys, more than 8 in 10 arc Christian, including about half who are Protestant and a quarter who are Catholic (Carrol, 2004). Because religion is an important component of individuals' lives, it is important to consider how religion and spirituality are relevant to clinical practice. Research suggests that many clients wish to include a discussion of spirituality in treatment (Griffith & Rotter, 1999). Spirituality and religion are important components of personality and identity development (Griffith & Griggs, 2001; Standard, Sandhu, & Painter, 2000). Research indicates the importance of spirituality and religion for positive functioning and health and wellness and the need for therapists to explore the importance of spirituality with their clients (Tolliver, 1997). Spirituality and religion are related, but different, concepts. Spirituality, which includes a notion of transcendence, communal spirit, and a relationship with a higher power, has been used as a source of support and a mechanism for resiliency for many people (Boyd-Franklin, 2004; Johnson, 1995). Spirituality includes a sense of unity or oneness, a connection to people, to nature, and to a higher power. It is connected to a sense of purpose and fulfillment in life. Spirituality is often reflected in the arts, including paintings, music, and body movement (Frame & Williams,

1996; Tolliver, 1997; Walsh, 1999). There are several identified universal spiritual needs (Fukuyama & Sevig, 1992, 1999). The first spiritual need is to develop a meaningful philosophy of life or a purpose for living (Griffith & Rotter, 1999). The second need is to develop a sense of transcendence, the notion of a greater or common good or of life being more important or greater than individual circumstances. The third need is to develop a deep, trustful relationship with a higher power. The fourth need is to develop meaningful relationships with people and nature, and the fifth need is self-actualization. The development of these needs is often conceptualized as a process or journey (Frame & Williams, 1996). Individuals who are farther along in the process of spiritual development are more likely to have a positive outlook on life, a sense of hope and faith, capacity for more intimate relationships and connections, and a sense of optimism. Understanding the spiritual journey may lead to greater self-awareness, consciousness, and a need for service to others (Fukuyama & Sevig, 1999).

Religion is defined as an organized practice of specific belief systems, traditions, institutional expressions of spirituality, and rituals reflective of spiritual beliefs (Dancy & Wynn-Dancy, 1994; Faiver, O'Brien, & Ingersoll, 2000; Frame & Williams, 1996). Religion consists of six components: ritual, doctrine, emotion, knowledge, ethics, and community (Fukuyama & Sevig, 1999). Ritual includes ceremonial behavior and practices, and doctrine includes teachings on the relationship with a higher power. Emotion includes the affective component of spirituality, and knowledge reflects understanding of teachings and principles. Ethics refers to notions of right and wrong, and community refers to psychological, emotional, physical, and social involvement. People with religious faith report higher levels of life satisfaction, personal happiness, social support, and empathy, along with lower levels of depression, blood pressure, and hostility (Griffith & Rotter, 1999). Although religion and spirituality are interconnected, spirituality represents a universal concept, and religion is associated with concrete expressions. Spirituality is personal and subjective, whereas religion tends to be social in nature and is often shared with groups of people or institutions (Standard et al., 2000). It is important to distinguish between people's spirituality and their religious faith or upbringing because some people report feeling spiritual while choosing their own way to worship or display it.

Religious beliefs and practices are an important part of identity development and follow a developmental model in a similar fashion to a spiritual journey. Griffith and Griggs (2001) developed a conceptual framework based on Erikson's and Marcia's identity developmental models. The diffusion religious identity status is characterized by a lack of interest in religion or an externally defined, self-serving form of religion. Individuals may define the relationship with a higher power as an instrumental exchange in which their needs are met. The foreclosure status is defined by conformity or acceptance of religious beliefs to gain acceptance from others. For children, this often includes the tacit acceptance of parental religious beliefs to secure parental approval. Many at this stage may begin to experience a spiritual or religious crisis that highlights the uncritical acceptance or endorsement of beliefs to gain approval. The moratorium status is characterized by an examination period and a critical examination of religious beliefs. This period may also include an exploration of a variety of religious faiths and traditions. The final status, achievement, occurs after the period of questioning and critical examination in moratorium. Here individuals integrate their religious beliefs into their identity and into their spirituality. They become an integral component of life functioning and influence thoughts, actions, and affective experiences. As with other developmental models, individuals can recycle from moratorium to achievement statuses; therefore, it is important for therapists to assess the status level of their clients (Griffith & Griggs, 2001).

Exploring religious beliefs may also lead to understanding culturally specific expressions of spirituality (Fukuyama & Sevig, 1999) and intragroup differences. For some individuals, spirituality is connected to the concept of animism—the belief that there is a universal life force that exists in all things, both animate and inanimate. The belief in spirits or forces leads to a belief in spiritual causes to mental illness or behavioral problems. Some clients will seek indigenous healers, such as shamans, *curanderos*, or faith healers, to find relief for symptoms. Many individuals believe that spirituality is an integral part of the wellness that provides a sense of balance in their lives. There is recognition of the unity of mind, body, and spirit. Many of the wellness models include spirituality along with physical, social, emotional, and mental health. Chandler, Holden, and Kolander (1992) argue, however, that spiritual health needs to be conceptualized as an interactional component of wellness with the other factors. Concentrating on behavioral change in clients without including wellness and spirituality may lead to recidivism of the original symptoms or presenting problems (Chandler et al., 1992).

Finally, it is important to understand that there are both positive and negative components to spirituality and religious practices (Faiver et al.,

2000) and that often people can be harmed or wounded by negative experiences. Some religious tenets or rules can be restrictive of behavior or individual expression. Religious beliefs can foster levels of guilt over behaviors and a sense of worthlessness. Guilt can occur from religious teachings and include negative behaviors, excessive guilty thoughts, and affective experiences, including depression and anxiety (Faiver et al., 2000). Individuals struggling with religiously controversial issues, such as homosexuality and abortion, may also feel wounded by religious tenets (Fukuyama & Sevig, 1999). There are also many positive aspects of religions and spiritual beliefs. Religion can mark rites of passages or developmental or transitional periods of life (Fukuyama & Sevig, 1999). Spiritual beliefs can help individuals cope with trauma, grief and loss, or interpersonal difficulties. Spirituality can also help people find self-worth, meaning, and fulfillment in life and increase physical health.

There are three stories in this section. Frank's story is one of a minister who learns to follow God more closely. As you read his story, notice the change in his religious identity across the life span. Bob's story, in contrast, is one of a minister whose changes in religious identity lead him to leave the ministry to serve in other capacities. Katie's story is about how her religious identity changed because she fell in love with someone of a different faith. All three stories highlight how religion and spirituality intersect with self-concept and psychological functioning.

Ten

Frank's Story

Hearing God's Voice

There are some people whose lives reflect confidence, security, and hope. They seem assured of their future, even when facing circumstances that are confusing, unclear, or uncertain. When pressed, these individuals often discuss how their spirituality and religious beliefs sustain them, how they have a personal relationship with a higher power that gives them strength. For them, religion is not just a set of rituals, traditions, or teachings; it is a vital component of who they are. They are what they believe, and their lives reflect this. Fukuyama and Sevig (1992) discuss individuals who are farther along on their spiritual journeys. They are optimistic, hopeful, and faithful and report comfort with the ebbs and flows of life. They report higher levels of intimacy and connection and an appreciation for reverence, aesthetics, and beauty. They also report higher levels of life satisfaction, personal happiness, social support, and empathy and lower levels of depression, blood pressure, and hostility (Griffith & Rotter, 1999). This first story on religion reflects these principles. Frank is a minister who describes his spiritual and religious development and the intersection of religion with self-concept. Frank reports a close relationship with God and the ability to hear God speaking to him and directing his life. The reader should pay attention to the role of religion in Frank's life and how this relationship influences decisions, values, and expectations. The reader is also invited to pay attention to personal reactions to the religious themes in the story.

Frank's Story

My life is an assimilation of two cultures. I was born and raised in the West Indies Caribbean, and now I live in the United States of America. I am 51 years old. I spent 18 formative, foundational, and fantastic years in the Caribbean culture and at present have spent 33 years in the American culture. But there is a thread that binds both cultures, a common nexus that makes my life journey what it is. It has brought purpose and meaning as to why I was so destined. I speak of the church. The church was and is the nucleus of my cultural development, of my values and belief system and my identity. The Caribbean culture grounded me in the critical areas of my life: family, work, education, church, friendship, and community. The American culture took the grounding of the Caribbean culture and brought clarity to my cultural identity. I left the Caribbean with a small idea of what I thought I was to be careerwise. But it was the American culture (way of life)—you must get it yourself—that brought me to deepen and define my life's purpose.

The Caribbean culture is laid-back, slow. The American culture is fast paced, a rat race. In assimilating both cultures, I have learned to live in the middle—a pace that is necessary for my mental state and ability.

My Caribbean background is most interesting. With a British background (we were a colonial state by England), I learned the value of history, country, honor for the queen (our leader), respect for her governmental representative (governor of the Caribbean), and love for one's country. Because of this background, I was able to have a well-rounded education. I acquired a thorough background in English, math, geography, history (mostly British), biology (science), literature, and religious education. These subjects were drilled into me. Throughout my elementary and secondary education, religious education (the study of the Bible) was at the center.

I attended Baptist elementary and secondary schools and had devotionals each morning, which consisted of two hymns, scripture, and prayer. This deepened my appreciation for the great hymns of the church. My mother plays both the piano and the organ. We grew up with a piano in the house. I can vividly remember gathering around the piano as a family, singing these great hymns. They were so much a part of my life that even after all these years I can still remember all the stanzas of these hymns. Because my father was (and still is) the pastor of the Alpha Baptist Church, I spent my childhood and youth in Sunday school each Sunday and in Vacation Bible School two or three times a year. We attended a special afternoon Sunday school that was held at a neighborhood church. I recall the flannel-graph presentations, the great Bible stories, and the various White teachers. I did not know it then, but I was being deeply grounded in the scriptures, understanding the basic stories and becoming familiar with the major events and persons. One of my favorite Bible characters was and still is Samuel (see 1 Samuel 3:1–10, 19–21). At the Alpha Baptist Church, there were many Sundays when preachers of different ethnicities brought the message. I recall an Indian, a Canadian, and a British preacher; many American White and Black preachers; and preachers from the surrounding Caribbean islands. We grew accustomed to the multicultural flavor from the pulpit. And because my father is a free spirit, we never knew from Sunday to Sunday who would be bringing the message. In fact, when I came to Christ, a White preacher had presented the Gospel message. As I look back over those years, I appreciate very much being exposed to this concept—for the Body of Christ is truly multicultural.

There were three childhood experiences that shaped my identity:

1. When we moved to the elementary school to have church, there were very few members at that time. I recall one Sunday morning having severe earaches. I told my father that I was not up to going to church. He granted me permission to stay home. As I lay in bed, something began to happen to me. An overwhelming feeling came over me. I had an irresistible urge to be in church. Before I knew it, I was getting ready. This urge was so great that I walked the 4 miles to church. My father and mother were surprised to see me. I discovered later that it was the Spirit of God that drove me to the church. It was truly an incredible experience.

2. I recall attending an afternoon worship service of the Caribbean Baptist Union, the name of the group of churches with which our church was affiliated. That afternoon, my father was the scheduled preacher. During the sermon, I was standing outside because a great crowd had gathered. As I stood outside, I could hear my father preaching. Suddenly, something gripped me. I was moved to stop what I was doing. Like a camera zooming in to focus on the desired object, my eyes fell on my

father. For a few moments, I was mesmerized. I said to myself, "My God, my father is truly preaching!" It was a moment that was indelibly etched on my mind. I can still see myself in that mesmerizing moment.

3. I also recall when we moved to the present location of the Alpha Baptist Church, in the initial building for worship. Here a strange phenomenon occurred. When worship was over, as we prepared to leave the church, I stood behind the pulpit. In the presence of my father, my mother, and a few of my siblings, I said these words, "One day, I will preach from this pulpit." I was barely into my teens when these unforgettable words fell from my lips. I did not know at the time what this experience meant.

These three experiences were all so special, so spiritual and intoxicating that they became foundational in my walk with the Lord.

These snapshots were a prelude to the major purpose that the Lord had in mind for me. In August of 1971, after completing my high school education, I had my conversion experience and my call to preach. I was so taken by the message and convicted by the Spirit of God that before I realized it I was standing before the church confessing my sins and surrendering my heart and will to the Savior, Jesus the Christ. I was blown away that day. I never before had such an experience. I could not explain what happened, but I was sure of one thing—I would never be the same again. Many of my friends could not believe what had occurred in my life. They knew my father was a pastor, but my lifestyle was far from that of a Christian. Once they saw how serious and committed I was about my new experience with the Lord, they stopped asking questions. Today, they all call me Rev.

The church was the nucleus of my cultural experience in the Caribbean and still is the nucleus of my experiences in America. All that has happened to me has its roots in this sacred and hallowed community. It was God's plan all along to make me and use me as a preacher and later as a pastor. I had no clue about my career when I completed high school. I thought very little about what I would become. I understood much later that the reason for this lack of direction was because my future was already determined for me. It was God's design to keep me from other areas and interests, so I could be totally committed to what He wanted and had willed for my life. What seemed like a cloudy time, with no sense of direction, was, in reality, a time of preparation and assessing. I recalled that this was a silent time in my life. It was as if I were waiting for something to occur but was uncertain what it was. Then one day my father came to me and asked me if I was interested in going to college. At this point, my life was so empty and seemed so boring and monotonous that something needed to happen. Daddy was asking me if I wanted to go to college in Atlanta, Georgia. He was asking me about my future. I knew nothing about Atlanta, Georgia, or, for that matter, college. I did not have a clue. Because preaching was my calling, Daddy was asking me to pursue my studies in this area. He was asking me to matriculate at a particular seminary.

My appreciation for the church I was able to acquire from the passion of my father and the commitment of my mother. I watched them sacrifice their own money, possessions, and skills and time to build the ministry God had called them to perform. Many of their own automobiles were worn out from transporting members and potential members to the church. They labored untiringly. I saw them with my own eyes give money to pay other people's bills and support families who had children in college. They loved the Lord, and it showed in their care for others.

I was not aware of it but their love, attitude, and faith were being transferred into my heart, mind, and spirit. Much of what I do, believe, and practice today came from their great influence on my life. I am truly the son of Everett and Mary Adams. I believe that my pastoral heart and a passion for God's word I received from my daddy, and my musical tendencies and talent, along with a humble spirit, I got from my mother. I can pick up a song or hymn in a heartbeat. I even try to sing on occasion—one of my mother's great gifts. They love people and the church, and I understand why I do. It was instilled in me in my formative years.

I did not realize that coming to America meant leaving an established culture and migrating to a new and different culture. This was the first reality check I received. When I arrived in Atlanta, I noticed that there were very many Whites in the airport and on my way to the college. Spending time downtown and in the community, I saw more of them. I was thrown aback by all of the Whites. I had grown up in a predominantly Black country. Though many Whites visited as tourists, I usually did not spend much time observing them. My contact with them was very limited. I was accustomed to seeing Blacks in every area of my life—church, school, downtown, hotels, stores, and so on. I did not realize it at the time, but I was experiencing what is called cultural shock. It was a reality check for me. As I traveled to various locations, grocery stores, gas stations, restaurants, and dry good stores, I encountered great numbers of Whites.

They were everywhere. They seemed to be bombarding me and hemming me in from all sides. I could not get away from them. The limited number of Blacks I encountered, no doubt, magnified and intensified my bewildering experience. Only on the campus and in the church—predominantly Black institutions—was I comfortable and relaxed.

I could not turn to anyone because I wasn't sure what was happening to me. I did not feel any anger or hatred toward them, nor did I feel inferior or even segregated or discriminated against. I was mostly threatened by their presence. There were just so many of them—or too many of them. I had just not been accustomed to this kind of cultural interaction.

My experience of cultural shock in Atlanta was probably magnified by two unforgettable experiences I had as a youth in the Caribbean—one in my early youth, the other in my high school years.

When I was about 6 years old, we moved from the house that was left to my mother to my grandparents' house (my father's parents; my mother's parents died before she turned 6 years old, and she was adopted). We were serious about our playtime and outdoor activities. We were adventurous and played all over the area. At the east end of my grandparents' street was a tall wall. It seemed to stretch to the sky, but in reality it was about 12 to 14 feet high and about 3 feet wide. On the top of the wall's surface were broken pieces of glass set in the concrete, and in the middle were steel bars about 3 feet high, also set in the concrete. The steel bars were for the barbwire that was strung onto it—about six rows of the wire from top to bottom. As youth, we were unsure to the danger of this wall. We walked on the wall, seeing who could walk without stepping on the broken glass, while holding on to the wire, avoiding its sharp protruding spikes. At the time, we ignored the potential dangers and unaware as to why such a wall existed. As we followed the wall, we discovered that it was about 3 miles long, running north to south.

Then we noticed a distinct difference between the houses, roads, trees, and yards on either side. The houses on our side were poor looking, rundown; the houses on the other side were elaborate, richer looking. We did not pay much attention to it. We just believed that that was the way it was meant to be. We also noticed that only Whites lived on the other side, while Blacks lived on the poor side.

We then learned that the wall was constructed many years before to separate the natives (Black Caribbeans) from the immigrant Whites from Britain, who had become Caribbeans. It was a shocking discovery—that discrimination and segregation were a reality in our country. That discovery resonated in my spirit. Our lives went on. But today the wall is broken down in strategic places, and the country is independent.

The other experience occurred while I was a student in high school. Among the student body were a few Whites, but they were never treated any differently by most Blacks. One of them told us about a party and invited us to attend. Going to parties was the going thing in that day. When my friends and I arrived, we observed that it was a White party. The friend who ran with us in school responded in a strange manner. He acted like he did not know us and gave us the cold treatment. Our friend felt he was better than us. Needless to say, we did not stay long. We came away from this ordeal confused, angry, disappointed, and sorry for our friend. To say we had mixed emotions is an understatement.

These two experiences were very disturbing, but deep in my spirit I felt that these were the exception rather than the rule. Why do I remember them? I believe because they disturbed and sought to destroy the value and worth I gave to all people. I did not understand it then, but I do now. I had a respect for people, and that respect was not based on their color. It was truly painful and was registered in my memory banks. The reality of what people of color had to deal with was most disturbing.

The early years in America were very challenging. In my college, I lived with African Americans—Blacks from all across the country, from Africa and the Caribbean. The Americans treated me very strange. They asked questions like, "Do you have TV? Do you live in houses? Are there cars in your country? Do you live in huts?" I felt like an alien, and in reality I was—I was in a strange and unfamiliar country.

The proximity of the island to America had a great influence on my formative years—television, movies, food (McDonalds, Kentucky Fried Chicken, Burger King were among the favorites), and clothes. But these were all disconnected from the American culture because these businesses had to adjust to the Caribbean culture, use Caribbean ingredients, and so on. So I was introduced to the culture, but I discovered that living in the culture was an entirely different experience.

I remember thinking that maybe I had made a mistake by coming to America. The weather was entirely different. My first winter was unforgettable, especially because I did not bring an overcoat. I knew nothing about long johns and had never seen real snow, only snow on TV. I did not know it could get so cold. In the Caribbean, 55 degrees is very cold. I knew nothing about using heat. I was accustomed to driving cars on the left side; driving on the right was a traumatic experience. The food was seasoned and prepared differently. The impact of all of these experiences took their toll as I struggled to adjust, but the difficulty did not interfere with my studies. I was able to keep pace in that area.

The cultural lag did not affect my cognition, but it did affect my daily living. That first semester was the longest time of my life. I was truly relieved when my father sent my plane ticket for me to go home for the semester break. It was a break I really needed. It proved to be the difference for the rest of my college career.

My accent was an ongoing challenge, as people tried to understand me and I tried to understand them. They said I talked too fast, so I had to learn to slow down because, as a preacher, communication was most important. I was fortunate that there were two other Caribbean colleagues on campus, and they were able to buffer my trauma.

I also learned that my secondary education was solid. I spent many nights helping others with their writing, mathematics, English, and Greek, just to name a few. I realized how crucial and valuable a foundational educational background was.

In addition to my cultural adjustments in college, I had many, many fears. As a preacher, I was afraid to stand before people and speak. My fears were so great that I would attend chapel services in college on Mondays, Wednesdays, and Fridays, praying that no one would call on me to preside, to offer prayer, or read the scriptures. I was so relieved when others were chosen. I was very fortunate that no one ever called on me.

I recall on Sundays when I attended the Mt. Mariah Baptist Church in Smyrna, Georgia, that we were invited to dinner after church. Usually my pastor and I would attend these affairs. This was the best meal I received each week as a college student. But because I was afraid of simply being in the pulpit, I developed a nervous stomach. When I ate, I had to dismiss myself from the dinner table and proceed to the bathroom. There all of the delicious meal would find its way back up from my stomach. My fears were deep-seated and many times posed a very difficult problem. I read the scripture in church, but because of my fears, I would stumble over the words. Even familiar scriptures like the 23rd Psalm or the beatitudes became a challenging exercise.

One day, my first pastor in Atlanta became very curious about my inability, ineptness, and clumsy liturgical and clergical functions in the pulpit. He asked me point blank, "Have you been called?" (Being called means that the Lord selected an individual for the preaching ministry. It is not something that the person selects; he is selected.) It was a very penetrating question. I had never really thought about my call until he asked. It was a most propitious moment. Fortunately, I wasted no time in responding. I told him emphatically that I was; I went on to say that I was not sure about other areas of my life, but I was very sure that the Lord had called me into the gospel ministry. This was truly a defining moment in my life. My confidence soared, as the reality of God's hand on my life grew to an all-time high. This, however, did not mean that I was over my turbulence because my fears continued. My calling was sure, but the daily challenges of that call still lay heavy on me; overcoming my fears would linger for a number of years.

In fact, this question of being called was asked in 1971. It was in the early 1980s at the First Baptist Church in Frankfort, Kentucky, that I had a recurring dream. This dream terrified me, as well as my wife. I would wake up screaming in a voice that I could never naturally duplicate. The manifestation of a human figure, like the grim reaper, would suddenly appear. It would be moving toward me, and once it stood over me I would break out in this terrifying scream. It was a few years later that the Spirit of the Lord came to me and told me the meaning of this dream. He said that this dream was related to my fear of standing before people. Because I came from a small country church in Georgia to a larger congregation in Frankfort, Kentucky, the reality and trauma of my fear intensified. I knew I was fearful standing in the pulpit each Sunday, but I did not connect my fear with my dream. Once I made this discovery, my dream went away. Though I am not fully over my fear, the one thing that always blessed me was that I never stopped going to the pulpit, preaching, praying, speaking, or reading. No one knew that I was struggling with this fear. It did not polarize me or hinder me from standing. It did, on occasion, hinder my effectiveness. But again, no one knew it. The Lord has kept me. This is why Psalm 27:1 was my favorite verse—it reminded me of my fears and how the Lord helped me to deal with them, especially my major fear. Even after 30 years as a pastor and 33 years as a preacher, I still have my moments.

As I developed, it was clear that the church played a major role in my life. I did not know that this was the beginning of a total change. When I met and married my wife of 28 years, Renee, I had already completed 2 years in the pastoral ministry. Though it was a very small church, the challenge was nonetheless intense. She fit me like a hand in a glove. She was (and is) God's special gift to me. She has brought stability, integrity, and satisfaction to my life and to my ministry. Her role was critical in the 1979 decision to go to First Baptist Church.

The Lord's presence in my life was truly magnified when I came to preach at the First Baptist Church, in Frankfort, Kentucky. I was scheduled to preach the second Sunday in August for a friend. Two weeks before I was to meet my obligation, I received a telephone call from one of the deacons in Frankfort. They wanted me to come the same Sunday (second Sunday in August). I told the deacon that I already had an appointment and that they should reschedule me. My wife heard me and called me on the carpet. She told me to call the deacon back and tell him that I would accept the invitation. Then she told me to call my friend and tell him to reschedule me. I did so.

On the second Sunday in August 1979, I came to preach at the First Baptist Church. The side entrance was open, so my wife, my son, and I went in. The entrance led us into the educational section. My wife and son remained behind as I took the time to observe the sanctuary. As I walked into this beautiful sanctuary with its high ceiling, I heard something that would change my life forever. I heard the voice of God. He spoke to me! Now this was not an audible voice. But God spoke to my mind or in my spirit. He said to me, "You will be the next pastor!" I had never before in my life had such an experience. And when I heard the voice, there was no hesitation on my part. There was no doubt in my mind what I heard. And what I heard, I believed. I was dumbfounded. Then I walked into the vestibule. I noticed on the wall a plaque with all the names of the former pastors. Then it happened again. I heard the voice one more time. It said, "Your name will be next!" It blew me away! Again, I had no doubt. I was very sure that what the voice said to me would come true. Following that experience, the Lord used me to bless His people with His word. The church agreed that I should return. I did so for the next 4 months. It was on the first Sunday in February 1980 that they called me to be their pastor. It was truly awesome! What God said to me came to pass. I would have missed this important step in my development and ministry if it were not for God's voice and presence in my wife's life. He used her to help me be the preacher and pastor He knew I needed to be. This unique experience in my life was another defining moment. From then on, I heard God speak to me from time to time. My faith and confidence grew to an all-time high. My cultural identity had brought greater awareness and a more authentic and profound faith. I would grow another few inches in my walk with the Lord. Awesome!

That second Sunday experience made quite an impression on me. I was so sure that I would be the next pastor of the church that I went to the church I had been serving with as pastor and resigned the next Sunday. The next day, I called a potential employer. In a few weeks, they hired me as an editor of church literature. This one Sunday experience changed my life totally. I had given up my first pastorate and changed jobs. The church was central in my life's pursuits because the Lord had chosen to use me in this special way. I worked in a fast-food restaurant before being hired at the publishing board. But though I was the chief cook, I never—I said never—worked on Sundays. And in the restaurant business, Sunday is the biggest day. But again, my cultural identity was my guide and my gauge. It was becoming much clearer to me that it was the very foundation and fruit of my life. There have been a few challenges in my ministry. I recall on the first Sunday in February 1990 I received a small raise from the First Baptist Church and a 2-year extension on my position as pastor. I was very upset and decided to leave the church and go to another. In looking back, I see I overreacted. I sent out letters to potential churches and waited for their reply. (In the Baptist Church, candidates for the pastoral office communicate their interest in the pastorate by sending a letter of interest.)

After a few months, I heard from a vacant church in Oklahoma City, Oklahoma. They scheduled for me to preach in May of that same year. My wife and I flew to the city that Saturday and arrived in time for an interview (which I felt went very well). We were given a tour of the facilities. It was a new structure and a very beautiful building. On that Sunday, we attended Sunday school and morning worship. I taught the Sunday school lesson for that Sunday and brought the morning message. It was truly an awesome experience.

When we came away from that experience, my wife and I believed that this was where the Lord was leading us. In June, we were invited again. This time we drove from Kentucky to Oklahoma. Again, all went well. A few weeks later, a small delegation from the Oklahoma City church came to investigate my ministry in Frankfort, Kentucky. It was a very uncomfortable day because most of the members knew why they had come to worship with us. Somehow we made it through. The church was to call a pastor in a few weeks. I waited and waited and did not hear anything. So I decided to call. I discovered that the business manager of the church (one of the delegates who had come to Frankfort) and the others had given "an evil report" on me. They told the church that they were treated with disrespect and that my family and I were very rude and unkind to them. This, of course, was further from the truth. I recall being kind to them, even giving them extra food for their travel back to Oklahoma City. Then I learned later from one of the members that the business manager had called his own pastor for the job, and I was out of the picture.

As I pondered these events, the Lord came to converse with me. I will never forget what He said to me. He told me that He never gave me permission to go to Oklahoma City. He had nothing to do with it. He said that I took matters into my own hands and went ahead of Him. In fact, He told me that He had nothing to do with the whole experience. Then He went on to say that He should have permitted the church to call me. He told me that He should have allowed me to be the next pastor, so I could fall flat on my face. Then He said to me, "But I saved you from that tragedy. I will grant you my grace. But don't you ever try anything like this again. If you do, you will live to regret it."

I remember thanking Him for being so gracious and kind to me. And I recall saying, "Lord, I will never do anything like this again. If you want me to stay in Frankfort, Kentucky, for the rest of my life, I am prepared to do so. I will go where You want me to go. I will do what You want me to do. Wherever You lead, I will follow."

This was truly a humbling experience. And I learned a very important lesson—my life was not mine; it belonged to the Lord. He was the One who would determine where I would do ministry, and He was the One who would determine when and how I would do that. If this was not enough, when the Murrah Federal Building was bombed in Oklahoma City in 1995, the Lord told me "that He would have fixed it for me to be in that building." I was truly thankful for His grace. And my faith in Him went up another notch.

In was in June of 1991 that the Lord came to speak to me again. I had sent a letter of interest to two churches—one in Anderson, Indiana, the other in Chicago, Illinois. I only did so because a friend kept pestering me to do it. To be rid of him, I sent the letters. I did not expect to get a call. I was only trying to get rid of the constant annoyance about sending these letters. But on the last Sunday in June, my telephone rang. On the other end was the chairman of the board of deacons. He said to me that the church had received my letter, and they needed more information on me and three letters of reference. As I was hanging up the phone, I heard that voice in my ear—it was the voice of the Lord. He told me that I had better get ready, He was sending me to the Peace Baptist Church in Chicago, Illinois. I was blown away. But I knew it was the Lord because I had heard that voice many times. My wife and I were scheduled to leave for the

Caribbean that Monday. So I hurried to get my information together and was able to secure three letters of reference. It was truly amazing.

I want you to know that from June of 1991 to January of 1992, the Lord kept speaking to me and confirming in my spirit that I was to be the next pastor of the Peace Church. They did call me to be their next pastor. This was an incredible experience. Waiting for this to happen was very easy because almost every week the Lord spoke to me in some special way, confirming His direction for my life. From June to January is 7 months, but it was the Lord who helped me stay focused. I learned from Psalm 27:14 that "those who wait on the Lord, He shall strengthen their hearts." This is exactly what the Lord did. He kept me on track with His words of direction. Needless to say, this was among the most extraordinary experiences of my life. I never dreamt that the Lord would speak to me in this way. And, as I write these words, it has been 12 years since I was called to serve the Peace Church. God has been and is true to His Word. You do know, of course, that my faith in God grew to another level. I could not believe that God would bless such an insignificant and dispensable individual as me. He had favored me. But He has made it very clear that it was not about me—it was all about Him. He blessed me so that I could give Him the glory due unto His name. Awesome!

Two other experiences have occurred since I was called to serve the Peace Baptist Church. One had to do with obeying God and not man. The Lord told me to start a new program. But I could not vote on it. Opposition arose. A group of members met with me and asked me to resign from the church. They said that they would give me a reasonable pay plan and help me move. I told them that I would not.

My future seemed in jeopardy. But nothing became of this meeting because it was unofficial. But I prayed, and the Lord sent me four confirmations that following week. A card, a special cup with an affirming message on it, a telephone call, and a couple who bought me a suit and a pair of shoes. These affirming responses by the Lord were accelerating. The other had to do with prayer. I was invited to offer prayer at the city hall before the city hall members began their regular bimonthly meetings. As I completed my prayer, I closed by saying, "In Jesus' name, I pray. Amen." There was a little commotion about what I said. In the newspaper the next day, it was reported that I had prayed in Jesus' name. It was as though I had done something wrong. I was being made an example of because of my faith. I came away more determined never to deny my Lord or my faith, if anyone asks. As a resource, I was able to gain strength from God's word and from Neil Anderson's book *The Bondage Breaker.* I was able to turn to my pastor for guidance and direction. With a graduate degree in clinical psychology, and with more than 20 years of pastoral experience, he was able to give some sound and solid counsel. I discovered anew the importance of having a pastor and the importance of professional pastoral counseling. You are aware that my faith grew to another level.

God has helped me in many ways, but let me share one major experience with you. In July of 1996 my youngest brother died from complications with his blood pressure, which led to him contracting pneumonia. In fact, members of the Alpha Baptist Church were visiting our church, and they were preparing to leave for home the next day. I drove home after securing them, and when I drove up to my home, two cars were parked in the driveway. When I walked in, a deacon and the assistant to the pastor were sitting in the living room. When I saw them, I thought my father had passed, but after conversing I learned that it was my 35-year-old brother.

I communicated with my parents, and we grieved together as we remembered my brother and their son. I flew to the Caribbean after being made aware of funeral arrangements. We all gathered the day before to view and inspect the remains of my brother. Those moments we spent in the funeral home felt like a lifetime. We mourned, wept, and grieved as we saw him. The memories abounded as we sat and reminisced.

The next day, the service was to take place at the church. My father assigned me to bring the eulogy. I remember spending the days before in God's word. I recalled when the Lord confirmed the scripture that I was to use for the basis of my message. That scripture was Psalm 27:13–14. It is a very familiar passage. As I prepared my message, I remembered how that scripture began to minister unto me. It gave me so much comfort, strength, and peace. The more its points and principles unfolded, the stronger I became. And when I delivered that message ("God's Prescription for Our Pain"), I was truly strengthened. I couldn't believe it: The word of God has grounded me and lifted me. As I thought about my family, I felt a little bad because I had received so much from God's word. I remembered praying how good it would have been for my family if they had had the opportunity I had. God's word brought me through. I did not break at all during that time. It was not until a few weeks later, as I was sharing with my wife a minor detail about my brother, that the tears began to flow. But even that was a catharsis.

The final experience I will share has to do with my immigration and naturalization status. The decision about this status was again based on my cultural identity. When I got married, I applied for permanent residency in the United States. This immigration status would allow me to live and work in America and maintain my citizenship in the Caribbean.

My wife and I flew to the Caribbean to finalize my status. When we arrived and checked on my status, we discovered that we were missing some very important papers. This meant that my wife had to return to the United States without me. It took about three additional weeks for this status to be granted. It was a very stressful, anxious time full of tension and trepidation. My wife returned home reluctantly and in tears. But it proved to be an important time for us because it brought us even closer together.

So significant was my desire to be totally involved in the life of my congregation in Chicago that I was moved to become a U.S. citizen. This compulsion grew out of the need to be more involved in the political and social processes. Giving guidance and direction to others without being a citizen became a serious problem for me. I was uncomfortable telling others about participating in our community, when I did not have the proper credentials to do so. In July 1994, I became a citizen of this country. I had assistance with the application process by a very capable and caring citizen, who guided me through the whole procedure. It took me about a year of preparation and actually applying before I heard from Immigration and Naturalization Services. I appeared in federal court downtown Chicago, along with a number of other persons of various citizenry.

My parents came from the Caribbean, and many dignitaries and special friends from the community were present at the awesome celebration that was held that night at the church. I was overwhelmed by their support, and I shouted and thanked the Lord for again favoring me as He had done many times in the past. The following things have made a difference in my life:

1. A strong faith and confidence in God

2. The power of prayer—God's answers

3. The importance of associating with others of similar beliefs, who reinforce my commitment

4. The ability to counsel others, using the presence of God's spirit in my life

5. The strong support and stability from my lovely wife and precious family. (I am truly blessed. My wife and I are raising eight children, three of our son's

children, four adopted children, and a special daughter, who was graciously given to us by two of our grandchildren's mother. This blended family has taught me much about love, relationships, honesty, truth, discipline, and the value of a loving and peaceful home. This is interesting because I am from a family of 13 siblings. I am the fifth child and the third son. I guess what I experienced as a youth was so special that I have tried to duplicate it. Like my father and mother, who had no miscarriages and no twins, I am blessed with a special family. I thank God for each of them. Awesome!)

Content Themes

Frank's story describes a life that is not only influenced by but is guided by religion and a relationship with God. Frank describes an intimate and trusting relationship with God, the third spiritual need (Fukuyama & Sevig, 1992). Most of the adult decisions in Frank's life have been guided by God and serve as a demonstration of Frank's ability and willingness to be led. Frank was socialized into the Baptist faith as a child because his father and other extended family members served as ministers or religious leaders. These experiences, along with his religious training, shaped his cultural or religious identity. It is clear that religion has served as both a source of strength and a resource for Frank. His religion has also helped him to fulfill a calling and to develop a sense of fulfillment in his life and work.

Relationship With God

Most of the major religious faiths include a higher power, a deity that is in charge of human life and nature. The relationship with a higher power can provide strength and comfort, provide answers to life's challenges and dilemmas, and provide a sense of hope and faith. Fukuyama and Sevig (1992) identify this relationship as an important spiritual need and emphasize the nature of trust that exists in the relationship as important. The importance and influence of God in an individual's life is the first content theme in Frank's story. Frank's relationship with God changed as he grew and developed. As a young child, Frank was socialized into religion by his family through family devotions, church attendance, Sunday school, and vacation Bible school. His relationship with God also has early roots, although he may not have been able to articulate it as a child. He was often led by the Spirit to engage in particular activities. Frank describes three early experiences: being led to attend church despite being sick that morning, recognizing and feeling his father preaching during a service, and announcing that he would someday preach from the pulpit. Although he did not fully comprehend these experiences at the time they were occurring, it is clear to him as an adult that he was being led and directed by the Spirit.

Frank continued to grow in his relationship with God as an adolescent and adult. As he was reaching the developmental stages of completing identity and selecting a career, his relationship with God continued to grow and change. It was during high school that he completed his conversion experience and received the call to preach. It is interesting that although he knew he was being saved and receiving the call, he was still not completely sure of the situation. Although he was not certain of the direction, the socialization and training he received allowed him to be confident that his future was secure. As Frank's relationship with God continued to grow during young adulthood, the direction for his life that God gave was revealed more clearly to him. One pivotal moment came when a pastor asked if he was confident that he had been called, and he responded emphatically that he had been called. Finally, as Frank's relationship became stronger and as his identity became more secure, the guidance from God was more direct. He clearly describes his first experience with hearing God's voice, when he was serving as a guest preacher at a church. When he walked into the sanctuary, he heard God tell him he would be the next pastor of the church. This experience was almost replicated when he received his final placement, and God's messages to him were confirmed through other experiences. His ability to listen and heed God's voice demonstrates not only the significance of the relationship but also Frank's willingness to be molded and shaped by it.

Submission in Religion

The next important theme in Frank's story that is present in many individuals with strong religious faiths is submission. Many clinicians are familiar with the notion of submission or surrender because it is the first step in Alcoholics Anonymous and other self-help groups. The ability to release control, acknowledge weaknesses and limitations, is for many the first step or direction to change. Frank's story is full of experiences related to the development of the ability to be submissive to God and to religious teachings. The most powerful point in the story related to this theme is when Frank overreacted, or reacted from a personal stance, and decided to leave the First Baptist Church. He describes the interview process and his feeling that the Lord had approved his decision to leave the church. However, this move was not directed by God and proved to be a mistake for Frank, although a valuable learning experience about the importance of submitting to God's will. From that point forward, Frank learned to listen more carefully to God's voice and follow God's direction for his life.

There are several benefits from leading a surrendered life or being submitted: a sense of calling, a sense of fulfillment, and confidence in the future. One of the existential needs is a need to develop a sense of purpose or meaning in life (Fukuyama & Sevig, 1999). Many individuals question the purpose of life and their place in the world. Learning to be surrendered or submitted provides that sense of purpose and direction for people. It is clear that when Frank received his calling his life began to have more purpose and meaning. Being surrendered provides direction for vocational or career choices and allows individuals to experience direction for volunteer and charitable services and for marriage and child rearing. The second benefit to being surrendered is the sense of fulfillment that occurs. The existentialists discuss the process of self-actualization, a sense of personal fulfillment. People who live surrendered lives report not only understanding a purpose in their lives but also a sense of fulfillment for being aligned with their purpose. This is a repeated message in Frank's story—that as he continues to grow with God and understand his purpose his sense of fulfillment and joy continues. The third benefit is the sense of confidence in the future that comes from being surrendered. In Alcoholics Anonymous, Steps 2 and 3 refer to the power of surrendering. (Step 2: Came to believe that a Power greater than ourselves could restore us to sanity. Step 3: Made a decision to turn our will and our lives over to the care of God as we understood Him.) Surrendering control of life to a power that is greater provides a source of confidence. Frank learned to be more confident and was able to wait for God to provide both direction and confirmation in his life.

Religion as a Strength or Resource

The final theme in Frank's story is the role of religion as a strength and a resource. Religious teachings can help people resolve depressive and anxiety symptoms. Frank experienced social anxiety, particularly a fear of public speaking. He was anxious about reading scriptures and praying in his college years and speaking publicly in the beginning of his preaching ministry. His anxiety was so great that he would often have a "nervous stomach." It was after he reaffirmed his ministerial calling that his confidence grew and he was able to begin to overcome his fears. He later had a terrifying recurring nightmare, but through God's interpretation of the dream, he was able to diminish the fear.

Religion can provide comfort during times of loss and grief. Religious teachings on the afterlife and the role of man in relationship to God can be a source of encouragement. When Frank lost a younger brother, his relationship with God and his religious beliefs helped him to handle his grief; they provided strength even as he prepared for and delivered the eulogy. It is interesting that the same scripture served as a resource for dealing with the anxiety of public speaking and with his loss.

Clinical Applications

This section explores the clinical implications of Frank's story for counselors, including assessment of the importance of religion and a relationship with a higher power, techniques and interventions to use in treatment, and countertransference concerns.

Assessment

Frank's story suggests that clinicians need to assess three important areas in religion and spirituality for clients: the relationship with a higher power, existential concerns, and spirituality as a strength. The following questions are recommended.

Relationship With a Higher Power

Do you have a relationship with God (a higher power)?

Does this relationship serve as a resource, source of support, or comfort?

Do you feel positively connected to God (a higher power)?

Are there times when you have felt abandoned or neglected by God (a higher power)?

Existential Questions

Have you asked yourself these questions: Who am I? What is the meaning of life?

What is the purpose of my life?

How do your religious beliefs help you to answer or address these questions?

Do you experience a sense of fulfillment or peace? What are the conditions that contribute to these feelings?

Religion as Strength

Has your religion served as a source of strength?

Has your spirituality or religious beliefs helped you during times of crisis?

Has your spirituality, religious beliefs, or relationship with God (a higher power) provided comfort for depression or anxiety?

Techniques and Interventions

When working with people with strong religious faiths, it is often important to consult with religious leaders for clinical treatment. Consultation can be valuable to therapists for a number of reasons. First, scripture, religious teachings, and doctrine can serve as resources for the presenting problems of clients. Frank, for example, discussed how several scriptures provided comfort for him. It would be impossible for clinicians to have a good command of the teachings from all religious groups; consulting with a religious leader can provide assistance in this area. Second, most religious institutions and congregations can serve as a resource for financial, physical, and spiritual needs. Congregations can provide money, food, and emergency shelter services, and members of institutions can provide a sense of accountability for individuals who need reinforcement for changes made in clinical treatment. Many churches, mosques, and synagogues provide self-help groups that can reinforce therapy goals. Finally, many individuals consult religious leaders before or in conjunction with their search for clinical services. Consultation will help to provide continuity of services. Therapists should help clients address their relationship with God. The development of a trusted relatedness with a higher power is a spiritual need (Fukuyama & Sevig, 1992). As with any relationship, clients may experience times of anger or frustration with the higher power. For example, Frank found comfort in his relationship with God after the loss of his brother. One of us, Anita, worked with a client whose son had been tragically killed in an automobile accident. The client entered treatment for her depressive symptoms in relation to the death. When asked about her relationship with God, the client expressed an extreme amount of hostility with God over what she felt was a betrayal of her trust and love for Him. She also felt an extreme amount of guilt over her anger but felt that her anger was too strong to deny. The client was encouraged to read Bible passages reflecting individuals' anger and frustration and to note God's responses to anger. She was encouraged to discuss her anger with her priest and to join a support group on her loss. If the therapist had not asked directly about her relationship with God, she may not have helped her to completely or appropriately grieve the loss of her son. The loss for her also changed her perceptions of her role as mother and her life purpose. Again, the discussion of her relationship with God and the meaning of her son's death in relationship to her life helped her to move forward in understanding her purpose.

Clinicians should invite clients to bring scriptures to or share teachings and doctrines during the sessions. Clinicians can respond to the themes present in the teachings and use them to reinforce coping strategies. Clinicians may be confused about how to relate to the discussion of a higher power, from knowing how to address this power to understanding the client's relationship with the power. Griffith and Rotter (1999) discuss constraints in therapy around introducing discussions of God: proscriptive constraints, which prevent discussions of God from occurring, and prescriptive constraints, which limit the level of discussion. Clinicians should help clients to critically examine scriptures. They may also help clients find scriptures on love, forgiveness, marriage, anxiety, courage, faith, patience, and so on.

Countertransference

Stories like Frank's that unfold in clinical offices may provide a variety of reactions for counselors. Therapists often have strong reactions to religious dialogue presented in treatment, both positive and negative. Some therapists embrace the opportunity to discuss religion and see it as part of a holistic focus of treatment. Other therapists feel overwhelmed by the discussion of religion, particularly if they were not raised with a particular religious faith or practice. As with any other issue, clinicians must very carefully examine their reactions and monitor them, so they do not disrupt the treatment progress or therapeutic relationship. The countertransference issues presented in this story include difficulty integrating spirituality and religion into the treatment, issues involving discussions of God in the conversation, lack of comfort with personal spirituality, lack of knowledge of doctrine or teachings, and concerns that clients are rigidly holding onto beliefs or using religion as a crutch.

Discomfort With Religious Discussions

Historically, psychotherapists have been trained to treat psychology and religion as separate disciplines and have not included religion as part of the therapeutic process. Some counselors may be uncomfortable introducing religion, religious identity, and its influence into treatment for a variety of reasons. First, most of the ethical codes for social services professions prohibit professionals from imposing their values. Professionals may fear that introducing spirituality will cause clients undue anxiety or cause clients to fear that the therapist is attempting to proselytize the client (Walsh, 1999). Therapists should feel comfortable asking clients about their religion and including it in treatment, however. The introduction of the topic does not lead to attempts for either party to indoctrinate others on beliefs if appropriate boundaries are maintained. Therapists also may feel that spirituality and religion have no place in treatment because the primary focus should be on the role of behaviors or cognitions. Many individuals, however, do not have the concept of mind–body duality. Many religious faiths include the notion of body, mind/soul, and spirit. To ignore spirituality would be to ignore a major component of clients' lives (Fukuyama & Sevig, 1999). Wellness models include spirituality as well, and therapists who wish to engage in holistic treatment should include it despite their concerns about introducing the topic. Therapists should feel encouraged that the field is becoming more accepting of therapy in treatment; the latest edition of the *Diagnostic and Statistical Manual* (American Psychiatric Association, 2000) includes a discussion of religious identity (Walsh, 1999).

Discussions of religion with individuals with strong religious beliefs and convictions may also cause clinicians some discomfort, particularly clinicians who have unanswered questions about their own beliefs or their relationship with God. Therapists may feel inadequately prepared to address clients' concerns and feel as if they do not know doctrine or teachings well enough to be able to aid clients. As with any situation in which the therapist is less knowledgeable than the client, the counselors should allow the clients to lead the discussion and educate the counselor.

Differences in Religious Beliefs

Finally, therapists may have concerns that clients are rigidly holding onto beliefs or that they are using religion as a crutch. For example, a client facing a terminal disease may choose to deny medical treatment and pray for healing. Therapists may feel that clients are not working actively enough to engage in alternative treatment strategies because clients may insist that their faith and beliefs are enough. Clinicians may experience an ethical dilemma between respecting the client's autonomy and choice to wait for a higher power and intervening by encouraging self-direction for clients. Clinicians again are encouraged to consult with religious leaders about these issues. There may be times when clients become immobilized with fear and cannot think beyond their beliefs or times when clients are misinterpreting scripture. Religious leaders may be able to help clients expand coping skills and strategies.

TOOLBOX ACTIVITY—FRANK		
Discussion Questions	*Activities*	*Resources*
Content themes What other themes do you see emerging in the story that the author did not identify? **Assessment** Are there any questions you would like to ask Frank? **Interventions** What other interventions could you propose with Frank? **Countertransference** What countertransference reactions were emerging in yourself as you read this story? **Other scenarios** Imagine that Frank is coming to you several years ago or several years from now with a presenting problem. Imagine what that presenting problem could be. How might his religious identity have changed?	Research the difference between religion and spirituality. Write an essay examining how Frank's experience would have been different if he had been more spiritual than religious. Make a list of neighborhood or community clergy. Compile a list of resources offered by neighborhood religious services. Interview clergy about their religious teachings and perspectives on counseling.	**Suggested readings** Frame, M. W. (2002). *Integrating religion and spirituality into counseling: A comprehensive approach*. New York: Wadsworth. Fukuyama, M. A., & Sevig, T. D. (1999). *Integrating spirituality into multicultural counseling*. Thousand Oaks, CA: Sage. Richards, P. S., & Bergin, A. E. (1997). *A spiritual strategy for counseling and psychotherapy*. Washington, DC: American Psychological Association. Walsh, F. (1999). *Spiritual resources in family therapy*. New York: Guilford.

Eleven

Bob's Story

The Good Christian Son

In Bob's story we read about how he views himself in terms of his cultural identity and the shifts that occurred in his religious life as a result of family relationships, his move from the South to the Northeast, and his rethinking about his role in society and in his family. He also talks about what influenced his first career choice as a minister in an Evangelical Christian church and what accounted for the choice of his second career as a teacher. As you read, pay attention to his shifts in personality traits and in his understanding of his religious affiliation and other shifts in his cultural identity.

Bob's Story

I must admit from the outset that I was somewhat surprised that someone would even be interested in my story. What I mean by that is, when it comes to culture, I have often thought that my life was somewhat void of it. I'm just another White guy with a job, two children, and a wife. I have nothing special to offer in the way of a story, right? Upon further reflection, however, I have come to realize that one's cultural heritage is not about being impressive or unique. Rather, each person's history is more significant than he or she could ever imagine—at least to them and those with whom they come in contact. So what follows is a sort of snapshot of my life from a cultural and especially spiritual identity standpoint.

I was born in south central Kentucky in a town that had no hospital. My mother and father had to travel several miles to access the needed medical assistance for my birth. This was not seen as a hardship or even an inconvenience, just how things were. My mother was the daughter of a farmer and a homemaker. She was the youngest of 10 children, 7 daughters and 3 sons. My father was from another town in Kentucky. His father was a professional in the trucking industry, and his mother taught music. My father met my mother while he was a college student in music education. He was also the music director of the small rural Southern Baptist church where my mother was a member. My mother's ethnic background was Scottish and Welsh. Her maiden name reflects that heritage. My father's ethnic heritage was Dutch and English. I cannot say that these historical roots made any significant contributions to my cultural heritage. Both of my parents seemed to prefer the notion that they were "American," and that was all that was necessary to them.

In the region of Kentucky I grew up in, people tended to be either Baptist or "unbelievers." Being an unbeliever meant you did not believe the standard tenets of the Christian faith regarding Jesus, but, most important, being an unbeliever meant you were going to hell. This was not a happy proposition—eternal burning in a lake of fire, gnashing of teeth, and so on.

The Evangelical Christian faith was a significant part of both of my parents' lives from early on. It would prove to be a powerful influence in mine as well. I learned as a child that one's faith was an integral part of decision making. The question of what God's will was in a given situation or relationship was a constant quest: "Does God want my father to take that job?" "Would God be pleased if I were to date this girl?" On and on it went. As a young person, I couldn't help but wonder if God was really all that interested in such miniscule items in light of world hunger, war, and other such global challenges. However, the Bible speaks of God knowing the "number of hairs on your head." In light of that, my older brother and I were taught that God was therefore interested in every detail of our lives. I had friends who literally prayed for good parking places! Interwoven into this Christian heritage was the fact that I was a White male Southerner. I have extended family members who still characterize the Civil War as "the war of Northern aggression." There was significant pride in being born and raised south of the Mason-Dixon Line. I was taught that those to the north were not to be automatically trusted because of how they had treated us throughout history.

Exposure to persons of color was nearly nonexistent in my upbringing. My family was White. My community was White. My church family was White. In fact, my house was White! Appreciation for cultural diversity was not an intentional part of my upbringing. It came through the back door, so to speak. It came through the arts. I remember growing up in my White neighborhoods and being the only person who knew of Black musicians like Sammy Davis, Jr., Ray Charles, and Nat King Cole. I also knew of Latino musicians, such as Chita Rivera and Tito Fuente. My parents listened to music from different parts of the world, and, as a result, I grew to appreciate sounds that most of my friends did not even know existed. I believe that this exposure made me aware of a world beyond the South. My parents' appreciation for these artists taught me that beauty and talent are to be appreciated, regardless of its origin.

My father eventually left church music and began to teach music in the public schools. My parents listened to music and loved to watch old movies. I was exposed to various art forms at a very early age and began to gain an appreciation for music from around the world. Along with that, my parents had a commitment to treating all people with respect, regardless of skin color. This view was unique compared with the view of many of my friends. However, there was a merging of my ethnic and regional identity and my spiritual formation that is still difficult for me to distinguish at times. The world around me was seen through so many filters that it became difficult to determine the legitimacy of almost any perspective I adopted. Was I seeing things in a particular way because I was told to? Was I seeing things that way because I wanted to please those around me? These were questions that were nearly impossible for me to answer.

Interestingly, it was evident to me that while my older brother completely embraced his identity as a Southerner, he did not seem to embrace this quest for God's will. He was a person of fierce independence—much to my parents' chagrin. He engaged in all the significant no-no's that we were taught to avoid—smoking, drinking, dancing, card playing, and enjoying the opposite sex. I was not nearly as interested in what I was missing by not doing those things as I was concerned about the pain that my parents were experiencing as they began to conceptualize themselves as failures as parents. My mother and father could not understand why my brother, who is 4 years my senior, would not respond to their directions or change his behaviors in light of their sometimes harsh punishments. In fact, their hearts were breaking. I knew I could not do the same thing to them.

Thus, I decided to become the ideal Southern Christian son. I did well in school, attended church regularly, was involved in extracurricular activities such as sports and drama club, and held down a part-time job. I graduated as president of my senior class and was motivated to attend a southern state university my father and grandfather had attended.

During college I began to seriously consider my career options. What did God want me to do with my life? What would please my parents? Later I came to learn that these questions would be almost identical in my conceptualization of them. Ministry seemed like the most obvious choice for a career. God would be happy. My parents would be happy. My brother's deficits would be compensated for. My happiness was not a concern aside from how well I was meeting the expectations of others. As I look back at this time in my life, I can see where I was being driven by a culture of pleasing God and family, everyone but oneself. This self-deprivation was seen as humble and servantlike.

In point, it became clear to me upon reflection that many of my White Christian peers in the South experienced the same lack of personal agency and integrity. I might have disliked a person or disagreed with him or her, but that person would likely never know it. I was so consumed with being "nice" that how I really felt or what I really thought were altogether lost and unimportant. This inevitably led to forming inauthentic relation-ships. I did not feel the freedom or have the courage to interact with another honestly if there was a chance that the person might not like me or might not approve of me. Thus, my relationships could not be built honestly. It wasn't until later that I began to realize that it was only when my identity was based on authentic thoughts and feelings that relation-ships could be meaningful and fulfilling. My mother's death was a signif-icant factor in this shift of character.

It was too risky to not be seen as the good Christian son, so I never thought much about what I wanted. What if what I wanted wasn't Christian or, better yet, wasn't perceived as Christian to those to whom I relinquished my locus of control?

I majored in religious studies in college and after graduation went on to seminary where I received a Master of Divinity. I knew during my stud-ies that the field was not for me, but what could I do? Could I turn my back on God, my family? The time of study, while interesting, became uninteresting to me. I began to feel like I was the wrong person in the wrong place because the priorities of the people around me were not similar to my own. Although I might agree that the issues were important, they were not issues for which I wanted to dedicate my life, personally and professionally. However, because of my continuing fears of what others might think, I completed the degree and worked in congregational ministry for 12 years. I was never happy, but I was always faithful, or so I thought. The most pivotal moment that served as an important challenge to my culture of pleasing others and Christian fundamentalism came at the untimely death of my mother. She was 60 years old and had suffered a major heart attack. I was serving at a church 90 miles from home in a big city in Kentucky when I was called about her hospitalization. During the drive, I spent substantial time praying and asking God to heal my mother. I was confident that one like me who had sacrificed so much for God and family could expect that God would answer my prayers. After all, hadn't I completed a degree that I disliked and been involved in work that I hated for some time now? It was all for Him. He owed me!

My mother was not healed, and her death shook me. It shook my understanding of faith as well as family. I had never realized how matriarchal my family was. My mother led the family, and she often did so through guilt and manipulation. Who would lead us now? Who would dole out affirmation in accordance to our good behavior? Where would our sense of self-esteem come from now?

I became angry. I was angry at God, and I was angry at the church. My ministry at the church began to dissolve, and my wife and I moved to New York City for her to pursue graduate education. I worked for a while in computer and book sales. I was lost.

My name was given to a church in the New York area, and I took the position of minister because I believed I didn't know how to do anything else. Besides, shouldn't that put me back in God's good graces? Even though the church was made up of White, Christian, transplanted Southerners, things were not what I hoped they would be. The parishioners at this church were people like those with whom I had grown up. They were in the New York area because of career or educational opportunities, but they had not allowed themselves to become integrated into the culturally diverse surroundings that New York offered. They were seeking others like themselves with whom to worship. Within a year of starting at the church, I was unhappy again and found myself looking at classified ads. My wife encouraged me to seek counseling during the time, and I did so. I was forced to ask questions that challenged my understanding of God and how people make decisions. I was forced to answer a question that I had never allowed myself to ask before: "What did I want?" In my cultural understanding of spiritual self, this question had never been an important one. What I wanted was totally unimportant. In fact, it was something to be ignored or changed to please God and family.

I came to learn that what I loved about ministry was service, but what I struggled with was church hierarchy and spiritual oppression. The gifts that I had been given—effective communication and the desire to help others—transitioned well into teaching. I was able to do something meaningful, but I was free within it. This was new territory for me. I must admit that I still struggle with pleasing others, but I have come to learn that such influences are much more about my own history than with a God who is looking for ways to judge me.

Being a person of faith still serves me. Although the negative aspects motivated significant pain and dissonance, positive aspects of my faith, such as hope, justice, and service to others, have become quite valuable to me. These components of my faith help foster appreciation for what I have and a sense of mission to help those in need. Although this service is no longer motivated by my desire to prove my worth or please others, it is still a vitally important piece of who I am.

Further, my Southern heritage is also valuable. I was raised with very few luxuries and had to work very hard on family farms. The work ethic I was given has challenged me to try to earn the things I receive and not feel entitled to them.

Also, the commitment to family that I was taught, albeit somewhat unhealthy at times, has been tempered through the years with clear boundaries and emotional separation, which enables me to be a more effective husband and father. I have taken my family down home to Kentucky on several occasions and have shown my sons the little house where I was raised in a small town in Kentucky. They have seen the Confederate flags, and I have been able to teach them about the dangers of hatred and prejudice. They have seen my mother's grave, and I have been able to teach them about love and commitment to family.

I believe that I am nowhere near the same person culturally as a resident in New York City that I was as a child in a small town in Kentucky. Yet my skin color, family of origin, and Scottish and Welsh bloodlines remain the same.

Content Themes

There are two important content themes in Bob's story as he describes his religious identity development. The first theme is the socialization to religion that he experienced not only from his family but also from his community and the region in which he was raised. The second theme is his shift from a fundamentalist Evangelical perspective to his own sense of religion and spirituality.

Religious Socialization

For Bob, socialization for religion existed in the family and was reinforced through his community and the regional area where he was born. His family was of an Evangelical Christian faith, and religion was taught to the children as a way of life. Every part of his life was based in or grounded on Biblical teachings and following God. Although Bob felt uncertainty about the importance of God's direction in all parts of his life, he nonetheless followed family socialization and attempted to include God and His will as part of his life. The socialization messages on religion were so strong that Bob seems to have felt that there was little personal choice. In fact, he was distressed that his older brother seemed not to follow the norms set by the family and engaged in behaviors that upset his parents. To the degree that he took responsibility for sparing his parents suffering, he became "the good Christian son."

Bob also makes a strong connection between his geographic origin, the rural South, the Evangelical Christian beliefs of his relatives and peers, his work ethic, and his ethnicity. His religious socialization was enforced by his entire ecosystem. For him it is still difficult to distinguish between his ethnicity, his regional identity, and his religious formation. This is understandable because there is a relationship between geographic origin, ethnic background, and religious affiliation. Bob was raised in the Bible Belt, where religious affiliation, particularly Protestant and Evangelical faiths, is more important than other cultural or personality characteristics. The result of the internalization of the socialization led Bob to choose a career as a minister to please his parents and to become closer to God. What is most interesting is that Bob did not consider himself to have much choice in career selection because making choices that were pleasing to his family and God were a lifestyle for him and consistent with the rest of his ecosystem. Even though he knew during his studies that the field of ministry was not for him, he could not turn his back on God and his family.

Shift in Religious Identity

The evolving nature of Bob's cultural identity is seen most clearly in the shift in his relationships with God and the church and his change of career from minister to teacher. As Bob traces the beginning of the shifts that occurred in his life, he tells us of the three factors that led to the change: the untimely death of his mother and his subsequent anger at God, his lack of personal fulfillment in working in formal ministry, and his move from the rural South to the urban Northeast. His was a process that culminates in slow but progressive changes in the way he views his religious identity. He talks about shifting from a Christian fundamentalist perspective, which included having a personalized view of his relationship with God and a more literal interpretation of the scriptures, to a less fundamentalist view of his relationship with God.

Bob interprets his plunge into Christian fundamentalism and eventually the ministry as a career choice, as having stemmed from the behaviors of his brother, and as a way to please his brokenhearted parents. Although he was unhappy when entering the seminary, he describes how the sense of fulfillment or happiness seemed irrelevant. This changed, however, when his mother suddenly became ill. Because of his level of faith, Bob believed that his prayers for her healing would be answered. He also believed this because he had made sacrifices in his own happiness to serve God. Bob was confused and overwhelmed by his mother's death and felt disappointed by God. This was an extremely significant occurrence for him and in his words the "most pivotal moment," the one that seemed to initiate his change in religious beliefs. The experience of being lost that Bob described that extended to his career as a minister eventually led to his growing awareness and his acceptance of the lack of fulfillment that he felt in ministry. He moved with his wife and was able to obtain another position in the church. But it was shortly after accepting the position that he realized that ministry was not for him. His feelings led him to counseling. Such shifts from religious fundamentalism to more liberal views of religious doctrine are not uncommon as individuals begin to question their adherence to the beliefs of the family of origin. After his mother died, Bob may have felt more free to explore the meaning of his religious beliefs and less constrained to continue with fundamentalist religious beliefs solely to please his parents, which he was previously compelled to do because of his brother's behavior. With hindsight, he now experiences his previous way of life as inauthentic, lacking in personal agency or integrity.

Internal Migration and Religious Identity

Bob's discomfort and dissonance experienced in New York City amid what he describes as the segregated community of Southern Whites transplanted to the Northeast may have influenced his shift just as much as the death of his mother or his own search for authenticity. Internal migrations, such as the one experienced by Bob, from the more conservative rural South to the more liberal urban Northeast call for acculturation processes that may be just as relevant as the ones that take place when people move from one country to another. The sudden exposure to dramatically different cultural milieus within the same country may have an effect on an individual's cultural identity and religious beliefs or practices. It seems fair to wonder to what extent Bob's religious ideas would have shifted had he stayed in the South, in the same community, and around the same peers. At the same time, one wonders whether the seeds of change were already present in Bob, which may have made it possible for him to move in the first place, because those who move or emigrate are already open to the idea of dramatically changing their lives (Grinberg & Grinberg, 2000).

Clinical Applications

This section comprises assessment questions related to the theme of shifts in religious beliefs and in career choice.

Assessment

Conversations about religion are not always easy to conduct, particularly between therapists and clients. There is a well-documented historical relationship between secularism and psychotherapy that persists in the taboo of discussing a person's faith in depth in the culture in general and in the therapeutic situation in particular. Many therapists, especially if they are unfamiliar with the religious background of the client, may not consider themselves qualified enough to have these conversations. It is important, however, to assess the degree to which a person's religious beliefs, religious affiliations, and religious allegiance may shift according to a person's experience, place of residence, family events, and so on. If someone like Bob were to seek help at the time of the transition, how the therapist handles these issues is of crucial importance for the well-being of the client. It is also important to assess the career choices of individuals and how they arrived at those decisions because many people who are unhappy with their career choice may have a difficult time exploring family connections to their choice or may struggle while figuring out their future if it involves issues of self-determination or authenticity. Many counselors not specifically trained in dealing with the career issues of their clients may fail to address them. Following are some of the relevant questions therapists should ask.

Shifts in Religious Beliefs

Were there any events in your life that may have influenced your religious commitment, fervor, or affiliation?

Has your religious observance, commitment, fervor, or affiliation changed in the course of your life?

Did your parents have the same or different religious affiliations, observance, or commitment?

How has your siblings' level of religious observance, affiliation, or commitment influenced your relationship with them?

Shifts in Career Choice

How did you make your initial career choice?

How satisfied are you with your career choice?

Are you aware of familial pressures or traditions that may have influenced your career choice?

If you are switching careers, is it going to be viewed negatively or positively in your family?

Techniques and Interventions

There were critical events in Bob's life that took him on a different path than the one he was on originally. As Bob describes, his strong religious identity was initially shaped by events in his family, his parents' religious affiliation, the behavior of his sibling, his geographic origin, and his ethnic affiliation as a White, religiously conservative Southerner. At a certain point in his life, he determined that he needed to make a change of course, which took him onto a completely different track. Such dramatic switches can be difficult for the therapist to follow, support, and elicit, particularly if the therapist is of a different religious orientation than that of the client or if the therapist thinks that he or she has not been trained in dealing with career-related issues. Therapists often treat career, religious, or ethnicity issues as if they were special issues (Giordano & McGoldrick, 1996) rather than basic to understanding personal identity. No matter what stage of the life cycle individuals are going through, helping them sort through important career or religious paths may be one of the most vital benefits of therapy for those experiencing dramatic shifts in their life paths. Often, early career decisions and early religious affiliations are closely tied to identifications with family of origin, as in Bob's case. Helping clients tease out these early identifications with family of origin from the personal goals and aspirations may make a difference in clients' lives and help them go from living to please or appease others to a more personally fulfilling career or religious life. Therapists also need to help clients as they shift and change in their religious identity. Clients often experience loss or trauma that causes a shift in their thinking and religious beliefs. This can create a void that is difficult to fill. Focusing on the spiritual needs of clients (Fukuyama & Sevig, 1999) can be a way to help them begin to sift and tease out religious teachings and beliefs from their socialization experiences.

One useful technique to help clients sort out the different aspects of themselves is called Voice Dialogue and involves identifying parts of the self, naming them, and encouraging dialogues between the self and the part or between the different parts (Zweifel, 2002). Once a part is identified, the self can have a dialogue with the part and ask, "What is your job in my life? What do you want? What do you need? Do you get enough airtime? If you had more airtime, what would you do? What do you know about the other parts?" Eliciting an internal search-and-find mission can lead to integration and more effective decision making (Zweifel, 2002), particularly when it comes to choosing a path that involves lifelong commitments, such as a career or the fulfillment of spiritual needs. The Internal Family Systems Model (Schwartz, 1995) is another model that recognizes the multiple selves of the personality. Allowing the parts to surface is helpful for self-exploration, and that, in turn, can help solve dilemmas.

Countertransference

Clinicians sometimes hold strong opinions about issues that appear to be foreign, strange, or too "other." This can get in the way of sound clinical practice. If the therapist is not able to dissolve the negative countertransference, it might be important to refer the client to someone else. In general terms, it is not possible to conduct meaningful therapeutic work when the counselor is disgusted with, fearful of, or too critical of the choices of the clients.

Negative Reactions to Strict Religious Practices

Clinicians often have strong reactions to individuals raised and socialized with strict evangelical religious traditions. For many, the notion of restricting behaviors, such as dancing, playing cards, wearing makeup, or watching television, seems odd and unusual. However, this is often the case for clients, and clinicians need to be respectful of clients' beliefs. Attempting to teach clients that these beliefs are wrong or too restrictive can be damaging to the therapeutic relationship, particularly if these issues are not related to the presenting problem.

Overreaction to Clients Who Are Excommunicated

The other reaction that counselors often have is to overreact to the hurt that clients feel from their religious background. One of us, Anita, had a client who was excommunicated from her church and family and divorced from her husband because she took her child to the movies, a behavior that was strictly prohibited by the church. When students hear the story, they often become outraged at the church's and the family's response. Although this anger may be a natural reaction to the situation, expressing the anger and encouraging anger in the client may be inappropriate. The client in this case needed to grieve and mourn the loss of her only support system and to reconcile her relationship with God and her religious identity. Although expressing anger was certainly a part of her grieving process, the clinician who focuses too much on this feeling disrupts and hinders the therapeutic process.

Applying Voice Dialogue (Zweifel, 2002) or multiple self work (Schwartz, 1995) to the countertransference reaction might be a useful way for clinicians to observe the parts of themselves that are rejecting, disgusted by, or angry with the client's decisions, the client's family, or the client's church. Allowing a dialogue between the self of the therapist and the disgusted, rejecting, or angry part of the therapist may bring some interesting information to the surface that may dissolve the disgust or anger of the clinician, increase her or his empathy, and allow for some creative ideas for helping the clients move forward.

TOOLBOX ACTIVITY—BOB		
Discussion Questions	*Activities*	*Resources*
Content themes What other themes do you see emerging in the stories that the authors did not identify? How important is the theme of Bob's identity as a White Southerner? **Assessment** Are there any questions you would like to ask? **Interventions** What other interventions could you propose with Bob? **Countertransference** What countertransference reactions were emerging in yourself as you read this story? **Other scenarios** Imagine that Bob is coming to you several years ago or several years from now with a presenting problem. Imagine what that presenting problem could be. How might his religious identity be different? What if Bob had remained in the ministry?	Interview someone on important scriptures of their choice, specifically regarding terms such as *love, forgiveness, guilt, anger, sin,* and *redemption.* Engage in a discussion about the themes of scriptures and discuss their relationship to spiritual issues. Write an essay on how your own religious beliefs have influenced your career selection. Interview others on the relationship between spirituality and career or volunteer experiences. Write an essay about your familial religious socialization process.	**Suggested readings** Burke, M. T., Chauvin, J. C., & Maranti, J. (2003). *Spirituality in counseling and therapy: A developmental and multicultural approach.* New York: Brunner-Routledge. Cloud, H., & Townsend, J. (1995). *12 "Christian" beliefs that can drive you crazy.* Grand Rapids, MI: Zondervan.

Twelve

Katie's Story

Catholic and Jewish? How Can It Be?

For some individuals, religion is a ritual imposed on them in childhood by their parents, a distant set of memories about church services or school. For others, religion is a practice, a routine that was begun when they were young and is continued through adulthood (Griffith & Griggs, 2001). Yet for others, it is a vibrant, active component of their identity. It shapes who they are and how they function. And the practices and rituals associated with religious beliefs are a way to connect with God, or a higher power; with other believers; and, most important, with oneself. The teachings and doctrines provide a blueprint and guide for living. Work, child rearing, volunteer services, and daily practices are guided by religion. Religion is often conceptualized as a developmental process; connections to religious beliefs change as people grow and mature cognitively and spiritually (Fukuyama & Sevig, 1999; Griffith & Griggs, 2001). Connection to religion also changes as people meet developmental milestones, including graduation, marriage, and child rearing. And religious beliefs change when people face crisis, trauma, or stressors; many people use these times to question spiritual beliefs and their relationship with God.

Katie's story follows this developmental focus. She was raised in the Catholic tradition, and her beliefs and connections changed with her developmental progress. The most important challenges to her religious faith came when she decided to engage in an interfaith marriage and had children. As you read the story, reflect on the intersection of religion, developmental milestones, and life transitions. Also note how current events influenced Katie's development, indirectly influencing her religious beliefs.

Katie's Story

I was born and raised a Catholic, but I did not become one until I married a Jew. I was a Latin-chanting, chapel-veiled, genuflecting, rosary-clicking, Friday-fish-eating Baby Boomer of a Catholic. When I was born in 1954, I was quickly whisked off to the local parish church to be baptized, lest I wind up in limbo if I died a quick death (and which was worse: SIDS or limbo?). My own mother (apparently a secondary player in my spiritual growth) did not attend the ceremony because she was readying for the gathering of relatives. And it would be a large crowd! This Catholic family had grandparents with farm roots, so large families were the norm. The collateral and collective nature of this family beckoned all aunts, uncles, and cousins to mark all major life passages. These gatherings were often colored by which one of my 41 first cousins (on my father's side of the family alone) was wearing the white dress of baptism, or adding the veil, or wearing the grown-up suit for First Communion. The predictable holidays, Holy Days of Obligation, and the Seven Sacraments marked the passage of annual time. These moments brought the certainty and sure knowledge that rote rituals and memorized prayers often provide, especially to the passive viewers that so many Catholics had become. We were dictated to by the rigors of the dogmatic Church rules that directed our practices. Religion was my cultural identity, the sole source of what made me both belong and be distinctive. In my White, upper middle-class suburban family, there were only vague hints about any ethnic component to our family: like the Wednesday night sauerkraut and sausage dinners or times when my aunts and uncles sang German songs around our piano. I realize now that at that time an Irish Catholic marrying a German Catholic was considered an out-marriage and subject to derogatory terms, such as "shanty Irish." So one ethnic group was expected to take a backseat, and usually this ethnicity belonged to the wife.

Besides, no one had lived on "the old sod" for four generations. I was American, an American *Catholic*. (Wait! Which was the noun and which the adjective?) I learned the fate of John F. Kennedy when my principal, a nun, came into the class and said, "Our Catholic president has been shot." Yes, I went to Catholic schools, no questions asked. That was what good Catholics did. In my youth, there were only two religions: Catholic and Public, each with their own schools. We, of course, knew which one was better because we were told at both church and school that we were The One True Faith. If we Catholics were true, then that meant everyone else's religion was false, right? (They did not call the schools parochial for nothing!)

At school, I dutifully memorized the answers to our Baltimore Catechism, those concise nuggets of theology and dogma that served as the basis of our faith. They are ingrained so deeply into my long-term memory banks through daily repetition and drills that I can today recall the lessons in my first-grade primer almost 45 years later:

Q: Who made the world?

A: God made the world.

Q: Who is God?

A: God is the creator of heaven and earth and of all things.

Q: What is man?

A: Man is made up of body and soul.

Q: How did God make you?

A: God made me in his image and likeness.

Q: Why did God make you?

A: God made me to know Him, to love Him, and to serve Him in this world and in the next.

This made Catholicism seem so easy. Here were all these clear answers—and without the questions ever being asked. Just memorize them and practice. All you need is a good memory. If I did my catechism well, at Confirmation, when the Bishop called on me, I would be able to recite the right response, bringing honor, not shame, to my family.

Weekends were marked by Sunday mass with both Mom and Dad, often after weekly Saturday confession. Mass was one of the few times we were together as a family. Church and services piqued our senses because

Catholicism was richly filled with unusual sights, sounds, and smells at that time: incense, chants, the jingle of little bells, holy day pageants, wimpled nuns, collared and cassocked priests. Spectacular, yes—but . . . It was still Latin mass. Now isn't that something a young child can relate to? We were estranged, marginalized from the adult world as we tried to sit there for the hour listening avidly for God's phone number (*Et-cum-spiritu-tu-o*). We would try to follow along in the missals (usually a First Communion present, along with a rosary, from a godparent). We could sound out the prayers phonetically, but actually translate them? Make the words meaningful? No. We were present in body but absent in spirit. The religion of my youth was something that I performed by going through the motions, like a perfect little marionette tied to the long line of family before me. My puppet practices were not hallowed but hollow, wooden. I learned I was not alone; the whole Catholic Church was chafing under the rigidity of the institution that theologian Martin Marty once termed as "mind-numbing boredom."

I was an adolescent who reached not the Age of Reason but rather the Age of Give-Me-a-Reason-Why-Not. James Fowler in his seminal work *Stages of Faith* (1981) considers adolescence a watershed moment in faith development, a time when minds and hearts expand their worldviews and either conform to the conventions and standards of the past or break apart the ordered clusters of their values, beliefs, and practices.

I questioned what I had been told was unquestionable; I wondered, though I risked being punished for imagining. If I ever asked those tough "why" questions, the good nuns said, "It's a mystery," which seemed a theological version of the parental "because I told you so." (It really refers to the Greek word *mysterios,* or "drama," but no one told us that.) The problem with Catholic education was that you actually got educated. No longer willing to accept all precepts and practices on blind faith, I wanted to see deeper, and rote rituals and strict rules were blocking me.

The winter of my discontent, fortuitously, coincided with the Church's own. Just as I could hear my inner strains of "Somebody better liven things up around here for me, or I will bail," along came Pope John XXIII, his successor, Pope Paul VI, and the Second Vatican Council, or Vatican II. The *aggiornamento,* the "shaking up" of the Church that Pope John put into motion, played out before my eyes in high school.

In a short period of time, the sensations of my old Catholicism were changing as if overnight—literally it seemed. One day, my favorite English teacher was wearing a tight wimple around her face and a long habit, and the next day she had—gulp!—hair! And at mass, they turned the priest around to face the pews. And it was in English! I took communion not placed on my tongue but in my hand, though I had been told in my First Communion preparation that if we ever touched the host our hand would wither. And it didn't! Ha! I was introduced to new titles and words: "People of God," "ecumenism," and "ecumenical." The changes were exciting, odd, hard, scary, and fun. They were more than cosmetic: No longer expected to be passive, I was actually invited to participate in the life of the Church. I was watching. I was relearning and reexamining and beginning to look deeper to find my own place in a new spiritual world.

My aunts and uncles and my father grumbled and complained mightily about the changes, the guitar masses ("Those Hootenanny masses," my father said), and, sotto voce, the infallible pope. Ah, yes, they were like Israelites in the desert, grousing at Massah and Meribah about the lack of food, water, and the leadership of that lousy Moses. After all, look what he made them do! Leave slavery! For what? Freedom. But the new way to the Promised Land was messy, hard, and uncomfortable. And they wanted to go back to Egypt! Biblical truth indeed because the first human response to change is usually resistance, and the second is fear or complaining. Change is a struggle, awkward and stressful. Yet is this crisis a problem, a catastrophe? Or might a radical, new energy to practice be an opportunity for rejuvenation, much needed for spiritual growth?

From 1967 to 1971, I rehearsed these new changes at an all-girl Catholic high school (free from embarrassing myself in front of boys!). My widening vistas saw peers all over America in the throes of massive changes: gender roles, politics, social activism, and so on. I tried on all sorts of nouns and adjectives as well: woman, outspoken, liberated, performer, blond, scholar. I was an eager shopper in an exciting identity mall.

A college education was a given in our family. My father was a first generation college graduate who came from the poverty of the Depression and quickly worked his way through undergraduate and medical schools, graduating at 21 years of age. When it came my time to choose a college, I made a very bold move—educationally, geographically, psychologically, and spiritually. I chose a non-Catholic university in a major metropolitan area 350 miles from my northern Kentucky family-of-origin, a university that attracted students from all over the country and the world—Columbia College. I chose theater as a major, a jolting departure from the sciences so valued by my surgeon father and my mother, his nurse, who had reared me. This departure from the family circle was unheard of in my extended family and probably raised some eyebrows at the time. My beloved mentor in high school, who ironically was then a cloistered nun, encouraged me. (She has since left the convent.) I loved both my college years and the sprawling city of Chicago. Here I stayed, continuing the process of finding myself as a young adult through college and my 20s. I stayed loosely connected to the practices of my Catholicism, still not exactly tied down.

My first job was teaching at a private all-girl Catholic high school, but I left that after 4 years to act in the theater instead of simply teaching it. The work hours of theater (and the various day jobs) conflicted with regular Sunday church attendance. I no longer saw myself as Catholic with a capital C but catholic, universal. I was just one fiber in this whole vibrant multicultural tapestry of my adopted city, Chicago.

Was This a "Crisis" of Faith?

In my early 30s, I fell in love, deeply, surprisingly, and irrevocably, with my best friend and could never look at life without him beside me. With him, I never felt more fully in touch with my truest self. What? A transplanted suburban Kentucky, Catholic girl wanting to spend the rest of her life with this urban Chicago, Jewish boy? But there we were. Religious traditions and cultural differences stared us in the face. And we cared deeply enough to care about it. Falling in love reawakened our spirituality, and thus, so naked and tentative, we began exploring our different symbol systems for faith. Obstacles and changes create disequilibrium. You can either run away, stay stuck in the emotion of uncertainty, or adjust and cope. I was too old, determined, and educated to freeze and too much in love to leave. We encountered the official naysayers in our discovery's way. Indeed, one rabbi railed, "Don't do it. Break up right away! Think of what you are doing to the Jews! Your marriage will fail." Another said, "Technically, you do not exist." Because I was then working at a school renting from a Catholic Church, I sought a different tack. "Let's go see one of the priests next door," I suggested. My fiancé was convinced we would be shunned or shamed there, too. Mentors are, first, angels—surprise strangers marking turning points in lives. We met Father Rick Matthews, the archdiocesan director of young adult ministry in Chicago. We sat down one afternoon at Chicago's Old St. Paul's Church and talked about our hopes.

"Are you in love?" he asked.

"Oh, yes," we replied, beaming.

"Then we are all in the presence of God," he said.

"I suppose it would be easier if I were Catholic, though," my fiancé suggested.

"But being Jewish is who you are," Rick said. "Why should you change that about yourself simply because you are in love with Katie? I think it must be wonderful to be Jewish. In fact, if I weren't Catholic, I'd be Jewish myself."

Then I asked, "What would you suggest about how we should raise our children?"

"What do you do for yourselves?" asked Rick. "You can't expect your kids to do anything except what you as parents are doing with them. That's a sure way to make religion a source of conflict."

"Makes perfect sense," we said, thinking about the pejorative words that sent us in this priest's direction in the first place.

"Katie goes to church and I go to temple," Daniel said. "Should we take them to temple on Friday night and church on Sunday morning?"

"Absolutely," said Rick.

"Won't they be confused?"

"You can help them understand the differences—and the similarities."

"What should we teach them religiously—Judaism or Catholicism?" I asked.

Rick smiled. "I would teach them both. How can you do otherwise? You two are going to be your children's most important teachers. How can you not?" Daniel was slightly incredulous. I made mental notes. (Five years later these seeds took root.)

As our meeting with Father Matthews ended, we asked him if there was a support group that he knew of for couples like us. "There isn't one that I know of," he said, wagging a finger. "But I've been thinking of starting one." (And what that wagging finger foretold!)

The Wedding Plans

Any engaged couple previews the marital adjustment of the first 5 years in the wedding plans. As an interfaith couple, with additional familial and cultural differences, obstacles seemed compounded. Here is a brief glimpse of our navigations:

> The Wedding List: His list of 45 friends and relatives for "a small wedding" made me laugh. I had a Catholic family. So 250 relatives and a handful of friends came.

> The Ceremony: The Baltimore Catechism taught neither wedding etiquette nor Canon Law. Though I envisioned a beautiful backyard wedding, my church could not allow it outdoors. My Reformed Jewish fiancé did not have the visceral reaction that many Jews feel about entering a church and did not mind being married there. (It was a small hint of how he generously entered all kinds of arenas other Jews might not.)

> The Celebrants: We wanted a priest and a rabbi, and that put both of our mothers in a spin. My mother was convinced she would have to bribe or blackmail the pastor. She knew that in her generation interfaith couples seeking the Church's blessing were forced to convert and wed in nondescript, private ceremonies, hidden away in the priest's rectory. Not many of us "people-in-the-pews" knew that in 1965 *Nostra Aetate* had been issued, the Church's official acknowledgment of Judaism as a means of salvation and its hope of rebuilding the special relationship between the two faiths that had been broken apart by painful history. This had paved the way for priests, including our pastor, to happily and publicly perform these interfaith ceremonies between Catholics and Jews. Indeed, it was finding the rabbi that was the rub because traditional Hallachic (ritually observant) law frowns on marrying outside of Judaism. Fortunately, Cincinnati is home to Hebrew Union College, one of the key U.S. centers for educating Reform rabbis. We were referred to several studying there and immediately felt comfortable with our first encounter with Rabbi Weiss.

> "The Paper": The vestiges of the medieval Catholic Church's fastidiousness about civic record keeping still exist today. The Church bureaucracy keeps great records on births (baptisms), marriages, and deaths. A couple with one non-Catholic is asked to sign a document colloquially called "The Paper" or "The Promise." In the Church of my youth, an interfaith couple was most often a Catholic marrying a Protestant, and I knew that both of them were required to promise to raise the children Catholic, with the subtextual tone of "On pain of death of your immortal soul."

It came to that moment that both Daniel and I dreaded. It was not that we were in disagreement about our children; we were not. We wanted our children to know both religions, but, yes, we would call them Catholic if we had to. Based on the Jewishness of Jesus and the Church's ecumenism, its content allows for more of both. Still . . .

Father John Walsh at Old St. Paul's met with us that day, immediately quelling our queasiness. He explained that Daniel need only acknowledge that I had made this promise. I was promising that in good faith "I would do all within my power" to raise the children Catholic, but sometimes our power might be great and other times not. The Promise opens up the conversation, not closes the door. And furthermore, the marriage is more important. Father Walsh—and indeed his entire parish community built around hospitality, acceptance, outreach, and ecumenism—remains another angel in our lives, another person saying, "Come on! Do not be afraid!" There we have found a home.

> The Ceremony: Even after we secured the two clergy in Kentucky, it dawned on all four of us that there was no prepared text that these two men could plug in the names and that the assembled would be able to follow. What resources did we use to thwart another obstacle? We tapped into our basic skills and talents. Daniel is a media writer, and we both were theater majors. We wrote our own ceremony. Because it was unlike anything our family had seen, people in the pews paid alert attention.

And the Rest of the Story . . . ?

A wedding is one day, but a marriage is daily. Our intercultural differences led us forth in unpredictable ways. For the first time in my adult life, I joined a parish; Old St. Paul's had made both of us—both!—feel welcome and valued for who we are. Daniel's Jewishness is considered quite special there, and never was he asked to change who he was. He also kept his membership at his temple where he grew up but eventually left over the rabbi's stance on interfaith marriage, and we joined two other temples.

God is sneaky. Beware the wagging finger! A little less than a year after our 1987 wedding, Father Matthews told us after mass that the interfaith couples' gathering we talked about might be getting off the ground. In June we met for the first time with Father Matthews and the late Father David Monts. This meeting spawned the Catholic-Jewish Couples Group of Chicago, which still exists today. About a year later Rabbi Albert Sachel joined us. A grassroots support group that we help lead, its membership list has approximately 300 couples in varying stages of relationships. Some people come for one or two meetings; some stay for years. Our monthly meetings address a variety of topics, and we have spun off special interest groups for those planning weddings and birth ceremonies.

> Teach your children diligently.
>   —Deuteronomy 6:7

When couples marry, children often follow. In interfaith families, when children come, and the wrestling with early rites of passage are put to rest, the lingering question of "What exactly will we teach the children?" soon arises. There were other families in the group whose children were roughly the same age as ours. Sending our children to a traditional religious education program alone did not feel quite right, yet could there be such a thing as a Catholic-Jewish Sunday School? If so, what would this look like? Rick Matthew's advice from years ago to teach them both still resonated. Certainly no established Jewish education program could really teach about Christianity, unless briefly presented as comparative religion. We thought that even suggesting such a course of action would cause rabbis or Jewish educators to shake their heads sadly or even become angry. Indeed, the Union of American Hebrew Congregations (the central organization of Reform Judaism in America) has issued a directive to its religious schools that children who have had religious instruction in other faiths should be discouraged from enrolling in Jewish education programs.

So, as with our wedding ceremony, we rolled up our sleeves and tapped into another talent, education. With seven families we started our own grassroots religious education program, The Family School, in 1993. Housed at Old St. Paul's, it is a bimonthly, parent-taught cooperative. There we strive for religio-cultural competence in two-faith community settings.

I developed a 9-year, K–8 curriculum during the summers, wrote four student texts, and composed a parent curricular overview and guide to teaching the weekly lessons in the curricula. People think I'm nuts, amazed that I would devote all this time for no pay. I knew we were trailblazers, breaking apart and putting together pieces of hidden pathways to the Spirit. I was invigorated, intellectually and spiritually! I did this for three not-so-simple reasons: (1) People told me it couldn't be done, and I wanted to dig in my heels and prove them wrong (a life theme perhaps?); (2) I did not want my own children to learn drivel and junk; and (3) if I were constructing this for my own kids, then why not share my efforts with others now and those to come behind me? Like any good curriculum, I never feel like I am finished, but it is finally in a form that I can share with future Family School families as well as other groups starting out across the country with similar hopes and dreams just like mine and Daniel's back in 1987.

Practice, Practice, Practice: A Practicing Catholic

The expression "I am a 'practicing Catholic'" fascinates me. When I hear it, I want to say right back, "And what the hell does that mean? Aren't we all just practicing?" Usually the phrase is a status report: "I am an active member of this club." Or it is shorthand for expected behaviors: "Yes, I go to church every Sunday, take communion, receive reconciliation at least twice a year (Christmas and Easter obligation, you know), get those ashes on my forehead, fast during Lent on Ash Wednesday and Good Friday, practice only natural birth control" and so on. (That's not fully me.) This expression too often summarizes the external life of the practitioner, not the internal; the extrinsic, not the intrinsic; the level of religiosity, not the depth of spirituality.

The phrase "I am a nonpracticing Catholic" fascinates me, too. Do pieces of your childhood identity ever totally go away? Or is this too just shorthand for the absence of regularity of the rote practices, a hint that you got out of the discipline or habit?

So today I say with a subtle, wry curl at the corner of my lips, "Yes, I am a practicing Catholic," but that means I am still trying to get it right—the untidy discovery part that is active spirituality. I do not practice my faith because I know it all; I practice because I don't know and want to know more. Weekly rituals are no longer rote routines but reminders or catalysts, so repetition and practice are no longer drudgery. The much-maligned Baltimore Catechism of long ago did teach me this (much to my adult surprise): Discipline, repetition, imitation, routine, and regularity are learning tools. Like music, dance, and drawing the basics must be practiced before you can infuse them with your creative spirit to make it become art, transcendent, divine. This reshaping is the start for growing into faith, of being-in-becoming the beloved of the God of love.

If religion is the lens through which we tease out our faith and spirituality and shape our focus of how we see the realities of our world, then today I wear bifocals. Intermarriage woke me up spiritually, or, as the metaphor says in Jesus' baptism stories, "the heavens opened." After 17 years with Daniel, I honestly think of myself as both Catholic and Jewish. It is not that I am Jewish but that I see my own Catholic practices and stories better, brighter, clearer through the added prism of the rich history, teachings, and traditions of another faith, indeed the very faith that gave mine birth. I like the threads of connection there. This is Catholicism within the light of Judaism. I am comfortable in both worship communities when it is inclusive of diversity, not pejorative.

Indeed some former Catholics do not practice because of the Church's controversial teachings, theological differences, or the psychic pain because of its myriad scandals, such as clergy abuse. I sadly know why some people want to say, "Screw the Catholic Church." Catholic history, past and present, is full of less than holy intentions and gestures filled with power and malice, not love and compassion. Yet would I, could I, drop my Caucasian identity because of our repugnant history of slavery and racism? I can't. I have to find ways to reconcile and forgive, without ever forgetting. Many vocations and roles form parts of my identity, past and present: teacher, actor, waitress, mother, counselor, writer, and wife. I think that what threads these realms—religion, arts, education, and psychology—is this common root: an attempt to take the ordinary human experience and somehow transform it into the extraordinary, whether in body, mind, or spirit. The quality that distinguishes an art, religious practice, or career as disgraceful or grace-filled is the answer to this question: "Am I stuck in an empty, rote, dull space? Or am I vibrantly, dynamically seeking connection?" That indeed makes the ordinary extraordinary. To that I strive in all I do.

My spiritual life is richer because I have been forced to venture into cultural language and stories that were once unfamiliar. Many Catholics gloss over those marvelous Hebrew scriptures. I now enjoy mining these new metaphors for little sparks lighting the way to see kaleidoscopes of "truth." My favorite for life, ethics, and faith is Jacob wrestling with the angel. He wants to reconcile his past mistakes and goes to see his estranged brother. He wrestles all night with "a stranger" and comes out of this close-encounter-of-the-divine-kind wrenched, bruised, and limping but changed, even with a new name: *Yakkov*, "the liar," becomes *Yisrael*, "he who wrestled with God and prevailed." Like the old Catholic girl falling in love with a Jew, Jacob's old self gives way to the new future for him and all his children. By marrying Daniel, I have been converted, and for the better. I changed my identity, and my future. That's metanoia!

Renewed, deepened faith practices risk changing the comfort of one's set worldview. But my sense of spirituality is that it is messy, uncomfortable, but then ultimately soothing to the limping self. "Spirit" happens in sneaky, surprising eureka moments. In encountering anything novel or life altering, a fevered sense of struggle, anxiety, and strangeness ensues. If you are curious and deeply engaged in breaking apart schemas, mindsets, and rote practices, change will follow. It requires energy to increase knowledge, but only fear can hold you back. (A biblical, angelic motif is, "Do not be afraid.") Humans, not animals, can choose between right and wrong and can push toward transcendence. Do we stay in place, held back by fear, or wrestle with the angel? The higher self may emerge, but the past identity may also linger, pained and limping.

Socrates tells us that an unexamined life is not worth living, and I concur. Any dynamic practitioner of a vocation based on the ethics of care, trust, change, and growth—be it an artist, a musician, an actor, a dancer, a painter, a theologian, a parent, a spouse, a counselor—has to break apart the basic frameworks of the field and reshape it to make it fit his or her own, however kaleidoscopic that framework might become. Otherwise, we risk becoming stagnant, succumbing to our own entropy, and hence dull, dead, lifeless. Dynamic encounters challenge us, and being shaken up makes for personal, professional, or spiritual transformation. First, you have to open all your many eyes (those cultural and spiritual visions) to fully see. Different lenses can take the lead at different moments. Only then will you move beyond life's barriers into the realm of the possible.

Fate and choice have taken me from the closed system of the 50s South to the horizons of the pluralistic 21st century metropolis. My spirit has opened infinite vistas, and I can never be the same. (Love and age have seen to that.) I no longer see my identity as I once did as a child, a teen, a young adult, a middle-aged woman. At this midpoint, I no longer see God in the same way either: God is no longer just a noun but also a verb. I can no longer be cerebral about the human atrocities committed both in the past and today, often done in the name of my God. I hurt because that is not my God.

I chose and vowed to love and honor my beloved, my Daniel. How could I honor him if I were judging the "other" as good or bad? As "us" or "them"? I am a Jacob, wrestling to find out what is valuable and desirable and discarding or restructuring what is dissonant or devalued. I have had to leap, to release, to let it go, to reach out anew. I embraced the "stranger" and made him mine. Together we reconciled our choices to fit our future hopes with fewer barriers for our children to knock down.

Our future, our children! They will forge their own life path. Oh, yes, I would be hypocritical to bind them too tightly to the family ties of our pasts. It is their journey. Their parents only prepare them with some basics: traditions, values, ethics, curiosity, wonder, and stories. (Oh, never forget the stories! Wrestle those images.) Practice may be rote and dull at times. Give it time. Yet we are really only launching their cultural boats, hoping with all our might that they land happily in body, mind, and spirit on the welcoming shores at a place where "otherness" doesn't divide their futures. To you both: Bon voyage. Peace be with you. Go with God. Go with Good. Shalom.

Content Themes

Katie's story reflects the developmental process of religious beliefs and describes how it changes across time to reflect life transitions and current events. It seems as if Katie's religious beliefs were an important component of her childhood but strengthened and changed throughout adolescence and high school and certainly when she decided to marry someone of a different faith. Katie's story demonstrates how spirituality and religion permeate all aspects of a person's life and actively influence and affect decision making. There are four important themes. The first theme is the developmental process of religious identity, which corresponds to milestones and life transitions. The second theme is the importance of religion in important decisions, particularly marriage and child rearing. The third theme is the role of socialization in religious identity development. The final theme is the relationship between current events, or the macrosystem and exosystem, in religious identity development.

Religious Identity Development

The development of religious faith and religious identity corresponds to other developmental components, including cognitive development. James Fowler (1981) identified a six-stage model of faith development. In the first stage, intuitive-projective (ages 3–7 years), individuals' religious beliefs are based on stories or messages taught by their parents. Because of children's cognitive capacities, the stories are primarily fantasy in nature. The second stage, mythical-literal, corresponds to concrete cognitive functioning and includes children's process of separating fantasy stories from reality. The third stage, synthetic-conventional, usually occurring during adolescence, includes a tacit acceptance of values and symbols from the religious faiths and practices. The fourth stage, individual-reflective, is a questioning stage in which people make their beliefs explicit. Individuals question not only their beliefs but also the context in which they developed. The fifth stage, conjunctive, includes a deepening sense of faith and an integration of beliefs. The final stage, universalizing faith, includes integrating ethical principles, including justice and love. It should be noted that, as is the case with most developmental models, individuals may not progress through the stages as outlined.

Katie's spiritual journey seems to follow this path. Her participation in Catholic traditions began in infancy, when she was baptized in the Church. During her school-age years, she participated in Catholic schools, and she was indoctrinated with the teachings of the Church through school and religious services. Katie's school-age development seems to reflect Stage 2. For Katie, religion was a rote practice, a part of family functioning, which she took literally and examined in a concrete fashion. Katie reports questioning teachings but being silenced by her teachers. One wonders if she tacitly accepted the teachings at that point, confident in her parents' acceptance of the teachings and doctrine. When Katie entered high school, she began questioning some of the teachings she had previously accepted, partly due to the empowerment she felt from the civil rights movement. She may have entered Fowler's fourth stage during adolescence due to the changes that were occurring within society. Although the primary doctrine of the Church did not change, there was more input from the laity within the service and more participation from parishioners.

When Katie entered college and began to work, as is the case with many, she participated less in religious services, focusing on other developmental tasks. Katie continued to move through the stages as she decided to enter an interfaith marriage. Religious beliefs that had perhaps become routine suddenly took on new meaning as she was faced with the prospect of needing to choose which religious faith to practice. For Katie, love conquers all, and Katie and Daniel examined their faiths within the commitment of the relationship. Although Katie began the challenges of young adulthood, entering and completing college and establishing a career, her participation in religious activities waned. But certainly the prospect of marriage and the challenge of choosing or defending faith helped Katie to reconnect with spirituality.

There are many issues that may propel individuals into Fowler's fifth stage, conjunctive, in which beliefs are reexamined and integrated. For Katie, it was certainly the decision to marry that caused her to examine her faith and to more fully embrace, accept, and make Daniel's faith a vital part of her life, beginning with the wedding ceremony. Following marriage was childbirth, which led to a new examination of beliefs. For Katie, the prospect of raising children in an interfaith marriage, providing the opportunity to study and embrace both religious traditions, moved her to the sixth stage of development, universalizing faith. People often choose to expose their children to religious teachings, even those who no longer actively practice their faith, to allow their children to choose whether to participate in religion as adults. But because Katie's faith was more developed, she decided not just to expose teachings and practices to her children but to enrich their lives. She was an active participant in their teachings by preparing curriculum for their studies.

Decision Making

Religious beliefs and teachings often influence decision making for individuals. Scriptures and teachings, along with religious leaders, are sought for guidance and advice. Religion influences values and determines rules and roles in interpersonal relationships, career decisions, and child-rearing practices. It is clear that Katie was influenced by her religion as she progressed through development. First, Katie's socialization through school reaffirmed values and teachings in the Catholic faith and within her family. For Katie, options for her future were defined by roles prescribed by the Church. When Katie was entering adolescence, the teachings of the Church were beginning to expand, allowing her to have the freedom to explore more options. These changes allowed her to choose to relocate across the country to attend a non-Catholic university, a choice that may not have been available to her before the Church began to expand. Katie's next major decision was to choose a career. She chose teaching and theater as a profession and decided to teach at a private, all-girl Catholic high school.

Following developmental trajectories, the next major tasks for Katie were marriage and child rearing, and, as with other aspects of her life, her religious teachings were used as guidance. Although she was taught not to marry someone who was not a practicing Catholic, love had other plans for her, and she fell in love with a Jewish person. Perhaps guided by the changes within the Church and its impact on her identity as an adolescent, she decided to follow her heart. This was not a light decision for her, and she and her fiancé decided to seek advice on their marriage. Not only did religion influence her participation in the marriage, but it also dictated the nature of the wedding ceremony, the first challenge to the interfaith relationship. Their commitment to the process led them to develop a support group for interfaith couples. The second challenge came in the attendance of worship services, as the couple decided to worship together in a parish that was accepting of his belief in Judaism. The final area of decision making in Katie's story is of child rearing, specifically religious teaching and training.

Family Socialization

Katie describes the role of the family in the development of her religious identity. Katie was born into a German and Irish Catholic family, and the extended family worshipped together and played a role in her religious development. They were a part of her baptismal ceremony, and the family worshipped and fellowshipped together for all major ceremonies. Katie spent the weekends worshipping with her parents and participating in Saturday confession. The family often dialogued about religious teachings, reflecting and mirroring the teachings from mass and the Catholic school. The extended family, along with her father, for example, expressed discomfort with some of the changes that were happening in the Church, particularly the modernization of the masses. They also expressed some concern about the interfaith marriage, the wedding ceremony, and the influence on children. Katie is continuing the family socialization of religious beliefs through her child rearing. She actively developed a curriculum so that her children would receive rich teachings in both Catholicism and Judaism. By ensuring her children's religious education, Katie is working toward securing their futures and aiding them in their spiritual development. Her advice to them, "Practice may be rote and dull at times. Give it time. . . . To you both: Bon voyage. Peace be with you. Go with God. Go with Good. Shalom."

Influence of Current Events

Bronfenbrenner's (1977) ecosystem model of development is relevant for understanding religious development. The sociopolitical issues and human rights concerns throughout the world often influence religious teachings and tenets. When Katie began to question her religious teachings and doctrine, the Church also began to respond to the zeitgeist and make changes within policies and the services. Katie experienced high school during the rise of the feminist and civil rights movements, which led to changes in her religious role models. Katie openly embraced the changes that occurred in the services, from having the priest face the congregation to changes within the Eucharist, but her family was resistant to the changes that were happening. Today there are social justice issues and policy issues that present moral dilemmas for individuals, along with teachings within churches and denominations. Various religious faiths wrestle with issues including abortion rights, civil rights, and same-sex marriages. Individuals, like Katie, look to religious teachings and leaders for guidance. For example, Katie had more freedom to attend colleges and explore careers due to changes within the Church. She was also not as bound to traditional gender role expectations.

Current sociopolitical issues also affected the possibility of mate selection. A generation ago it would have been more difficult to marry someone of a different religious orientation. Changing attitudes, behaviors, and immigration patterns have literally transformed the past tendency toward homogeneity in mate selection patterns. Intermarriage rates have increased for all ethnic, cultural, and religious groups in the United States (Crohn, 1998). Katie falls into that category by marrying a Jewish man.

Clinical Applications

Assessment

There are two primary areas of assessment for spirituality and religion as illustrated in this story: religious identity and development and the influence of religion on decision making. First, clinicians should assess the religious socialization practices and teachings of childhood and adolescence. Teachings influence values, decisions, judgments, and relationships, so it is important to assess these early teachings with clients. Because the relationship with religion changes according to developmental stages, it is important to assess how these changes have influenced clients. It is equally important to ask these questions of clients who are no longer practicing a religious faith because individuals often leave religious institutions because they have been harmed or hurt by particular teachings. The second area of assessment includes the influence of religion on decision making. Clients often seek religious teachings or religious leaders when making choices, and it is important for therapists to understand how these are affecting clients. The following questions are recommended for assessing the importance of religion:

What is your religious background? Were you raised or socialized in a particular religious faith?

How important is your religious background to you?

How important was religion during your childhood?

How important are religious teachings and practices to you?

Are you currently participating in religious or spiritual practices?

How have your religious beliefs or your connection to religion changed during your development?

How do your religious beliefs influence your decisions? Do you seek religious leaders for advice in decision making?

How are your religious beliefs related to your presenting problem?

Techniques and Interventions

Examination of Specific Religious Teachings

Therapists need to help clients examine and explore their specific religious beliefs in treatment. As individuals progress through religious identity development, they begin to question their religious beliefs, separate perceived facts from myths, and understand how their beliefs are related to values and decisions. It is important for therapists to assist clients in their exploration, particularly because their beliefs are related to the presenting problem. It may also be helpful for couples who become overwhelmed by differing religious doctrine to discuss spirituality and spiritual needs. The couple may find more commonality in their sense of purpose in life or transcendence, for example.

Interfaith Relationship Issues

Only since the 1970s have churches and religious faiths sanctioned or allowed interfaith marriages; many people have been raised with teachings and practices that prohibited and did not recognize interfaith marriages. Clients who are contemplating these marriages may experience some trepidation because they may feel as if this decision goes against religious teachings and family rules. Therapists can assist clients in two ways. First, clinicians can help clients to outline the important doctrines and teachings from their religions and to find a compromise about worship services, rituals, and traditions. Premarital counseling should help clients explore and face their families' reactions to the marriage. Discussions about how to spend the holidays, particularly the religious holidays, need to be included in the treatment. Counselors can be helpful in assisting clients in the discussion about the actual wedding ceremony as well. Counselors should encourage clients to have realistic discussions about the religious socialization of the children if the couple is planning to have them. Clinicians should suggest to clients that the original conversations in premarital counseling have to be repeated with major life transitions, stressors, or crises. For example, parents may be agreeable about having a civil service ceremony but insist that their grandchildren be socialized in a particular way.

Interfaith couples who are already married or who have children are most likely to seek help when some event in the life cycle disrupts the family's balance (Crohn, 1998). Many couples attempt to deal with their religious differences by trying to forget the past or deny their differences in religious backgrounds or commitments. However, a major life event or trauma may make couples more vulnerable to conflicts around those issues. Many people revert to religious practices and rituals they have been socialized with to deal with the crisis or tragedy, even if, for the sake of being in this interfaith couple, they had denied or rejected their religious practices in the past. Helping couples clarify their needs, differences, worries, and anxieties about the religious differences is important. It is also important for the therapist to help interfaith couples create their own religious rituals, routines, and traditions.

Countertransference

Two areas of countertransference are raised in this story: moral dilemmas and confusion around interfaith relationships.

Moral Dilemmas

Katie's story and her religious identity show the influence of current affairs, sociopolitical issues, and the cultural ideology on functioning. Religion influences our decisions and behaviors. When teachings and practices of the church change, people are left confused over what to believe or how to behave. Likewise, individuals may experience a lack of change in religious teachings and think that their religious training and beliefs are not relevant to today and leave the church. Counselors will experience these same feelings and be confused about how to assist their clients. For example, a person with an unplanned pregnancy may be confused about whether to terminate the pregnancy, which would go against her religious training. Therapists are advised to be aware of their own positions and be careful not to impose them on their clients. A Rogerian approach that focuses on active listening may be useful in helping people with moral dilemmas (Rogers, 1980). The narrative approach that focuses on helping people understand the meaning they are constructing may also be beneficial in this area (Freedman & Combs, 1995).

Confusion About Interfaith Differences

Clinicians may become overwhelmed by working with clients who were socialized in two different religious traditions. Therapists who share a similar religious tradition and strong religious beliefs with one member of the couple may find it difficult to understand how and why the couple is interested in an interfaith relationship. Therapists with no religious training may underestimate the significance of the relationship and the troubles the clients will face. Clients need assistance in sorting out and prioritizing religious beliefs and family reactions. Clinicians may want to consult with religious leaders to assist in the process of helping the couple achieve a balanced view of their differences (Falicov, 1995).

TOOLBOX ACTIVITY—KATIE		
Discussion Questions	*Activities*	*Resources*
Content themes What other themes do you see emerging in the story that the authors did not identify? **Assessment** Are there any questions you would like to ask? **Interventions** What other interventions could you propose with Katie? **Countertransference** What counter-transference reactions were emerging in yourself as you read this story? **Other scenarios** Imagine that Katie married another Catholic. How would this marriage have shaped her religious identity? Imagine that Katie married someone of the Islamic faith. What challenges would they have?	Research a religious faith that differs from yours. Imagine marrying a person from that faith. Write an essay on the challenges you would have to face. Develop a list of essential religious teachings that you would want to share with your children.	**Suggested readings** Cowan, P., & Cowan, R. (1989). *Mixed blessings: Overcoming the stumbling blocks in an interfaith marriage.* New York: Penguin. Hawxhurst, J. C. (1998). *The interfaith family guidebook: Practical advice for Jewish and Christian partners.* Boston, KY: Dovetail. Rosenbaum, M. H., & Rosenbaum, S. (1998). *Celebrating our differences: Living two faiths in one marriage.* New York: Ragged Edge Press. Yob, I. (1998). *Keys to interfaith parenting.* Hauppauge, NY: Barron's Educational Series.

SECTION IV

Social Class

S ocial class and socioeconomic status influence behaviors, lifestyle, values, and functioning. *Socioeconomic status* is the term used to denote salary and income levels for individuals. Social class, a more inclusive term, includes wealth, salary and wages, real estate, educational levels, and assets (Kliman, 1998). Social class has sociopolitical connotations and carries with it sociological and psychological implications (Boyd-Franklin, 2003) because it is tied to issues of race and ethnicity. For example, poverty is associated with ethnic minorities, and middle-class values are connected to the White or dominant experience. The standards associated with social class are different according to racial and ethnic groups, so what constitutes a poor class in one setting may be a middle-class community according to that particular group (Boyd-Franklin, 2003). Additionally, there are numerous subjective representations of social class that may include people's relationship with social capital, human capital, or cultural capital. There can be a multiplicity of middle-class cultures, each with different values, motivations, and expectations (Liu, Soleck, Hopps, Dunston, & Pickett, 2004).

Typically, income, education, and occupation are used to place people in a hierarchical framework. There are five sociological social-class categories: the underclass, the working poor, salaried workers, managerial/ professional workers, and the nonruling capitalist class (Kliman, 1998). The underclass includes individuals who are near or below poverty level. Assumptions about the underclass include lower levels of education (high school diplomas or less), illiteracy, and laziness. Members of the underclass are also assumed to be less psychologically sophisticated than members of other classes, to not have the capacity for insight or long-term psychotherapy. Members of the underclass are also assumed to engage in criminal activity or illicit behaviors, including gang involvement, drug dealing, prostitution, robbery, and burglary. In fact, criminal activity in the underclass is often glamorized in the media, including a focus in news reports and in movies such as *Boyz 'N the Hood, Colors,* and *Striptease.* The working poor include individuals whose employment involves manual labor or menial tasks. Assumptions about the working poor include that they have limited education, most likely a high school diploma or GED. They are seen as hard workers but still not psychologically sophisticated. They are not considered cultured or refined.

The salaried workers class is reflective of the middle-class images in this country. Members of the salaried workers class often are employed in positions that require high school diplomas or college experience. Members of this class are seen as more psychologically sophisticated than members of lower classes. The professional/managerial class is equivalent to the economic upper middle class, although from the sociological model they may have lower income levels than the salaried workers class. They are assumed to have some college experience, most likely to have completed a college degree and graduate studies. They are more likely to participate in fine arts and culture, enjoying the educational experiences of museums, plays, and concerts. This social class is assumed to be psychologically sophisticated, capable of insight, and good candidates for psychotherapy. The nonruling capitalist class is equivalent to the upper class and considered to contain most of the total wealth of the country. Although they are often assumed to come from "old money," their educational levels vary. They are assumed to be the most cultured and refined, attending the symphony and opera, and to have high levels of psychological sophistication. The stratified view of social class is limited because strict hierarchical ideas of social class are insufficient for understanding how people perceive themselves or are perceived by others (Liu et al., 2004).

Understanding social class is important because social class is related to values and resources and is a primary factor in intragroup differences. One of the most important values related to social class is the relationship to education. Education is seen as providing access to opportunities and resources. The importance of education and the belief that education can aid in career development vary according to social-class status, with members of the upper class often placing more importance and value on education. Although a higher educational level can lead to career development and higher salaries, some individuals in the lower classes may feel that the pursuit of higher education will not bring benefits, or they may doubt their ability to afford continuing education. Therefore, it is important to explore the differences in career aspirations and career expectations. Career aspirations refer to the dreams or ideals that individuals hold regarding career choice and occupational status. Most of us begin dreaming about careers at an early age, with our hopes of becoming doctors, police officers, or nurses. Career expectations refer to the beliefs that individuals hold about the likelihood of attaining a particular position, including the likelihood of completing a particular educational level. Career aspirations and expectations may differ drastically. For example, a child of a recent immigrant may dream of practicing medicine in this country but not expect to attend medical school due to the economic need to work to bring additional family members to the country. An African American student may aspire to become a lawyer but not expect to achieve this goal due to a lack of role models in the community or a financial inability to attend college.

Finally, social class is related to values of spending and access to resources. Total wealth includes salary and income, assets, real estate, stocks and mutual funds, and professional level (Kliman, 1998). Social-class standing allows individuals access to resources, including credit lines, loans, and temporary assistance during financial crises. Members of the working class often do not meet the requirements for public benefits or social service benefits (Breunlin, Schwartz, & Mac Kune-Karrer, 1997), and they may not be able to afford loans for additional resources. In addition to educational opportunities, social-class status also provides access to health care services. The cost of medical care has to be considered when understanding an individual's functioning. Individuals without health insurance can incur significant amounts of debt if sickness occurs. It is important to assess clients' access to resources because it often influences priorities for individuals and the assumptions held about members of particular classes. If a family is coping with providing meals, it is unrealistic to expect the family to be interested in focusing on self-esteem or actualization. When providing therapy for those in poverty or members of the working class, different types of interventions that focus on providing resources or coordinating services may be warranted. Spending habits and priorities regarding savings plans also are influenced by social class. Members of the middle class may face issues regarding consumerism and the accumulation of debt (Breunlin et al., 1997). Therapists should remember that counseling services might contribute to the debt or financial difficulties that clients sometimes face.

Clinicians are probably most familiar and comfortable working with clients who come from middle- or upper-class backgrounds (Roland, 1996). Most clinicians are from the middle class, whereas a great number of clients come from a lower- or working-class background, so it is important for clinicians to be exposed to some of the unique characteristics and issues these clients face. Counselors have to address their own reactions to social class and classism. Social class is related to classism, which is defined as prejudice directed toward someone of a different social class. Downward classism is the typical classist idea involving prejudice and discrimination against people perceived to be in a lower social class. But individuals can also express upward, lateral, and internalized classism (Liu et al., 2004), paralleling issues with racism. Additionally, psychotherapy is a middle-class, Western invention (Robinson, 2005; Roland, 1996; Sue & Sue, 2007), but in the United States, a large percentage of consumers of counseling services are from lower-class backgrounds. Understanding the values associated with social class as they influence therapeutic services is important.

This section includes two stories. The first describes Carla's struggles to overcome the multigenerational effect of poverty. Note the legacy and influence of teenage pregnancy and the lack of education on social class. In the second story, Anthony discusses the influence of a change in socioeconomic status on self-concept and identity development. Anthony's mother moved to the working class after her divorce, and Anthony struggled with alienation and isolation for much of his childhood and adolescence as a result. The reader is encouraged to think about how to work with people in various social-class levels.

Thirteen

Carla's Story

One More Mile

S ome of the most difficult commercials to watch on television portray starving children, with sad faces and protruding stomachs. The narrator pleads for pennies a day, so children can be rescued from poverty and hunger. They are always shown in distant, underdeveloped, third world countries, far from the comforts of America. The commercials convince us that poverty is an issue for other countries. And yet census data indicate that 12.1% of individuals and families live in poverty within the United States. It is hard to imagine, but children here often struggle to find meals, and if they were shown on a television commercial, these U.S. children might closely resemble the children from third world countries.

Socioeconomic status influences values and functioning. For those in poverty, decisions are made in view of available resources and satisfaction of current needs. Social-class standing, with the accompanying sociological implications, includes assumptions about characteristics of people. Those in the lower or working class may struggle to find employment and educational opportunities. This leads them to decisions that often go against the dominant middle-class standards and values and at times may be illegal. What often occurs is a cycle of poverty or lower-class standing, connected to feelings of confusion, depression, helplessness, and hopelessness. Carla's story is one of overcoming the cycle of poverty. She represents clients who are struggling to meet basic physical survival needs, to the neglect of other psychological needs. As you read, notice the connections between middle-class standards issues of race and oppression. Also notice the generational patterns of social-class status and the role of education in relieving poverty.

Carla's Story

I'm a 48-year-old brown-skinned woman; maybe I even have a few hidden freckles. I'm a little-past-middle-age Black woman who decided to return to school after being out for what seems like an eternity. I never understood about being Black because my skin color is brown, or at least it is one of the colors you see in a box of crayons. I was born and raised in Dallas, Texas. It took me a long time to be able to identify myself as a Black, African American, or Negro. I accepted Jesus as my savior and Lord about 15 years ago. Well, actually, I know that Jesus has always been a part of my life, ever since I was a little girl. I have overcome a lot of obstacles in my life. I know the Lord was present in my life, and this is the only reason I made it this far; as the old women from my culture used to say, "on a prayer and a wing," meaning praying and soaring on the celestial throne of God.

I refused even at an early age to let my color dictate to me. By this, I mean when I was growing up it was like a crime to be Black, even if you knew you were Black. "One more mile" is what I call this autobiography because of all the obstacles of being Black, poor, and raised in a single-parent home, though this life still came with benefits. The only thing I felt that the White people could not take from me was my color. Eventually, my mother explained it was not the color, and if you're really going to make a White person dislike you, get an education. I was 7 years old. What did I know about color or education? I just knew I was treated differently because of the color of my skin.

I knew there was a difference by the time I turned 7 in the second grade. The White children dressed better, and they even had better lunches. White children seemed to have better homes, every necessity any human could want, including me. This had me asking myself questions about my Black identity and how come I could not give this evil, bad color back. How come I could not trade me in for a White version that got respect, that did not go hungry, that did not want for a pretty dress? I heard people talking about the new bleaching cream that had just come out. I thought maybe if my mother bought some, I could use it and turn White. It should have been a requirement not an obligation for children, no matter what nationality, to not be deprived of the essentials of life, such as food. All my girlfriends, the ones who were White, always spoke about their mothers and fathers. My Black girlfriends would speak of their mothers and their fathers visiting. Most of the time, it would be them visiting their father and stepmother. The average Black family when I grew up only knew that the so-called American dream pertained to a White family—a mother, a father, and their children. But the American dream to some Black families was mother and maybe a stepfather. I know I had some Black girlfriends who actually told me that their mother told them Mr. Welfare was their father, meaning the public aid assistant for needy families was their father.

These are the words that played in my head that my mother would tell us: "When you leave this house, you become actors and actresses. No matter what's going on around you, it's not about you, and keep your head up and a smile on your face. Always keep people on the outside, never let them on the inside." See, my mother believed that if people knew that calling you names and treating you bad bothered you, then they knew how to push you emotionally. But if you ignored them and let them call you names, they could not get control over you mentally or physically because you refused to play in their hands.

The challenges of school coming up in the 1960s and 1970s were true for most Black children. You had to work harder because the books were a year behind and the teacher was not adapted to teaching Black children with their "incorrect" language—no proper pronunciations of language, only the language learned in the home. So, if your mother had a southern accent, you would also have that same accent. Trying hard to talk like the White man or White woman or White kids was like having a full-time job. The only time I was able to sound White was when I was repeating some disturbing things some White child had said to me.

Being the second eldest of seven children was hard. We lived in a kitchenette apartment. My mother and father were separated at this point. I did not know or understand what this meant at the time. With no resources, this was all my mother could afford. When I asked my mother about my father, she said he was in the army. I noticed that all of my friends' fathers were always at home and not in the army. I would tell my mother that my friends' fathers were at home; she would state that my friends' fathers were White—like I knew what that meant. All I knew was

Maggie had a father, and my father was in the army because we were Black and poor, and if he had been White, he would not be in the army. At 6 years of age, what did I know?

When my mother and father were together, all they did was fight. My mother was an alcoholic, and my father was abusive. After they separated, her only relief was more alcohol. No money, no help, we weren't eligible for assistance from public aid until my mother proved that she was not getting assistance from my father, who was of course in the army. She never missed sending my siblings and me to church services in the morning because they served breakfast, and sometimes that was a meal we did not have at home. In that day and time, you did not tell what went on in the home; you just endured, no matter what happened in your life.

I would go to my White friends' houses because they always had food. Later on, I found out that my mother was barely 13 when she married my father, and my father was 18—a shotgun wedding. My mother was pregnant, and back at that time, you married the man, no ifs, ands, or buts. After my mother and father went their separate ways, times became unreal. But, as I said earlier, one more mile—I could go on; because of God this was possible. Sometimes my mother would play like we had an expensive steak, and it would only be peanut butter and jelly for breakfast, lunch, and dinner. We received public assistance because my father was not in our home and my mother had no other way to support us. Literally, trying to raise seven children alone took a toll on her, and she started escaping in a bottle of liquor. She was a strong Black woman. Married at 13 she did not have a childhood. She had to be a wife. Culturally, being a Black child meant that you became grown at an early age. Being a Black woman meant that you were considered the strong, I-can-take-anything woman, the man's backbone, the mother and father. You did not have rules and regulations pertaining to raising your children and being the missing father; you made it up as you went along. The way my mother handled my father not being there was to become the substitute, and her seven children ended up a substitute for her.

When I turned 10 years old, some glimmer of light came into my life— my mother went on the wagon. My mother was getting public assistance and had found a part-time job in the hospital. We moved to a larger apartment, one with three bedrooms. With six siblings, that was like living in a mansion compared to the kitchenette, which was one room less than living in a small studio apartment. Even though I have experienced many dilemmas in my past that included different types of rejection,

I know my mother did the best she could under the circumstances—a Black woman with no education, no husband, and seven children to raise by herself. We always had dinner at 4:00 p.m., no later than 5:00 p.m., and took our baths and were in bed by 6:00 p.m. At 7 years of age, I knew how to iron, wash, and cook. When I turned 9, I realized from some inner feeling and from other children in the community where we lived that my mother was very young and Black. She had her first child when she was 13 years old and was married. The child died in her arms. She had a nervous breakdown and received no help to deal with her grief and the death of her child. She was a child, a Black child in the 1950s, with no coping mechanism to help her endure depression and grief over her lost child. African Americans did not believe in going to psychologists. When I was much older, it was told to me that you did not want the community in which you live to think that you were crazy. My grandfather was a preacher, so he tried to console her when my grandmother would let her go to her father's house. When it became overbearing, they sent her back to her husband's family since he was the one who caused the problem.

My grandmother used to tell me that she could tell the Lord her problems. Why pay the White man money to talk to them when they would only have the White man answer for a Black problem? My grandmother was from the South, where she picked cotton; sometimes I would ask her about picking cotton. She would laugh and say, "I did not pick cotton; I used to be the lady of night." My grandmother had problems going to a regular medical doctor. She had all types of remedies, such as goose grease if you had the mumps or a swollen gland. We used Father John cough syrup and cod liver oil for most if not all sicknesses. There were all types of remedies that the Black woman used to keep from going to the White doctor for a Black illness. Just like my grandmother at one time did not understand the logic of going to a White man's doctor.

My mother at 14 and pregnant again was devastated for a young girl—not just a mother and wife but a young girl. My mother was an only child, so she had no brothers or sisters she could talk to. The lack of love in my mother's life had my mother seeking love; this would be a cycle my family would go through. My mother did not embrace us and say "I love you" because she did not know how. This is how my mother ended up with my father; she dressed up and pretended to be something she was not. I did not know that I had a grandmother until I was 13. I had never seen this woman; I had only heard about her. My mother did not know how to be a mother at 13 and 14.

My mother's drinking problem was getting worse. Children and Family Services came out. I remember someone called on my mother, but when the family services came out, we denied the charges because we were taught that what happened in the house stayed in the house. We knew my mother was sick. I remember at one time we did not have any lights. I was about 13. We told all our friends who came over that we were religious, and we used candles because we were not allowed to use lights for a week. But this was when my mother was supposed to get her public aid check and get the lights back on. This was a very rundown apartment we lived in that needed a lot of work, but it was all my mother could afford to pay for with seven children. I was 14 and a freshman in high school. My sister and I would have to walk because my mother did not have car fare for us to get to school. Thank God that we were on public aid; at least we were able to eat free lunch at the school. One more mile I would have to overcome. I thought I found the solution to my mother's drinking problem. My mother loved to drink vodka, and she would leave the bottle in the refrigerator. So I told my sisters if we drank half of the vodka and put water in the bottle, she would not be as drunk. This proved to be disastrous because my sisters and I were just as drunk as our mother.

Without the proper help, such as psychologist or psychiatrists, my mother went into her own world. Just when I thought that things couldn't get any worse, my mother started disappearing for 3 to 4 days, and we would not even have food to eat. I had three younger siblings who did not have friends' houses where they could go visit and stay for dinner. This became the responsibility of me and my two other siblings to provide the necessary food for the younger siblings.

At 14, I had to do something. I met this young man who worked in a store right across the street from my house. He was 18, and he liked me a lot. I couldn't say I liked him the same, but I did not know what having a relationship or love was all about. My mother was not stable; she did not know love or how to express it. I was able to secure food because he liked me. We started dating; I told him I was going on 17 years of age, that vicious cycle I talked about earlier. One more mile—there is nothing free in life. I had to decide whether to have a sexual encounter with this guy to keep feeding my siblings and myself. Especially since I lied and told him I was 17. Families had unity but no help. Your family stuck together no matter what. At 15, I found out I was pregnant. At gym one day, I got really sick and went to the nurse, and she did a pregnancy test. The school informed me that when I began showing, I would have to quit until I had the baby or they were going to drop me out of school because the school was not insured for this type of problem. I lost a lot of friends because their mothers would not let them be friends with me because they would become pregnant. Even I did not realize that it was not contagious.

My mother was laid off her job, but she was still receiving public aid. I signed up to go to Dante Skill Center to secure a clerical certificate, while I was waiting for my child to be born. I was under the NYC-II Program (Neighborhood Youth & Counseling Program) for Black people whose parents were not working or were getting assistance from the government and whose children were not going back to high school. After my daughter was born, I did go back to high school and the Dante Skill Center in the evening. This was against the law, but I needed the money, which was $154, to help support my siblings and my daughter. It wasn't much, and the government paid the rent.

One of my mother's drunken friends had cut the gas on illegally, and Human Services paid for our lights because I had a new baby. One day I came home from school, but before I got there I just knew something was wrong. First, I passed by this lounge my mother loved to go to. They told me that my mother and daughter had been in there earlier, and they had collected about $20 from people in the lounge who said my daughter was really cute. When I finally got to my house, my mother was passed out on the floor and my baby was crawling around eating off the floor. I picked up my baby, and I cried and wished for a normal family like the White family I saw on television. I made up my mind that I had to move.

I took my money and rented a room owned by my girlfriend's mother, Ms. Shells. It was a men's rooming house that housed men. My baby's father would come and spend the night, so I would not be scared, but he had also become very abusive. When my baby's father went to jail, this was the best thing I figured could happen, so I could move. I went to the public aid office to get assistance, but they told me that as long as I was underage, my mother still had to get the check for my children and me. I had two children by the time I turned 18.

While at the public aid office, I ran into a girl I went to high school with. I was standing waiting for the bus with my new baby and my eldest little girl, who was 2 years old. I began to cry, but I did not have anywhere to go, and I was really worried about my children. Social Services only helped adults. I knew now how my mother must have felt, all alone and no one to go to. I really needed psychological help, but I did not know what that meant at the time. I just heard people say this. I was depressed and felt there was no hope, but I still had a strong sense of spirituality that God was enough in spite of what I was going through. The girl told me to come home with her and talk to her mother and maybe we could work out something so I would not be on the streets. I told her mother all the money I received was $154 from training school and that I had 2 more months and then I would be graduating from there.

A new home is what I received and some special friends. I slept on the floor of my girlfriend's bedroom with my 2-year-old child and my 3-month-old baby. Once I put the children to sleep, I would go to these two lounges across the street from each other to get milk and diaper money from the men at the lounge. This is how I would do it. Once a week, I would go sit at the bar; the men would give me money for cigarettes and to play the jukebox and buy myself a drink. I would order a soda and pocket the rest of the money and tell them I was going to the washroom. Then I'd leave. I was able to do this until I started getting checks from school. My baby wasn't on formula like other babies because I could not afford to buy it. I did not even have a medical card to take her to the doctor. The medical card was the poor people's insurance. My baby survived as well as myself on what I could muster up.

I only knew Black antidotes—alcohol, drugs, and men, anything that would give us what we considered a little peace in the White man's world. My friend's mother agreed to keep the children while I attended business college downtown. This was a government program for poor people who want to get a trade and a stipend for car fare. The school had 6 spaces out of 100 for poor families to go to school to earn a trade. They had a special scholarship, so you had to show that you were really poor and could not even afford to come to school. I put in an application and was accepted because I had a high school diploma. About 90% of the students at this school were White. One of the significant life events that happened to me while in this school was, besides my teacher being White, I became one of her prized students to use in class to the other White students as "the poor Black student who was able to come to school on scholarship"; she would tell them, "If she can make it, you people should make it that much more."

The teacher used to tell me that I was Black; she must have figured I did not know that. Then she would say that I would never learn how to type because my hands were like a dwarf's—too short to reach the keyboard. The reality of the situation is that culturally I was not White, but I was not an idiot, either. The teacher always used the three Black students as her escape to try to make the White students succeed.

I was used to the dilemma of racism and some White people speaking as if we learned by example, by looking and not by using our brains. I used my teacher to inspire me to complete the program, and everything she said I could not accomplish I did better than accomplish. I graduated from the program with honors, and I graduated out of the 12-month program typing 73 words a minute. Education was always a big part of me; my mother stressed the importance of it. This is when I met the man that would become my husband. I was seeking love when I did not know what love was. I got married because I got tired of trying to support myself and get by on my own. I signed up at YMCA College, majoring in court reporting and music. These dreams were put on hold temporarily. At 18 and with two children, I married but did not know the man or his family.

I was married 23 years. In all the years I was married this was past a challenge. The marriage was not made in heaven. I had encountered a family who believed in selling drugs and gang banging. I finally got tired, two more children later. I moved to the opposite side of town than my husband with my four children, no job, nothing to support my family. I had quit my state job to move and have food for my children and to get away from my husband. So I started sending out resumes and putting in job applications.

One more mile—I had to have closure. Sure, life had thrown me more lemons, but I was always able to make lemonade, and after my divorce from this man, I decided to better myself by going back to college. I had been doing temporary work for several years and decided something had to happen for the better. At this point, I needed to seek psychological help, social services, and anything or anybody who could explain why it may have been destiny that I would still be going through hell, just because it never came easy being a Black person.

Presently, I'm working as a secretary. I completed a double degree in criminal justice in a college that has a returning adult program. Eventually, I want to work in juvenile probation or a juvenile correctional center or perhaps even one day open up a facility that would help young pregnant girls survive the system.

One more mile of culturally challenging things—I kept seeking to better myself and become something I saw all my life. You are not disabled because you are Black, White, or green. You disable yourself because you give up and allow yourself to believe that education is only for White people. This story has just lightly touched the events that I dare not share with anyone except my God and children because they have always been a part of my big picture. I know if it had not been for the grace of God and His mercy, I would have not lived to tell my story.

Content Themes

Carla's story teaches us about the influence of social class and socioeconomic status on functioning, values, and behaviors. It is clear from the story that Carla's family lived in a generational cycle of poverty, with accompanying feelings of helplessness and depression. Because both Carla and her mother had children as teenagers, they were limited on the available sources of public aid and other resources, exacerbating the issues of poverty and leading to questionable solutions. Carla's story also highlights the importance of education as a means of changing or shifting in socioeconomic status. Finally, the intersection of social class with dominant standards, race, and oppression is highlighted in the story.

The Impact of Poverty

Carla's mother was poor, and although it is not mentioned in the story, Carla's grandparents may have been working class or poor as well. Carla's mother had her first child as a teenager and was unable to support her family once the relationship with the child's father dissolved. To receive public aid, she had to prove that she was not receiving financial assistance from her husband. Although she was eventually awarded aid, by the time she had seven children, the aid did not provide enough support to be able to sustain the children. Carla's mother ended up abusing alcohol as a way to overcome the depression and helplessness she felt from her circumstances. It seems as if she felt she had no way out of poverty, probably because she did not receive financial or emotional support from her family of origin and did not receive enough government support to feed her children.

The influence of poverty is apparent throughout the story. The first effect was the hopelessness and negative emotions that were felt by the family members. It appears that Carla's mother attempted to make the most of situations—for example, helping the children to feel as if their meals were more luxurious than they were. The level of poverty in the family often kept them from having minimal survival needs met. However, having children at a young age with little support eventually seemed to take a toll on her. She began to drink more and to leave her children unattended and without supervision. When individuals need to receive services but are denied for a variety of reasons, feelings of depression occur. The inability to see a way out of poverty, combined with real physical needs, extends the depression to a sense of hopelessness and helplessness. One can only imagine the pain that Carla's mother experienced not being able to provide for her children's basic needs and in seeing them hungry and negatively comparing themselves to others. The injustice of the situation without the voice to be heard can lead to increased helplessness. There is also a sense of shame that comes from being in poverty. The second effect of poverty is that it often forces children to behave in ways that are older than their biological age. Older siblings often have to be responsible for the care and support of siblings; they often need to drop out of school to work part-time jobs to feed siblings. It is clear that Carla felt this responsibility for her younger siblings. Older siblings often serve as intercessors at school for parents who may be unable to attend conferences. This creates role ambiguity and confusion for siblings who are forced to take on responsibilities before they are ready (Kliman & Madsen, 1999). In gang- and drug-infested neighborhoods, children often work selling drugs to make up for the lack of funding provided by public aid.

This of course is the third effect of poverty: the choice to engage in risky or illegal behaviors to meet basic survival needs. Boyd-Franklin (2003) discusses the necessity of street survival skills that is often a part of the culture of poverty. Although selling drugs may not be the best long-term solution, for many it provides more immediate and substantial cash than working a minimum wage job or receiving part-time wages. Fortunately, Carla's family was able to receive some assistance from public aid, churches, the school, and friends, so none of the children had to turn to drugs to provide money for the family. Carla, however, did engage in questionable behaviors to provide for her younger siblings. Carla had to find ways to find money for food and was placed in the vulnerable position of needing to exchange sexual favors for money. This behavior continued even after she began to have her own children. Even when making more healthy choices, the consequences may be negative. Carla married as a way to gain financial support but ended up in an abusive relationship.

The final effect of poverty is the intergenerational transmission of poverty. In poor families, the family life cycle between generations may be compressed (Kliman & Madsen, 1999). Young mothers, with or without partners, may be raising children at a much younger age than their middle-class counterparts. By the time a poor mother has grandchildren, it is not unusual for a middle-class mother to have her first child. This pattern can be repeated from one generation to the next. Although Carla attempted to provide money for the family, she became pregnant, propelling her into poverty. She had to quit high school because she was pregnant, which prevented her from finding suitable employment. The end results for Carla were feelings of helplessness, hopelessness, and depression similar to what her mother experienced. Carla was fortunate that another family took her and her children in until she completed school and could begin working. Many individuals remain in a cycle of poverty (Boyd-Franklin, 2003). Parents are unable to care for their children, who begin to make decisions that keep them in the lower socioeconomic status. There are generations of families, for example, that remain in public housing because they cannot develop enough resources to move. Carla does not discuss her children, but it is possible that they are also receiving public assistance and maintaining the generational cycle of poverty.

Lack of Access to Resources

One of the major consequences of living in poverty or being in the working class is the lack of resources available to individuals and families. Although the U.S. government offers subsidy programs, they often do not provide enough to fully support families. Many of the welfare-to-work programs in states, introduced by the 1996 Personal Responsibility and Work Opportunity Reconciliation Act, offer limited assistance to families, for example, 5 years of funding to engage in training and job placement. When the 5-year period is over, people are removed from welfare rolls and have to become financially independent. Individuals with mental disorders that prevent them from maintaining full-time employment are unable to earn a living wage. Those not able to work due to child care concerns are left without public assistance. Members of the working class often make too much money to receive assistance but lack sufficient income to provide for families.

The effect of poverty tends to be even more severe on women and children of color (Boyd-Franklin, 2003; Robinson, 2005). The percentage of minorities in poverty is disproportionately higher than that for White people (Boyd-Franklin, 2003; Kliman & Madsen, 1999). Individuals in impoverished rural areas may have less access to resources (Sayger & Heid, 1990; Weigel & Baker, 2002).

Although Carla's family received public assistance, it was not adequate for taking care of the seven siblings. Her mother had to rely on support from other social service organizations. Carla also spent time with friends and ate at their homes. She was also able to participate in the free lunch program at school, and that sometimes served as her only meal. Carla faced barriers of her own after she had her first child. She reports that social services and public aid were provided at the time only to individuals over the age of 18 years. The lack of access to resources led Carla and her family to cheat the system—for example, they had utilities turned on illegally, and Carla enrolled in a program illegally to earn an education to find employment. Many individuals often remain single but live together, receiving benefits illegally. Other individuals lie about their age to receive services.

Oppression and poverty increase vulnerability to chronic stressors (Boyd-Franklin, 2003). This is related to increases in drug and alcohol abuse and chronic health problems. And the lack of resources extends to medical services and therapeutic services. Carla did not have enough money to provide appropriate nutrition for her daughter. Fortunately for Carla, her baby did not require medical attention because she could not have afforded quality medical care for her. Women of color often have the least amount of access to medical and psychological services (Robinson, 2005). Many individuals remain in poverty if they have to have extensive medical care and build up debt from medical bills. In fact, individuals often become poor due to medical concerns that are not covered by insurance. Individuals in poverty often do not receive psychological services as well. Because their primary focus is on food, clothing, and shelter, despite feelings of depression or anxiety, therapy is not seen as an option. If individuals are able to enter treatment, they are more likely to attend sporadically due to difficulty with transportation or work schedules (Boyd-Franklin, 2003). They may also feel that it is not necessary to participate in insight-oriented work and rather want the therapist to serve more as a case manager or advocate in social services organizations. The lack of availability of therapeutic services can be detrimental for individuals and families in poverty who experience chronic stress and trauma and exposure to violence, gang activity, crime, and drugs and alcohol (Boyd-Franklin, 2003).

Importance of Education

Carla's story highlights the importance of education as a means out of poverty. Her mother became pregnant for the first time and married at the age of 13 years, preventing her from completing high school. The lack of a high school education probably contributed to her being unable to find suitable employment to care for her children. Carla repeated this cycle, becoming a teenage mother, which forced her from high school. Carla's mother stressed the importance of education, so Carla continued to pursue vocational training, even using illegal means to continue. Education proved to be a way out of the lower socioeconomic status for her. She eventually completed her college degree, despite occurrences of racism along her educational path. Many do not have that opportunity or the heroic personal characteristics or perseverance to sustain the path despite chronic exposure to racism.

Link to Race/Dominant Values

The exposure to middle-class norms and values has an influence on individuals of all class levels, particularly due to the prevalence of television viewing. Aponte (1995) discusses the "new poor," who are bombarded with images of wealth, greed, and consumerism via television, leading to a sense of injustice, helplessness, and sometimes rage. For Carla, these images were not viewed via television but in vivo through her attendance at predominantly White schools. As a child, Carla combined the notions of race and class, with wealth and comfort associated with being White and poverty with being Black. Carla early on felt a sense of injustice about the lack of equity in resources. In addition to class associations, Carla connected family structure with race, believing that only Whites had intact nuclear families, whereas Black families were predominantly single-parent households. Many African Americans view economic situations, educational opportunities, and employment through the lens of race (Boyd-Franklin, 2003).

Clinical Applications

Assessment

Clinicians must assess the influence of both social class and socioeconomic status on clients for a number of reasons. Social class determines the level of access to resources. Participating in therapeutic services is in many ways a luxury and can become a financial burden to clients who do not have insurance to cover payment. Clients in lower social classes and who have psychological disorders of a neurological or biological basis may not be able to afford to maintain medication. They may also have some unaddressed medical concerns that are contributing to the presenting problems. Socioeconomic status is also linked to basic and psychological needs of individuals. Clients may have more pressing concerns than behavioral change, such as providing food and shelter. The following are recommended as questions to assess social class:

What is your current income, wage, or salary level?

Are you making enough money to meet basic needs?

Are you receiving financial assistance? Does this assistance allow you to meet basic needs?

What is your educational level?

Are you receiving a living wage?

Do you have access to appropriate medical care?

Do you have a budget? Are you able to maintain your budget?

Are you in debt?

Techniques and Interventions

Social-class standing should influence treatment goals and interventions. Many clients in poverty are referred through third parties, such as court or legal systems or schools. Although it is important to address the treatment concerns of the referral source, therapists may also need to serve as case managers with other social service agencies and as advocates for clients. Aponte (1995) calls for therapeutic services that address the ecosystem of the client, noting the importance of interventions at the individual, family, and community levels. He outlines three general goals for treatment of the poor. First, the poor need to feel control over their lives, particularly ownership of therapy. This need serves to counterbalance the sense of helplessness that often develops due to the lack of available resources and the inability to meet basic needs. The second goal for treatment is to help clients to develop a sense of purpose or meaning in life. Children who live in the housing projects of large urban areas often are pessimistic about reaching 18 years of age due to violence in the neighborhood. This pessimism contributes to a sense of meaninglessness. The lack of gainful employment or the ability to contribute to society may also add a sense of futility about life. Clients need to move beyond basic survival needs to address other psychological needs, including a sense of meaning and fulfillment. The third goal of treatment is to focus on changing the community in which clients live and function. Again, therapists need to be willing to expand beyond providing individual counseling. Therapists need to remember that the client's therapy goals may be focused more on present-oriented or basic needs. Clients at the poverty level may enter treatment for depression or anxiety, but the inability to meet basic needs or the lack of available resources often exacerbates psychological symptoms. Clients in this social class may appear infrequently in treatment. They may call clinicians to be seen on an emergency basis, which generally involves an immediate family crisis, a situation with work, or a medical need. Insight oriented or long-term therapy may be deemed by the clinician as useful, but clients may identify other uses for the therapist, including assistance through crises. Behavioral approaches and brief therapeutic approaches may be most helpful for clients.

Special care needs to be taken to establish a working alliance with clients of economically disadvantaged backgrounds. Initiating a clinical encounter with an assessment of strengths, coping, and resilience factors may be most beneficial to the establishment of the therapeutic alliance (Kilpatrick & Holland, 2009).

If clients are engaging in illegal activity, they may not feel comfortable disclosing information in treatment. For example, a single mother may be living in public housing with her children's father but may be unwilling to acknowledge her partner for fear of losing benefits if the living arrangement is discovered by the government. Clinicians have to consult the ethical codes of their professions and state laws regarding reporting criminal activity. In all cases, it is important to provide informed consent for reportable offenses as part of establishing the therapeutic relationship. Therapists working with clients in rural areas need to address dual relationships in treatment, particularly because therapists are advocating for them and seeking resources (Sayger & Heid, 1990; Weigel & Baker, 2002).

Family Therapy

Family therapy, particularly structural therapy or ecostructural therapy (Aponte, 1995), is also recommended for individuals who are economically poor (Minuchin, Colapinto, & Minuchin, 1998). Families often lose structure as children, especially older siblings, take on more adult and parental responsibilities. Children may also be called on to serve as parents to their own parents, who are incapacitated due to depression, anxiety, or substance abuse. It is also not unusual for multiple generations to be living together and for parents to be treated as siblings of their children. Family therapy can help to restore structure to families, empowering parents. Home therapy or home visits are recommended for treatment (Aponte, 1995). Home visits may help the clinicians meet with the families or clients on a weekly basis. The visits also provide the therapist with an opportunity to see the clients' living space and community and to meet important family members. Visiting the home also provides the clinician with the opportunity to deliver more informal psychotherapy groups as a benefit to the community.

Community Interventions

Clients also need to be empowered through community interventions. Therapists may need to help clients coordinate services through various agencies and may need to serve as advocates for clients. Boyd-Franklin (2003) recommends developing an ecomap, a diagram of the agencies and services that clients receive. The diagrams help to coordinate services and serve as a tool to help clients empower themselves.

Parent Education

A common experience of poor families is to be referred for services by the state Children and Family Services agency, schools, and community counseling centers. Typically, parent education programs consist of a teacher with a curriculum telling parents how to be better parents. This involves several underlying assumptions: that the parents are bad parents, that the teacher knows how to parent the children of these parents better than the parents themselves, that the parents are going to absorb a curriculum they had no input in designing, and that after the teacher teaches the curriculum, the parents are going to have an "aha" moment and become better parents of their children after they gain insight into their mistakes. When parents do not demonstrate that they have learned the correct way of parenting the children, they are labeled unmotivated, resistant, or abusive. In the United States, protecting the family often means controlling the family (Iglehart & Becerra, 1995). With the worthy goal of protecting the children from abusive and neglectful parents, institutionalized violence in the form of curriculum-based parent education is exerted on the family in disrespectful and damaging ways (Minuchin et al., 1998).

Traditional parent education curricula are generally not designed with regard to the social-class status of the parents and are delivered by providers who are not involved in the community, with little input from the parents. Culturally sensitive parent education can start by involving the targeted parents in a needs assessment of the community. Abuse and neglect do not take place in a vacuum but are part of a community that needs help with affordable housing, employment, health care, and other issues. Even parents who are mandated to take parenting classes can be encouraged to become collaboratively involved in the identification of their needs and the implementation of the needed changes as the stages of change, the motivational interviewing, and the solution-focused models demonstrate (De Shazer, 1988; Miller & Rollnick, 1991; Prochaska, Norcross, & Di Clemente, 1995). When parents identify parent education as one of their needs, they are much more likely to benefit from it. For meaningful change to occur, counselors should not be thinking for their clients and should not be their "surrogate frontal lobe" (Hoyt, 2001, p. 113). A facilitated discussion could take place in a school, for example, with a facilitator who poses questions to the group. These discussions can take place during parent university days and parent–teacher conference nights, in day care centers, or in community youth programs, and they may be more successful than curriculum-based parent education programs.

The following are some of questions that a parent educator could use to springboard discussions. The questions are intended to elicit answers from the parents themselves and not from the facilitator.

What are the best ways to motivate a child?

What works when it comes to getting kids to do what the parent wants?

What works to modify a child's behavior? What does not work?

How do you get a child to stop/start doing something?

What did your parents do when you were a child that worked?

What did your parents do when you were growing up that didn't work?

What did you learn about how to raise your children from the ways your parents raised you?

When you know what works, can you implement it? How so?

What hinders your implementation of what works?

What are the characteristics of a good mother/father?

What are the characteristics of an ineffective mother/father?

Is there anything you do/don't do that makes you feel like a good mother/father?

Is there anything you do/don't do that makes you feel like you are not a good mother/father?

Do you know what happens to you that makes you behave in one way and not another way with your children?

Make a list of what works for you. Now make a list of what does not work. When do you do things from one list and when do you do things from the other list? What do you notice about the two lists?

When parents are given an opportunity to talk about the best way to change a child's behavior, they often say that patience works and screaming does not. When asked for the best way to raise a child's self-esteem, parents often say that praise, love, and attention are better than punishment and neglect. In other words, parents generally already know what works and what does not.

Countertransference

There are many areas in which therapists may have strong personal reactions. Working with people of differing social-class levels may invoke strong feelings, value differences, and ethical dilemmas. Clinicians should carefully monitor their reactions, especially when working with people in lower social-class levels.

Feelings of Helplessness

The first typical reaction of clinicians is to overidentify with feelings of helplessness and hopelessness (Comas-Diaz & Jacobsen, 1991). It can be frustrating to hear stories of deprivation and hunger, especially when children are involved. Clinicians who feel overly sympathetic may offer solutions that clients have already tried or solutions that are not viable, inadvertently enhancing the frustration of the clients. They may feel guilty for their own middle- or upper-class status (Robinson, 2005).

Therapists may also be tempted to cross therapeutic boundaries to take care of clients by offering money or transportation services. Clinicians may also be tempted to provide housing for children in poverty. Therapists may also engage in the parallel process of helplessness and hopelessness, leading them to provide false hope to clients or to make clients feel stuck in treatment. The frustration may lead therapists to blame the clients for their circumstances.

Feelings of Anger

The second reaction is to feel angry with the clients, particularly if clients seem to have values different from the middle-class clinicians' (Gorkin, 1996). A common complaint in supervision is that clients have inappropriate spending habits or values around money. Therapists may also be angry with clients who are wearing expensive clothing, shoes, or jewelry. Many clients, however, buy designer clothing at thrift stores or secondhand stores or receive donated clothing from companies or social services organizations. Many clients spend money on nice clothing because they feel that it is important to look presentable and decent: "We may be poor but we don't have to look poor" is the philosophy that is often presented by individuals in poverty. Maintaining appearances can be a way to maintain a sense of self-worth and dignity. It is important to remember that clients have free will and autonomy and can choose to spend money as they see fit. If therapists feel that the value differences hinder the therapeutic relationship, they should discuss their concerns with the clients. Clinicians may also feel angry with clients who engage in illegal activities to provide for themselves and families. Therapists may be able to see the shortsightedness of illegal solutions but have difficulty with helping clients find more suitable solutions. Therapists may also face an ethical dilemma when hearing about illegal activity regarding their duty to report the activity to the police. Clinicians need to check with state regulation boards.

Standard English

Clinicians may have difficulty with clients in lower social-class backgrounds who do not speak Standard English proficiently (Robinson, 2005; Sue & Sue, 2003). Similar to working with immigrant clients, therapists may struggle with understanding slang terms. Clinicians may also assume that clients who do not speak Standard English are illiterate or unintelligent or have difficulties learning.

TOOLBOX ACTIVITY—CARLA		
Discussion Questions	*Activities*	*Resources*
Content themes What other themes do you see emerging in the story that the author did not identify? **Assessment** Are there any questions you would like to ask Carla? **Interventions** What other interventions could you propose with Carla? **Countertransference** What countertransference reactions were emerging in yourself as you read this story? **Other scenarios** Imagine that Carla is coming to you several years ago or several years from now with a presenting problem. What might that presenting problem be?	You are a single parent planning to attend the local community college this year with the goal of transferring to a 4-year college in 2 years. You are currently receiving food stamps and a housing subsidy and have a part-time salary of $9,000. Two courses cost $600. Plan a monthly budget including costs for housing, utilities, food, child care, transportation, entertainment, and miscellaneous expenses. Research the application process for public housing and public welfare programs in your state. Research the application process for unemployment benefits.	**Suggested readings** Kotlowitz, A. (1992). *There are no children here: The story of two boys growing up in the other America.* New York: Anchor. Minuchin, P., Colapinto, J., & Minuchin, S. (1998). *Working with families of the poor.* New York: Guilford. **Websites** www.hud.gov www.doleta.gov

Fourteen

Anthony's Story

From Radical to Bohemian to Suit Me

O ur social-class status distinguishes us from other people, yet it is sometimes so invisible that, although differences between us are recognized, we do not attribute them to class. The differences in class and socioeconomic status begin in childhood. For example, there are certain brands of blue jeans or sneakers that children just "must have" because everyone is wearing them. Other differences can be seen at lunch in the cafeteria, through distinctions between the meals purchased through free lunch programs to homemade meals of peanut butter sandwiches or left-over veal. It is clear that some people are poor: They seem to be unkempt, may smell, and have to eat free lunches. And it is equally clear that some are rich: They drive their own cars to high school. These are the visible differences that are superficial, and although they are at times linked to popularity or attractiveness, social-class issues are not generally labeled as such. But it is important to recognize that social class is also linked to values, standards, and norms for behaviors—less visible characteristics.

Individuals are socialized within a particular social-class structure. Although social class is fluid, the values associated with it are developed through childhood socialization (Robinson, 2005). Social class is linked to values, including the importance of education, vocation, and achievement. Class is related to interpersonal relationships, influencing activities people share. Relationships with authority figures, whether they are treated with respect or disdain, are often determined through social-class socialization. Socialization begun in childhood is reinforced in high school, as adolescents begin to make decisions on vocational aspirations and college attendance. Decisions are often based on parental income level, the perception of opportunities, role models within the community, and family expectations. When faced with the challenges of adulthood, issues of social class and accompanying values come to the surface.

However, the values of social class may emerge at earlier times in individuals' lives, particularly if change occurs in socioeconomic class levels. The predominant media image is that of a positive change in class standing. Television is filled with shows where individuals can go from rags to riches. The American dream of being able to own a home and have a family is something that is aspired to by many. In fact, one of the stereotypes of immigrants is that they come to the United States for economic gain, to be a part of the American dream. Rarely does one think of social-class change in the opposite direction: of losing income. But many Americans are laid off, fired, or downsized from their positions. Parents divorce, sometimes causing women and children to move to poverty level. This change in class standing can influence self-concept and identity development. Anthony's story is one of changes within social class. The reader should note the effect that change in social-class status has not only on his self-concept and identity but also on his social activities and interpersonal relationships.

Anthony's Story

An old Italian jibe states, "How do you get an Italian to keep quiet? Easy. Tie his hands behind his back." The truth fundamental to the joke is that Italians are, by and large, an expressive bunch who routinely gesture in their storytelling.

While growing up, I confess, my family expressed their private joys, public triumphs, and collective pain in storytelling. To them, no subject was considered either too taboo or too sacrosanct. Political correctness, a virtue embraced by the larger culture, was largely absent from my family. Decorum was judged by the level of audience interest. Through their frequent retelling, the stories grew in revision and refinement.

At an early age, I was taught that plainspoken pilgrims and their pursuit of religious freedom shaped America. By inference, they built a dominant culture and extended its benefits to the world.

My family, on the surface, appears to embody this story. With historical veracity, I can trace my lineage back to the founding of the nation as a registered son of the Mayflower. This fact, coupled with my Anglo-Saxon sounding surname suggests that I am ethnically White. Granted, I realize that by tracing my lineage back to Plymouth Rock I admit English heritage, but an uncomfortable fact emerges: I can only claim 1 immediate ancestor in 16 as Anglo Saxon. That ancestor, my grandfather, is not strictly English himself. He is a mix of English and black Irish. My name aside, I strain to understand what it means to be White.

As family lore and history books explain, the black Irish were the survivors of the unsuccessful Spanish naval invasion of England. As fate would have it, they washed up on Irish beaches and married the local girls. In 1930, my grandfather married a Sicilian woman after his arrival from Tennessee. She, an Italian immigrant, had ancestors who emigrated from France in the 1800s. It appears that not all of Napoleon's soldiers returned home after the war.

The lineage on my mother's side is equally as convoluted. My maternal grandfather, a southern Italian, married a Scottish-Hungarian woman. As a result, both my father and my mother grew up in bicultural households with prevailing Italian cultural norms. As a result, I trace my identity back to Italian, Hungarian, Scottish, Irish, English, and French ancestors— Italian American, for short.

The social patterns embedded in an Italian heritage are obvious from the media images. My family is loud, emotionally extravagant, and profligate in storytelling. Communication was, and is, next to impossible without operatic gestures and crescendoing falsettos. To paraphrase Shakespeare in literature and my family in life, "All is but a stage."

Indeed, not only is life a stage but a loud one at that. My family routinely performed at dinnertime. Dinner was both an open forum and, simultaneously, an audition. Moreover, if someone's story became boring and uninteresting, it was then expected, if not required, that another family member save dinner from destruction and take up the reins of conversation. Outside the family, we dichotomized relationships into the tidy categories of family and everyone else. Notwithstanding, different measures of conduct applied. In times of stress, the family turned to itself for strength and excluded the demands of the dominant culture. Usually, this was accomplished through sarcasm and aloof observation. Stock phrases would be taken out of our cultural vault and deployed against any of the dominant culture's claims on our time, our money, or our allegiance.

Not surprisingly and tragically, we became firmly convinced of our own cultural integrity. In retrospect, after making the necessary concessions to the family's fear of change, I have since come to view their traits in terms of strength and resilience, rather than simple fear and ignorance. A few short years into my life and my parents' marriage, they divorced. As a result of their divorce, my family's finances plummeted. A sharp thud later, I awoke to form a fuzzy picture of my financial standing vis-à-vis the other 7-year-olds in the area.

Not long after, as I sat on my front stoop in my Sedgefield jeans with the knees blown wide apart, I collected my thoughts. I quickly reasoned that the new erratic dinner schedule was not due to spontaneity, novelty, and stoicism, nor was it a passionate commitment to child-centered learning. It was a consequence of the divorce. Scarce meals accompanied my mother's erratic work schedule. I plummeted in all the relevant measures of physical fitness: height, weight, and resistance to illness. Other consequences soon followed. Baseball, a pastime in the neighborhood, required strict attention to detail: uniforms, snug caps, well-oiled gloves, and a litany of bats, wooden and aluminum. Moreover, it required a basic understanding of the concepts strike zone, catching technique, and swinging basics. Shell-shocked from my father's rapid exit, I found all this talk overwhelming and alienating. As a result, I shied away from organized sports.

Not long after her divorce, my mother returned to her childhood home with me and my brother in tow. We toddled along, only later becoming aware that our postcard-perfect smiles opened closed doors. My grandfather insisted that he provide a second phone line in his home. Magnanimously and publicly, he trumpeted this as a grand gesture to provide for his children. The sleek burgundy phone with its 10 feet of unspooled line sat on a faux-mahogany table. Later, he used this gift, this phone, to whisper his illicit passion into his mistress's ear. I would often sit in the jagged, dry silence trying to swallow my revulsion.

Implicitly, I understood the exchange: shelter for silence. My grandmother, however, played by another set of rules. Stammering over herself in convoluted emotional somersaults, she lashed out, and my grandfather remained complicit in his silence. Quickly, I became the convenient alibi for his indiscretions and an unwilling accomplice in his attempts to shelter time, money, and emotional availability from his wife, my grandmother.

Her legendary rants pierced my already fragile psyche. Before long and fully realizing the consequences of the Faustian exchange, I simply tuned out. Amid the emotional abuse, willful manipulation, and emasculating atmosphere, I realized the road to happiness would be a bumpy one. To survive, I stripped down my expectations to a bare minimum and deeply buried my emotional needs. I understood that if I could survive until college, I could unpack my troubled identity.

Growing up in such an environment, I attempted to lessen the stigma of poverty by controlling my environment. Initially, I enforced this by not placing myself in any potentially embarrassing situations where my deprivations would be exposed. Often, when confronted with a happy two-parent family with a bright economic future, I ridiculed them. Importantly, it must be noted that rarely were these thoughts verbalized. Eventually, I turned the ridicule inward on myself. Often this cycle culminated in a racing heart rate, a constriction of my vision, and a near blackout.

To cope with what I saw as a debilitating condition, I recast the entire experience into my family's far-left political language. My earliest childhood recollections include a moment where my mother cooed over me: "Who is my little radical?" Prompted, I responded that indeed I was her little radical. With Pink Floyd's "Dark Side of the Moon" wafting in the background, I was strongly encouraged to never work for the corporations because they were evil incarnate.

My mother's idealism, countercultural spin, and politics led her in the early 1970s to entertain some unconventional notions of mainstream culture. In short, a radical group recruited my mother to bomb an abortion clinic. After deliberation, she refused, but only after considering the repercussions on her two infant sons. Her beliefs framed the radical-left character of the family's politics.

Later, I trained myself to crucify any hope of economic betterment, and I purged myself of friendships and experiences that could conceivably testify to other alternatives. Surprisingly, I found that poverty was quite resistant and had a life of its own, replete with its self-sustaining mores, norms, and values. By the time I entered college, I began to question my conclusions. As a student in the early 1980s, I unflinchingly sized up the local high school. Consequently, I understood that my future lay elsewhere.

Seeking to escape a substandard education, I, along with a handful of resolute ragtag urban city dwellers, clambered onto the bus. We peered out at the passing urban landscape as our bus bent its way to the north transit terminal considered by all Westsiders to be the equivalent of the

Brandenburg Gate. There, I exchanged the frayed city green for the crisp suburban blue. After running the gauntlet across the city's edge, I longingly gazed on suburban West Park's ample lawns and sturdy stone homes. I traveled a snug suburban mile to Carnegie College Prep, an academy for the well-heeled.

Again, I was the kid with the Anglo last name but misplaced Italian heritage. Even more to the point, as a city dweller, I was regarded as disadvantaged and potentially violent. As a result of having a confused heritage, a questionable pedigree, and a checkered financial legacy, I soon became marginalized and encountered difficulty in assimilating.

Inside the classroom, I adjusted to the academic demands. However, outside the classroom, I strained to find common ground with my classmates because their conversations revolved around experiences beyond my reach. I could not identify with the gated communities, the downtown business internships, and the jaunts to Europe. I felt I needed stories and experiences of my own to counter the wide net cast by Carnegie College Prep. Confused, I tried to put an affirming spin on my shame. Inwardly, I agreed with the stereotypes to create a "violent identity" for myself. I concluded that I would always remain a second-class citizen, a poster child for the downtrodden—in short, a pity project. I hardened my childhood flirtations with alcohol, drugs, and gangs into a more active participation.

Working in the city at a local banquet hall opened the door to the purchase, barter, and, often, the outright theft of hard liquor. Jack Daniels, marijuana, and hash became my drugs of choice, and my friends who passed through the criminal system gave me instant clout in the rarified air of Carnegie College Prep.

In a Conradesque way, I became the anti-wonder-boy of the community. I dealt them alternative stories, beautifully tragic, to counter my own sense of inadequacy. I tried to project myself as an embodiment of their upper class fears.

After years of this borderline self-destructive behavior, I gladly parted with this ill-fitting identity and embraced Christianity. I traded my alcoholic tales and drug-induced visions for a new story of redemption and healing. At last, I felt I had a road map to reconstruct my fractured sense of self. Although I successfully eliminated most of the destructive symptoms of my pain, the root confusion still remained. During the nonthreatening environment of college, I attempted to clarify my struggle. I attempted to patch my identity together with spiritual and aesthetic glue. Comical in retrospect, I endeavored to solve my questions by transcending them.

Clove cigarettes, Echo and his Bunnymen, and late-night Marxism—bohemia beckoned, and I felt the allure irresistible. In defining myself as an artist, I felt I could leave all the inconvenient talk of heritage, ethnicity, and duty behind and replace it with the lively topics of beauty, inspiration, and class warfare. After my best imitation of Jasper Johns, and an unsuccessful storming of a government building to protest late-night Nicaraguan romps by the Contras, I grew tired of being so countercultural.

I concluded that being a Bohemian was a definite dead-ender. Against my better radical judgment, I fancied that there may be something to the tired talk of heritage, ethnicity, and duty. But before beginning a systematic exploration of my roots, I took a 10-year detour through second-generation Asian America.

After college, my childhood imps of despair and fatalism feverishly gnawed on my relationships. I lived with a robust fear of the "spontaneous meal" or the "unplanned movie." I feared if my social encounters drifted into unexpected expenses, I would meet three equally unsettling choices: (1) invent an indecorous excuse, (2) accept someone's charity, or (3) commit myself to an expense I could ill afford. As a result, any sustained effort at intimacy became difficult. A cycle of shame and anxiety danced in my head. I reasoned if I chose friendship over finances, the unexpected would create feelings of worthlessness, a loss of control, and a sense of being less than masculine. After surveying these thoughts, I often returned to the cycle of anxiety and blackouts. So I chose to limit my relationships. With good reason, I equated my singleness with my financial situation.

With an eye on the inevitable emotional hangover, I routinely stayed in on weekends. I reached out to the Christian community, and they thankfully responded.

I firmly believe that my God has an incredible sense of humor. He took me, an angry and broken Italian American, and placed me into the tightly woven community of second-generation Korean American Christians. This Asian faith community provided the reliable and predictable behavior I needed to heal my identity, while I deconstructed my Anglo Italian, liberal artistic upbringing. In time, and only after receiving much support, wisdom, and healing, I began to test the limits of my adopted culture. Soon, a majority of my social life centered on the Korean community. I became a youth pastor to a Korean church, roomed with a second-generation Korean American, and socialized almost exclusively within the Korean American community.

Thankfully, I healed my identity in a community dedicated to the pursuit of truth and harmony. These two ideals balanced the excesses of my

heritage. Later, when I became confident of my identity, I found it necessary to separate my ethnic identity from my growing spirituality. That
necessitated a break from the Korean American community.

Struggling against post-college poverty, I perceived that my socioeconomic position sharply contrasted with my aspiration to be White. I persis-
tently wrestled with my sense of belonging. My pigmentation allowed me
to pass for White in the dominant culture, whereas my mannerisms frequently aroused suspicion. Often, I was asked to tone down because I
caused distraction. It was explained to me that "most people do not act like
that." This variance created in me a desire to further define myself according to my family's radical political legacy.

I entertained two questions: "How could I, a second-generation radical, push the envelope beyond the limits set by my former hippy
parents?" and, second, and not as crucial to my identity but imperative to
my immediate survival, "How can I eat regularly?"

Thankfully, I found an acceptable balance of these two competing
needs. I betrayed my family's mores, values, and trust. I snapped a conservative navy blazer into place and laced up for success. I decided that I
needed to work for the corporations.

Working as an agent, I received a regular paycheck, which alleviated
my immediate financial crisis. More important, my job served as a convenient wedge between me and my near-hysterical mother. It allowed me
the necessary psychological space to complete my identity formation.

Inwardly, I delighted in the shrewdness of my seemingly mundane
career choice; I valued it as the pièce de résistance of my post-college
identity development. However, in the long run, I could not separate this
job from my emergent identity. Eventually, I found the job ill suited for
both my temperament and my sense of belonging. Suffice to say, I could
not reconcile the White, affluent business world with my ethnic and class
understanding. In retrospect, I should have been tipped off by the constant lunchtime dry heaves.

I left the corporate world after a 2-year stint and went headlong into
teaching. Initially, I resisted the idea because it reflected my father's fail-
ings, himself a public school teacher. After, taking inventory of my gifts,
talents, and temperament, I realized that the road to healing ran straight
through my father's profession.

My 6-year journey to teaching was difficult and offered little immediate relief. In my pursuit of my dream, I culled eight meals from my
weekly budget, compromised on air quality with my apartment's toxic

mold, and studied late into the night amid the sounds of the bustling city rats scurrying under the floorboards.

Undeterred, I courted my present situation with a ripening sense of purpose. I taught for 6 years as a substitute teacher while pursuing my teaching certificate. While back in school, I separated from both the radical notions of my childhood and the Asian culture that supported my healing. I found peace and a growing sense of my identity.

I left the Asian community to deepen my spirituality. Ironically, as I left, I reconciled with my father and found a faith community that fit both of us. It was there that I met my wife, an Asian American.

My wife and I continue to explore our shared bicultural/biracial experience. Importantly, our cultural differences are undergirded by a common faith.

The most noticeable differences in our marriage revolve around time management, conflict style, and in-laws. Our conflict with time might humorously be relegated to the time differential between Los Angeles and Seoul. Small underlying conflicts have occasionally spilled into larger cultural messes. My Italian heritage gives full vent to emotional expression. As a result, most of the cultural cues of tone, facial expression, and nonverbal language are readily understood. In the same vein, Korean culture relies on a subsequent series of cultural cues, protracted periods of silence, and nonverbal protocol to express meaning.

To illustrate, my wife and I temporarily shared living space with a couple while our home was being built. While seated on a couch rapt by CNN's coverage of the second Gulf War, I observed our Korean American friend express, albeit nonverbally, a sense of displeasure. Moreover, as I readily understood her mild displeasure, I intuited it had nothing to do with the war or my viewing of it.

After a quick internal check of possible offenses, I concluded none existed. As a result, I continued watching the broadcast. Later, this friend exploded into unmitigated rage. On the surface, she explained that she was angry that I neglected to bring in the newspaper. It soon became evident that her rage was directed at my reluctance to probe for a more complete understanding of her distress and my unwillingness to respond to her discomfort with a kind act of service. The Korean word *nunchi* expresses this dynamic. From my predominately Italian American understanding, *nunchi* is tantamount to being held an emotional hostage. My inner Tony Soprano mumbled, "If she's gotta' problem with me, then she needs to tell me." My cultural paradigm informed me of three things:

People need to take responsibility for their own discomfort, responsibility involves expression, and if people choose to not verbally communicate their anger or frustration, then the problem resides with them.

In contrast, the Korean concept of *nunchi* places great emphasis on the nonverbal and demands a response by the recipient. Additionally, the act of verbalizing is viewed as somehow diminishing the value of the exchange. I have since translated *nunchi* into the more readily understood concepts of being empathic, thoughtful, and proactive. Still, the cultural assumptions of the role verbal expression plays in relationships present ongoing challenges. Returning to the nature of in-laws, I have, of late, more fully embraced my mother-in-law. Our relationship has gone through a series of awkward steps but has culminated into full acceptance with the birth of her grandson. Initially we were on a first-name basis, which reflects the American value of informality. Now, often I refer to her as *Chung-mo-nim*, the Korean term of respect given by a son-in-law. Occasionally, I refer to her as Nana, my son's version of "Grandmother."

Building on this belief, I have come to understand that my ethnic identity and sociocultural history, along with the indwelling of the Holy Spirit, define me.

The answer to my own identity struggle is a complex one. Recently, I have rejoiced in the fact that I can lay claim to a bicultural identity. My identity remains primarily rooted in my faith but is open to new experiences. The intensity and raw emotionality of my Italian heritage is being refined in my marriage to a Korean American. Emotional expressiveness is giving way to thoughtful restraint. Storytelling is ceding ground to acts of service.

Content Themes

Anthony's story is rich with images around social class and socioeconomic status and their influence on self-concept and identity. There are two central themes in the story: the influence of changes in social class and the influence of dominant middle-class values.

Changes in Socioeconomic Status and Social Class

The first major content theme is the change in social-class status that Anthony experienced and the influence of this change on his self-concept and identity. When his parents divorced, it is likely that he dropped from middle-class status to working class. His mother moved to her parents' home because she may not have been able to afford her own place and perhaps because she wanted to receive child care for her children. It is not uncommon for individuals, particularly women, to move into a household with their parents or extended family members immediately following a divorce to save on housing costs, reduce child care expenses, and receive emotional support. If individuals do not have family for financial support, the change in social standing most likely would be from the middle class to poverty level. Anthony's mother was fortunate to be able to relocate with her parents. Nonetheless, there must have been a drastic change in status because Anthony reports consequences to his physical status.

The changes had effects on Anthony's development and social activities. The initial effect was on his peer relationships in the neighborhood, which seemed to result from changes in family structure and social class. When the children in the neighborhood talked about baseball, Anthony became overwhelmed and began to withdraw. When in high school, Anthony experienced a similar disconnection from his peers. He was not able to associate through the middle- and upper-class activities and discussions. Anthony felt the other students assumed that because he was from the city he was "disadvantaged and potentially violent." He began to construct his identity based on the stereotypes projected onto him and his inability to connect with his peers. Unfortunately, Anthony chose to participate in illicit activities to define himself.

Anthony's transition is similar to the character portrayed by Judd Nelson in the movie *The Breakfast Club*. His peers were all more financially stable and seemed to come from intact nuclear families. To hide his shame and embarrassment, he took on the role of the delinquent. His real personality, of being sensitive, empathic, and caring, was revealed as he spent time with the other characters. Many adolescents who feel alienated and disconnected from the mainstream may choose this path to define themselves; the tough-guy stance serves as protection against rejection and hurt. Had Anthony continued with his behaviors, he may have ended up dropping out of high school or possibly imprisoned. Fortunately, his desire to be able to feed himself helped him to find career direction and to pursue college. Anthony also found solace in the Christian community.

The sense of social isolation continued after college and after he entered the workforce. Anthony decided to reenter school to pursue his teaching career, which left him on a tight budget. He became fearful of being invited out for spontaneous outings because he could not afford meals, movies, or activities outside of his budget. Anthony chose to isolate himself from peers and to remain single due to the shame of his social-class position. Unfortunately for Anthony, the pressure to fit within the dominant culture continued through young adulthood, college, and employment. It also continued to influence interpersonal relationships.

Dominant Class Standards

Anthony begins his story discussing his mixed ethnic heritage and his claim to the Italian American culture. His family sounds as if they were loud and boisterous, shared many heated discussions, and enjoyed each other's company. Of course, even in the introduction, Anthony discusses his relationship with the dominant culture and his feeling of separation from it. Although racially he identifies with being White, it is clear that, for Anthony, his cultural identity is more rooted in his Italian American heritage than in his Whiteness. However, examining his relationship to social class and interpersonal relationships, it is clear that his socialization was influenced by dominant White, middle-class values, which he eventually internalized, even though he fought them earlier.

White middle-class values include the importance of individualism; independence; autonomy, achievement, and competition; the Protestant work ethic; a future time orientation; status and power; and ownership of goods and property (Robinson, 2005; Sue & Sue, 2003). Although some of Anthony's values may have differed from the mainstream values due to ethnic variations, it is also likely that they differed due to social-class status. Anthony was able to attend a high school noted for academics and to pursue college, so it is clear that he endorsed the mainstream values of achievement and autonomy. He reported that his college experience was "nonthreatening." When choosing a career, however, the socialization that Anthony experienced influenced his choice, which differed from mainstream values. He reports that his mother was a "hippie" who taught him that valuing money was inappropriate. The notion of status and power and ownership of property, goods, and assets may not have been important or a priority for the family. However, his quest to stay aligned with his family's values contradicted his need to eat and support himself, so he attempted to acculturate to the dominant mainstream values and began to work for a corporation. Working in this environment was unsettling for Anthony, however, and seemed to make him physically sick. The differences in values may have been too overwhelming for him.

Making the choice to leave corporate America and to pursue a teaching career returned Anthony to his working-class status. He followed the Protestant work ethic by attending school to earn his teaching degree, so he meets the dominant standards in some regards. However, few would take the option of leaving a well-paying job to move to a place where rats could be seen or heard, making his choice different from the choice other White middle-class men would have made. One wonders if this option would have been available to him if he were married and had children.

Clinical Applications

This section addresses assessment concerns, techniques and interventions, and countertransference issues.

Assessment

Social class influences values, standards, and norms for behavior, along with interpersonal relationships. Therapists need to assess clients to determine how they have been socialized regarding class. Therapists also need to assess changes within generations as well as within individual lifetimes regarding socioeconomic status. Clinicians may also want to assess how social class influences interpersonal relationships and their clients' internalized classism. Internalized classism can manifest itself in "anger, frustration, feelings of failure, anxiety or depression related to not being able to meet the demands of his or her economic culture" (Liu, Soleck, Hopps, Dunston, & Pickett, 2004, p. 109). The following assessment questions are recommended:

What is your current social class level?

Has there been a change in your social class? Have you recently received a promotion or raise at work? Have you been downsized, laid off, or fired?

Has there been a change in your family's social class?

What messages did your parents or other family members give you regarding finances or economics? Were you encouraged to save money or plan for the future?

What messages did you receive regarding education, achievement, or career aspirations?

How were your relationships influenced by your socioeconomic status?

To assess internalized classism, the following questions are recommended:

How do you view your own social class in relation to your friends, neighbors, or relatives?

Has that view changed over time or did it remain the same?

How comfortable/uncomfortable are you with members of a different social class?

How do you feel about disclosing your social-class status to other people?

How do you understand the reasons for your economic successes or your failures?

Techniques and Interventions

Anthony's story teaches about the influence of social class on self-concept and interpersonal relationships. Clinicians need to be sensitive to changes in social class and how the changes influence functioning. A number of techniques are recommended for treatment.

Dominant Values

First, clinicians need to address social-class norms and standards and help clients who feel as if they differ from the norms. Middle-class values predominate in the media, along with the drive for consumerism, and influence self-concept and self-esteem. Clinicians should help clients understand how their socialization experience, values, and self-concept are related to social class. Exploring childhood experiences around social class might be a useful way of helping clients elicit values related to class. Focusing on clothing, toys, games, and accessories may be a useful way for clinicians to begin. Children are socialized early about the importance of material goods; in preschool, friendship changes based on who has the best new toy. By school age, children use ownership of goods as a way to assess worth and to measure self-esteem. These messages may be supported by parents who often go into debt to buy extravagant gifts for children during holiday seasons and birthdays; birthday parties are even becoming expensive affairs, with goody bags and treats for children who attend. The macrosystem and general cultural ideology of consumerism reinforce these values.

Helping clients explore the relationship between their self-concept and their class-related values may elicit an awareness previously not present about how they go about selecting their mate, their careers, and other lifestyle options, and are intimately related to their socialization and to their social class. For example, often clients consider themselves "less than" in terms of their social-class standing and their background and may wrongly assume that they do not have access to certain professions or future mates solely based on a self-deprecating view of themselves and on their social class. A woman with a professional degree who was raised in a working-class environment may feel that she is not a suitable partner for a professional man raised in the upper middle class, although their current social class is the same. Others may consider themselves "more than" and avoid making a professional or occupational choice because they may consider themselves above it. For example, executives who are downsized may refuse to accept employment under a certain salary level or a particular title.

Many dual-career families may feel like failures because they cannot obtain the same status that previous generations could obtain living on one income (Kliman, 1998). As disparities in income grow and media images continue to depict upper middle-class comfort that few people can afford, therapeutic conversations about historical phenomena and class disparities may help normalize this issue and decrease shame for these couples and families. Having clarifying conversations with clients can be revealing and life changing.

Clients should also be encouraged to discuss educational and career goals and their relationship to social class. The Protestant work ethic is part of mainstream culture, along with the notion of the importance of achievement, accomplishment, and status. Again, children are socialized with these messages and, therefore, may be encouraged to prepare for standardized tests and to begin to think of a vocation at an early age. Clinicians should discuss individuals' career expectations and aspirations, especially when working with adolescents, because these aspirations and expectations may differ based on social class. For example, a teenager growing up in an inner-city area may aspire to become a physician. However, due to expectations about the cost of college and medical school, the lack of role models within the community, and the lack of access to information regarding available scholarships, the adolescent may decide that pursuing college is an impossible dream. Clients of all ages should be assisted in finding resources to pursue career aspirations and vocational goals.

Budgets

Many live with high levels of debt; it is easier to buy items on credit today than at any other point in history, an effect of the interaction of the macrosystem ideology of consumerism and the chronosystem in which consumer spending is seen as the answer for economic recessions and slowdowns. Although it may feel out of the arena of treatment, therapists should explore financial wellness with clients. Teaching clients how to balance a checkbook and avoid credit card debt can be an important tool for fiscal responsibility. Clients should also be encouraged to develop reasonable and manageable budgets for living expenses. Living in debt, with the fear of being pursued by creditors, can create undue stress and pressure for individuals. As we saw in Anthony's story, it can also lead to a sense of social isolation. Clinicians should refer clients to reputable non-profit credit counseling agencies. Therapists must be cautioned that the cost of therapeutic services can exacerbate the financial stress clients face. Even if clients make a small copayment, the cost of therapy should be carefully considered and included in budgets. Therapists are encouraged to follow suggestions present in many of the ethical codes and consider providing pro bono services; this may be a preferred option, along with a reduced fee, for clients who are in need of treatment services but experiencing financial stress.

Countertransference

It is tempting for counselors to avoid or ignore issues of social class in the counseling relationship when counselors perceive themselves as being of the same social class as their clients. However, it is important for counselors not to assume that their clients share similar worldviews and expectations, even if they are perceived to belong to the same social class. Hearing stories such as Anthony's can elicit emotional reactions in clinicians, including sadness and sympathy for his social-class differences and confusion about his financial choices. The importance of mainstream middle-class values and their influence on counseling also need to be addressed. Anthony experienced social isolation throughout school based on his perception of alienation from his peers. Clinicians who have experienced a similar sense of isolation based on social class may overidentify with clients such as Anthony. This hinders therapists' ability to display genuine empathy for clients. Therapists who were socialized and raised in the middle and upper classes may associate clients such as Anthony with delinquent or criminal behaviors. Stereotyping clients also hinders the development of the therapeutic relationship.

Differences in Values

Therapists may feel confused about Anthony's decision to struggle financially by leaving a job in a corporation to pursue a teaching degree. Becoming wealthier seems to be a part of the mainstream values because status, power, and financial gain are valued. Individuals with education who choose to live in poverty are viewed as deviant. "Being poor in American society and staying poor is not valued. Being poor and then becoming rich is often admired; the values of hard work, pulling oneself up by one's bootstraps, change, and perseverance are showcased" (Robinson, 2005, p. 178). Special care may have to be taken to work with clients whose value systems differ from mainstream middle-class norms. Therapists need to determine what is "normal" according to their social-class socialization and how that perception of normal influences their perceptions of clients.

Finally, clinicians should remember that counseling occurs within a particular context and follows mainstream values (Sue & Sue, 2003). In addition to valuing independence and autonomy in individuals, counseling reinforces the notion of hard work, perseverance, and self-control. This includes the concept that change is the responsibility of clients and emphasizes an internal locus of control. Clients whose cultural values are different from the mainstream may expect different approaches to treatment.

Classism

Counselors have to address their own reactions to social class and classism. Social class is related to classism, which is defined as prejudice directed toward someone of a different social class. Downward classism is the typical classist idea involving prejudice and discrimination against people perceived to be in a lower social class. But individuals can also express upward, lateral, and internalized classism (Liu et al., 2004), paralleling issues with racism. Counselors need to assess their own level of internalized classism and examine whether downward, lateral, or upward classism are present in the interactions with their clients.

TOOLBOX ACTIVITY—ANTHONY		
Discussion Questions	*Activities*	*Resources*
Content themes What other themes do you see emerging in the story that the author did not identify? **Assessment** Are there any questions you would like to ask Anthony? **Interventions** What other interventions could you propose with Anthony? **Countertransference** What countertransference reactions were emerging in yourself as you read this story? **Other scenarios** Imagine that Anthony decided to remain in his corporate position for fear of being poor. How would you help him deal with his stress?	Conduct a values auction. Determine which values are most important to you and how they are related to social class (see Pedersen & Hernandez, 1996). Write an essay about the social class values you hold and their influence on psychotherapy.	**Suggested readings** Ehrenreich, B. (2002). *Nickel and dimed: On (not) getting by in America*. New York: Owl Books. Shipler, D. K. (2004). *The working poor: Invisible in America*. New York: Knopf.

SECTION V

Sexual Orientation

Sexual orientation is the romantic, sexual, or emotional attraction to another person. It is important to distinguish sexual orientation from other concepts with which it is often confused. Sexual orientation is different from biological sex, which refers to the physical sexual characteristics with which people are born. Sexual orientation is also different from gender identity, which is the psychological sense of being male or female. Finally, sexual orientation needs to be distinguished from the term *gender*, which can be defined as the socially constructed adherence to cultural norms for feminine and masculine behavior, thoughts, and feelings ("Answers to Your Questions," n.d.).

Sexual orientation cannot be viewed as a dichotomous variable because it exists along a continuum that ranges from exclusive homosexuality to exclusive heterosexuality and includes various forms of bisexuality ("Answers to Your Questions," n.d.; Elze, 2006; McClellan, 2006). The traditional polarization of sexual orientation into two discrete categories, homosexuality and heterosexuality, leaves out bisexuality and other sexual orientations (Division 44, 2000). An understanding of the differences among gender identity, gender expression, and sexual orientation is important. Sexual orientation refers to one's sexual attraction to men, women, or both, whereas gender identity refers to one's sense of oneself as male, female, or transgender, and gender expression is the behavioral expression of either the gender identity or the sexual orientation ("Answers to Your Questions," n.d.).

Homosexuality can be defined as the orientation of people who "identify inwardly as male or female in accordance with their genitals, and whose primary erotic attraction is to their own sex" (Johnson, 2004, p. 79). Bisexual individuals can experience sexual attraction to both their own and the opposite sex, regardless of their behavior (McClellan, 2006).

Anywhere between 2% and 10% of the population is gay or lesbian (Smith & Gates, 2001). It is difficult to estimate the number of people who identify as gay, lesbian, or bisexual because there is a fear of discrimination or victimization by identifying as other than heterosexual (Smith & Gates, 2001). The "Don't ask, don't tell" policy in the U.S. military, which advocates for hiding one's sexual orientation in order to serve in the military (Gates, 2004), mirrors the written or unwritten policies in work, family, and social environments where people do not feel free to reveal their sexual orientation.

Same-sex intimacies have been documented in all historical periods. Although same-sex behavior has always existed, sexual orientation is a relatively new concept, and the idea of homosexuality as a category is only about 100 years old (*GLBT Fact Sheets*, n.d.; Roseneil, 2002; Tully, 2000). Homosexuality went from being considered a sin to a medical and scientific category (Miller, 1995) viewed as deviant, pathological, and criminal (Moses, 1982). Though considered to have had liberal views for his time, Freud's view of homosexuality as arrested development contributed to the belief that homosexuality is learned behavior, and can, therefore, be cured. The medically oriented approach resulted in viewing gayness in terms of mental illness with a slant toward rehabilitation (Moses, 1982). Treatments that were often forced upon patients included induced seizures, nausea-inducing drugs, electroshock, covert sensitization, having gay men masturbate while viewing pictures of a nude woman, lobotomies, castration, and implantation of "normal" testes (Hunter & Hickerson, 2003). The members of the early American psychiatric establishment maintained that homosexuality could be corrected with treatment until 1973, when the American Psychiatric Association altered its position by declaring that homosexuality is not a mental disorder. The classification of homosexuality as a mental disorder was not changed until the 1987 revised edition of the third edition of the *Diagnostic and Statistical Manual of Mental Disorders* (*DSM-III*) (Hunter & Hickerson, 2003).

Currently, conversion therapies or reparative therapies have been rejected as unscientific by the American Psychological Association (DeLeon, 1998), the American Psychiatric Association, the American

Psychiatric Association Commission (2000), the American Counseling Association (Whitman, Glosoff, Kocet, & Tarvydas, 2006), and the National Association of Social Workers (Hunter & Hickerson, 2003).

The rise in social activism movements spawned by the civil rights movement is a recent development. The gay liberation movement was born at the time of the Stonewall Rebellion of 1969 in Greenwich Village, which was an important historical marker of the gay civil rights movement (Miller, 1995). While homosexuality, bisexuality, and transgender issues are "coming out of the closet" (Blumenfeld, 2000, p. 261), so is the backlash against this trend. Hate crimes against lesbians, gays, bisexuals, and transgenders are on the rise.

The relationship between sexuality, sexual orientation, and gender is a complex one involving multiple cultural, biological, social, and genetic aspects (Birke, 2002). Current scholarship regarding gender socialization generally reveals a description of a permanent interaction between biological and cultural/constructivist perspectives (Mitchell & Black, 1995). Gender socialization is understood as a complex psychological and social construction, not as a simple extension of either anatomically based reproductive capacities or brain physiology. In terms of gender socialization, this means that people are not only born as male or female, but "learn to be women and men" (Lorber, 2000, p. 204) in reciprocal interactions between anatomy, social expectations of male and female behavior, and other complex, gender-based socialization experiences, such as gender role expectations and gender role responsibilities (Moses, 1982). Genes, hormones, and biology contribute as much as social practices to the construction of gender socialization. It is now understood that, as with anything else that is human, gender identity cannot be thought of as devoid of the influence of culture.

The controversy surrounding the origins of sexual orientation has strong political, religious, and social implications. Research on the origin of sexual orientation shows contradictory and inconclusive data. Scientists do not know what "causes" homosexuality, any more than they know what "causes" heterosexuality. The complex interactions among genes, sex hormones, prenatal, and environmental determinants has not been elucidated. In addition to genetic and other biological factors, it is suspected that a multitude of environmental and psychosocial factors may have a profound influence on the sexual differentiation of the brain, and later, on the development of children and adolescents (Birke, 2002).

Regarding the need to understand the origins of homosexuality, important questions arise. If homosexuality were not a stigmatized behavior, would there be an interest in finding out the reasons for its origin? Why is there not a similar push to find out the reasons for heterosexuality? If heterosexuality was not viewed as the norm, from which homosexuality deviates, would the question: "What makes people gay?" have any meaning at all? There is a lot at stake in the answers to these questions. Some supporters of gay rights contend that finding the genetic markers of homosexuality would end the controversy and advance the gay rights cause by reducing discrimination and putting an end to the idea that homosexuality can be contagious (Birke, 2002). Other scholars contend that, on the contrary, focusing on the causes and origins of homosexuality is itself a homophobic activity that merely reinforces the prejudices. From that point of view, "What makes people gay?" is not an important or even a relevant question (Blades, 1994).

To frame the issue of homosexuality as one that oscillates between biological determinism and social constructionism only is to attempt to simplify the complexity of the issues. Some examples of that complexity follow. First, there may be numerous forms of homosexuality and heterosexuality. Some authors contend that homosexuality is fixed and cannot be changed or consciously chosen ("Answers to Your Questions," n.d.; Butke, 2002). Other authors argue that sexual orientation is fluid and that people can fall anywhere along a continuum (Roseneil, 2002), and that "there is not a homosexuality, but homosexualities" (Nardi, 2002, p. 46). Second, sexual behavior cannot be the only dimension considered; fantasy, sexual attraction and desire, love, self-identification, and culturally sanctioned expectations and behaviors also need to be taken into consideration. Third, there is diversity within sexual orientations and there can be different typologies of gays, lesbians, or bisexuals. For example, in "Latin bisexuality" found in some Latin American societies, men may engage in overt same-sex behavior, and as long as men play the active or "insertive" role, they are not considered homosexual (Esterberg, 2002, p. 219).

For most people, sexual orientation emerges in early adolescence without any prior sexual experiences. It appears that men, on average, know that they are gay earlier than women (Arey, 2002). Many men and women generally report knowing they were gay from very early on, but some women awaken to their lesbian sexual orientation later in life. It is unclear whether a postadolescent awakening is even possible, whether it is a result of the denial and repression of earlier homosexual feelings or tendencies, or whether it is a reflection of differences between men's and women's origins of homosexuality (Esterberg, 2002).

The lack of full consensus surrounding many of the issues about sexual orientation is a reflection of the lack of available knowledge but is also a reflection of the profound social, cultural, and political implications of each position.

When counseling gay, lesbian, or bisexual (GLB) clients or their families, it is important for clinicians to take into account exposure to homophobia, the ethnicity of the individual, and experiences with the coming-out process, among others. GLB clients may be at risk for suicide and substance abuse, among others. With gay and lesbian youth it is important to assess for family support and resiliency factors. Clinicians might work with GLB clients directly or with their siblings, parents, spouses, or children and should be aware of the preceding clinical issues. Professionals need to be comfortable making assessments, asking appropriate questions, and providing help in finding support. Counselors need to be aware of state regulations and ethical guidelines regarding exceptions to confidentiality around issues of HIV and AIDS disclosures to third parties, and that there are multiple pathways toward the successful synthesis of an individual's sexual identity.

This section includes Karen's story, told by a woman who discovered, after having been married for several years, that she was attracted to another woman. We read about her journey toward self-knowledge, self-expression, and self-acceptance.

Fifteen

Karen's Story

Midlife Growing Pains

Karen writes about her 14-year marriage to Steve, the discovery of her attraction to another woman, and the steps she took after that discovery. She tells us about her subsequent relationships, her unfortunate encounters with violence and homophobia, and how she dealt with her family of origin and the work-related issues of her coming out. As you read, notice the fluctuations in her identity awareness.

Karen's Story

At the age of 35, I began another growth spurt. This change crossed many dimensions including physical, cognitive, emotional, social, familial, occupational, and sexual. After 14 years of marriage to Steve, my high school sweetheart, I found myself being attracted to a woman. This attraction was causing me to question my integrity as a woman, a friend, and a married wife. Never before had I felt such incredible exciting stirrings inside, nor such torment. Whether or not to act on these feelings and desires became a weight that I carried with me in all settings. What would this do to my marriage and more importantly my friendship with Steve? What would happen at work, since Gwen, the woman I was attracted to, was a coworker at the school where I was a librarian? What would my friends say? What about family? Is this a choice or is this something that has been building inside of me, remaining dormant until I was ready to face it? Is this love or just lust? Is it the person you love regardless of their gender? Is this adultery if it is with the same sex? Why is God doing this to me? And finally, am I going crazy?

I shared some of my questions separately with Steve and my best friend, Meg. To my amazement, both of them were not surprised that I had this attraction. They had always suspected or at least acknowledged the possibility that I might have lesbian tendencies. This was an incredible surprise to me that they had thought this but had never talked with me about it. I cannot remember ever entertaining the thought but I always found myself open to differences in people, welcoming diversity, enjoying the study of relationships and social interactions in psychology, feminism, humanism, and the role of faith and the values of independence, responsibility, caring, and resiliency. I had strayed from the religious teachings of my Southern Baptist upbringing many years before and preferred a more secular view of faith. This allowed me to attend churches that were welcoming to people from all walks of life and to not pass judgment on others. However, this did not keep me from judging myself.

The conversations Steve and I were to have over the next couple of months became more and more difficult. The stirrings grew. An overwhelming curiosity and desire to explore collided with my devotion to him, my life on the farm, and my fear of what might come. As I moved into the spare room and came home later and later, so that I could spend time just being with her, I could see the toll that this was taking on him. This tender man had supported me emotionally and economically while I worked on my master's degree in library science. He surprised me with weekend getaways to the beach. He held me even when I was writhing in tears over what I was going to do with these feelings. How could I end a marriage that so many of our friends idealized? And that I idealized? The guilt and pressure mounted, but then so did the stirrings.

As I spent time with Gwen during the work week, I began to have an awakening deep inside. Almost as if discovering a part of me that had been waiting for the door to open for the light to come in. I drove away from her on our meetings yearning for both solitude to think it all out and planning for when we could meet next. I began to feel alive in a way I had never felt possible. In my past, I was prone to bouts of melancholy and perhaps a cynical if not pessimistic view of life. This experience was leaving me soaring to heights and depths I never knew possible. I was recognizing beauty all around me, feeling fortunate and blessed, tapping into physical energy to function on less than 3 hours of sleep, eating ravenously or not eating at all and crying in rages of self-hate and blame. The full gamut of life revealed.

Whoever said the coming-out process is a spiritual one was correct. Learning who you are as a sexual human being after decades of never having to think about it at all makes you question your whole purpose of life. As I began to redefine myself, my old support systems began to change. I couldn't talk about what was happening to me but to a couple of close friends. As the strain of my actions began to take a toll on my relationship with Steve, resentment, bitterness, and anger began to be the undercurrent of our talks. I moved away from my home on the 85-acre farm within 6 months to a one-bedroom condo in town. I began a Dr. Doolittle sort of push me–pull me routine with Gwen.

I sought help from conversations with God and a therapist, began taking medicine for sleep, and walked on eggshells around my family and at work. I was not prepared to talk with my parents and siblings and struggled with how to explain why I had moved out.

My family was very supportive of my decisions and never pried. For this I am extremely thankful as I don't know how I would have handled their questions about "why." Being the youngest of four children and sometimes forgotten, more formally educated and the one everyone considered "different" gave me some freedom from the inquisition that others might have in their families. I felt supported by them because "blood takes care of blood" but I did not feel close enough to them to share this part of my life even though all of my immediate family lived in the same town. I'm sure they talked among themselves and wondered why the perfect marriage was failing, but few questions were asked. My parents checked on me routinely and always offered to help if I needed them.

While living in the condo, I spent a good deal of time at Gwen's house. She lived in a very rural setting, which gave me comfort since leaving the woods, river, and meadow of the farm. One drizzly afternoon, we took her dog for a walk down the dirt road past her house. While walking back home we passed a car that had stopped at a bridge over the small river that was full from the rain. Soon after passing the car, it pulled up ahead of us and stopped. We walked on by thinking it unusual but unaware that the man, a stranger in the car, had intentions of harming us. He got out of the car with a baseball bat and struck Gwen in the leg, then came after me. He hit me in the knee as I shoved my umbrella in his face. I yelled for Gwen to run, and we both took off with him following us. Gwen fell down, and I turned to defend both of us. I began talking to him in as calm a voice as I could muster, told her to run and then I began running backwards still telling him that he needed to go home to his family and leave us alone. He finally turned back to his car and we got to her house and locked the door. Physically, Gwen was okay, but I had ligament damage to my knee. Later that night, my father drove both of us to a convenience store where the police had apprehended the attacker and I gave a positive ID. In court, we learned of several previous charges for this man including several for assault on a female. He received more jail time for his assault on us. As we were leaving the courtroom, members of his family called out words of profanity to us intermixed with words like "dyke," "lesbian," and "fags." Was this to be my first experience of sexual orientation discrimination? Even my landlord said to me that there is a lot of hate out there for lesbians when he learned of the crime, but I had never spoken to him about my sexual orientation. Did this mean that I now was attaining the appearance of a lesbian? Was I being outed by just my looks and my presence with Gwen? What was going to happen at work? Could I get fired?

At work I found support not condemnation from the faculty and administration. When I returned to work on crutches, people showed genuine concern for my health and never asked too many questions. My school library colleague was wonderful. She introduced me to feminism and goddess-based faith through tarot cards and readings that I had never encountered before. She opened her home to Gwen and me and began to share more of her personal life with me to help me understand that everyone has questions they are searching answers for. Her husband shared in this support and became a consistent ally. She even spoke individually with a student who was passing a note around about Gwen and me being lesbians. She was an incredible safety net and her understanding allowed me to begin to develop my own understanding of what was happening.

The depth of darkness I found myself slipping into from time to time after leaving the farm was directly related to the fact that I had planned my whole future around my infallible belief that Steve and I would be together as friends, if not husband and wife, forever. When he began dating again, I realized that he could be happy with someone else but that perhaps I couldn't if it meant losing contact with him forever. The woman he was now living with became intensely jealous, and contact with him was stressed and awkward. I wanted to come home, but he was in a different place now, and I had to accept the change.

About 3 months after the assault incident, Gwen and I moved in together in a small rental house in the country. Anytime you share living space, there are changes and compromises to be made. Here is a journal entry during that first few months together.

June 4—I went for a walk this afternoon looking for nothing but then something. I went up the start of a logging road cut through the woods with poison ivy and all. Then I got on another red clay road to the top of the mountain. At the top I looked around some to check out where I could go next time I wanted to hike. The logging road looked like a big gash that had begun to heal some but had many scars running through it becoming smooth yet jagged in places. I asked the trees if they talked. The response was a cry—not a new cry but a mourning sorrowful one. The woods were still in recovery from the damage done by the road work. The gash and scars were still very sensitive and healing slowly. Yet, the trees had learned that life continued, things were constant as before. The wind still blew, the birds came, and leaves were new and green. It was as though a metaphor existed for me on the ridge. The scars were the changes in my life, the loss of the relationship with Steve, the cuts in my heart. Still very sensitive but healing, recognizing that some things are the same: friends, family, interests, laughter and play. This brings me to wondering why I am reluctant to make a greater commitment to Gwen. I keep trying to hold on to the image of the relationship with Steve as perfect and it is the relationship with Gwen that has created the wound that I now carry as a scar. Yet standing on that ridge with the trees looking at the road, I realize it is the relationship with Steve, the silence, the anger with him and with myself that has created the wound. I keep wanting to blame Gwen for the scar but it's not her. She is one of the constants that helps the woods [me] gain the energy and strength to heal and look beyond the road.

Why can't I let this happen? Maybe it's like the road. My scar is still quite sensitive and changing in its look every day. Maybe once I can go beyond the focus of the scar I can really heal and breathe easy again.

While we were living together, Gwen quit her job to go back to school to become a physical therapist. To the public, family, and some friends we were housemates saving money for other adventures. To our close friends, we were a couple. It was not possible to show public forms of affection as I still worked in the school setting and it just didn't feel safe even in a town as progressive as the one we lived in.

It was on a trip to Atlanta to visit some of Gwen's gay friends that we were able to be more open. It was also on this trip that I learned how to not look gay. We went out to a local restaurant that is frequented by gay men, lesbians, and bisexuals. I began to take notice of the women's hair and clothing. Many of these women did not fit the stereotype. They did not have short hair rather they had long flowing, permed, curled, bunned, or braided hair. They wore dress suits, makeup, jewelry, skirts, and feminine blouses and carried pocketbooks. I laughed out loud when I realized that I could not tell who was gay and who wasn't. From this experience, I coined the notion that you can tell a lesbian by her haircut, and whether or not she wears a black belt with a silver buckle and carries a pocketbook. I became very conscious of how I dressed, keeping long hair, wearing brown belts, and carrying a pocketbook. I even had people whom I outed myself to say, "No you're not, you don't look or act like one."

The relationship with Gwen lasted for 7 years. When I look back on the experience with her, I can sometime feel remorse for the losses I and others endured for me to follow what felt natural. The journal writing during this time of forming a new identity allowed me a chance to express what was heartfelt and sometimes unthinkable to say out loud. The breakup with Gwen left me swirling into a period of self-doubt, condemnation, resentment, and ultimately depression. I allowed myself to become physically sick, dehydrated with rapid weight loss, intense anxiety, and stagnation in my growth. I sought the comfort of friends, my family, therapist (a new one), a church support group, a women's support group, and antidepressants. My whole world was reeling with confusion about direction, questioning of my ability to survive the emotional pain of the loss. Here I had chosen to be in a relationship with a woman that led to the loss of my home, friends, my sense of identity, changes in my approach to work, social settings, and family gatherings, and the dreams of the future I had shaped while married, and now that relationship was over. My whole outlook on life had changed. How could this have happened?

I turned to reading as much as I could on Buddhist beliefs about attachment and letting go, forgiveness, and how to be alone. I didn't like being alone, yet I knew this was what I needed to do to learn how to survive. I reached out to others, who were incredibly patient with me. I joined a social organization for lesbians to meet others and have new lesbian friends to hike and go to the movies with. I sought out lesbian retreats. And yes, I was looking for a companion to fill the void left by Gwen.

At this point I was and am still today not totally convinced that I am a lesbian. My experience with Gwen allowed me to open up to parts of myself that needed to come to the surface if I was to continue to grow as a human being. I find the definition of bisexuality more fitting for me, but then that brings up another set of concerns. No one really wants to hear that you are bisexual because that means you are a frustrated lesbian or you can't make up your mind.

After Gwen I dated some women, entertained the idea of dating a male friend of a friend, flirted a little with people of both genders, and finally decided to enter a doctoral program. I had always talked about wanting to work at the collegiate level even when I was married and just finishing my undergraduate degree. This was the dream of the future I had kept in my head since I was 18 years old. Now at 42, I began to save as much money as possible to make the commitment to a doctoral program without the help of a partner. I found a person who became a friend to share my house with and take care of my pets while I was in school during the week. And in 2 years, I was through with my coursework and ready to reenter the real world again. It was in November of the second semester I went to a movie with Savannah, a woman whom I had worked for during the summer months. I had stopped looking for "the one" by this time, especially since my studies dominated my time and thoughts. Much to my surprise when I dropped her off after the movie, she asked, "Was this a date?" I didn't even know she was interested in women, let alone me. We will be celebrating our third year together this winter as I continue to increase my awareness of my sexual identity. I don't believe sexual orientation is a continuum for me. I think it is much more fluid and especially for women who discover these aspects of themselves later in life. I read a book titled *From Wedded Wife to Lesbian Life* edited by Deborah Abbott and Ellen Farmer and was able to see myself in many of the stories. I have learned that women (and men) at midlife can have growing pains, and we must listen to them in order to know how to heal.

I completed my dissertation on the training of school administrators on issues of sexual orientation and today, I am an assistant principal, and I teach part-time at the university about research, multicultural education, and the education of children and adolescents. I rely on my 15 years of experience working in schools to provide examples and scenarios for class discussion. I have also given myself the gift of being out with my students at the university. I realize that I am taking a risk by doing this, but at this time in my life I really don't like hiding who I am. Yet, you will most likely not see me holding my partner's hand in public. Being aware of my surroundings and of the prejudice that exists in many people's views allows me to keep a balance that sometimes is frustrating but very real.

All of my siblings now know of my orientation. My father is deceased and my mother is supportive without asking questions. My longtime friend Meg, who is now the mother of two boys, has told me to feel comfortable showing affection with my partner in front of them. It is so freeing to know that they and others are welcoming of people who are not heterosexual, and that my orientation is seen as only part of who I am. Yesterday I put up grape jelly from my own grapes and tomorrow I will make squash casserole to share with friends who just had a baby. Who knows what next week might bring?

Content Themes

In this story, Karen tells us of her journey of coming out both to herself and to those around her. She shares her difficulty in coming out to her family. Karen also addresses the confusion that she experienced coming to terms with her bisexuality and reveals to us that the process has not completely ended for her. We sense her confusion with labels and her desire to "love whom she loves" regardless of their gender. The final theme that we learn from her story is her shame and internal judgment about who she is becoming.

Coming Out

The disclosure of a gay or lesbian sexual orientation, also known as "coming out of the closet," needs to be understood as a process rather than an event (Morrow, 2006). Coming out is a twin process that involves several areas. First there is coming out to the self, or thinking of oneself as gay or lesbian, and second there is coming out to others, in which one identifies as gay or lesbian to other people (Moses, 1982; Morrow, 2006). The coming-out process can be understood as related to the individual's level of identity development. There are several models of sexual identity formation (Cass, 1979; Coleman, 1981; Fassinger & Miller, 1996; Fox, 1995; Grace, 1992) that conceptualize the development of sexual identity as consisting of stages. When working with GLB (gay, lesbian, bisexual) adolescents and adults, it is important to understand at what level of identity development they place themselves (Ryan & Futterman, 2001). Cass's sexual identity formation (SIF) model proposes six stages of coming out: (1) identity confusion; (2) identity comparison; (3) identity tolerance; (4) identity acceptance; (5) identity pride; and (6) identity synthesis (as cited in Hunter & Hickerson, 2003).

The focus on identity development models, however, while important to foster self-acceptance in a hostile environment, can be also limiting and simplistic (Miceli, 2002). Ryan and Futterman (2001) present coming out as a process that involves: "recogniz[ing] the impact of stigma, . . . unfold[ing] over a period of time, . . . increasing acceptance of a 'homosexual' identity, and . . . disclosure to nongay persons" (p. 3). The process of coming out and the realization of society's negative reactions is often managed by GLB individuals without support and modeling from parents or other family members (Ryan & Futterman, 2001). This lack of support can lead to feelings of isolation, more feelings of stress, and a greater chance of being victimized by others. It is also imperative that GLB clients be allowed to identify and define themselves, and that the counselor does not do the labeling for them (Savin-Williams, 2005). Though labels can be liberating, they can also be considered reductionist and unable to capture the full extent of sexuality. "Identity terms box [gays and lesbians] in . . . and oversimplify a complex aspect of the self" (Savin-Williams, 2005, p. 18). It is important to help clients understand that there are multiple trajectories and that there exist several different ways of synthesizing and developing their sexual identity (Yarhouse, Tan, & Pawlowski, 2005).

Coming out can lead to negative repercussions, including loss of job, family, and friends (Ryan & Futterman, 2001). As this story suggests, coming out can also lead to victimization and violence, which increases the fear of disclosing one's sexual orientation (Ryan & Futterman, 2001). Hunter and Hickerson (2003) discuss working with clients to identify the possible repercussions of disclosing sexual identity in order to assess realistically what the client will be able to handle. Morrow (2006) addresses the possibility of rejection from the family and the subsequent loss of one's parents when coming out. Clients may want to carefully consider each context in their lives to decide when, where, how, and to whom disclosure is appropriate (Hunter & Hickerson, 2003). Hunter and Hickerson (2003) also suggest that "clients . . . make disclosures when they are feeling positive about themselves rather than when they are feeling vulnerable. They should feel prepared instead of making impulsive or reactive disclosures" (p. 252). Counselors may utilize techniques such as visualization or role-plays in order to help clients rehearse coming out to others (Hunter & Hickerson, 2003).

The coming-out process for ethnic minority individuals may present additional challenges and an understanding of their cultures (Hunter &

Hickerson, 2003). Morrow (2006) discusses the cultural implications of coming out for African American GLB people, such as strong religious ties that value heterosexuality, emphasis on traditional gender roles, valuing procreation, and devaluation of same-sex relationships. Some considerations when working with Asian American GLB persons would be fear of rejection by families, lack of understanding from parents, fear of bringing shame onto the family, and stigma associated with utilizing mental health services (Hunter & Hickerson, 2003; Morrow, 2006). In Latino cultures, there is often a strong tie to Catholicism, an emphasis on traditional gender roles, and procreation-based values (Hunter & Hickerson, 2003; Morrow, 2006). When working with Native American clients, Hunter and Hickerson (2003) suggest assessing the level of acculturation and cultural values, and helping clients to find a "culturally relevant way to come out" (p. 258).

The other aspect of the coming-out process involves its effect on the parents, children, and peers of GLB youth and adults. Gays and lesbians and their parents are often not prepared to handle the effect of the coming-out process on the extended family because the cultural milieu can be discriminatory and stigmatizing. The disclosure of a GLB orientation could be distressing to the parents, siblings, and other relatives. Family members' reactions can also be conceived as a process not unlike that of the grieving process and can include alternate states and varying degrees of denial, rejection, acceptance, tolerance, embarrassment, shame, guilt, and loss. The reactions of the parents of gay and lesbian offspring may depend on their age, their ethnicity, and their religious background. Also, their experiences in dealing with past crises, their degree of acceptance of differences, past exposure to gay people, and the availability of support and information (Herdt & Koff, 2000) may impact the nature of their reaction. Some parents go through a grieving process that may include wondering what they did "wrong" to cause the homosexuality of their children, embarrassment, or a feeling of loss of the illusion of having a "normal" child. Other parents' love and devotion to their children help them to find strength and a new way of looking at the world, overcoming a system that stigmatizes and tyrannizes their children. Clinicians will need to be aware that parents will move through these patterns at different rates, to allow them time, and to stay "with" them as they move through the phases toward acceptance (Hunter & Hickerson, 2003). Hunter and Hickerson (2003) suggest helping parents with these emotional responses, encouraging them not to trivialize their children, respecting the courage their GLB children had in coming out to them, and helping them dispel their misconceptions, stereotypes, and negative attitudes toward GLB persons. Some questions that parents may have when discovering their child's GLB identity might be as follows: (a) How did it happen? (b) Is it permanent? (c) What kind of future is there for my child? and (d) What about disclosures outside of the family? (Hunter & Hickerson, 2003).

In her story, Karen describes going through the process of coming out as an adult while she is in a heterosexual marriage. Though most people come out to themselves generally at a younger age, Karen's is not an uncommon experience. Karen felt that her marriage was "everything," yet she found herself attracted to another woman. This realization started a process of self-evaluation and self-questioning. Karen's terms for her coming out to herself were "an awakening" and "stirrings inside." She talks about "discovering a part of herself" that she had not previously known.

Karen's coming out to others proved just as difficult, as it often is. She describes her difficulties talking to the members of her family. For many GLBs, coming out to friends, coworkers, the community, and people at the store, on the street, and in all other public areas of a person's life is a continual struggle, in part because others have the assumption that an individual is straight. It is not surprising that Karen would experience difficulty in coming out to others and find it overwhelming to do so. In Karen's coming-out process, she experiences a lot of discomfort in Cass's identity confusion stage. When in this stage, she feels very confused about her sexual orientation, her desires, her needs, and her self-concept (Hunter & Hickerson, 2003). She also goes back and forth in her feelings, sometimes thinking of her husband and her marriage, and sometimes thinking of Gwen and their relationship. Although the feelings that she has in this stage are expected, when working with clients in this stage counselors would need to understand the enormity of the confusion and the flip-flop nature of the client's feelings. As people move through all the different aspects of the coming-out process, they may move backward and forward, as Karen does, hesitating and affirming at different times in a fluctuating, nonlinear manner. The fact that Karen is not totally comfortable holding hands in public may be a reflection of her continued struggle that may be due to the geographic area where she resides, in which case it would constitute a self-protective measure, or may be due to her internalized homophobia, or both.

Bisexuality

Like Karen, many lesbians tend to have their first same-gender relationships later than gay men do (Tully, 2000). Women may be conditioned by society to have relationships with men, and often marry in their twenties. For lesbians whose sexual orientation may be unfolding at the same period in their lives, this can create confusion for those women who may have internal feelings of same-gender attraction but are conditioned by society to marry men (Burgess, 1997). Because of the expectation to have children, many of these women may have already had children with the man whom they have married when they begin to come to terms with the feelings that they have toward other women (Burgess, 1997), as happened to Karen.

Kinsey suggested in the late 1950s that bisexuality was much more widespread than previously thought, and he argued that exclusive heterosexuality and exclusive homosexuality were the two poles of a continuum and that most people could be placed somewhere in the middle (Esterberg, 2002). Bisexuality is also diverse, and a case could be made for a typology of bisexuality. But attempts at defining the types and categories of bisexuality encourage labeling and stereotyping. Karen expresses that she is not comfortable labeling herself as lesbian, and although she identifies as bisexual at this time, she is not comfortable with society's view of that label either. The way that an individual feels or acts sexually may change over time, just as it did in Karen's story. Because Karen and others may see their sexuality as fluid, not as a continuum, trying to identify themselves with a label at any given moment may prove a difficult task (Feinberg, 1996). Rosario, Schrimshaw, Hunter, and Braun (2006) suggest that sexual identity development is a process of finding congruence among sexual orientation, sexual behavior, and sexual identity. Rosario and colleagues (2006) state: "[I]dentity formation consists of becoming aware of one's unfolding sexual orientation, beginning to question whether one may be GLB, and exploring that emerging GLB identity" (p. 47). Because GLB individuals are usually not raised in a community of others who are like them where they would learn about that identity, as the sexual identity development process takes hold, these individuals often seek out gay-related social activities and sexual experiences (Rosario et al., 2006).

The complexity involved in a bisexual orientation presents its unique struggles. The bisexually oriented individual cannot look to heterosexual society or homosexual society for support of that identity (McClellan, 2006). The prevalent dichotomous view of sexual orientation is a factor that presents confusion for those who may identify as bisexual (Hunter & Hickerson, 2003; McClellan, 2006). Hunter and Hickerson (2003) go farther and state: "Because of the stereotypes and myths associated with bisexual persons, they may have trouble attaining social validation from heterosexual and gay and lesbian persons" (p. 248).

Recent scholarly literature based on lesbians and bisexual women suggests that sexual identities are far more changeable in the course of the life cycle than originally thought and that identity development does not necessarily occur in only one direction (i.e., from straight to gay or lesbian; Esterberg, 2002). What is important is to allow individuals to define how they think of themselves, as Karen is doing. It appears that, in terms of sexual history or behavior, "it is the meaning they make of their experiences that leads some women to think of themselves as bisexual and others as lesbian" (Esterberg, 2002, p. 220). Karen seems to have resolved the fact that she has been attracted to others both heterosexually and homosexually, and accepts this piece of herself. She has realized that she is not completely heterosexual and has accepted this part of herself, yet she still struggles with what her identity truly is. She frames the self-evaluation of her identity as fluid and changing, yet in her own words, she became very conscious of how she dressed and presented herself because she did not want to appear lesbian. She mentions that she is "not totally convinced" that she is lesbian, feels that the definition of bisexual is more fitting, and states that her "sexual identity awareness keeps forming," and she also says that she would most likely not hold her partner's hand in public. Karen is out to her family and friends, has extensively researched issues of sexual orientation, and expresses that she does not want to hide who she is. Karen recognizes that her sexual orientation is one piece of who she is and continues to work on developing awareness of that piece of herself.

Shame and Internal Judgment

Karen talks about judging herself. As Kaufman and Raphael (1996) state, "Embedded in these judgments are distinct, though sometimes hidden, expressions of shame" (p. 6). Shame is deeply rooted in our selves and is formed from the judgments of others and then internalized; it preys on self-esteem, affecting identity and sexual intimacy (Kaufman & Raphael, 1996).

Some factors that may perpetuate feelings of shame in Karen are society's stigmatization of homosexuality and the relative acceptance of homophobia. The historical condemnation of homosexuality provides a framework of judgment, criticism, and inferiority that, once internalized, produces shame (Kaufman & Raphael, 1996). This shame causes some to hide in fear, which Karen expresses at different points in her story. Heterosexism is another factor that may contribute to judgment, as it "functions to shame anyone who is different and . . . [often] silence[s] lesbians and gay men in many situations where their heterosexuality is assumed" (Kaufman & Raphael, 1996, p. 95). Another significant factor that contributes to shame is the feeling of powerlessness that gay men and lesbians experience due to their sexual preference (Tully, 2000). The attack on Karen and her partner by the male stranger may have reinforced judgment, shame, and feelings of powerlessness.

Clinical Applications

This section explores the clinical implications of Karen's story for counselors, including assessment of sexual identity and level of comfort with being out, techniques and interventions of use, and countertransference issues.

Assessment

Assessment of Identity

When working with clients who are exploring acknowledging their sexual orientation to themselves and others, it will be important to assess how they choose to identify, what they are struggling with, and how they feel about themselves and their families. What to ask depends on the age of the clients, their level of self-acceptance or rejection, their fears or their shame, and the nature of their families and other social support systems. Some individuals will be comfortable discussing these issues with a counselor sooner than others, some are comfortable in certain circles (i.e., among the GLB community), and some are not comfortable at all for a long time. These differences need to be respected, and clients should not be pressured to move in a direction they are not ready to go, according to their level in the gay and lesbian identity development models.

It is important to assess sexual attraction, behavior, and fantasies as well as sexual and emotional attractions.

Following are some questions that counselors can ask clients who are presenting with issues dealing with their sexual orientation. Before asking these questions, it is important to find out whether clients are comfortable discussing issues regarding sexual thoughts, feelings, or behavior with the clinician.

Who do you mostly socialize with?

Which sex or sexes are you attracted to?

Which sex or sexes are in your fantasies, daydreams, and dreams?

With which sex or sexes do you engage in sexual relations?

How are you dealing with what is happening to you (from self-acceptance to shame)?

How do you label or identity yourself (lesbian, gay, bisexual, or an identity other than these)?

How comfortable or uncomfortable are you discussing issues regarding what is going on with your parents, siblings, friends, and colleagues?

What messages have you received from society about your sexual identity?

How, if at all, is your sexual orientation related to your presenting problem?

Techniques and Interventions

Helping Clients With Their Coming-Out Process

One of the most important functions that counselors, psychologists, and social workers can engage in is helping GLB clients with their coming-out process. This involves several areas. First, it is important to help clients assess whether or not coming out, and to whom, is a wise decision. For example, for teenagers who live in religiously conservative environments and are financially dependent on their families, coming out may put them at a high risk of homelessness. For people who live in remote rural areas, or in city neighborhoods that may not be safe, it might be more protective not to come out. Second, it is important to educate clients that coming out to oneself may involve getting over self-loathing, disgust, or denial. Not all GLBs will express these negative emotions, but for those who do, it is important to help clients understand that this is a normal aspect of coming out to oneself, and that these feelings can be overcome. This is a particularly important topic, because self-loathing, inner conflicts, denial, and disgust with one's own characteristics can lead to self-destructive behaviors. To deal with self-loathing and lack of self-respect, strategies may need to be implemented that include educating clients about the myths associated with sexual orientation, helping clients learn coping strategies to deal with homophobia, encouraging clients to conduct research on the realities of gay and lesbian life, and seeking out role models and gay-friendly people. Clinicians can encourage clients to seek support from online bulletin boards or community groups to develop a family of friends, find out information about HIV and AIDS, and become acquainted with the faces of internalized homophobia. Finally, clinicians can help clients with the process of coming out to others. Clients need to know that the coming-out process involves steps such as: planning, timing, anticipating the reactions of others, dealing with frustrating experiences, and weathering bad responses. They also need to know that disclosure to the closest family members is often the most difficult task (Bass & Kaufman, 1996; Signorile, 1995).

Feelings of Shame and Internal Judgment

Gay and lesbian clients may have feelings of shame that result from internalized homophobia or internalized judgments. Directing clients to identify and understand these feelings may help them to lessen the feelings of shame. Kaufman and Raphael (1996) suggest working with the client to develop self-esteem, find self-nurturing activities, participate in self-forgiveness, re-own previously disowned parts of the self, and develop a positive identification of oneself as gay or lesbian in order to dissolve feelings of shame. Working to create a self-affirming identity, a whole and integrated self, and self-value can help clients to transcend their feelings of shame and empower them (Tully, 2000). Kaufman and Raphael (1996) suggest refocusing attention as a tool for releasing shame, whereby an individual refocuses his inward attention, such as inner scrutiny and self-consciousness, into attention outside of himself or herself. This could be accomplished by encouraging clients to focus on external things when they are experiencing internal judgment. Another technique suggested by Kaufman and Raphael is changing scripts, or modifying self-shaming scripts into self-affirming scripts. Additionally, encouraging clients to get in touch with gay community resources, gay subcultures, and to form families of choice result in the reduction of shame (Tully, 2000).

Countertransference

Counselors need to cultivate awareness of their reactions to GLB clients and their expectations for gender role behavior, their homophobia, their heterosexism, and their acceptance or rejection of their clients' choices. Clinicians' countertransference reactions may vary depending on whether clinicians are GLB or not.

GLB Clinicians

Clinicians who are GLB may identify too much with the experiences of their clients and fail to be helpful (Hunter & Hickerson, 2003). As in other clinical situations, the dangers of identifying too much with a client may prevent clinicians from listening to the uniqueness of their client's story and fail to recognize the differences (Hunter & Hickerson, 2003). Thinking that they know "what is best" for them, GLB clinicians may push clients in a direction they are not ready to go, or may fail to push clients who might need some encouragement, affirmation, or assertiveness. A GLB clinician of color working with another sexual minority of color might minimize clients' other problems, or be at risk of engaging in dual relationships (Lowe & Mascher, 2001). It is important for clinicians to provide education, recommend interventions, and make suggestions to clients without projecting their own experiences or agendas onto their clients.

Clinicians Who Are Not GLB

Excessive Curiosity or Guilt. Clinicians who are not GLB, on the other hand, may have excessive curiosity about the client's sexual behavior and other issues of which the clinician may not be sufficiently aware. It is important for the clinician to learn from sources other than the client some basic information, so that session time can be spent on client-specific issues. Insecure therapists may feel uncomfortable, guilty, or inadequate dealing with sexual minority clients and may act out or lack boundaries (Lowe & Mascher, 2001).

Wish to Change or Rejection. Some counselors may accept working with GLB clients as long as they do not have to deal with relationship issues, because they feel an intense rejection of the clients' sexuality. If a counselor feels the need to change a client or reacts with much distress, then referral should be considered (Morrow & Tyson, 2006; Moses, 1982).

Clinicians who do not support gay and lesbian human rights need to refrain from working with GLB clients because it may be unethical to work with a population that the therapist does not support (Twist, Murphy, Green, & Palmanteer, 2006). However, the issue of referral based on ethical principles of competence or differences in values is complex and has important ethical and legal ramifications. Counselors who would be comfortable helping a GLB individual client but refuse to counsel clients on relationship issues on the grounds that homosexual relationships go against their religious beliefs might be violating important ethical principles. Recent court decisions (Herman & Richter Herlihy, 2006) indicate that using religious beliefs to justify refusing services based on sexual orientation violates the principle of beneficence, the first—and possibly the main—obligation of a clinician (*American Counseling Association Code of Ethics*, 2005).

TOOLBOX ACTIVITY—KAREN		
Discussion Questions	*Activities*	*Resources*
Content themes What other themes do you see emerging in the story that the authors did not identify? **Assessment** Are there any questions you would like to ask Karen? **Interventions** What other interventions could you propose with Karen? **Countertransference** What countertransference reactions were emerging in yourself as you read this story? **Other scenarios** How would Karen's life be different if she had children? As a counselor, how could you help her? Imagine that Karen came to you after her initial struggles with the attraction to another woman. What could you have said to her upon finding out that she is a teacher in an elementary school? A high school?	Compile a list of the resources available for GLB youth in your community. Interview clergy who perform commitment ceremonies and those who do not. Write a paper about the differences. Include how this information could help you as a counselor.	**Suggested readings** Abbott, D., & Farmer, E. (Eds.). (1995). *From wedded wife to lesbian life: Stories of transformation.* Freedom, CA: The Crossing Press. Bass, E., & Kaufman, K. (1996). *Free your mind: The book for gay, lesbian, and bisexual youth and their allies.* New York: HarperCollins. Burgess, C. A. (1997). The impact of lesbian/gay sensitive policies on the behavior and health of lesbians in the workplace. In W. K. Swan (Ed.), *Gay/lesbian/bisexual/transgender public policy issues.* New York: Harrington Park Press. Jennings, K. (1994). *One teacher in 10: Gay and lesbian educators tell their stories.* Los Angeles: Alyson Books. Nava, M., & Dawidoff, R. (1995). *Created equal: Why gay rights matter to America.* New York: St. Martin's. Sinclair, A. (1995). *Coffee will make you Black.* New York: Harper Paperbacks. **Videos** *Claire of the Moon* *De Colores: Lesbian and Gay* *If These Walls Could Talk 2* *Latinos: Stories of Strength, Family, and Love*

SECTION VI

Disability

Like other cultural variables, the construct of disability is multifaceted and complex. Disability is a factor that covers a broad spectrum of individuals. Disability has been defined as "a physical or mental impairment that substantially limits one or more of the major life activities of an individual" (Americans with Disabilities Act, 28, C.F.R. §36.104); major life activities include behaviors for sustaining life, daily living skills, and sensory activities (Beecher, Rabe, & Wilder, 2004). Disabilities, then, can range from visible physical difficulties or challenges (i.e., being in a wheelchair, blindness, or hearing loss) to invisible or hidden disabilities (i.e., mental disorders, learning disorders, or chronic illnesses) (Beecher et al., 2004). Disabilities may arise from birth defects, have genetic or biological causes, or be caused by accidents and injuries. The treatment or consideration of disability, therefore, encompasses a variety of approaches as is related to the nature of the disability and its connection to the presenting problem in treatment.

Psychologists and counselors are not adequately trained to attend to issues of disability in treatment (Pledger, 2003; Thomas, 2004). Treatment has been either relegated to rehabilitation psychologists or counselors, or psychiatrists. Even when treating individuals with mental disorders, social service professionals may not consider that person to belong to the class of individuals with disabilities. Studies indicate that about 19% of the population in the United States is reported to have some type of disability (Beecher et al., 2004), which suggests that therapists need to be trained to integrate disability into their work and to treat individuals with dignity (Anderson & Middleton, 2004). In fact, it has been argued that counselors are trained not to see disability, leading to the marginalization of people with disabilities in therapeutic services (Smart & Smart, 2006). Moreover, able-bodied social service providers may inadvertently participate in stereotypical thinking and may have a difficult time understanding issues of oppression and discrimination with respect to individuals with disabilities (Anderson & Middleton, 2004).

There are two main concerns that should be addressed in treatment: models of disability and integration of disability into identity.

There are four models of disability that provide a theoretical framework for understanding disabilities (Smart & Smart, 2006). The biomedical model, which examines disability through a medical lens, is the one that is most widely accepted by the general public and is considered an older paradigm of disability (Pledger, 2003). In this model, the disability has at its root a medical cause or basis, and therefore should be treated medically. The strength of this approach is emphasis on biological bases for treatment. This approach, however, is limited because it places the sole focus on the individual, allows for society to stigmatize individuals with disabilities, and ignores environmental factors in both the etiology and treatment of the disorder (Smart & Smart, 2006).

The next two models, the functional and the environmental models, include systemic and environmental factors in the conceptualization of disability (Smart & Smart, 2006) and represent newer paradigms (Pledger, 2003). Both models include a focus on the interaction of skills, abilities, and functioning of the individual along with physical functioning. These models differ from the medical model in their inclusion of the influence of the environment on the manifestation and the treatment of the disability. These models also remove the stigma of disability by focusing on the role of the environment in reducing challenges to those who are disabled (Smart & Smart, 2006).

The final model is the sociopolitical or minority model of disability (Smart & Smart, 2006). This model is designed to explain the daily life of individuals and incorporates experiences with discrimination and prejudice. Disability is seen as a social construction and not solely as a medical issue. People with both visible and invisible disabilities face negative stereotypes and bias from others, who may feel that individuals with disabilities are disadvantaged and less capable of full functioning. According to the model, individuals with disabilities should be considered minorities and ensured civil rights as other minority groups in this country. The commitment to achieve social justice for those who are marginalized due to their disabilities and the advent of the disability rights movement in the United States, which advocates for the rights of individuals with disabilities through social activism and advocacy, are good examples of the sociopolitical or minority model of disability (Israel, 2006; Palombi & Matteson Mundt, 2006).

One benefit of the sociopolitical model of disability is the recognition of the importance of the individual defining and integrating the disability into self-concept and identity. For many, disability is one of several important identity components. Disability is integrated in a manner that is similar to racial/ethnic and gender identity, beginning with an awareness of the disability, and a passive acceptance of societal views on the disability, which may mimic the medical model. Individuals progress to acceptance, embracing the disability as a positive and valued feature of the self (Gibson, 2006).

Finally, clinicians should be aware of intersectionality concerns with disability. "Typically, the disability is not the single defining characteristic of the individual; rather the disability is one of several important parts of the individual's self-identity" (Smart & Smart, 2006, p. 29). Ability status will interact with race/ethnicity, gender, social class, and immigration status. Additionally, individuals with disabilities from diverse cultural backgrounds may experience oppression from membership in two or more marginalized groups (e.g., gender, sexual orientation, social class) (Gibson, 2007). "For example, a young African American man with schizophrenia would probably experience more prejudice and discrimination than a Euro-centric man who is blind" (Smart & Smart, 2006, p. 33).

This section contains the story of David, who became paralyzed from a sports injury as an adolescent. As you read his story, you will be introduced to the concepts of working with someone with acquired visible disabilities. Note, as you read, the challenges in integrating his disability into his identity, along with the influences of oppression as he copes with his disability.

Sixteen

David's Story

Broken Neck, Intact Spirit

I n this chapter, we read the story of David, an individual paralyzed in a tragic sporting accident. His story describes his and his family's efforts to cope with his disability. The story also includes his process of developing a disability identity, which differed from his identity as a White able-bodied man. As you read his story, pay attention to his level of grief and loss of his able-bodied status and the integration of himself as a paralyzed individual into his self-concept. Notice the areas of oppression and discrimination he faced, and his steps to advocate for himself and others.

David's Story

"Life is difficult." I once read these three trivial words in a book, but never knew how true to life and impactful they would be until one fateful fall evening. Before I begin, let me back up and tell you more about who I am and how I got here. I am a Caucasian male raised in a small conservative town in Maine by hard working middle-class parents. My compassionate mother juggled raising three rambunctious children, me being the eldest, and has worked the same secretarial job since high school. As a young child, I observed my mother selflessly dedicating her free time and energy to those in need. My mother would often bring food to the elderly, volunteer at church, and have children from the children's home stay with us during holidays. I absorbed my mother's compassionate nature towards the disadvantaged. My uncompromising father has devoted over half his life laboring for the shipping industry. Even after working all day, he would come home to work in the yard or repair the house. Growing up I spent many of my weekends toiling over a project my dad refused to pay someone else to do. I still remember the words of my dad pushing me to better myself as I helped with his undertakings, "Son, if you're going to do it half way, then don't do it at all!"

As a child with too much energy for my size, I incorporated my father's hard work ethic to my life and found my outlet in sports. All of my dreams and aspirations were encapsulated in being the best athlete possible. Nothing else mattered except for excelling in sports; my drug was sports. I got a rush from the dirt, sweat, and blood produced by two rival opponents clashing. I found my niche in hockey because it combined my love of contact sports with a prosperous future I aimed to achieve. My dream was to be a professional player. Of course, life does not always follow along with dreams.

Here is where my story takes a turn of unforeseeable events leading me to never forget that life is difficult. The most significant event impacting my life and cultural identity happened on September 21, 1982. At that time, I was the strong, confident, fearless captain of my freshman high school hockey team. I did not have a care other than playing hockey. I had an adolescent belief I was invincible and that nothing could hurt me. As a 15-year-old that thought he knew everything, my world was turned upside down when I was tragically injured in a hockey accident that left me paralyzed from the neck down. The accident took place when I was flipped head first after trying to steal the puck. In that split second, my life was changed forever! I had broken my neck shattering my fourth and fifth vertebrae while severing my spinal cord. I fell limp like a sack of potatoes face first on the ice unable to move a muscle with my body feeling as if it were on fire. I was awake for every excruciating moment and terrified for my life. I had no idea what was wrong with me.

It took 45 minutes, which seemed like an eternity, for the ambulance to arrive and paramedics to reach me on the ice. As I lie listless on the ice, the paramedics cut off my dirty sweat stained hockey pads. They put an oversized neck brace on me and strapped my body to a loading board to get in the ambulance. I remember crying while telling my mother I loved her not knowing if I would ever get the chance again.

When I arrived at the hospital, I was immediately rushed into the emergency room and put into traction, which consisted of metal rods being screwed in my skull. While I struggled in and out of consciousness, the doctor was informing my traumatized parents that if I made it through the night I would never walk or be able to do ANYTHING again. After making it through the first and next few nights in the hospital, I was in total shock. Unfamiliar words like "spinal cord injury," "paralyzed," "quadriplegic" and "handicap" kept being used in my presence but never connected with me. It was as if I was watching from afar and emotionally detached. After the shock began to dissipate, the gravity of my situation set in. I had a disability!

Even though I had an unbelievable amount of love and support in the beginning from family, friends, and well wishers, I still felt alone. I thought that no one knew what I was going through. During that solitary time, I had many dark days and restless nights to reflect on who I was and who I would become. I started questioning my worth. I wondered what, if any, contribution I could ever have to society as an individual in a wheelchair unable to walk. I had no real knowledge of individuals with disabilities. I used to feel sorry for and pity people that were different and had disabilities. Now I was one of those people.

During those daunting days of coming to terms with my disability, my faith was my bedrock. For a child raised Baptist and taught that God is an angry God looking for an opportunity to punish sinners, I never questioned why I got hurt or got angry with God. I guess I never believed that I was being condemned or punished for some heinous sin that required God to paralyze me. I also had so many people from different Christian denominations and religions coming to visit and pray for me that the angry God image dissolved. The love and support I felt from these multi-religious beings assisted in my initial strengthening of a secure positive outlook as a future disabled person, even though I have had significant life events that challenged my faith and relationship with people that I thought empathized with my situation. I once had a close respected neighbor that I looked up to tell me that if my faith in God was strong enough I would not need to use a wheelchair. After he told me that, I thought that maybe there was more I should or could be doing spiritually to help regain my ability to walk. At that time, I had no idea how to respond or rebut my neighbor's judgment on my faith. I was still young and believed my elders were always wiser. It took a long time to mentally grasp that there was nothing I was doing wrong that kept me paralyzed and dependent on a wheelchair. I had to rely upon trusted people and do much soul searching to realize that I was OK even with a disability.

Having a disability, I have come to realize that I am perceived as different and not always in a good way. I came to this epiphany one day while attending a social work class in pursuit of my bachelor's degree. My professor wrote five labels on the board and asked everyone to stand beside the label they believed would have best chance of getting a job. I was taken aback when the students parted and I could see everyone standing by all the labels except one. The label read "Quadriplegic with Master's degree." I was shocked to discover that everyone in the class viewed people with disabilities as a lesser group. Until that time, I did not see my disability separating me from other people. After leaving class, I felt as if I were not equal to others because I had to use a wheelchair to get around. A harsh reality opened my eyes to the fact that I was no longer looked at as a Caucasian male or majority of the population. I was seen strictly for my disability.

Therefore, after spending over half my life with a spinal cord injury and using a wheelchair, I have come to identify most with my disability not my race or gender. I identify with my disability because, unfortunately, it is most noticeable to other people. It is difficult to hide a three hundred pound power wheelchair. I am not ashamed of who I am because of my spinal cord injury, but I do realize that because I use a wheelchair to get around and do not quite fit the status quo I draw peculiar, sometimes pitiful and many inquisitive looks from others.

I have had many occasions when people I do not know come up to me and inquire about my disability. Before even asking, "How are you?" or "What's your name?" I've been asked, "What's wrong with you?" "Why can't you walk?" or "Car wreck, huh?" I am often amazed at other people's reaction to my disability. Though, children's uninhibited curiosity humors me the most. I remember one young boy asking his mother, "Why is he riding in a big baby stroller?" as we passed by each other in the doctor's waiting room. Another child once yelled to his mom in amazement in the middle of a restaurant, "Mom, look! It moves!" when he saw my wheelchair rolling. I do not have a problem with curiosity about my disability, but I do have a problem with people judging me and telling me they know exactly how I feel and what I am going through.

Another reason I identify most with my disability is because of how much it consumes my life. From the time I wake in the morning having someone dress me, put me in my wheelchair and prepare my breakfast, until the time I am transferred back into bed at night I am constantly aware of my disability. It was a surreal and shocking feeling to lose total independence and the ability to walk at 15. I had many psychological battles to overcome in order to rise above my physical losses. Twenty-seven years later and many battles won I still occasionally fight to not let my physical disability turn into a mental disability/crutch.

At times, my disability has been a challenge and made life difficult. Due to my spinal cord injury, I require many unbelievably priced adaptations for daily living. My $16,000 wheelchair has taken the place of my legs because I am unable to walk. I look at my wheelchair with ambivalence. As much as I hate having to use a wheelchair, I have no other means of moving. My wheelchair has turned into my best friend because of how much I depend on and trust it to work for me. Besides a wheelchair, I need accessible transportation to get around. I cannot go and jump in any vehicle because my wheelchair will only fit in a modified van. It cost near $20,000, not including the cost of vehicle, just to adapt a van for me. I also necessitate a bathroom specially equipped with wide doorways and roll-in-shower. Since I need so much and am dependent on others, it has been a financial, emotional and psychological hurdle to not feel like a burden.

When I first got hurt, I was unable to move anything but my neck. I had to depend on others for the simplest things like scratching my nose or feeding me. Having my independence snatched away from me so quickly was surreal and by far the most difficult part of adapting to my disability. It was the little things I lost that were taken for granted and so devastating to my ego and recovery. Before I got hurt, if I wanted to shave or brush my teeth I just got up on my own free will and went in the bathroom and did it. It was so humiliating and humbling to ask someone to brush my teeth and watch them do it as I stared in the mirror and remembered the young independent man I once was.

The loss of my physical independence left me with two options, give up on life or keep on fighting. Fortunately I strive for a challenge and chose to keep fighting. I vividly remember when I decided to not let my disability get the best of me. After 4 weeks in the hospital, I was immediately taken to inpatient physical rehab in another state. I had no expectations of what was in store for me or how soon I would have to make a life altering decision. Upon reaching the three-story monolithic rehab that specialized in spinal cord injuries, I was wheeled in on a gurney and taken directly to the room I would call home for the next 4 months. Before I even reached my room, I was startled by a low painful moan that came from a gentleman I was to know as my roommate. As the nurse's aides wheeled me into the room, I was shocked to hear that my older rugged looking roommate was repeatedly moaning to his family, "Just let me die, just let me die!"

I soon found out that my roommate had a recent spinal cord injury and was coming for rehab just like me. As my roommate continued to moan to his family, my mom had to leave the room to fight back tears. I remained stoic for the sake of my family, but inside of me I was an emotional volcano ready to erupt. I felt so unbelievably hopeless, sad, and confused. I began to wonder, "Is this what I had to look forward to as an individual with a disability? Was I going to eventually follow the path of my roommate and wish for nothing more, but to lie there and die?" After my family and his had all left for the night and all was quiet, I lay in bed and forced myself to make a decision. It was at that moment that I chose to get busy living and make the most of my life no matter the circumstances.

My perseverance and dedication to regaining as much as possible in rehab eclipsed anything I had ever done before. I had two major neck surgeries within 2 months of each other requiring metal screws and steel plates to realign my spine. With the surgeries and a grueling 4 months of intensive inpatient physical, occupational and respiratory therapy, I started slowly regaining the ability to move parts of my upper body. The greatest triumph I ever achieved in my life happened after 3 months of being in rehab. I had been consistently working 8 hours a day putting all my effort into my rehabilitation. I never complained or griped about what the therapist challenged me [to] do even though it pushed me to every physical limit I had. When I first started rehab, I could barely move and only shrug my left shoulder upwards.

During my third month of being in therapy, I was working out in the gym one day and my occupational therapist asked me to shrug my shoulder and try pulling my hand up to my face. It took all my effort and determination to clumsily sling my hand up to my face and across my nose as it fell back in my lap. The excitement and joy the feel of my hand touching my nose brought me to tears. That was my first glimpse of hope towards my physical recovery. The accomplishment of being able to scratch my nose again was sweeter than any goal I had ever scored.

After getting out of rehab, I came home to a house that was totally inaccessible for me. My bedroom was up a flight of stairs I could not reach with a wheelchair. The bathrooms downstairs were too narrow to enter. To top it off the rehab sent me home with a wheelchair I could not push or control. I slept, bathed and used the bathroom in our living room for my first 6 months after being discharged from rehab. For some reason though, it never really seemed to bother me. I think I was so happy to be home and with my family that the inaccessibility of my house seemed trivial. I never knew how much I missed and relied upon them until I was taken away due to rehab.

My family and close friends were there for me in the much needed time when I returned back to high school. It was a culture shock to abruptly leave school as "David the jock" and return 5 months later as "David, the guy in a wheelchair." I was self-conscious as to how students and especially my friends would look at and think of me. I was afraid people would reject me or treat me different because I was using a wheelchair. All of these fears were gradually lessened from being treated as the same old David, but with certain limitations. My family and most of my friends stood by me and I never felt any different around them even though I was different.

I was also insecure as to what to expect from the opposite sex. I wondered if girls would still like and be attracted to me even with a disability. The girlfriend I had before I got hurt found my disability too difficult to handle and broke up with me before I even got out of rehab. I blamed my inability to walk and loss of independence for our split which made me even more insecure. Before I was injured, I thought that girls paid attention to me solely because of my physical ability and looks.

Soon after I got back to school, I was asked by a girl to a high school dance. I learned from her that I had many more qualities to offer which overshadowed my loss of physical ability. I grossly underestimated the importance of treating a girl with respect, personality, charm, and intelligence. I slowly began to feel more comfortable dating again and more importantly who I was as an individual with a disability. My self-esteem was no longer linked to my physical prowess, which made my transitioning back to school that much easier.

While missing a whole semester of my freshman year, I was able to catch up with my class and graduate on time with a 3.7 GPA. It was during my high school years that I began focusing more on my mental capabilities. I started seeking new career paths that required my mind instead of my physical ability. I stopped pursuing my dream and future career in hockey and worked on getting into college.

After graduating high school, I took a dreadful leap and moved out of my family's house and comfort zone and went to college in another town. I moved into the dorms and discovered how much I had been sheltered and relied upon others. I had to adjust to a new city, college life and being away from the friends and family that helped me physically and emotionally. I was forced to do what I could for myself. I tried to not depend on people to drive me places and worked on driving myself. Eventually, after months of drivers training and two wrecks I had the liberating feeling of driving myself to wherever I pleased.

Though my disability has caused many obstacles for me, it has also served as a foundation of strength. If I can live through a traumatic injury and intrepidly carry the signs of my loss, then I can handle most anything that comes my way. My disability has helped me to see life in a fresh and totally different perspective. Now I am more thankful for what I have and can do instead of being unhappy about what I cannot. From my disability, I have learned many valuable lessons.

I have learned how important having a sense of humor is for my sanity. There have been many times I could look at my life and feel pitiful for my circumstances. Instead I decided to find the humor in my quandaries. Such as the time I was riding with a friend to a much anticipated football game. Two streets before reaching the stadium my friend abruptly turned a sharp corner which caused me to uncontrollably lean over the side of my wheelchair until I fell completely onto the floor of the van. As my frightened friend slammed on the brakes and frantically jumped to help me up, he was perplexed by the huge smile on my face. With a laugh I told him how I had always wondered what the floor smelled like. I discovered life is too stressful to take everything seriously.

My cultural identity as an individual with a disability has helped me to empathize with other minorities in ways I never could before. Prior to my injury, I never took notice of or had much compassion for minorities. I was part of the majority as a Caucasian male and never had family or friends that I recognized as minorities. Therefore, I never saw and was ignorant to the fact that any injustices were committed against others. After I became disabled, it was as if a light had been turned on and everything around me was unfamiliar. There was a lot of ugliness I saw and disgust that I felt towards societal barriers and those that put them there. For example, the restaurants I used to love eating at looked totally different because I could not get in many of them due to their inaccessibility for wheelchairs. Also I found it difficult to address these accessibility impediments because some people believed that the problem was mine and not the individuals or establishments that made the restaurants inaccessible. Because of this, I have had no other choice but to become an advocate and voice for the disabled.

When I initially got hurt, I viewed societal barriers to the disabled as just the way things were. I accepted that I would be limited as to where I could go and what I could do. After a few years, I began to get frustrated and fed up with the injustices I saw and experienced. Such as the time my sister and I tried to get in a popular barbecue restaurant in my hometown. Excited and hungry for the mouth watering burgers the restaurant was known for I quickly lost my appetite after five minutes of being there due to their inaccessibility. After struggling to get up a wheelchair ramp that was too narrow and steep for my wheelchair, I had to have my sister pick up on my three hundred pound chair and turn it just to get me in the narrow double doors of the restaurant. I should have known what to expect next from the hassle it was to get in the restaurant. As I got my first glance into the restaurant, I saw nothing but a sea of people and counter tops that rose way above my head denying me access to order my meal. While my sister ordered my meal, an older Caucasian female with food stained apron came to seat us. As I looked around the seating area, I saw nothing that would accommodate my wheelchair without me being stuck in the aisle blocking the only walk-way. Everyone was beginning to stare at me and the waitress as she bunglingly tried to rearrange tables. In the end, my sister and I had to try and eat outside in the 95 degree heat while we watched everyone on the inside in the cool air conditioning.

From this incident and many similar experiences, I felt compelled to fight for the rights of the disabled. I have contacted restaurant proprietors, written letters to newspapers and been on local television news addressing the injustices endured by disabled. I try to let everyone know that our "Separate but Equal" society is not as equal as it seems if you look hard enough. Though great strides for the disabled have been accomplished with the inception of the Americans with Disabilities Act, there is more work to be done. I realized long ago that change does not take place without breaking the status quo.

I have learned that having a disability does not control or limit the way I live my life. I believe I can do most anything that an able-bodied person can do. Since my injury, I have regained enough upper body strength to brush my teeth, shave, and feed myself. It has been difficult at times, but I currently live on my own and work a full time job. I also have had the pleasure of snow skiing in the Colorado Mountains, paragliding over the Pacific Coast, snorkeling in the Great Barrier Reef, playing harmonica with a blues band and achieving my PhD. I found that my only disability is when I allow it to become one.

Even though I miss walking and the independence I once had, I would not take back the journey that led to my spinal cord injury or time thereafter. I never imagined the way my disability would shape my life and others'. I have been able to touch and inspire other people in a way that I could not have able-bodied. Though it is a physical and psychological climb over the struggles of living with a disability, I have become stronger because of it. In the end, I want to look back at my life and be able to say, "I may have broken my neck, but I did not let it break me."

Content Themes

David's story reflects an individual who became disabled from a serious and significant injury, and many of the content themes, including adjusting to the disability and integrating disability into identity or sense of self are reflective of that process. Other content themes that may be more easily generalized for people born with both visible and invisible disabilities include grief, loss, discrimination, and stereotypes of individuals with disabilities.

Grief and Loss Issues

As David describes in his story, his journey to disability identity status happened after a tragic accident that occurred during a sporting event. David was in the process of developing his sense of self, his professional and career goals as an able-bodied person. When the accident first happened, he was unsure whether he would survive and was unable to fully comprehend the prognosis given by his physicians. What is interesting about his story is his initial inability to connect his current ideas about himself with the diagnosis he had been given; he states that now he is in a category of individuals he had previously pitied.

David's initial reaction to his paralysis parallels models of grief and loss that speak to shock and denial. Due to the nature of the injuries and moving in and out of consciousness, David was in shock and disbelief regarding the nature and extent of his injuries. When David fully realized he would be paralyzed for life and entered rehab, he had to make a choice to survive and continue to grow. David recalls listening to his roommate begging to die. While David does not articulate long periods of anger or bargaining that is typically included in stages of grief, he does describe the periods of questioning and doubt as he began to cope with and accept his disability. David realized he had a choice to accept his status and make the most of his life. He made a conscious and deliberate choice to live and to attempt to recover as much of his functioning as possible.

David does not describe the grief process of his family in adjusting to the disability. His mother had to leave the room during rehab due to the cries of his roommate, which suggests the challenges and difficulties she experienced in assisting her son. David's ability to cope with his grief may have been supported by the strength of his family and their ability to process their grief over his paralysis appropriately.

Adjusting to the Disability

There are several factors that helped David to recover both physically and emotionally and to adjust to the disability. First, he seemed to have full support of family and friends. His family helped in the recovery process and had the resources to help make his home accessible. Family members often experience grief and loss in the same way, and often may not be able to attend to the individual. This does not seem to be the case for David. He was anxious to return to school after having been the jock and was pleasantly surprised that his peers responded to his character and personality. He is invited to a dance and able to resume his social life. Second, David describes his faith and religious beliefs as an invaluable coping resource after the accident. What is remarkable is that even after he is "invited" to be critical of God, he maintains his steadfast faith throughout his recovery. Third, David had the cognitive skills to be able to catch up on his schoolwork and to develop alternate career plans. If David had not been able to cope cognitively, he may have had different outcomes emotionally.

Disability Identity Development

Again, before the accident, David saw himself as most adolescents do, as invincible and with a bright future. He took advantage of his privileged status as an able-bodied White male adolescent. After the disability, David had to cope with his new status as an individual with disabilities. Models of disability identity development describe the process of moving through awareness of the disability status to acceptance (Gibson, 2006). David had several pivotal moments that propelled him through his identity development. The first experience occurred in the first night of rehab when his roommate was moaning suicidal statements. David made a deliberate decision to live with his disability. Another pivotal moment occurred during rehab after he was able to move one of his arms. The ability to scratch his nose, a behavior most take for granted, helped him to focus on his strength and potential and propelled him further in his identity development. The third pivotal moment occurred when David was in college when the other students chose being disabled as the least likely to attain career success. While David was shocked, it further helped to motivate him to continue with his life goals and dreams. David shifted from seeing himself as a White man to a disabled individual because that is the first thing others associate with him. He has not chosen the label as a limitation but as a sign of strength and resilience. He has a PhD, enjoys outdoor sports and activities, and has a rich social life. His disability seemed to affect his body but not diminish his spirit or zest for life.

Discrimination

David experienced discrimination and negative stereotypes due to his disability. He recalls how the students in one of his college courses selected a disabled person as the least likely to be successful, and how that highlighted the negative beliefs and assumptions that many have about individuals with disabilities. What is remarkable is that David was in college with the students who still had negative biases despite their prior interactions with him.

Resilience and Social Justice

David also describes limitations to accessibility in public places and the embarrassment that occurs in attempting to receive services or be able to frequent restaurants. Utilizing to the fullest his personal resilience, he becomes actively involved in issues of advocacy and social justice by challenging the status quo and fighting for accessibility in his state. By doing that, he joins the ranks of those who manage to turn oppressive and adverse experiences into meaningful life missions (Schwarzbaum & Thomas, 2008). His experiences with discrimination helped him to become an advocate for himself and to be more empathic and sensitive to ethnic minorities.

Clinical Applications

This section addresses assessment concerns, techniques and interventions, and countertransference issues.

Assessment

It is important for clinicians to include an assessment of the role and influence of disability. Even if the disability seems unrelated to the presenting problem, clinicians need to assess the nature of the disability, adjustment to the disability and coping skills, and discrimination and oppression. Therapists need to understand the relationship of intersectionality of disability with other cultural factors.

The following questions are recommended:

What is the nature and extent of the disability?

How did you first react to the onset of the disability, illness, or injury?

How did others react?

What has been helpful to your adjustment?

What barriers do you face? Are you experiencing financial difficulties?

Have you experienced any forms of discrimination due to your disability?

How does your disability interact with other components of your identity?

Has the way you think about your disability changed over time?

Techniques and Interventions

Clinicians need to develop competency skills in disability for a number of reasons. First, therapists need to be able to select appropriate evidence-based interventions that concern disabilities and the intersection of other factors. Second, therapists need to understand oppression and discrimination that clients with disabilities may face, and they need to be able to advocate for clients and influence policy (Pledger, 2003). Service providers need to understand the extent and nature of the disability and the influence on the functioning and performance of the client. Therapists also need to be able to accommodate individuals with disabilities in their offices and treatment centers, as the Americans with Disabilities Act of 1990 mandates that psychologists, counselors, and social workers provide equal access to treatment (Beecher, Rabe, & Wilder, 2004). Accommodations need to include written and verbal materials for individuals with vision and hearing impairments (Hunt, Matthews, Milsom, & Lammel, 2006).

Grief and Loss

Therapists need to work closely with individuals with disabilities and their families to address grief and loss concerns, particularly if the disability is in response to an injury. Families who have children born with deformities or birth defects will need to grieve the dream or expectations that they had for their children while simultaneously being encouraged to maximize the growth and potential of their child. Helping individuals to use family and friends for support needs to be encouraged. Integrating spirituality and religion may also be useful in coping with the disability and dealing with grief and loss. Clients may have to reconcile their beliefs about God or a higher power while addressing the disability. Clients also need to be encouraged to use discernment in discussing their religious and spiritual beliefs with others. David, for example, could easily have become discouraged from his discussions with others, but instead chose to rely on his faith. Clients should also be persuaded to use religious institutions as sources of financial and emotional support, and to provide respite for caring for those with disabilities or the chronically ill. If the disability is not the presenting problem, providers will still need to be sensitive to grief issues that may be related to the disability. For example, if the client is interested in pursuing career counseling, the therapist will need to address how the disability affects choices.

Finally, clinicians will need to include a careful assessment of life satisfaction, as this tends to be lower than for those who are not disabled, with the exception of those who report feeling in control of their disability (Sue & Sue, 2003). Depression may accompany the disability, or the disability may exacerbate depressive symptoms (Hunt et al., 2006). Assessing for suicidal ideation will be critical for clients who are suffering from injuries or chronic illnesses.

Fostering Resilience

Acceptance of the disability will have to include a realistic assessment of the level of functioning and performance that the individual will have. Clinicians will need to incorporate strengths and areas of resilience for the client. Providers also need to help clients to discuss societal barriers and limitations, including issues of accessibility (Smart & Smart, 2006). Helping clients to empower themselves or advocating for services can be effective tools for coping with grief and loss concerns. Therapists do need to be careful not to impose their values on clients or encourage them to work beyond their limits, however (Smart & Smart, 2006).

Career Counseling

A counselor working with David could have incorporated career counseling to help him adjust his long-term goals. Due to negative stereotypes of individuals with disabilities, they may not be encouraged in the school system to pursue a wide variety of careers. The Individuals with Disabilities Education Act requires that children with disabilities who are between the ages of 3 and 21 be given special education services. The services provided depend on the level of the disability and functioning of the individual, and may not include a career focus. Students who enter college are largely responsible for accessing resources on college campuses and may not have knowledge of services provided (Beecher et al., 2004).

Intersectionality

Therapists must be careful not to assume that the disability is the most important cultural variable of clients. Some clients may enter treatment to help specifically with the disability. Others may have other cultural factors that are more important to their identity that need to be addressed in treatment. Counselors need to consider the relevance of each category of identity and gather information about what is important to the client (Hays, 2001). For example, a Latino who is blind may want to address limitations for employment due to discrimination as an ethnic minority as well has issues with sight. In a qualitative study of lesbians with disabilities, participants and counselors discussed the distress in the therapists' inability to integrate sexual orientation and disability (Hunt et al., 2006).

Process of Therapy

Due to the nature of the disability or chronic illness, it may be more challenging to engage in work with individuals with disabilities. Beecher and colleagues (2004) have recommendations on working with this population.

First, they note that establishing rapport may take more effort. People with disabilities or chronic illnesses may not be able to attend weekly sessions. Special efforts may need to be made to accommodate the client to enhance the therapeutic alliance. The importance of the counselor using basic skills has been mentioned by individuals with disabilities in the research (Hunt et al., 2006) and cannot be overstated. However, specific measures need to be taken into consideration depending on whether or not the client is using assistive devices. For example, it may be inappropriate to touch clients' walkers, wheelchairs, or prosthetic devices because they function as an extension of the individual's body (Hays, 2001). Second, individuals with a disability may display low self-esteem or learned helplessness, especially if they have internalized negative assumptions or expectations. Again, therapists will need to find ways to empower the clients and serve as an advocate for receiving appropriate services. Third, clients with disabilities often experience inconsistencies with their health or level of functioning from day to day. Therapists can be instrumental in helping them to adjust. Finally, individuals with disabilities may experience social isolation in addition to discrimination from others. Clinicians need to help clients build social support networks.

Countertransference

The medical model that conceptualizes disability holds that the disability is a medical issue and an individual concern (Smart & Smart, 2006). This approach, which is widely held by many, leads to stigmatization of individuals with disabilities. Because most clinicians are not trained to work with this population, it is crucial that an assessment of countertransference issues that may occur be examined prior to engaging in clinical services.

Pity

Many service providers have adopted the medical model and may feel pity for their clients. Because of limited experience with individuals with disabilities, some clinicians may focus on the limitations and feel sorry for their clients, leading to expressions of sympathy and not empathy in their work. Clinicians may need to engage in dialogues with clients regarding the relationship, and clients should be invited to provide feedback (Smart

& Smart, 2006). Therapists need to give equal focus to areas of strength and resilience in their clinical work, and process feelings of pity in supervision and consultation. Feelings of pity may also lead clinicians to be self-conscious during sessions. For example, therapists may use an empathic response such as "I'm hearing you say" or "I see your point," and then become worried that their statements are upsetting or offensive to the clients.

Curiosity

It is okay to inquire about the disability and its influence, but be careful not to ask questions solely out of curiosity. Therapists need to assess the nature and intensity of the disability but only in relation to the work and not to become better educated about disabilities. Clients may see their disability in a positive light. Clinicians should be careful not to exploit the client's perspective to satisfy their curiosity regarding the disability. Counselors are encouraged to learn as much as possible about disabilities outside of the therapeutic relationship to minimize the impact of countertransference (Hunt et al., 2006).

TOOLBOX ACTIVITY—DAVID		
Discussion Questions	*Activities*	*Resources*
Content themes What other themes do you see emerging in the story that the authors did not identify? **Assessment** Are there any questions you would like to ask David? **Interventions** What other interventions could you propose with David? **Countertransference** What countertransference reactions were emerging in yourself as you read this story? **Other scenarios** Imagine that David was an African American football player dreaming of getting a college scholarship when he was paralyzed. What themes might you have seen emerging in his story? Imagine that David's accident took place when he was 45 years old, not 17. What could be some differences in terms of his identity issues and/or development?	Compare and contrast the disability rights movement, the civil rights movement, and the gay rights movement. Report the similarities and differences to your classmates. Go on a walking or driving survey of your block, neighborhood, or campus, paying attention to issues of accessibility, safety, transportation, architecture, and physical environment. Write a report on changes that need to be made to increase access for people in a wheelchair. Compile a list of adaptive technologies that make access to a job or independent living more likely.	**Suggested readings** Prondzinski, R. (2008). *Another fine mess you've gotten us into: The life and adventures of a quad.* Bloomington, MN: Nasus Publishing. Selzer, M., & Dobkin, B. (2008). *Spinal cord injuries: A guide for patients and families.* New York: Demos Medical Publishing. Thomas, P., & Harker, L. (2005). *Don't call me special: A first look at disability.* Hauppauge, NY: Barrons Educational series. **Videos** *Breaking the Waves* *The Diving Bell and the Butterfly* *Frida* *The Ten Commandments of Communicating With People With Disabilities.*

Appendix A

Author Guidelines

You are invited to write a cultural autobiography, a story of your life, your identity, and your experiences. The story should tell who you are, how you see yourself, and how you arrived at your perceptions. There is no set format for the story; it should be as creative or reflective of your life as you would like. The following questions are general guidelines to assist in writing the chapter. You do not need to answer each question, nor are they intended to be included in a particular order.

How do you identify yourself?

What factor do you most identify with as your cultural identity? Why? What significant events in your life have contributed to your cultural identity? What meaning does it provide for your life?

What is your most distinguishing cultural factor? Does it differ from the most important? If so, how? Why?

Has your cultural identity served as a detriment, challenge, problem, difficulty, or deterrent in your life? Has your cultural identity felt like a burden? If so, how? What childhood message(s) did you receive about your cultural identity/background?

How has your cultural identity served as a source of strength in your life?

Have you used your identity as a coping skill/problem-solving tool? If so, when and how?

Does the factor that you identify most strongly with differ from the cultural factor with which others identify you? How has that affected your identity development?

Are there significant life events associated with this factor?

Have you encountered any difficulties with your cultural identity? If so, what kind? How have you coped with them? What resources have you needed to cope with them? How have the difficulties attributed to your identity?

What strengths do you associate with your cultural identity? What are the areas of pride associated with them?

Appendix B

Multicultural Genogram

The genogram is a useful tool for assessing families and determining multigenerational patterns, significant life events, rituals, roles, and the nature of relationships between family members. The genogram often provides direction for treatment. The multicultural genogram provides all the information listed previously but includes an assessment of worldview that often affects behaviors of members. Worldview can be defined as an individual's perception of his or her relationship with the world. Specific questions on cultural factors can be included in the genogram to enrich the process.

Ethnicity

1. What is the ethnicity of each family member?
2. What roles does ethnicity determine for different members?
3. What roles are assigned due to ethnicity?
4. What are similar characteristics across various ethnic groups?
5. What are differences between ethnic groups?
6. How is conflict handled according to ethnic groups?
7. How do family members handle conflicts across ethnicities?
8. What are specific rules for marriage and child rearing according to ethnicity?

Immigration/Acculturation

1. What is the family's history of immigration?
2. When did individual members migrate to America and why?
3. Are there plans to return to the country of origin?

4. What difficulties did the family face during immigration?

5. Has each member acculturated to the majority culture?

6. Is there conflict between members who retain the culture of origin and members who have acculturated?

Gender

1. What is the role of gender for each member as defined by the ethnicity/ culture of origin?

2. What behaviors, characteristics, beliefs, and values are defined by gender?

3. How are gender roles divided in the family? In the family of origin?

4. How is conflict between gender roles handled?

5. How do beliefs about gender roles influence child-rearing beliefs?

Socioeconomic Status (SES)

1. What role/meaning does SES have for members?

2. Does class differ across generations?

3. What resources are available to members due to SES?

4. Has there been a change in current SES?

Spirituality

1. What is the family's religious history?

2. What characteristics, values, and beliefs are influenced by religion?

3. If members differ according to religion, what are the similarities in values and beliefs?

4. What are the differences in values and beliefs according to religion?

5. How are conflicts due to different religious values resolved?

Other areas of concern include:

Majority/minority status

Sexual orientation

Regional background

Physical disabilities

Source: Adapted from Thomas, A. J. (1998). Understanding worldview and culture in family systems: Use of the multicultural genogram. In *The Family Journal: Counseling and Therapy for Couples and Families, 6,* 24–32. Reprinted with permission.

References

Aciman, A. (2000). *Letters of transit: Reflections on exile, identity, language and loss.* New York: New Press.

Almeida, R., Woods, R., Messineo, T., & Font, R. (1998). The cultural context model: An overview. In M. McGoldrick (Ed.), *Re-visioning family therapy: Race, culture and gender in clinical practice* (pp. 414–429). New York: Guilford.

American Anthropological Association. (1998). *American Anthropological Association statement on "race."* Retrieved May 14, 2010, from http://www .aaanet.org/stmts/racepp.htm

American Counseling Association code of ethics. (2005). Alexandria, VA: American Counseling Association.

American Psychiatric Association. (2000). *Diagnostic and statistical manual of mental disorders* (4th ed.). Washington, DC: Author.

American Psychiatric Association Commission on Psychotherapy by Psychiatrists (COPP). (2000). Position statement on therapies focused on attempts to change sexual orientation (Reparative or conversion therapies) [Electronic Version]. *American Journal of Psychiatry, 157,* 1719–1721.

Americans with Disabilities Act of 1990, 28, C. F. R., §36.104 (2002).

Anderson, S. K., & Middleton, V. A. (2004). *Explorations in privilege, oppression and diversity.* Belmont, CA: Wadsworth.

Answers to your questions about sexual orientation and homosexuality. (n.d.). Washington, DC: APA Office of Public and Member Communications. Retrieved May 17, 2010, from http://www.apa.org/topics/sexuality/ orientation.aspx

Aponte, H. (1995). *Bread and spirit: Therapy with the new poor.* New York: Morton Press.

Arey, D. (2002). Gay males and sexual child abuse. In L. Aronson Fontes (Ed.), *Sexual abuse in nine North American cultures: Treatment and prevention* (pp. 200–235). Thousand Oaks, CA: Sage.

Ashemberg Straussner, S. L. (2001). Jewish substance abusers: Existing but invisible. In S. L. Ashemberg Straussner (Ed.), *Ethnocultural factors in substance abuse treatment* (pp. 291–317). New York: Guilford.

Atkinson, D., & Hackett, G. (2003). *Counseling diverse populations.* New York: McGraw-Hill.

Bass, E., & Kaufman, K. (1996). *Free your mind: The book for gay, lesbian, and bisexual youth and their allies.* New York: HarperCollins.

Beecher, M. E., Rabe, R. A., & Wilder, L. K. (2004). Practical guidelines for counseling students with disabilities. *Journal of College Counseling, 7,* 83–89.

Berger, K. S. (2008). *The developing person through the lifespan* (5th ed.). New York: Worth.

Berry, J., Phinney, J., Sam, D., & Vedder, P. (2006). *Immigrant youth in cultural transition: Acculturation, identity, and adaptation across national contexts.* Mahwah, NJ: Lawrence Erlbaum.

Beth-Shalom, U., & Horenczyk, G. (2003). Acculturation orientation: A facet theory perspective on the bidimensional model. *Journal of Cross Cultural Psychology, 34*(2), 176–188.

Beyebach, M., & Escudero Carranza, V. (1997). Therapeutic interactions and dropout: Measuring relational communication in solution-focused therapy. *Journal of Family Therapy, 19,* 173–212.

Birke, L. (2002). Unusual fingers: Scientific studies of sexual orientation. In D. Richardson & S. Seidman (Eds.), *Handbook of lesbian and gay studies* (pp. 55–71). Thousand Oaks, CA: Sage.

Birman, D. (1994). Acculturation and human diversity in a multicultural society. In E. J. Trickett, R. J. Watts, & D. Birman (Eds.), *Human diversity: Perspectives on people in context* (pp. 261–284). San Francisco: Jossey-Bass.

Blades, E. (1994). The causes of homosexuality are irrelevant. In M. E. Williams (Ed.), *Opposing viewpoints: Homosexuality* (pp. 47–51). San Diego, CA: Greenhaven.

Blumenfeld, W. J. (2000). Heterosexism. In M. Adams, W. Blumenfeld, R. Castaneda, H. Hackman, M. Peters, & X. Zuniga (Eds.), *Readings for diversity and social justice* (pp. 261–266). New York: Routledge.

Boyd-Franklin, N. (2003). Race, class, and poverty. In F. Walsh (Ed.), *Normal family processes* (pp. 260–279). New York: Guilford.

Boyd-Franklin, N. (2004). *Black families in therapy: Understanding the African American experience* (2nd ed.). New York: Guilford.

Bradford, D. T., & Munoz, A. (1993). Translation in bilingual psychotherapy. *Professional Psychology: Research and Practice, 24*(1), 52–61.

Breunlin, D. C., Schwartz, R. C., & Mac Kune-Karrer, B. (1997). *Metaframeworks: Transcending the models of family therapy.* San Francisco: Jossey-Bass.

Bronfenbrenner, U. (1977). Toward an experimental ecology of human development. *American Psychologist, 32,* 513–531.

Burgess, C. A. (1997). The impact of lesbian/gay sensitive policies on the behavior and health of lesbians in the workplace. In W. K. Swan (Ed.), *Gay/lesbian/bisexual/transgender public policy issues* (pp. 35–48). New York: Harrington Park Press.

Burke, M. T., Chauvin, J. C., & Maranti, J. (2003). *Spirituality in counseling and therapy: A developmental and multicultural approach.* New York: Brunner-Routledge.

Butke, M. (2002). Lesbians and sexual child abuse. In L. Aronson Fontes (Ed.), *Sexual abuse in nine North American cultures: Treatment and prevention* (pp. 236–258). Thousand Oaks, CA: Sage.

Carrol, J. (2004). *Religion is very important to 6 in 10 Americans.* Retrieved on June 24, 2004, from http://www.gallup.com/content/login.aspx?ci=12115

Cass, V. C. (1979). Homosexual identity formation: A theoretical model. *Journal of Homosexuality, 4,* 219–235.

Chandler, C. K., Holden, J. M., & Kolander, C. A. (1992). Counseling for spiritual wellness: Theory and practice. *Journal of Counseling and Development, 71,* 168–175.

Clauss, C. S. (1998). Language: The unspoken variable in psychotherapy practice. *Psychotherapy, 35*(2), 188–196.

Coleman, E. (1981). Developmental stages of the coming out process. *Journal of homosexuality, 7*(2–3), 31–43.

Comas-Diaz, L. (1987). Feminist therapy with mainland Puerto Rican women. *Psychology of Women Quarterly, 11,* 461–474.

Comas-Diaz, L., & Jacobsen, F. M. (1991). Ethnocultural transference and countertransference in the therapeutic dyad. *American Journal of Orthopsychiatry, 61,* 392–402.

Crohn, J. (1998). Intercultural couples. In M. McGoldrick (Ed.), *Re-visioning family therapy: Race culture and gender in clinical practice* (pp. 295–308). New York: Guilford.

Cross, W. E., & Cross, T. B. (2008). Theory, research, and models. In S. M. Quintana & C. McKown (Eds.), *Handbook of race, racism, and the developing child* (pp. 154–181). Hoboken, NJ: John Wiley.

Dancy, J. J., & Wynn-Dancy, M. L. (1994). Faith of our fathers (mothers) living still: Spirituality as a force for the transmission of family values within the Black community. *Activities, Adaptation, and Aging, 19,* 87–105.

Daniels, R. (2002). *Coming to America: A history of immigration and ethnicity in American life* (2nd ed.). New York: HarperCollins.

DeLeon, P. H. (1998). Proceedings of the American Psychological Association, Incorporated, for the legislative year 1997: Minutes of the Annual Meeting of the Council of Representatives, August 14 and 17, Chicago, Illinois; and June, August and December 1997 meetings of the Board of Directors [Electronic version]. *American Psychologist, 53,* 882–939.

De Shazer, S. (1988). *Investigating solutions in brief therapy.* New York: W. W. Norton.

Division 44/Committee on Lesbian, Gay, and Bisexual Concerns Joint Task Force on Guidelines for Psychotherapy with Lesbian, Gay, and Bisexual Clients. (2000). Guidelines for psychotherapy with lesbian, gay and bisexual clients. *American Psychologist, 55*(12), 1440–1451.

Ellis-Hill, C. S., & Horn, S. (2000). Change in identity and self-concept: A new theoretical approach to recovery following a stroke. *Clinical Rehabilitation, 14,* 279–287.

Elon, A. (2002). *The pity of it all: A history of the Jews in Germany 1743–1933.* New York: Metropolitan Books.

Elze, D. E. (2006). Oppression, prejudice, and discrimination. In D. F. Morrow & L. Messinger (Eds.), *Sexual orientation and gender expression in social work practice* (pp. 43–78). New York: Columbia University Press.

Epston, M. (1993). Internalized other questioning with couples: The New Zealand version. In S. Gilligan & R. Price (Eds.), *Therapeutic conversations* (pp. 183–189). New York: W. W. Norton.

Erikson, E. (1968). *Identity, youth, and crisis.* New York: W. W. Norton.

Esterberg, K. G. (2002). The bisexual menace: Or, will the real bisexual please stand up? In D. Richardson & S. Seidman (Eds.), *Handbook of lesbian and gay studies* (pp. 215–227). Thousand Oaks, CA: Sage.

Faiver, C. M., O'Brien, E. M., & Ingersoll, E. R. (2000). Religion, guilt, and mental health. *Journal of Counseling and Development, 78,* 155–161.

Falicov, C. J. (1995). Cross-cultural marriages. In N. S. Jacobson & A. S. Gurman (Eds.), *Clinical handbook of couple therapy* (2nd ed., pp. 231–246). New York: Guilford.

Falicov, C. J. (1998a). The cultural meaning of family triangles. In M. McGoldrick (Ed.), *Re-visioning family therapy: Race culture and gender in clinical practice* (pp. 37–49). New York: Guilford.

Falicov, C. J. (1998b). *Latino families in therapy: A guide to multicultural practice.* New York: Guilford.

Falicov, C. J. (2003). Immigrant family processes. In F. Walsh (Ed.), *Normal family process* (3rd ed., pp. 260–279). New York: Guilford.

Fassinger, R. E., & Miller, B. A. (1996). Validation of an inclusive model of sexual minority identity formation on a sample of gay men. *Journal of Homosexuality, 32,* 53–78.

Feagin, J. R., & Sikes, M. P. (1995). *Living with racism: The Black middle-class experience.* Boston: Beacon.

Feinberg, L. (1996). *Transgender warriors: Making history.* Boston: Beacon.

Fordham, S. (1988). Racelessness as a factor in Black students' school success: Pragmatic strategy or Pyrrhic victory? *Harvard Educational Review, 58,* 54–84.

Fowler, J. E. (1981). *Stages of faith.* New York: Harper & Row.

Fox, D. R. (2003). Awareness is good, but action is better. *Counseling Psychologist, 31*(3), 299–304.

Frame, M. W., & Williams, C. B. (1996). Counseling African Americans: Integrating spirituality in therapy. *Counseling and Values, 41,* 16–28.

Freedman, J., & Combs, G. (1995). *Narrative therapy: The social construction of preferred realities.* New York: W. W. Norton.

Fuertes, J. N. (2004). Supervision in bilingual counseling: Service delivery, training, and research considerations. *Journal of Multicultural Counseling and Development, 32*(2), 84–94.

Fukuyama, M. A., & Sevig, T. D. (1992, November). Integrating spirituality and multicultural awareness [Workshop presented at Loyola University, Chicago].

Fukuyama, M. A., & Sevig, T. D. (1999). *Integrating spirituality into multicultural counseling.* Thousand Oaks, CA: Sage.

Garcia-Prieto, N. (1996). Puerto Rican families. In M. McGoldrick (Ed.), *Re-visioning family therapy: Race culture and gender in clinical practice* (pp. 183–199). New York: Guilford.

Gates, G. (2004). *Gay men and lesbians in the U.S. military.* Retrieved May 17, 2010, from http://www.urban.org/publications/411069.html

Gergen, K. (1991). *The saturated self: Dilemmas of identity in contemporary life.* New York: Basic Books.

Gibson, J. (2006). Disability and clinical competency: An introduction. *California Psychologist, 39,* 6–10.

Gibson, J. (2007). Clinical competency and culturally diverse clients with disabilities: The case of Linda. In M. E. Gallardo & B. McNeill (Eds.), *The clinical casebook of multicultural psychology: Implementation of culturally proficient treatment strategies.* Mahwah, NJ: Lawrence Erlbaum.

Giordano, J., & McGoldrick, M. (1996). European families: An overview. In M. McGoldrick, J. Giordano, & J. K. Pierce (Eds.), *Ethnicity and family therapy* (2nd ed., pp. 427–441). New York: Guilford.

GLBT fact sheets. (n.d.). Retrieved May 17, 2010, from http://www.aglp.org/pages/cfactsheets.html

Gonzalez, G. M. (1997). The emergence of Chicanos in the twenty-first century: Implications for counseling, research and policy. *Journal of Multicultural Counseling and Development, 25,* 94–106.

Gorkin, M. (1996). Countertransference in cross-cultural psychotherapy. In R. Pérez Foster, M. Moskowitz, & R. Javier (Eds.), *Reaching across boundaries of culture and class: Widening the scope of psychotherapy* (pp. 160–173). Northvale, NJ: Jason Aronson.

Grace, J. (1992). Affirming gay and lesbian adulthood. In N. J. Woodman (Ed.), *Lesbian and gay lifestyles: A guide for counseling and education* (pp. 33–47). New York: Irvington.

Green, R. J. (1998). Race and the field of family therapy. In M. McGoldrick (Ed.), *Re-visioning family therapy: Race, culture and gender in clinical practice* (pp. 93–110). New York: Guilford.

Greene, B., White, J. C., & Whitten, L. (2000). Hair texture, length, and style as a metaphor in the African American mother-daughter relationship: Considerations in psychodynamic psychotherapy. In L. C. Jackson &

B. Greene (Eds.), *Psychotherapy with African American women: Innovations in psychodynamic perspectives* (pp. 166–193). New York: Guilford.

Greene, B. A. (1992). Racial socialization as a tool in psychotherapy with African American children. In L. A. Vargas & J. D. Koss-Chioino (Eds.), *Working with culture: Psychotherapeutic interventions with ethnic minority children and adolescents* (pp. 63–81). San Francisco: Jossey-Bass.

Grieco, E. M., & Cassidy, C. R. (2001, March). *Overview of race and Hispanic origin: Census 2000 brief.* Retrieved May 13, 2010, from http://www.census.gov/prod/2001pubs/c2kbr01-1.pdf

Griffith, B. A., & Griggs, J. C. (2001). Religious identity status as a model to understand, assess, and interact with client spirituality. *Counseling and Values, 46,* 14–24.

Griffith, B. A., & Rotter, J. (1999). Families and spirituality: Therapists as facilitators. *Family Journal: Counseling and Therapy for Couples and Families, 7,* 161–164.

Grinberg, L., & Grinberg, R. (2000). *Psychoanalytic perspectives on migration and exile.* New Haven, CT: Yale University Press.

Gushue, G. V. (1993). Cultural-identity development and family assessment: An interaction model. *Counseling Psychologist, 21,* 487–513.

Hays, P. (2001). *Addressing cultural complexities in practice.* Washington, DC: American Psychological Association.

Helms, J. E. (1995). An update of Helms's White and people of color racial identity models. In J. G. Ponterotto, J. M. Casas, L. A. Suzuki, & C. M. Alexander (Eds.), *Handbook of multicultural counseling* (pp. 181–198). Thousand Oaks, CA: Sage.

Herdt, G., & Koff, B. (2000). *Something to tell you: The road families travel when a child is gay.* New York: Columbia University Press.

Herman, M. A., & Richter Herlihy, B. (2006). Legal and ethical implications of refusing to counsel homosexual clients. *Journal of Counseling & Development, 84,* 414–418.

Hernandez, M., & McGoldrick, M. (1999). Migration and the family life cycle. In B. Carter & M. McGoldrick (Eds.), *The expanded family life cycle: Individual, family and social perspectives* (3rd ed., pp. 169–184). Boston: Allyn & Bacon.

Hines, P. M., Garcia-Preto, N., McGoldrick, M., Almeida, R., & Weltman, S. (1992). Intergenerational relationships across cultures. *Families in Society, 73,* 323–338.

Hopson, D. P., & Hopson, D. S. (1992). *Different and wonderful: Raising Black children in a race-conscious society.* New York: Fireside.

Hoyt, M. (2001). Cognitive-behavioral treatment of posttraumatic stress disorder from a narrative constructivist perspective: A conversation with Donald Meichenbaum. In M. Hoyt (Ed.), *Interview with brief therapy experts* (pp. 97–120). Philadelphia: Brunner-Routledge.

Hughes, D., Rodriguez, J., Smith, E. P., Johnson, D. J., Stevenson, H. C., & Spicer, P. (2006). Parents' ethnic-racial socialization practices: A review of research and directions for future study. *Developmental Psychology, 42,* 747–770.

Hunt, B., Matthews, C., Milsom, A., & Lammel, J. A. (2006). Lesbians with physical disabilities: A qualitative study of their experiences with counseling. *Journal of Counseling and Development, 84,* 163–173.

Hunter, S., & Hickerson, J. C. (2003). *Affirmative practice: Understanding and working with lesbian, gay, bisexual, and transgender persons.* Washington, DC: NASW Press.

Iglehart, A. P., & Becerra, R. M. (1995). *Social services and the ethnic community.* Prospect Heights, IL: Waveland.

Imber-Black, E., Roberts, J., & Whiting, R. A. (Eds.). (1988). *Rituals in families and family therapy.* New York: W. W. Norton.

Ingoldsby, B. (1995). Poverty and patriarchy in Latin America. In B. Ingoldsby & A. Smith (Eds.), *Families in multicultural perspective* (pp. 335–351). New York: Guilford.

Isom, D. (2002). *Me, I got many parts: An exploration of racialized gender with African American youth.* Unpublished doctoral dissertation, Loyola University Chicago.

Israel, T. (2006). Marginalized communities in the United States: Oppression, social justice, and the role of counseling psychologists. In R. L. Toporek, L. H. Gerstein, N. A. Fouad, G. Roysircar, & T. Israel (Eds.), *Handbook for social justice in counseling psychology: Leadership, vision, and action* (pp. 149–154). Thousand Oaks, CA: Sage.

Javier, R. A. (1996). In search of repressed memories in bilingual individuals. In R. Pérez Foster, M. Moskowitz, & R. A. Javier (Eds.), *Reaching across boundaries of culture and class: Widening the scope of psychotherapy* (pp. 225–242). Northvale, NJ: Jason Aronson.

Johnson, A. C. (1995). Resiliency mechanisms in culturally diverse families. *Family Journal: Counseling and Therapy for Couples and Families, 3,* 316–324.

Johnson, O. S. (2004). *The sexual spectrum: Exploring human diversity.* Vancouver, British Columbia, Canada: Raincoast Books.

Johnson-Powell, G., & Yamamoto, J. (Eds.). (1997). *Transcultural child development: Psychological assessment and treatment.* New York: John Wiley.

Kaufman, G., & Raphael, L. (1996). *Coming out of shame.* New York: Doubleday.

Kerwin, C., & Ponterotto, J. G. (1995). Biracial identity development: Theory and research. In J. G. Ponterotto, J. M. Casas, L. A. Suzuki, & C. M. Alexander (Eds.), *Handbook of multicultural counseling* (pp. 199–217). Thousand Oaks, CA: Sage.

Kilpatrick, A. C., & Holland, T. P. (2009). *Working with families: An integrative model by level of need* (5th ed.). Boston: Allyn & Bacon.

Kirkpatrick, D. D. (2005, February 11). House passes tightening of laws on immigration. *New York Times,* p. A13.

Kliman, J. (1998). Social class as a relationship: Implications for family therapy. In M. McGoldrick (Ed.), *Re-visioning family therapy: Race, culture, and gender in clinical practice* (pp. 50–61). New York: Guilford.

Kliman, J., & Madsen, W. (1999). Social class and the family life cycle. In B. Carter & M. McGoldrick (Eds.), *The expanded family life cycle: Individual, family and social perspectives* (pp. 88–106). Boston: Allyn & Bacon.

Kuo, B. C. H., & Roysircar, G. (2004). Predictors of acculturation for Chinese adolescents in Canada: Age of arrival, length of stay, social class, and English reading ability. *Journal of Multicultural Counseling and Development, 32*(3), 143–154.

LaFrombroise, T., Coleman, H. L. K., & Gerton, J. (1993). Psychological impact of biculturalism: Evidence and theory. *Psychological Bulletin, 114,* 395–412.

Lewis, T. F., & Osborn, C. (2004). Solution-focused counseling and motivational interviewing: A consideration of confluence. *Journal of Counseling and Development, 82*(1), 38–48.

Liu, W. M., Soleck, G., Hopps, J., Dunston, K., & Pickett, T., Jr. (2004). A new framework to understand social class in counseling: The social class worldview model and modern classism theory. *Journal of Multicultural Counseling and Development, 32*(2), 95–122.

Lorber, J. (2000). "Night to his day": The social construction of gender. In M. Adams, W. Blumenfeld, R. Castaneda, H. Hackman, M. Peters, & X. Zuniga (Eds.), *Readings for diversity and social justice* (pp. 203–213). New York: Routledge.

Lowe, S., & Mascher, J. (2001). The role of sexual orientation in multicultural counseling. In J. G. Ponterotto, J. M. Casas, L. A. Suzuki, & C. M. Alexander (Eds.), *Handbook of multicultural counseling* (pp. 755–778). Thousand Oaks, CA: Sage.

Marcos, L. R. (1976). Bilinguals in psychotherapy: Language as an emotional barrier. *American Journal of Psychotherapy, 30,* 552–560.

Marcos, L. R., & Urcuyo, L. (1979). Dynamic psychotherapy with the bilingual patient. *American Journal of Psychotherapy, 33*(3), 332–338.

McCarthy, J., & Holliday, E. I. (2004). Help-seeking and counseling within a traditional male gender role: An examination from a multicultural perspective. *Journal of Counseling and Development, 82*(1), 25–30.

McClellan, D. L. (2006). Bisexual relationships and families. In D. F. Morrow & L. Messinger (Eds.), *Sexual orientation and gender expression in social work practice* (pp. 243–262). New York: Columbia University Press.

McGill, D. W., & Pierce, J. K. (1996). American families with English ancestors from the colonial era: Anglo Americans. In M. McGoldrick, J. Giordano, & J. K. Pierce (Eds.), *Ethnicity and family therapy* (pp. 451–466). New York: Guilford.

McGoldrick, M. (2003). Culture: A challenge to concepts of normality. In F. Walsh (Ed.), *Normal family process* (3rd ed., pp. 235–259). New York: Guilford.

McGoldrick, M., & Giordano, J. (1996). Overview: Ethnicity and family therapy. In M. McGoldrick, J. Giordano, & J. K. Pierce (Eds.), *Ethnicity and family therapy* (pp. 1–27). New York: Guilford.

McGoldrick, M., Giordano, J., & Pierce, J. K. (1996). *Ethnicity and family therapy.* New York: Guilford.

McGoldrick, M., & Preto, N. G. (1984). Ethnic intermarriage: Implications for therapy. *Family Process, 23,* 347–364.

McIntosh, P. (1998). White privilege: Unpacking the invisible knapsack. In M. McGoldrick (Ed.), *Re-visioning family therapy: Race, culture and gender in clinical practice.* New York: Guilford.

McKinley, J. C. (2005, January 6). A Mexican manual for illegal immigrants upsets some in U.S. *New York Times,* p. A5.

Mead, J. C. (2004, June 20). Ticket to nowhere. *New York Times,* p. L1.

Mezzich, J. E., Ruiz, P., & Muñoz, R. A. (1999). Mental health care for Hispanic Americans: A current perspective. *Cultural Diversity and Ethnic Minority Psychology, 5*(2), 91–102.

Miceli, M. S. (2002). Gay, lesbian, and bisexual youth. In D. Richardson & S. Seidman (Eds.), *Handbook of lesbian and gay studies* (pp. 200–214). Thousand Oaks, CA: Sage.

Migration Policy Institute. (2004). *Coming to America: Two years after September 11, 2001.* Retrieved May 13, 2010, from http://www.migrationpolicy.org/pubs/Immigration_Since_9-11.pdf

Miller, N. (1995). *Out of the past: Gay and lesbian history from 1869 to the present.* New York: Vintage Books.

Miller, W. R., & Rollnick, S. (1991). *Motivational interviewing: Preparing people to change addictive behaviors.* New York: Guilford.

Mills, N. (Ed.). (1994). *Arguing immigration.* New York: Touchstone.

Minuchin, P., Colapinto, J., & Minuchin, S. (1998). *Working with families of the poor.* New York: Guilford.

Mirkin, M. P. (1998). The impact of multiple contexts on recent immigrant families. In M. McGoldrick (Ed.), *Re-visioning family therapy: Race, culture and gender in clinical practice* (pp. 370–384). New York: Guilford.

Mitchell, S. A., & Black, M. J. (1995). *Freud and beyond: A history of modern psychoanalytic thought.* New York: Basic Books.

Morrow, D. F. (2006). Coming out as gay, lesbian, bisexual, and transgender. In D. F. Morrow & L. Messinger (Eds.), *Sexual orientation and gender expression in social work practice* (pp. 129–149). New York: Columbia University Press.

Morrow, D. F., & Tyson, B. (2006). Religion and spirituality. In D. F. Morrow & L. Messinger (Eds.), *Sexual orientation and gender expression in social work practice* (pp. 384–404). New York: Columbia University Press.

Moses, A. E. (1982). *Counseling lesbian women and gay men.* St. Louis, MO: C. V. Mosby.

Nardi, P. M. (2002). The mainstreaming of lesbian and gay studies? In D. Richardson & S. Seidman (Eds.), *Handbook of lesbian and gay studies* (pp. 45–54). Thousand Oaks, CA: Sage.

Nava, G. (Director). (1983). *El norte* [The North] [Videotape]. (Available from Filmco A/S, 9718 Glenoaks Blvd., #A, Sun Valley, CA 91352)

Nichols, M. P., & Schwartz, R. (2001). *Family therapy: Concepts and methods* (5th ed.). Boston: Allyn & Bacon.

Nieto, S. (1999). *The light in their eyes: Creating multicultural learning communities.* New York: Teachers College Press.

Nieves, E. (1999, July 30). California calls off effort to carry out immigrant measure. *New York Times*, p. A1.

Palombi, B. J., & Matteson Mundt, A. (2006). Achieving social justice for college women with disabilities: A model for inclusion. In R. L. Toporek, L. H. Gerstein, N. A. Fouad, G. Roysircar, & T. Israel (Eds.), *Handbook for social justice in counseling psychology: Leadership, vision, and action* (pp. 170–184). Thousand Oaks, CA: Sage.

Pedersen, P., & Hernandez, D. (1996). *Decisional dialogues in a cultural context: Structured exercises.* Thousand Oaks, CA: Sage.

Pérez Foster, R. (1996). Assessing the psychodynamic function of language in the bilingual patient. In R. Pérez Foster, M. Moskowitz, & R. Javier (Eds.), *Reaching across boundaries of culture and class: Widening the scope of psychotherapy* (pp. 243–264). Northvale, NJ: Jason Aronson.

Pérez Foster, R. (1998). The clinician's cultural countertransference: The psychodynamics of culturally competent practice. *Clinical Social Work Journal, 26*(3), 253–269.

Phillips, R., Munt, G., Drury, J., Stoklosa, M., & Spink, J. (1997). Dropouts in family therapy. *Australian and New Zealand Journal of Family Therapy, 18*(2), 115–118.

Phinney, J. S. (1996). When we talk about American ethnic groups, what do we mean? *American Psychologist, 51*, 918–927.

Pledger, C. (2003). Discourse on disability and rehabilitation issues: Opportunities for psychology. *American Psychologist, 58*, 279–284.

Prochaska, J. O., Norcross, J. C., & DiClemente, C. C. (1995). *Changing for good.* New York: William Morrow.

Quintana, S. M. (1998). Children's developmental understanding of ethnicity and race. *Applied and Preventive Psychology, 7*, 27–45.

Quintana, S. M., Castenada-English, P., & Ybarra, V. C. (1999). Role of perspective-taking abilities and ethnic socialization in development of adolescent ethnic identity. *Journal of Research on Adolescence, 9*, 161–184.

Rahman, O., & Rollock, D. (2004). Acculturation, competence, and mental health among South Asian students in the United States. *Journal of Multicultural Counseling and Development, 32*, 130–142.

Richards, P. S., & Bergin, A. E. (1997). *A spiritual strategy for counseling and psychotherapy.* Washington, DC: American Psychological Association.

Robinson, T. L. (2005). *The convergence of race, ethnicity, and gender: Multiple identities in counseling.* Upper Saddle River, NJ: Prentice Hall.

Rockquemore, K. A., & Laszloffy, T. A. (2003). Multiple realities: A relational narrative approach in therapy with Black-White mixed-race clients. *Family Relations, 52*, 119–128.

Rogers, C. R. (1980). *A way of being.* Boston: Houghton Mifflin.

Roland, A. (1996). How universal is the psychoanalytic self? In R. Pérez Foster, M. Moskowitz, & R. Javier (Eds.), *Reaching across boundaries of culture and class: Widening the scope of psychotherapy* (pp. 71–90). Northvale, NJ: Jason Aronson.

Rosado, R. J. (1992). *The effects of pretreatment orientations on the utilization of treatment by Spanish speaking Hispanics, bilingual Hispanics and non-Hispanics in treatment at a child guidance center.* Ann Arbor, MI: University Microfilms International.

Rosario, M., Schrimshaw, E. W., Hunter, J., & Braun, L. (2006). Sexual identity development among lesbian, gay, and bisexual youths: Consistency and change over time. *Journal of Sex Research, 43*(1), 46–58.

Rosen, E. (1995). Mourning in different cultures: Jewish families. In F. Wash & M. McGoldrick (Eds.), *Living beyond loss: Death in the family* (pp. 194–200). New York: W. W. Norton.

Rosen, E., & Weltman, S. (1996). Jewish families: An overview. In M. McGoldrick (Ed.), *Ethnicity and family therapy* (pp. 611–630). New York: Guilford.

Roseneil, S. (2002). The heterosexual/homosexual binary: Past, present and future. In D. Richardson & S. Seidman (Eds.), *Handbook of lesbian and gay studies* (pp. 55–71). Thousand Oaks, CA: Sage.

Ryan, C., & Futterman, D. (2001). Lesbian and gay adolescents: Identity development. *Prevention Researcher, 8*(1), 1, 3–5.

Savin-Williams, R. C. (2005). The new gay teen: Shunning labels. *Gay & Lesbian Review Worldwide, 12*(6), 16–19.

Sayger, T. V., & Heid, K. O. (1990). Counseling the impoverished rural client: Issues for family therapists. *Psychotherapy Patient, 7*, 161–168.

Schwartz, R. (1995). *Internal family systems therapy.* New York: Guilford.

Schwarzbaum, S. (1995). The effect of a combined pretherapy orientation on Hispanic clients' utilization of counseling services. *Dissertation Abstracts International, 57* (01B), 0710.

Schwarzbaum, S. (2002). Drop out from counseling services by low income Latinos/as: Historical and current explanations. *Illinois Counseling Association Journal, 149*, 25–37.

Schwarzbaum, S. (2004). Low-income Latinos and dropout: Strategies to prevent dropout. *Journal of Multicultural Counseling and Development, 32*, 296–306.

Schwarzbaum, S., & Thomas, A. J. (2008). *Dimensions of multicultural counseling: A life story approach.* Thousand Oaks, CA: Sage.

Selman, R. L. (1971). Taking another's perspective: Role-talking development in early childhood. *Child Development, 42*, 1721–1734.

Sicard, C., & Heller, S. (2003). *U.S. citizenship for dummies.* Indianapolis, IN: John Wiley.

Signorile, M. (1995). *Outing yourself: How to come out as lesbian or gay to your family, friends, and coworkers.* New York: Random House.

Smart, J. F., & Smart, D. W. (2006). Models of disability: Implications for the counseling profession. *Journal of Counseling and Development, 84,* 29–40.

Smith, D. M., & Gates, G. (2001). *Gay and lesbian families in the United States.* Retrieved May 18, 2010, from http://www.urban.org/publications/1000491.html

Speight, S. L., Myers, L. J., Cox, C. I., & Highlen, P. S. (1991). A redefinition of multicultural counseling. *Journal of Counseling and Development, 70,* 29–36.

Standard, R. P., Sandhu, D. S., & Painter, L. C. (2000). Assessment of spirituality in counseling. *Journal of Counseling and Development, 78,* 204–210.

Sue, D. W., & Sue, D. (2003). *Counseling the culturally diverse.* New York: John Wiley.

Sue, D. W., & Sue, D. (2007). *Counseling the culturally diverse.* New York: John Wiley.

Sue, S. (1998). In search of cultural competence in psychotherapy and counseling. *American Psychologist, 53,* 440–448.

Thomas, A. J. (1998). Understanding worldview and culture in family systems: Use of the multicultural genogram. *Family Journal: Counseling and Therapy for Couples and Families, 6,* 24–32.

Thomas, K. R. (2004). Old wine in a slightly cracked new bottle. *American Psychologist, 59,* 274–275.

Thompson, G., & Ochoa, S. (2004, June 13). By a back door to the U.S.: A migrant's grim sea voyage. *New York Times,* p. A1.

Tolliver, W. F. (1997). Invoking the spirit: A model for incorporating the spiritual dimension of human functioning into social work practice. *Smith College Studies in Social Work, 67,* 477–486.

Tomm, K. (1988). Interventive interviewing: Part III. Intending to ask lineal, circular, strategic and reflexive questions. *Family Process, 27,* 1–16.

Tomm, K. (1989). Externalizing the problems and internalizing the personal agency. *Journal of Strategic and Systemic Therapies, 8,* 54–59.

Torres, L., & Rollock, D. (2004). Acculturative distress among Hispanics: The role of acculturation, coping, and intercultural competence. *Journal of Multicultural Counseling and Development, 32,* 155–167.

Tully, C. T. (2000). *Lesbians, gays, & the empowerment perspective.* New York: Columbia University Press.

Twist, M., Murphy, M., Green, M. S., & Palmanteer, D. (2006). Therapists' support of gay and lesbian human rights. *Guidance & Counseling, 21*(2), 107–113.

U.S. Census Bureau. (2000). *Fact sheet: Population finder.* Retrieved May 24, 2010, from http://factfindeer.census.gov/servlet/SAFFFactsCharIteration

Vazquez-Nuttall, E., Romero-Garcia, I., & De Leon, B. (1987). Sex roles and perceptions of femininity and masculinity of Hispanic women: A review of the literature. *Psychology of Women Quarterly, 11,* 409–425.

Vogel, R. (1999). A control mastery approach to short-term couple therapy. In J. M. Donovan (Ed.), *Short-term couple therapy* (pp. 63–100). New York: Guilford.

Wald, M. L. (2004, December 9). U.S. to specify documents needed for driver's licenses. *New York Times,* p. A36.

Waldegrave, C. (1998). The challenges of culture to psychology and postmodern thinking. In M. McGoldrick (Ed.), *Re-visioning family therapy: Race, culture and gender in clinical practice* (pp. 404–413). New York: Guilford.

Walitzer, K. S., Dermen, K. H., & Conners, G. J. (1999). Strategies for preparing clients for treatment: A review. *Behavior Modification, 23*(1), 129–151.

Walsh, F. (1999). Religion and spirituality: Wellsprings for healing and resilience. In F. Walsh (Ed.), *Spiritual resources in family therapy* (pp. 3–27). New York: Guilford.

Walters, M., Carter, B., Papp, B., & Silverstein, O. (1988). *The invisible web: Gender patterns in family relationships.* New York: Guilford.

Ward, I. (Producer). (1997). *The ten commandments of communicating with people with disabilities* [Videotape]. Available from Irene Ward and Associates, P. O. Box 2038, Syracuse, NY 13220–2038.

Watts, R. J., & Abdul-Adil, J. K. (1997). Promoting critical consciousness in young, African-American men. *Journal of Prevention and Intervention in the Community, 16,* 63–86.

Weigel, D. J., & Baker, B. G. (2002). Unique issues in rural couple and family counseling. *Family Journal: Counseling and Therapy for Couples and Families, 10,* 61–69.

Weiner-Davis, M. (1993). *Divorce busting: A step-by-step approach to making your marriage loving again.* New York: Simon & Schuster.

Weissbrodt, D. (1998). *Immigration law and procedure in a nutshell* (4th ed.). Eagan, MN: West Publishing.

Whiston, G. (1996). Working-class issues. In R. Pérez Foster, M. Moskowitz, & R. Javier (Eds.), *Reaching across boundaries of culture and class: Widening the scope of psychotherapy* (pp. 143–158). Northvale, NJ: Jason Aronson.

Whitman, J. S., Glosoff, H. L., Kocet, M. M., & Tarvydas, V. (2006). Exploring ethical issues related to conversion or reparative therapy [Electronic version]. *Counseling Today, 49*(1), 14–15.

Wright, M. A. (1999). *I'm chocolate, you're vanilla: Raising healthy Black and biracial children in a race-conscious world.* San Francisco: Jossey-Bass.

Yarhouse, M. A., Tan, E. S. N., & Pawlowski, L. M. (2005). Sexual identity development and synthesis among LGB-identified and LGB dis-identified persons. *Journal of Psychology and Theology, 33*(1), 3–16.

Ziegler, P., & Hiller, T. (2001). *Recreating partnership: A solution-oriented, collaborative approach to couples therapy.* New York: W. W. Norton.

Zweifel, J. (2002). *Will the real me please stand up?* Naperville, IL: Nell Thurber Press.

Index

About the Authors

Anita Jones Thomas, PhD, is a counseling psychologist with specializations in multicultural counseling and family therapy and is currently an associate professor at Loyola University Chicago. She received a bachelor's degree in human development and social policy from Northwestern University and a master's degree in community counseling from Loyola University Chicago. Her doctorate in counseling psychology was received from Loyola University Chicago. Her research interests include critical consciousness, racial identity, racial socialization, and parenting issues for African Americans. She has also conducted training seminars and workshops on multicultural issues for state and national professional organizations in counseling and psychology, hospitals, and corporations and has served as a consultant for human service organizations. Dr. Thomas has served on and chaired the Committee on Children, Youth, and Families of the American Psychological Association and the Task Force on Resilience and Strength and Black Children and Adolescents.

Sara E. Schwarzbaum, EdD, LCPC, is a professor in the department of Counselor Education and a coordinator of the Master's in Couple and Family Counseling Program at Northeastern Illinois University in Chicago, where she supervises and trains future family counselors. She is also a couples therapist in private practice in Chicago. She has a master's degree in clinical psychology from Buenos Aires, Argentina. She received her doctoral degree in counseling with an emphasis in family therapy from Northern Illinois University. Formerly, she was the coordinator of the Latino Family Counseling Program of Lake County, Illinois, where she provided services for Latino families and trained bilingual clinicians. She is the coauthor, with Anita Thomas, of *Dimensions of Multicultural Counseling: A Life Story Approach.* She has also written articles that have appeared in the *Psychotherapy Networker, Counseling Today,* and other publications. She is a consultant, trainer, and presenter at state and national conferences where she frequently conducts workshops on clinical issues with Latino clients, the multicultural competency of clinicians, psychotherapy with immigrants' families, and couples counseling.